EU Law and Economics

EU Law and Economics

ARMIN STEINBACH
Professor of EU Law and Economics, Department of Law, École des Hautes Études Commerciales (HEC) Paris, France

OXFORD
UNIVERSITY PRESS

OXFORD
UNIVERSITY PRESS

Great Clarendon Street, Oxford, OX2 6DP,
United Kingdom

Oxford University Press is a department of the University of Oxford.
It furthers the University's objective of excellence in research, scholarship,
and education by publishing worldwide. Oxford is a registered trade mark of
Oxford University Press in the UK and in certain other countries

Co-funded by the European Union. Views and opinions expressed are however
those of the author only and do not necessarily reflect those of the
European Union or the European Education and Culture Executive Agency (EACEA).
Neither the European Union nor EACEA can be held responsible for them.

Published in the United States of America by Oxford University Press
198 Madison Avenue, New York, NY 10016, United States of America

British Library Cataloguing in Publication Data
Data available

Library of Congress Control Number: 2024947766

ISBN 9780198920885

DOI: 10.1093/9780198920915.001.0001

Printed and bound by
CPI Group (UK) Ltd, Croydon, CR0 4YY

MIX
Paper | Supporting
responsible forestry
FSC® C013604

The manufacturer's authorised representative in the EU for product safety
is Oxford University Press España S.A. of el Parque Empresarial San
Fernando de Henares, Avenida de Castilla, 2 – 28830 Madrid (www.oup.es/en).

Preface

The ambition of this book is not to demonstrate that economics could remedy the insufficient rigour of the EU legal discipline, nor to question the self-sufficiency of legal science. The productive contribution of economics to EU law aims to offer complementary insights into the understanding of EU rules and principles, to uncover empirical premises that are implicit in (normative) legal provisions, and to highlight (in)consistencies between legal and economic views. EU Member States transfer centralized power for some competences, while not for others, inviting us to ask whether their proper understanding should be interpreted through the legal principles of conferral of powers and subsidiarity (law), or through the economic concepts of preferences, spillovers, and economies of scale (economics). EU law oscillates between rigidity and flexibility, provoking us not only to ask *what* compliance with EU law means (law) but also *why* compliance occurs (economics); and the actions of institutions created through the Treaties should not only be understood as exogenous events to be measured against a binary 'law–unlawful' standard (law) but as an endogenous function of interest, control, and sanctions (economics). More fundamentally, cooperation through law, established by primary law or created through deliberate policy-maker decisions in EU secondary law, does not just exist as a pre-defined positivist legal benchmark (law) but as the outcome of cooperation motives shaping institutional, procedural, and substantive arrangements (economics).

With the *why* of Treaty-making, competence allocation, and rule-compliance being a largely disregarded analytical category for lawyers, the inquiry into motives for state conduct are core for an economic analysis, channelled through preferences and payoffs. Instead of a binary legal standard, economics examines incentives, welfare, efficiency, and distribution. It is the consequentialist orientation of economics that adds value to a law-only perspective on EU law. By extending the hypothetical *homo economicus* to the 'state economicus', rational choice is a fruitful tool for the study of EU law. Whether economics is the 'queen of the social sciences' or whether it just 'colonized other disciplines by seeming to point the way toward understanding the rational basis of human behavior'[1]—it certainly offers multiple approaches to study the legal framework in a way that legal scholarship as a norm science fails (and is not intended) to uncover.

[1] Liran Einav and Leeat Yariv, 'What's in a Surname? The Effects of Surname Initials on Academic Success' (2006) 20 Journal of Economic Perspectives 175.

Law as a norm science applies EU law to specific circumstances entailing questions such as: Is a certain Member State's conduct in compliance with the Treaties? Is a directive the lawful choice of legislation in a given policy area? Does the Treaty cover a union institution engaging in a certain activity? Economics has no methodological tools for interpreting texts. Economics cannot decide whether a certain set of facts can be subsumed under a norm or whether a certain action is legal or illegal. Law as an applied science of norms has developed a canon of interpretative methods, inferred from national practices and legal traditions, from international law, for example how to interpret treaties, or even from genuine sources in EU law, such as the *effet utile* interpretation of EU law. Economics enriches the legal canon of interpretation through its ability to assess the effects of EU rules on actors making choices within EU law, allowing interpretations that consider both desirable and undesirable outcomes (including incentives). As an auxiliary science, economics supports both lawyers as applied norm scientists and as technical law-makers. In the best scenario, law draws from this social science insight regarding the real consequences of norms. What can become an interdisciplinarily informed judgement is up to the legal scholar who must decide whether the extra-judicial insight can be imported into and reconciled with the established legal *intra*disciplinary requirements.

What is of interest to economists—real effects, the consequences for incentives, distributional effects, and welfare implications—is not necessarily the benchmark of legal doctrine. It is an established reference point for EU law designed to achieve efficient results, particularly in specific fields such as mergers, antitrust, state aid, procurement, trade, and investment law all of which integrate economics. Yet, this contribution fundamentally aims to shed light on an understanding of institutional, procedural, and substantive EU law beyond legal rigour.

Challenging legal standards and interpretative methods leads inevitably to the portrayal of economics as an intrusive, dominant, overarching science, one that fosters critical resistance and suspicion from other disciplines towards cross-disciplinary outreach. This (mis)perception arises from economics imposing its prescriptive perspective on areas where law practices self-constraint. Legal science is relatively limited compared to economics in establishing normative claims or empirical observations that go beyond its narrow mission as applied norm science. Law is not a science of values. In order to determine what justice is, it must revert to non-positivist legal and moral philosophy if it does not limit itself to a purely positivist representation of existing laws. As a reflection of this, consider lawyers' limited salience in public policy debates compared to the omnipresence of economists offering policy and politics advice. As a normative economic analysis of law, economics provides normative guidance through its different instrumental lenses: traditional welfare economics emphasizes allocative efficiency; institutional economics stresses the role of mutual consent in rule-setting; and fiscal federalism theory explores whether and how public goods should be supplied at EU level.

Economics goes well beyond the positivist *de lege lata* approach to which EU law, as an applied norm science, is bound. Normatively vocal, economics relegates the law to an auxiliary function in bringing normative economics policy choices into proper legal terms. This study seeks to uncover the normativity that economics can unfold on how Treaties *should* be designed and modified *de lege ferenda* in order to be incentive-compatible and efficiency-enhancing, building on economic tools as diverse as game theory, agency theory, and contract theory; how to modify the division of competences between the EU and Member States; determining where flexibility or rigidity should be incorporated into EU provisions and prescribing when breaches of EU law should be accepted rather than remedied; and identifying which public goods should be delivered on the European rather than Member States' level and how to implement it.

Overall, social sciences are descriptively meaningful in their complementary role, offering law the kind of information that a norm science is unable to produce on its own. Again, this does not imply that EU law should in all cases be re-designed on the basis of economic benchmarks. Distributional effects and morality are concerns that underpin notions of justice often standing in the way of an economics-only perspective. Nevertheless, economics can respond to a wider set of non-economic considerations by offering second-best or third-best solutions giving law-makers leeway to prioritize goals other than economic ones. Its comparative strength both in *lege lata* and in *lege ferenda* analysis arises from the array of empirical tools that economics has available as a social science, allowing it to account for unintended side-effects of regulation, distributional consequences, and costs and benefits, information that does not contradict the interpretative canon of law but complements it. EU law has long ago integrated the comparative disciplinary advantage by requiring impact assessments for all EU legislation, with economics as a powerful supplier of this tool. What it cannot do is translate its insights into consistent legal texts or into proper legal interpretation, make legislative choices, or determine the standard of legality review. This work remains under the authority of legal scientists. But it is this collaboration between social science and law, legal norms and empirical effects, and economic normativity and legal positivity, which makes the interaction between both disciplines a fruitful exercise—be it through integrated analysis or through a division of labour building on each other's insights consecutively.

Like all interdisciplinary inquiries, a law and economics approach has its limitations. On the one hand, legal scholarship is forced to open law to the methodologies of social sciences. In an interconnected world in which legislation requires considerable knowledge to anticipate the resistance and reaction of real-world actors to evolving rules, practitioners—much more than (continental European) academia—have acknowledged that a law-only perspective remains deficient, acknowledging that social science insights are vital to ensure regulation and rule-makers choose sound policy goals and achieve intended effects. And yet, the integration of economics into law has evolved at variable rates across the different fields of law. While law and economics has advanced well beyond the state of a nascent field (at least in its home country, the United States), it remains understudied with regard to EU law. One reason for this may be the limited openness of continental legal disciplines to cross disciplinary boundaries. Given the scope and depth of various legal fields to which law and economics has devoted attention, including the study of international law, its application to EU law is still comparatively underdeveloped (except in the fields that are inherently economic such as competition law). Recognizing the value of studying the law through the lens of economics begins with a proper representation of the discipline in universities' curricula. From there it can influence how academics, practitioners, and judges utilize this complementary tool set. Europe lags significantly behind the United States in this regard, where exposure to law and economics in law schools has profoundly influenced judicial decision-making, leading to more economically reasoned judgments.[2] Recourse to extrajudicial resources is still too often inhibited by struggles with methodological transfers and transdisciplinary communication hurdles.

[2] Siying Cao, 'Quantifying Economic Reasoning in Court: Judge Economics Sophistication and Pro-Business Orientation' (2022) New Working Papers No 321.

Brief Contents

Detailed Contents

PART IV. *WHO* COOPERATES UNDER EU LAW

PART V. *WHAT* TO COOPERATE ON IN THE EU

Economic and migratory motion

[illegible]

PART I
BASICS

Introduction to Part I

The usefulness of studying European Union (EU) law based on the categories of *why*, *how*, *who*, and *what* is not inherently self-evident. Cooperation between states has been examined from a range of discipline-specific perspectives. By way of example: scholars of international relations have explored 'cooperation problems' and 'characteristics of the states', using the former term to account for how the interests and constraints that govern the actions of cooperating parties can explain certain design features of international agreements.[1] Lawyers, and especially EU lawyers, structure their analysis with recourse to positive legal texts and what they define in terms of relevant institutions, sources of law, and policy instruments.[2] Scholars of law and economics, by contrast, have often focused on public international law and international law compliance.[3]

Taking positive EU law—that is, primary and secondary law, as well as the associated institutional and procedural frameworks—as a point of analytical departure, inquiry into the *why*, *how*, *who*, and *what* of cooperation paves the way for the integration of various disciplinary perspectives. Some of the 'cooperation problems' described in the international relations literature, such as the enforcement or commitment problem, are related to *how* states use EU law to cooperate: institutional and legal arrangements are tools that represent 'how' the benefits of cooperation are obtained. Enforcement issues are also of interest for lawyers and for scholars of law and economics, but they should be distinguished from the underlying motives as to *why* cooperative relations are established (or eschewed) in the first place. Scholars of international relations interested in how relations are 'designed' have focused on five broad dimensions of international organizations (such as the EU).

[1] Barbara Koremenos, *The Continent of International Law: Explaining Agreement Design* (Cambridge University Press 2016).

[2] Craig de Búrca, *EU Law: Text, Cases, and Materials* (Oxford University Press 2020).

[3] Andrew Guzman, *How International Law Works* (Oxford University Press 2008) 22, 33, 71, 119, 183; Jack L Goldsmith and Eric A Posner, *The Limits of International Law* (Oxford University Press 2006) 23, 83; Joel P Trachtman, *The Economic Structure of International Law* (Harvard University Press 2008) 72, 119, 208.

Treating states as rational actors that shape an international organization (the independent variable), they identify a range of dependent variables, including membership rules; the range of issues addressed; the centralization of responsibilities; rules for controlling the institution; and the flexibility of arrangements.[4] Certain features—namely, flexibility and centralization—are of essential importance from an economic perspective, and of relevance for the EU (*how* and *why*), while others may be better understood from an actor-centric perspective that considers incentive structures and associated aspects of game theory, including the view that EU institutions are 'agents' acting on behalf of Member States as 'principals' (*who*).

With a view to 'centralization', we find interdependencies between form and substance, for 'centralization' not only refers to the empowerment of supranational authorities to monitor, mediate, and sanction, but also to the distribution of substantive competencies between EU-level institutions and Member States. Thus, our *why* captures more fundamentally the core motivational drivers for EU members to enter into binding EU law and subject themselves to a constraining institutional framework in the first place. By contrast, the *how* inquiries into the specific institutional and procedural design of the EU—that is, the way it centralizes responsibilities, maintains flexibility, and legislates and enforces EU law; the *who* is actor-oriented and focuses on the economic underpinning of Union institutions acting as administrators, legislators, and adjudicators of EU law, each of them guided by individual incentive structures through (more or less) legally defined control and sanction regimes. Furthermore, the *what* inquiries into the specific policy fields and competencies of the EU from an economic perspective.

EU lawyers typically struggle with the *why*. EU public lawyers ask questions regarding underlying motivations only in very limited cases (eg to determine the relevant legal basis for public policies); they exhibit almost no interest in the rationale for creating EU primary law in the first place or for crafting the peculiar EU institutional framework. By contrast, asking *why* is a key research question posed by scholars of international relations and economics. And it is precisely this perspective that we seek to render fruitful for legal analysis. One prospective benefit of such an approach is to furnish economically informed metrics for assessing *how* competences between the Union and Member States *should* be allocated. Such an approach, which clearly goes beyond positivist considerations of how competencies *are* allocated in the Treaties, promises to appeal in particular to legal scholars, given the importance they attach to systematic definitions and doctrinal consistency. By the same token, legal analysis of the instruments set forth by the Treaties can be expanded by asking *why* and *when* these instruments should be used.

International lawyers traditionally ask questions of *who* is bound by law or *who* can invoke certain rights: While the Westphalian legal order from which modern

[4] Koremenos (n 1) 42.

international law emerged was tied to the state-only approach, the emergence of international organizations and individuals in the international law arena has given rise to an array of new legal issues.[5] International relations scholars have also sought to account for the shift in focus from states to non-state actors, recognizing the non-state actors as active agents that make and change rules in global governance.[6] Unlike lawyers, who generally consider states to be the sole source of authority (even going so far as to consider domestic affairs irrelevant to international public law[7]), international relations and economic scholars endeavour to add granularity to the *who* in international law by breaking up the 'billiard ball' and looking inside the state—for example, by applying a political economy perspective that explains the actions of domestic state actors, a perspective relevant to the multilevel and multi-institutional framework of the EU. Likewise, with methodological and normative individualism as an operational benchmark, economics speaks to the perennial legal issue of who is the subject of legitimacy in the EU, that is, in whose interest the EU should act. Principal–agent considerations enter the analytical sphere of *who* acts, which is alien to a legal assessment that determines the *who* with sole reference to the competences, rights, and obligations enshrined in the Treaties.

[5] Roberto Virzo and Ivan Ingravallo, *Evolutions in the Law of International Organizations* (Brill/Nijhoff 2015).

[6] Deborah D Avant, Martha Finnemore, and Susan K Sell, *Who Governs the Globe? (Cambridge Studies in International Relations, Series Number 114)* (Cambridge University Press 2010).

[7] Article 27 of the Vienna Convention on the Law of Treaties 1969.

1

Meandering between rational choice, realism, constructivism, and institutionalism

A few words of explanation regarding the methodological arsenal of this work are necessary, that is where it sits on the spectrum between realism and constructivism, between rational choice and behavioural economic scepticism. Building on mainstream economic theory and International Relations literature, this work harnesses rational choice theory as its dominant analytical approach, given its power to account for the behaviour of various actors, whether individuals, firms, non-governmental organizations (NGOs), or states. The rational choice model presumes that actors seek to maximize their interests in decision situations marked by constraints. This perspective takes EU Member States as the analytical point of departure and suggests that the design of EU institutions, including core legal principles (eg conferral or subsidiarity), are deliberate architectural choices made by Member States as the 'masters of the Treaties'. Over time, this perspective has proven excessively narrow, as the EU as an organization has evolved to become an actor itself when acting through its institutions—for instance, when it adopts secondary law, when judges of the ECJ perform their judiciary function, or when Union institutions are involved in Treaty amendments, as is perhaps most visible through the supranational character and supremacy of EU law over national law. This makes the EU different from other international organizations which have, from a rational choice perspective, largely been viewed as a derivative function of Member State interests.[1] While Treaty changes were ultimately decided and ratified by the EU members, these changes have contributed to the emergence of the EU as an autonomous actor.

It is the supranational character of the EU that has emancipated it from typical analytical perspectives in international law, and with this in mind, we must reconsider our assessment of the EU from the standpoint of law and economics, for the EU cannot be studied solely as the expression of Member State will; rather, the EU has been emancipated from being a 'dependent variable' to assume the status

[1] Barbara Koremenos, Charles Lipson, and Duncan Snidal, 'The Rational Design of International Institutions' (2001) 55 International Organization 761; Eric Posner and Alan O Sykes, *Economic Foundations of International Law* (Harvard University Press 2013) 84.

EU Law and Economics. Armin Steinbach, Oxford University Press. © Oxford University Press 2025.
DOI: 10.1093/9780198920915.003.0001

of an 'independent variable'. This is a methodological extension that may be disruptive to traditional legal perspectives founded on the *Kompetenz-Kompetenz* of Member States as 'masters of the Treaties'. To be sure, institutional development in the EU is not solely driven by the deliberate choices of Member States, but also by the autonomous behaviour of EU-level institutions. To take this institutional autonomy into account is essential, and it requires us to look beyond the EU as a blind agent of Member State will. One important and groundbreaking example of EU autonomy is the legal innovation introduced by the ECJ's rulings concerning the direct effect and supremacy of EU law, which have been the driver for legal and institutional intervention of the EU into Member States' legal orders.

We will discuss the various rationales that underpin EU cooperation from a rational choice perspective—a perspective that inherently treats the EU as a 'dependent variable'—but we will also look at the various EU institutions that act as rational choice actors—for example, by examining interactions between EU institutions involved in policy formulation or adjudication from the perspective of game theory. It may be plausible to view the EU as a 'dependent variable' during the initial development of the EU Treaties. This is less the case when Treaty amendments occur, because Member States are the pivotal actors under the Treaty revision procedure (Article 48 Treaty on European Union (TEU)). By contrast, with a view to the adoption of EU secondary law, it is plausible to assume that the outcomes depend on the actions and interests of Union institutions, given their indispensable consent for the law-making process.

The predominant assumption underpinning a rational choice assessment is that state preferences are exogenous, as domestic policy is mostly not taken into account in the law and economics literature, nor in international relations scholarship.[2] However, the notion of evolving preferences that has been posited by the constructivist view represents a deviation from the rational choice postulate. In essence, constructivist approaches focus on the social construction of identity between actors in international relations.[3] Accordingly, international norms, including international and EU law, have a constitutive function in the sense that they help to give form to the wishes and preferences of states.[4] Yet it is not only

[2] Koremenos (n 1) 12.

[3] In line with critical theorists for a detailed discussion, see Alexander Wendt, 'Constructing International Politics' (1995) 20 International Security 71, 71 f.: 'Critical IR "theory", however, is not a single theory. It is a family of theories that includes postmodernists (Ashley, Walker), constructivists (Adler, Kratochwil, Ruggie, and now Katzenstein), neo-Marxists (Cox, Gill), feminists (Peterson, Sylvester), and others. What unites them is a concern with how world politics is "socially constructed", which involves two basic claims: that the fundamental structures of international politics are social rather than strictly material (a claim that opposes materialism), and that these structures shape actors' identities and interests, rather than just their behaviour (a claim that opposes rationalism).'

[4] cf also Martha Finnemore, *National Interests in International Society* (Cornell University Press 1996) 128: 'The fact that we live in an international society means that what we want and, in some ways, who we are shaped by the social norms, rules, understandings, and relationships we have with others. These social realities are as influential as material realities in determining behaviour. Indeed, they are

constructivists who point to the changeable preferences of states. Public choice offers a similar understanding by considering interactions with domestic constituencies.[5] Notably, state preferences may change as a result of changes in domestic politics. In the case of the EU, the situation is further complicated by the multilevel governance structure that involves several actors interacting with each other in decision-making, both horizontally between Union institutions, but also vertically between the EU and Member States, adding complexity and additional strategic aspects to the analysis. Under these circumstances, we must abandon the assumption that states are animated by stable preferences and instead pursue positive analysis of the context in question, rather than employing general models.[6] The more public choice considerations add complexity to our understanding and prediction of state interests—that is, the more we construct state preferences as a function of domestic policy issues—the less we can draw general predictions about the conduct of EU states. This is problematic for an economic analysis that seeks to achieve generalizable results. At the same time, assuming that states are unitary actors would preclude such considerations altogether. It thus would appear plausible to adopt both perspectives—that is, to view states as unitary actors animated by concern for national welfare while relaxing this assumption when warranted by contextual factors.

Constructivists acknowledge that ideas and beliefs—and not just material interests—determine the behaviour of states, and are therefore relevant in promoting compliance with law.[7] In their seminal discussion of constructivist theory, Finnemore and Sikkink assert that 'norm cascades' can function as causal chains that induce compliance with international law norms.[8] In their view, norms arise when 'norm entrepreneurs' try to convince states to accept new norms. In a second phase, a critical mass of states accepts the norms, and they 'cascade' down to the remaining states. In the final phase, the norms are accepted and internalized, thus giving rise to a preference for norm compliance. However, rationalists categorically reject this description of the preference formation process. One can use the constructivist logic to explain the sequential spread of EU law into Member State domestic law. Once the ECJ had ruled that EU law had direct effect or supremacy over national law (a judicial innovation not directly derivable from the Treaties), it

what endow material realities with meaning and purpose. In political terms, it is these social realities that provide us with ends to which power and wealth can be used.'

[5] Andrew Guzman, *How International Law Works* (Oxford University Press 2008) 128.

[6] Steven P Croley, 'Theories of Regulation: Incorporating the Administrative Process' (1998) 98 Columbia Law Review 1.

[7] Alexander Wendt, 'Constructing International Politics' (1995) 20 International Security 71; Jeffrey T Checkel, 'Why Comply? Social Learning and European Identity Change' (2001) 55 International Organization 565.

[8] Martha Finnemore and Kathryn Sikkink, 'International Norm Dynamics and Political Change' (1998) 52 International Organization 887.

was the domestic courts of Member States who first accepted this interpretation of EU supremacy when applying European law domestically, and Member State governments subsequently accepted such arrangements, rather than striving for any form of rectification through Treaty amendment.

Unlike constructivists, who accord importance to law as a socially constructed identity that leads to a 'culture of compliance',[9] realists do not see law as a relevant source of authority that can positively determine state conduct. They downplay the importance of international law, and they predict state conduct—and, by extension, compliance with EU law—only as a function of power and preferences, with states always pursuing selfish interests.[10] Rational realists such as Goldsmith and Posner have characterized large parts of public international law as 'cheap talk'.[11] Distributive rationalists, by contrast, are somewhat less radical; while they agree with realists that power is deployed to advance the interests of the state, they do not argue that international institutions are wholly inconsequential. For advocates of this line of thought, institutions are shaped by power politics, and there is no reason to expect that institutions are designed to improve social welfare.[12] This is a view that does not convincingly apply to the EU law context, however. On the one hand, most EU institutions (the Parliament, the Commission, the ECJ) represent Community interests, and EU actions will often diverge from dominant Member States preferences (here we find a point of contrast to member-driven organizations such as the International Monetary Fund and World Trade Organization). On the other hand, the voting weights in the European Parliament and Council tend to disproportionately favour small states. Last but not least, early recognition of the direct effect of EU law by the ECJ can be seen as a pursuit of EU common interest *against* the original intention of (powerful) EU Member States.

Over time, international relations and international law have become increasingly interwoven. It was the contribution of institutionalism to show that collaboration between states could function even in the absence of a centralized enactor or enforcer of law.[13] Discourse has relied heavily on the notion of 'regimes'

[9] Thomas M Franck, *The Power of Legitimacy among Nations* (Oxford University Press 1990); Louis Henkin, *International Law: Politics and Values, vol 18* (Brill 1995); Stephen J Toope and Jutta Brunnée, *Legitimacy and Legality in International Law: An Interactional Account* (Cambridge University Press 2010).

[10] Hans J Morgenthau, 'Positivism, Functionalism, and International Law' (1940) 34 American Journal of International Law 260, 260; as well as Hans J Morgenthau, *Politics Among Nations: The Struggle for Power and Peace* (Alfred A Knopf 1978); John J Mearsheimer, *The Tragedy of Great Power Politics* (updated edn, Norton & Company 2014); Richard H Steinberg, 'Wanted—Dead or Alive', *Interdisciplinary Perspectives on International Law and International Relations* (Cambridge University Press 2012).

[11] Jack L Goldsmith and Eric A Posner, *The Limits of International Law* (Oxford University Press 2006) 175.

[12] Lloyd Gruber, *Ruling the World: Power Politics and the Rise of Supranational Institutions* (Princeton University Press 2000).

[13] Robert O Keohane, *After Hegemony: Cooperation and Discord in the World Political Economy* (Princeton University Press 2005); Duncan Snidal, 'Coordination versus Prisoners'

in international relations, a term expressing the body of norms, principles, procedures, and rules around which actors' expectations converge in a given area of international relations.[14] Consequently, international relations soon developed an interest in international law, partly driven by the former's 'legalization'.[15] From this perspective, legalization is a particular kind of institutional design, one that imposes international legal constraints on states through three dimensions—precision, obligation, and delegation. This strand in the international relations literature has furnished a bridge for international lawyers to connect to international relations theory.[16]

Traditionally, the subject of analysis in the (private) law and economics literature is how law made at the macro level creates incentives on the micro level for individual states, citizens, or firms. With either rational choice or behavioural economics as a methodological premise, this micro legal perspective centred on individual decision-making has been particularly productive for the study of research questions in private law. Unlike the vast economic literature on private law, our focus on public law—and by extension international law and EU law—faces the challenge that collective entities take decisions, not individuals alone.[17] As the economic analysis of competition law shows in exemplary fashion, the unit of analysis was traditionally the firm *in toto*, rather than the individuals who manage it.[18] In the context of legal scrutiny—for example, when it concerns managerial liability under corporate law—the 'black box' is opened to look at individual conduct within the corporate structure.[19] At the international law level, but likewise in EU law, institutions such as the EU Commission, Council, Parliament, or ECJ take collective decisions. The analytical challenge is thus to determine how individuals (state representatives, EU commissioners, or parliamentarians) produce decisions at the macro level in collective bodies when they act, vote, or decide. Economic insight drawing from principal–agent analysis, public choice theory, and game

Dilemma: Implications for International Cooperation and Regimes' (1985) 79 American Political Science Review 923.

[14] Stephen D Krasner, *International Regimes* (Cornell University Press 1983).

[15] Judith Goldstein and others, 'Introduction: Legalization and World Politics' (2000) 54 International Organization 385, 386.

[16] Anne-Marie Slaughter, Andrew S Tulumello, and Stepan Wood, 'International Law and International Relations Theory: A New Generation of Interdisciplinary Scholarship' (1998) 92 American Journal of International Law 367; Goldsmith and Posner (n 11) 16.

[17] Anne van Aaken, 'Behavioral Aspects of the International Law of Global Public Goods and Common Pool Resources' (2018) 112 American Journal of International Law 67.

[18] Paolo Buccirossi and others, 'Deterrence in Competition Law' (2014) SFB/TR 15 Discussion Paper, No 285.

[19] Robert H Sitkoff 'An Economic Theory of Fiduciary Law', in Andrew S Gold, and Paul B Miller (eds), *Philosophical Foundations of Fiduciary Law* (Oxford University Press 2014); Jonathan R Macey, 'Corporate Social Responsibility: A Law & Economics Perspective' (2014) 17 Chapman Law Review 331.

theory may yield various insights that add nuance to the assumption of a 'unitary' institutional will.

By a similar token, lawyers are not typically confronted with the need to distinguish between collective bodies and the individuals that compose them when assessing the conduct of institutions. Either they declare the individual's action irrelevant by simply equating the individual's action with the state (as per Article 7 of the Vienna Treaty Convention), or they count the individual as one element in the formation of collective decision-making (such as the Council representative or parliamentarian counting towards the majority requirement). Alternatively, they consider individuals as actors who are subject to Treaty constraints (such as EU commissioners appointed by the Commission president), or the individual as entirely hidden behind the decision of the collective organ, like at the ECJ, where the law only applies formal criteria to individual judges (such as independence), in contrast to economic analysis, which seeks to understand *why* a judge acts the way they do.[20] Overall, the legal discipline cares little about the motivations (the *whys*) that animate individual representatives in collective decision-making bodies.

In the field of economics there are different ways to account for state conduct: First, states are assumed to be *state oeconomicii* that pursue the self-interest of national welfare. This pragmatic rational-choice approach will be deployed as the default lens when discussing rationalist motives for why states subordinate themselves to EU law (the *why*). This approach is naturally compatible with realist approaches that emphasize inter-state power relations and that downplay the relevance of international norms. From this perspective, the state remains the unit of analysis and is considered to act based on a given set of preferences under a given array of constraints. In this way, states are treated as 'billiard balls' or as 'black boxes'; state preferences are exogenous and monolithic.[21] The merit of this approach is that it reduces complexity and simplifies the act of analysis. Assuming that states have monolithic preferences is obviously a simplifying reduction. Clearly, the 'state' is an aggregation of various actors, each of whom may pursue divergent preferences. The relevant decision-makers change in composition over time, as do the relevant domestic policy constraints, making the supposition of iron-clad 'state preferences' problematic, not least due to the flux these preferences may experience over time.[22]

Second, when dissecting EU law-making, one can understand EU decision-making as a function of the interaction between idiosyncratic institutions, whereby

[20] Jens Frankenreiter, 'The Politics of Citations at the ECJ—Policy Preferences of E.U. Member State Governments and the Citation Behavior of Judges at the European Court of Justice' (2017) 14 Journal of Empirical Legal Studies 813.

[21] Anne-Marie Slaughter, 'Remarks, the Big Picture: Beyond Hot Spots & Crises in Our Interconnected World' (2012) 1 Penn State Journal of Law & International Affairs 286.

[22] Eric Posner and Alan O Sykes, *Economic Foundations of International Law* (Harvard University Press 2013) 18.

Member States, the ECJ, and the EU Commission, Council, and Parliament act as 'micro agents' under the 'macro constraint' of the Treaty framework. This perspective can draw not only on public choice theory to focus on institutional interests, but can also tap a growing body of scholarship in international relations that considers how domestic political processes mediate cooperation at the international level. Gourevitch's 'second image' and Putnam's two-level game are examples of early contributions to this stand in the literature.[23] Third, in response to a constitutional law perspective that emphasizes legitimacy as a critical element of the EU's multi-level and multi-institutional architecture,[24] economics questions whose preferences the Union institutions are accountable to—that is, the preferences of the 'citizens of Europe', Member States, or Member State electorates. With (legal) legitimacy and (economic) preferences serving as mutually enriching concepts, this approach to the analysis of EU law-making devotes particular attention to the optimal allocation of competences between the EU and Member States.

[23] Robert D Putnam, 'Diplomacy and Domestic Politics: The Logic of Two-Level Games' (1988) 42 International Organization 427.

[24] Dieter Grimm, *Europa ja - aber welches? Zur Verfassung der europäischen Demokratie* (C H Beck 2016) 29.

2
A cursory review of economic methods

This analysis does not rely exclusively on one specific analytical approach. Rather, it aims to present various interpretations based on a variety of analytical perspectives. This chapter briefly introduces the methods most frequently applied in this study and highlights their connection to EU law. With a view to the EU law regulation of public policy in Member States, *public-good analysis* is used to assess collective action dilemmas as well as rationales for cooperation within the EU. The 'Europeanization' of public goods is a driver of European integration, as trends toward internationalization and globalization have been giving public goods such as peace, security, monetary stability, and climate protection an increasingly pan-European dimension.[1] This necessitates multilevel governance institutions to limit the collective action problems posed by intergovernmental politics. In this vein, the transfer of competences from Member States to the EU in tandem with the establishment of supranational governance structures aims to deliver public goods that could not be achieved through Member State action alone.[2] Public good analysis and federalism theory offer guidance on when and under what conditions the delivery of public goods in the EU should be provided at the EU level or, conversely, at the level of the Member State. These approaches also offer insights into how the allocation of competencies by the EU Treaties can optimize the effective provision of public goods.[3] For example, the existence of externalities, economies of scale, and economies of scope offer economic metrics by which to enrich the application of the legal principle of subsidiarity (Article 5 TEU), and grant an economic dimension to the assessment of competency allocation. Fiscal federalism theory and its concern with the responsiveness of public-goods provision to the preferences of the citizenry also furnish links to insights from other disciplines.[4] Preference heterogeneity, a core criterion in fiscal federalism for determining the proper level of regulation, is well-suited for drawing attention to the value of democratic participation and of protecting personal rights and liberties. This literature speaks more specifically to the level of government activity that should take place in order to

[1] Ernst-Ulrich Petersmann, *Multilevel Constitutionalism for Multilevel Governance of Public Goods: Methodology Problems in International Law* (Hart Publishing 2019) 190.

[2] Clemens Fuest and Jean Pisani-Ferry, 'A Primer on Developing European Public Goods' (2019) EconPol Policy Report, No 16.

[3] See below Chapter 5.1 and Grégory Claeys and Armin Steinbach, 'A Conceptual Framework for the Identification and Governance of European Public Goods' (2024) Working Paper 14/2024, Bruegel.

[4] Deil S Wright, 'Fiscal Federalism' (1974) 68 American Political Science Review 1777.

EU Law and Economics. Armin Steinbach, Oxford University Press. © Oxford University Press 2025.
DOI: 10.1093/9780198920915.003.0002

maximize the ability of citizens to influence actual decision-making.[5] In this vein, fiscal federalism theory generally favours local governance as a default position for enhancing democratic participation and accounting for local preferences.

Closely related to public goods analysis is the concept of *transaction costs*, which captures various dimensions of costs associated with cooperation.[6] Transaction costs analysis may offer a plausible explanation as to why cooperation within the EU takes place or why it does not.[7] Transaction costs can be multidimensional. By way of example, sovereignty costs are incurred whenever states cannot choose their national prerogatives and surrender competencies. In light of the transfer of competences to Brussels, some constitutional courts have argued that specific aspects of state sovereignty should remain under national control. Similarly, negotiation costs occur if EU states must engage in lengthy debate to find unanimity in the Council; contracting costs occur if the complexity of an issue is high; implementation costs occur when there is a burden of complying with EU directives and regulations; and monitoring costs occur when an institutional structure is established to administer an agreement or review compliance with EU law (eg the European Stability Mechanism, or ESM, established during the sovereign debt crisis). The use of transaction costs analysis paves the way for cost-benefit analysis that studies the behaviour of EU members seeking various forms of cooperation (eg differentiated rather than full integration). Transaction costs vary depending on a range of factors, including the number of EU states involved, the substance of the issue at hand, the degree of formality, and the institutional environment of the agreement.

The EU is based on international treaties, which are the main source of EU law, making *contract theory* a fertile analytical tool, as it is commonly applied to the assessment of international law.[8] The EU is an international organization built on many contracts in the sense that the EU Treaties cover a wide scope of substantive law, procedural rules, and institutional arrangements. Accession to the EU is predicated on the assumption that taking on the rights and obligations associated with membership will generate a positive net payoff. EU Member States delegate

[5] Albert Weale and Michael Nentwich, *Political Theory and the European Union: Legitimacy, Constitutional Choice and Citizenship* (Routledge 1998); Mareike Kleine, Javier Arregui, and Robert Thomson, 'The Impact of National Democratic Representation on Decision-Making in the European Union' (2022) 29 Journal of European Public Policy 1.

[6] Building on seminal work, Ronald H Coase, 'The Problem of Social Cost' (1960) 3 Journal of Law and Economics 1; Ronald H Coase, 'The Institutional Structure of Production' (1992) University of Chicago Law Occasional Paper; Oliver E Williamson, 'The Economics of Organization: The Transaction Cost Approach' (1981) 87 American Journal of Sociology 548.

[7] Armin Steinbach, 'The Trend towards Non-Consensualism in Public International Law: A (Behavioural) Law and Economics Perspective' (2016) 27 European Journal of International Law 643, 646.

[8] Robert E Scott and Paul B Stephan, *The Limits of Leviathan* (Cambridge University Press 2006); Joel P Trachtman, *The Future of International Law: Global Government* (Cambridge University Press 2013) 318.

authority over a particular area of concern to the EU in exchange for cooperative gains (such as reciprocal commitments by the other Member States) or for the coordination gains achieved through centralization (such as harmonizing standards). The multiplicity of contracts to which Member States must accede is a distinguishing feature of the EU compared to other international organizations because it widens the number of agreeable solutions through cross-policy compensation, with asymmetric concessions on one contract (eg in agricultural policy) being compensated by asymmetry in other context (eg market freedoms). While subcontracts produce divergent benefits and costs for Member States, the complementarity of policy fields allows greater positive net payoffs than in narrowly designed international organizations.

The questions surrounding optimal Treaty design is a highly salient issue for contracting parties. A contract should be optimal from an *ex-ante* perspective, that is, it should incentivize the parties to invest in the contractual relationship in order to maximize anticipated mutual benefits. At the same time, however, the parties want to craft a contract that is also optimal *ex post*, that is, one that maximizes the benefits for parties even after possible uncertainties have arisen. These partially conflicting goals create tension, because each party wants to secure the other party's commitment, but *ex-post* inflexible commitments can compromise the goal of maximizing shared benefits. Specifically, unforeseen circumstances may cause the compliance cost of one party to exceed the benefits that it expected to generate from the contract.[9] Treaty specification and *ex-post* adjudication of the European Court of Justice (ECJ) are thus key to maintaining contractual gains under conditions of uncertainty.

Similar considerations apply to expected compliance with EU Treaties. EU members enter into a contract behind a 'veil of ignorance', that is, they do not know who might break the contract. In this situation, they are obliged to make a distinction between, on the one hand, 'intra-contractual flexibility', which applies to certain behaviour that is due to unforeseen external events and that is not tantamount to a breach of contract; and, on the other hand, 'extra-contractual flexibility', which refers to a breach of contract due to opportunistic behaviour, and which should trigger corresponding legal consequences. An optimally designed contract permits flexibility in the first case and provides for 'hard' law in the second case. While 'hard' law punishes those who violate the contract, extra-contractual flexibility punishes the party who abides by the contract. Parties can therefore express their contracts in rather vague provisions and delegate the interpretation to third parties (ie EU Commission administration, and ECJ adjudication) in order to ensure the necessary flexibility *ex post*, at the price of raising the uncertainty regarding the net payoff from cooperation *ex ante*. This interpretative framework allows us to

[9] Scott and Stephan (n 8) 61.

study the optimal degree of specificity that contracts should contain, and the functionality of 'rules' and 'standards' under conditions of uncertainty[10]—parameters which, in the EU context, are fulfilled by 'regulations' and 'directives'. This has a direct connection to economic arguments for 'efficient breaches' of contract, a term that refers to voluntary breaches of contract when adherence would lead to even greater economic losses.[11] While such a perspective is incompatible with the binding *pacta sunt servanda* rule, breaches of EU obligations may be the efficient response when EU Treaties do not offer sufficient flexibility or when other contractual partners prevent an efficient adaption of the EU Treaties as a selfish holdout strategy.[12]

The interactions between EU states can also be likened to the decisions made by players in a game. Indeed, economic analysis has made extensive use of the techniques furnished by non-cooperative *game theory*. One limitation of game theory is that it precludes consideration of exogenously binding contracts.[13] Hence, for international law to be effective, the contractual arrangements must be self-enforcing, because, unlike national law, international law lacks exogenous enforcement tools. In this way, the rules themselves must offer sufficient endogenous incentives for compliance. Compliance is assured because adherence is in the individual interests of the parties to the agreement. With a view to the EU, the cooperation literature shows that cooperation is possible in repeated games.[14] The interdependencies that exist between European states, including the Union-wide scope of many policies, entail repeated interaction of a cooperative nature. Incentive compatibility does not require positive net payoffs for all states and compliance on all occasions and under all contingencies, provided the long run benefits for adhering to a specific institutional setup are positive. Sanction mechanisms help to sustain defined institutional arrangements and also promote compliance, but this requires the actual imposition of sanctions when they are warranted. A key problem in this regard is that within international organizations, sanctions are endogenous, thus creating a second-order public good dilemma. As a consequence, sanctions are underutilized in the international law arena (see below Chapter 14). The EU, which has a supranational character, represents a hybrid case. Compliance with EU law rests on the generation of payoffs in a repeated game as well as retaliation in the event of

[10] Louis Kaplow, 'General Characteristics of Rules' in *Encyclopedia of Law and Economics* (National Bureau of Economic Research 1997); Cass R Sunstein, 'Problems with Rules' (1995) 83 California Law Review 953.

[11] Wenqing Liao, *The Application of the Theory of Efficient Breach in Contract Law: A Comparative Law and Economics Perspective* (Intersentia Ltd 2015); Melvin A Eisenberg, *Foundational Principles of Contract Law* (Oxford University Press 2018).

[12] Eric Posner and Alan O Sykes, *Economic Foundations of International Law* (Harvard University Press 2013) 25.

[13] Trachtman (n 8) 516.

[14] James W Friedman, 'A Non-Cooperative Equilibrium for Supergames' (1971) 38 Review of Economic Studies 1; Drew Fudenberg and Eric Maskin, 'The Folk Theorem in Repeated Games with Discounting or with Incomplete Information' (1986) 54 Econometrica 533.

misconduct by a third party (EU Commission and ECJ), rather than by the parties to the agreement, which can resolve the second-order public goods dilemma. The EU has increasingly built up an arsenal of sanction mechanisms, which are largely under the control of the Commission as a third party to Member States (alongside qualified majority voting on the Council). Non-compliance with EU law thus leads to considerable exogenous enforcement which resolves the second-order collective action dilemma, representing a point of contrast to public international law.

As the EU addresses many policy areas and encompasses multiple sector-specific commitments (subcontracts), one could reasonably presume that various games are underway in parallel.[15] From a game theory perspective, one could say that players are bound to each other in multiple ways, including through the links between games.[16] Suppose, for example, that Member States interact with each other and with the Commission in a game of fiscal supervision in which Member States have to decide whether to comply or defect. This game may be influenced by behavioural spillovers from a parallel game taking place on a more general level as part of inter-state relationships (eg within the European Council, in the interactions between heads of state). In this way, the state of play in an inter-state relationship or the likelihood of Member State coalitions (against the Commission) might impact the fiscal-scrutiny game and determine its payoff structure. More generally, EU Member States and EU institutions interact in a variety of contexts, with each Member State taking on different roles in each circumstance. In a 'rule-of-law game' a country might take a harsh stance vis-à-vis potential defectors to the EU rule of law while, at the same time, a 'fiscal-supervision game' might be underway in which that same EU member is much less concerned with the rigid application of EU rules, and these games could be linked.

This potential for interaction between games is at odds with an established legal doctrine: international agreements are considered to be self-contained regimes that are sufficient unto themselves for settling disagreements, and they also claim primacy over more general law. Accordingly, an issue occurring under the EU fiscal surveillance regime should be dealt with exclusively under the applicable EU fiscal rules—however, in a legal *and* political union, in which more than one game is going on at the same time, the fiscal dispute is unlikely to be resolved solely based on the application of fiscal rules. The additional discretion that the Commission and Council enjoy is likely to be determined by other games. What is legally designed as a self-contained regime is influenced in practice by other factors—which is good news for the compliance record under EU law, as the interrelationships between games may induce compliance in a way that makes the larger relationship between Member States self-enforcing.[17]

15 Trachtman (n 8).

16 Timothy N Cason, Anya C Savikhin, and Roman M Sheremeta, 'Behavioral Spillovers in Coordination Games' (2012) 56 European Economic Review 233.

17 Trachtman (n 8) 516.

Likewise, game theory may furnish an explanation for the institutional design of the EU. Consider for instance the judicial independence granted to ECJ judges. We can think of judges as participating in a power competition game with other officials. In contrast to the assumptions of positivist lawyers, for whom the Treaty's stipulation of independence is unquestioned, judges typically have their own preferences regarding the political order.[18] The court has a range of possible interpretations that can be brought to a legal text, and judges can satisfy their political preferences by exercising their power to interpret statutes. However, they must fear legislators overruling a court's judgment and, in the case of the EU, that national courts may not follow ECJ decisions, as domestic courts are obliged to apply EU law as interpreted by the ECJ.[19] From this, it stands to reason that that the ECJ will more aggressively apply its judicial discretion when the risk of legislative repeal or conflict with domestic courts is small (see below Chapter 20 c).

The EU is based on Treaties that are quasi-constitutional in nature. In this way, *constitutional economics* offers a fruitful lens for examining EU law. This school of thought, initiated by Nobel prize winner James Buchanan, seeks to abandon the prevailing focus on welfare economics (with its neoclassical 'maximization paradigm') as well as the rational choice theory that undergirds realist approaches to international relations.[20] By contrast, constitutional economics hinges on the premise of 'constitutional contract/exchange paradigms'.[21] Individual and collective gains are enabled by constitutional cooperation that improves the 'laws and institutions' of the economic and political order and protects the democratic expression of informed preferences. Constitutional economics redirects the focus of economic analysis away from individual utility maximization towards the design of markets and political arenas such that 'consumer sovereignty' in markets and 'citizen sovereignty' in political domains form the analytical and normative benchmark.[22] Normative constitutional economics calls for legal safeguards to ensure that the 'competitive order' (based on 'performance competition' and price mechanisms) remains embedded in a mutually coherent monetary order (that protects price stability and ensures fiscal discipline); democratic constitutionalism (that holds 'European network governance' accountable through multilevel competition, monetary, and other regulatory agencies); and social order (that

[18] Jeffrey J Rachlinski and Andrew J Wistrich, 'Judging the Judiciary by the Numbers: Empirical Research on Judges' (2017) 13 Annual Review of Law and Social Science 203; Cass R Sunstein, *Are Judges Political? An Empirical Analysis of the Federal Judiciary* (Brookings Institution Press 2006).

[19] Stefan Voigt, 'Iudex Calculat: The ECJ's Quest for Power' (2003) 22 Jahrbuch für Neue Politische Ökonomie.

[20] Geoffrey Brennan and James M Buchanan, *The Reason of Rules: Constitutional Political Economy* (Cambridge University Press 1985); James M Buchanan, 'The Domain of Constitutional Economics' (1990) 1 Constitutional Political Economy 1.

[21] Armin Steinbach, 'Constitutional Economics and Transnational Governance Failures', Constitutionalism and Transnational Governance Failures (Brill/Nijhoff 2024) 77.

[22] Viktor J Vanberg, 'Market and State: The Perspective of Constitutional Political Economy' (2005) 1 Journal of Institutional Economics 23, 27.

protects labour markets, welfare states, social justice, and judicial remedies).[23] Normative constitutional economics criticizes various aspects of neoclassical economics, including its focus on utility maximization and rational rent-seeking and the assumption of 'perfect market competition' without transaction costs. Gross domestic product as a welfare metric is also attacked given its failure to account for other important measures of human well-being, including the universal satisfaction of the populace's basic needs, the enhancement of 'human capacities' (AK Sen), and the protection of constitutional rights. The EU Charter of Fundamental Rights (EUCFR) guarantees civil, political, economic, social, and 'European citizenship rights', and thus does not only protect 'negative freedoms' (eg constraining abuses of public and private power). Articles 2 and 8 of the European Convention on Human Rights (ECHR) have prompted ever-greater number of courts to rule that environmental pollution and climate change infringe on human rights, thus furnishing a legal basis for addressing market failures. Combatting climate change, promoting sustainable development in cooperation with third states, and principles of 'environmental constitutionalism' (including the principles of precaution, prevention, and rectifying pollution at its source, as well as the 'polluter pays' principle) are included in the EU Treaty provisions on EU environmental policies (eg Treaty on the Functioning of the European Union (TFEU) Arts 11, 191–193).[24]

In the arena of international law, *Trachtman* posits that the allocation of jurisdictional power constitutes an assignment of *property rights*.[25] Accordingly, a wide range of activities by Member States can be conceived as an assignment of property rights, including the agreement on specific rules governing the legality of state conduct, the determination of state obligations and individual rights, and the delineation of competences between states (Union versus Member States) and between institutions (Council versus Commission). States seek to define property rights in order to facilitate coordination and to stabilize expectations. A primary function of property rights according to the literature is to guide incentives for achieving a greater internalization of external costs. Accordingly, a primary function of jurisdictional rules is that of shaping incentives to achieve a greater internalization of external costs among political units. At the same time, Member States, as the initial 'owner' of jurisdictional power, engage in property allocation based on whether this allows them to achieve gains. By viewing jurisdictional power as property, we can thus inquire into the optimal allocation of prescriptive jurisdiction in the EU—that is, how to allocate competences to authorize the use of public policies. An interesting conundrum arises in connection with the harmonization of rules within

[23] Ernst-Ulrich Petersmann and Armin Steinbach, 'Neo-Liberalism, State-Capitalism and Ordo-Liberalism: "Institutional Economics" and "Constitutional Choices" in Multilevel Trade Regulation' (2021) 22 Journal of World Investment & Trade 1, 20.

[24] Ernst-Ulrich Petersmann, 'Constitutional Pluralism, Regulatory Competition and Transnational Governance Failures' in *Constitutionalism and Transnational Governance Failures* (Brill/Nijhoff 2024).

[25] Trachtman (n 8) 10, 26.

the EU. Specifically, the assignment of property rights to the EU by Member States could be viewed as a means of collusion, as an anti-competitive use of property rights. Indeed, this assignment can be interpreted as an inappropriate restraint on interjurisdictional competition—for example, when the EU sets educational standards for lawyers or doctors, or establishes effectiveness standards for pharmaceuticals. Accordingly, the anti-competitive impacts of collusion in the domain of jurisdiction assignment must thus be taken into account; this is a concern that also arises in fiscal federalism theory (see Chapter 10 a).

As a multilevel governance order, the EU is also amenable to *principal–agent analysis*, a perspective that promises to shed light on the consequences of authority delegation at various levels of government. Here, a collective principal (the Member States) acting on behalf of another principal (national citizens) delegates authority to an agent (the EU) and institutional sub-agents (EU institutions) in order to accomplish particular purposes. Special attention can be devoted to each element in this multi-stage principal–agent chain. In this connection, controversy has been triggered by the delegation of authority to non-majoritarian institutions. Such delegation is typically motivated by one of two rationales: the first is the need for technical expertise (principals delegate certain functions to agents who possess required competencies, but also impose control mechanisms);[26] the second rationale is informed by the quest for credible commitments (in this connection, principals deliberately provide a considerable freedom of action to the agent so that this agent can adopt policy to which the principals themselves could not credibly commit).[27] Non-majoritarian institutions such as the Commission, the European Central Bank (ECB), and the ECJ have the following features: they delegate authority to govern specific domains of activity; they are not directly elected; and they enjoy considerable independence.[28] For economists, independence in this context means leeway for agents to act autonomously from pressures native to the political economy, in conjunction with the inherent risk that agents will pursue objectives that do not align with the preferences of the principal; associated shirking or self-dealing generates 'agency costs'.[29] Political scientists and lawyers have raised legitimacy as a core concern associated with the non-majoritarian character of EU institutions.[30] Measures designed to reduce legitimacy concerns

[26] Giandomenico Majone, 'Nonmajoritarian Institutions and the Limits of Democratic Governance: A Political Transaction-Cost Approach' (2001) 157 Journal of Institutional and Theoretical Economics 57; Giandomenico Majone, 'Two Logics of Delegation' (2001) 2 European Union Politics 103.

[27] Mark A Pollack, *The Engines of European Integration* (Oxford University Press 2003).

[28] Mark Thatcher, Alec Stone Sweet, and Bernardo Rangoni, 'Reversing Delegation? Politicization, De-delegation, and Non-majoritarian Institutions' (2023) 36 Governance 5.

[29] Eric W Orts, 'Shirking and Sharking: A Legal Theory of the Firm' (1998) 16 Yale Law & Policy Review 265; Susan P Shapiro, 'Agency Theory' (2005) 31 Annual Review of Sociology 263.

[30] Ben Crum and Deirdre Curtin, 'The Challenge of Making European Union Executive Power Accountable' in Simona Piattoni (ed) *The European Union* (Oxford University Press 2015); Deirdre Curtin, 'Challenging Executive Dominance in European Democracy' (2014) 77 Modern Law Review 1.

by limiting shirking and self-dealing generally establish supervisory arrangements. In this connection, it is necessary to strike an appropriate balance between *ex-ante* and *ex-post* accountability.[31] Yet another recommended means of shoring up legitimacy is to ensure a sufficiently specified mandate. In this way, some political scientists have reconceived the principal–agent problem in terms of 'input legitimacy' and 'output legitimacy'.[32]

The bold normative claims advanced by economists are at least partially to blame for the resistance that has arisen to the proliferation of economic thinking in neighbouring disciplines.[33] Accordingly, adequately distinguishing between positivist and normative metrics in economic analysis is far from inconsequential. The positivist conception starts from the premise that economics is primarily an epistemology, not a methodology. The economic toolbox hosts multiple methods, and all of them may be deployed for rational social scientific analysis.[34] Properly applied, economic methodologies simply generate relational descriptions. Good economics helps to identify the relationships between law, institutions, and policies and the outcomes that they generate. US President Harry Truman is widely credited with saying 'Give me a one-handed economist! All my economists say "on the one hand . . . [and then] on the other"'. Here, Truman was expressing his desire for straightforward economic counsel, rather than an ambivalent discussion of trade-offs and opportunity costs. In this tradition, economics is a consequentialist and self-conscious tool for analysing social life and the prospective effects of implementing policy measures, one that accepts that normative policy goals should be determined by values outside of the economics discipline.[35] Economics is most helpful to law when it offers complementary insight and tools—by studying empirical effects; by revealing the incentives that rules create for states and individuals; by highlighting welfare differences between two states of society; and by disclosing the stability of the legal equilibrium that binds two or more states. By contrast, the normative mode of the economic approach to law seeks to assess the desirability of certain objectives, typically efficiency. Yet it should be relegated to constitutions and law-makers to determine what normative goals society should pursue. Efficiency is not enshrined in constitutional documents, and legislators rarely pursue efficiency as a primary objective of policy. Employing efficiency as normative benchmark should thus been seen as a scientific exercise, one that

[31] Rosa M Lastra and Christina P Skinner, 'Sustainable Central Banking' (2023) 63 Virginia Journal of International Law 397, 436.

[32] Fritz W Scharpf, 'Economic Integration, Democracy and the Welfare State' (1997) 4 Journal of European Public Policy 18; Vivien A Schmidt, *Europe's Crisis of Legitimacy: Governing by Rules and Ruling by Numbers in the Eurozone* (Oxford University Press 2020).

[33] Liran Einav and Leeat Yariv, 'What's in a Surname? The Effects of Surname Initials on Academic Success' (2006) 20 Journal of Economic Perspectives 175.

[34] Trachtman (n 8) 1.

[35] ibid 2.

allows us to identify first-best choices in terms of efficiency while also acknowledging second-best choices, given the primacy of other objectives.

Descriptive and normative forms of economic analysis intersect when EU law is investigated using interrogative pronouns (eg who, what, why, how). Over the course of this book, various perspectives are adopted. When we discuss *why* EU members cooperate through EU law (and when they should), efficiency helps to identify rationales for addressing market failures; for tackling externalities; for unlocking economies of scale; and for reducing (transaction) costs. The *how* of cooperation is amenable to descriptive economic analysis—it can reveal the economic rationale for flexibility clauses in the EU Treaties; explain when Treaties are incomplete or overcomplete in specifying legal provisions; and explore the incentives arising from EU law enforcement. By contrast, the *how* may also entail economic normativity—for example, how the subsidiarity test should be applied from an economic perspective; when 'differentiated integration' should be the preferred course of integration; and how legislative choices between directives and regulations should be guided. Our discussion of the *who* of EU cooperation draws on descriptive analysis of public choice theory and principal–agent analysis to discuss the interactions among EU institutions. However, the analysis may be founded on the normativity of efficiency when exploring whether breaches of EU law motivated by efficiency considerations should be permitted in a departure from the *pacta sunt servanda* principle.

Economics is agnostic with regard to the state of the law—it informs the *lex ferenda*: economics advises how EU Treaties should be amended, how secondary law should be crafted, and how to redesign EU competences in the provision of European public goods.[36] *De lege ferenda* economic advice must be assessed in view of the legal barriers posed by the requirements for Treaty amendment. But economics is also helpful *de lege lata* when it informs how law should be interpreted—that is, the economic meaning that can be given to legal terms (eg subsidiarity). *De lege lata*, economic insight must be aligned with the legal canon of interpretation modes, in order to be transferable to the law. The hurdle to introducing economic analysis to the law is the lowest when the law explicitly incorporates economic concepts and benchmarks, such as in EU competition law (eg defining markets) or trade rules (eg determining 'like' products). Finally, the *what* of EU law cooperation addresses policy fields and legal areas that have been neglected in the law and economics literature. Inquiring into European public goods implies the development of a conceptual framework as to how the underprovision of public goods should be addressed—that is, what their economic case is, and what governance options the EU law menu offers to avoid a governance architecture à la 'one-size-fits-all' for European public goods. With the economic freedoms at the core of the

[36] Claeys and Steinbach (n 3).

EU integration project, the relationship between individual freedom and public policy intervention is one where efficiency concerns militate against preference heterogeneity. Finally, the Economic and Monetary Union is the field of law in which lawyers and economists have spilled most ink over the past decade, for it raises the fundamental question of how state organization principles interact with debt dynamics and instruments to contain debt.

PART II
WHY COOPERATE THROUGH EU LAW

Introduction to Part II

Scholars of economic analysis of law have devoted attention to the cooperation between states through international law and its institutions, including international organizations.[1] Comparatively little inquiry has been undertaken on the unique design of the EU.[2] Rational choice has been the dominant analytical benchmark, applied both by international relations scholars and economic scholars. This Part builds on the rational choice literature to the extent that it presumes EU members make deliberate decisions when designing EU cooperation, but we will account for competing perspectives to rational choice. Rational choice posits that states enter into contracts in the same way as individuals do when doing so makes them better off.[3] Indeed, EU law allows states to resolve problems of cooperation (public goods), coordinate with a view to stabilizing expectations (through reduced transaction costs), leverage the benefits of the Union's size versus decentralized Member State action (exploiting economies of scale), and avoid economic instabilities that one EU member inflicts on others (through negative externalities).

Yet, on a number of occasions rational choice tends to lack explanatory power due to its focus on optimizing states' conduct *within* existing rules rather than choosing rules in the first place. Clearly, rational choice theory offers game-theoretic rigour as to when states comply or defect from commitments,[4] how cost-benefit analysis determines rational state leaders' choices,[5] and when economies

[1] Andrew Guzman, *How International Law Works* (Oxford University Press 2008) 22, 33, 71, 119, 183; Jack L Goldsmith and Eric A Posner, *The Limits of International Law* (Oxford University Press 2006) 23, 83; Joel P Trachtman, *The Economic Structure of International Law* (Harvard University Press 2008) 72, 119, 208; Eric Posner and Alan O Sykes, *Economic Foundations of International Law* (Harvard University Press 2013) 84.

[2] Klaus Mathis, *Law and Economics in Europe: Foundations and Applications* (Springer 2014); Paul B Stephan, *Economics of European Union Law* (Edward Elgar 2007).

[3] Guzman (n 1) 121.

[4] Posner and Sykes (n 1) 27–31.

[5] Anne van Aaken, 'Behavioral International Law and Economics' (2014) 55 Harvard International Law 421, 434.

of scale serve as benchmarks to allocate competences.[6] Applying these tools analytically focuses on what the optimal outcomes are, in the sense of how individual states achieve net gains through interaction. Yet, this focus may be insufficient to explain why countries such as EU members agree to constitution-like Treaties like the TEU and TFEU, even when they, on many occasions, lead to unfavourable outcomes for EU members. Unlike optimizing rational choice *within* existing rules, we must therefore shift the analytical focus to the design of the rules themselves: that is, to the initial crafting of EU Treaty rules that determine the frame for future EU decision-making and policy actions. This implies shifting the perspective from economists' traditional focus on *mutual gains from exchange* to inquiry into how people may realize *mutual gains from joint commitment*, that is, from jointly accepting suitable constraints on their behavioural choices, as is the case for EU members subjecting themselves to EU law.[7] As alternatives to mainstream economics, constitutional and institutional economics have offered suitable conceptual frameworks to that end. In a nutshell, it posits that the benefits participants can expect from such constitutional commitments are not derived from specific anticipated outcomes, but are the overall benefits that result over time from having the continuing process of interaction and cooperation bound by suitable constraints.[8] For instance, EU members accepting jurisdiction of the ECJ surrender unilateral responses to retaliate whenever they see themselves treated unfairly by another state and accept the authoritative but unpredictable decision of the EU Commission and ECJ as enforcers of EU law. Put differently, a distinction between *interest in having valid rules* and *interest in complying with rules* should be made. The *interest in complying with rules* can refer to the effectiveness of rules, while *interest in having valid rules* connects to the acceptance of rules. Interest in having rules is a precondition for the stability of the legal order overall.[9]

Constitutional economics adds a further perspective: rational choice posits that what matters for the normative benchmark is the state's interests[10]—constitutional economics in turn emphasizes that it is the citizens' interest that matters. Hence, when considering the *why* and *how* of legal self-commitment in the EU, we should

[6] Guzman (n 1) 168–170.

[7] Geoffrey Brennan and James M Buchanan, *The Reason of Rules: Constitutional Political Economy* (Cambridge University Press 1985); James M Buchanan, 'The Domain of Constitutional Economics' (1990) 1 Constitutional Political Economy 1.

[8] Viktor J Vanberg, 'Market and State: The Perspective of Constitutional Political Economy' (2005) 1 Journal of Institutional Economics 23, 29.

[9] Abram Chayes and Antonia Handler Chayes, 'On Compliance' (1993) 47 International Organization 175, 183 f.: 'It is true that a state's incentive at the treaty negotiation stage may be different from those it faces when the time for compliance rolls around . . . Nevertheless, the very act of making commitments embodied in an international agreement changes the calculus at the compliance stage, if only because it generates expectations of compliance in others that must enter into the equation'.

[10] Tom Ginsburg and Richard McAdams, 'Adjudicating in Anarchy: An Expressive Theory of International Dispute Resolution' (2004) 45 William & Mary Law Review; Robert E Scott and Paul B Stephan, *The Limits of Leviathan* (Cambridge University Press 2006).

thus relax the rational choice perspective limiting us to using 'state interest' as a normative benchmark in favour of citizens' preferences.

In addition, behavioural economics offers modifications of the rational choice perspective: scholars working in the psychological proximity of economics have revealed the ubiquitous deviations from the theoretical tenets of rational choice.[11] For instance, rational choice posits states to be risk-neutral as the theoretical default[12]—behavioural economics has experimentally revealed loss aversion, a phenomenon in line with realist scholarship putting existential fear at the core of state concerns.[13] Also, even within the arsenal of rational choice, analytical tools do not produce consistent results, but rather different results. An 'economies of scale' perspective emphasizing costs advantages may inform the legal subsidiarity principle in a different direction than a utility-oriented perspective would do, emphasizing heterogenous preferences among EU members (see below chapter 10 b).

With this (limited) authority that rational choice can claim as analytically standard, we will explore the motives of EU members for entering into European cooperation. Examining core drivers for entering into binding self-commitments necessarily precedes an analysis of the variety of cooperation forms under EU law—the *why* precedes the *how*. Specifically, the *how* concerns the legal design of institutions; the sources of EU law; the interaction of Union institutions and EU members; the sense of rigidity of some rules or the flexibility of others; the integration with full versus limited EU membership; and the allocation of centralized EU powers versus decentralized members' competences. As a first step we should inquire into core rationales underpinning the employment of EU law as a commitment device.

Lawyers and economists look at cooperation differently. Lawyers, particularly European positivist lawyers, concentrate their doctrinal interest on binding laws, such as agreements or treaties.[14] Lawyers engage in systematic analysis, often taking recourse to a canon of interpretative methods, to inquire *what* the law says, and (to the extent that the meaning of law is clear) *how* the law should be applied to a set of facts. Economic analysis in turn precedes these questions—it asks *why* legal commitment exists, what drives countries to self-commit to certain conduct. From that angle, it is also discernible under what conditions states feel no longer bound by their legal commitment—an issue that lawyers consider beyond doubt by simple reference to *pacta sunt servanda* (Article 26 of the Vienna Convention). Economic analysis of law has highlighted that formalized and binding law does not

[11] Anne van Aaken and Tomer Broude, 'The Psychology of International Law: An Introduction' (2019) 30 European Journal of International Law 1225.

[12] Posner and Sykes (n 1) 50; Guzman (n 1) 122.

[13] Barbara Koremenos, Charles Lipson, and Duncan Snidal, 'The Rational Design of International Institutions' (2001) 55 International Organization 761, 782.

[14] Unlike under international law, customary law plays a minor role in EU law. On customary international law, see, eg, Guzman (n 1) 183.

deserve more attention than non-binding, informal, and soft versions of law, as they all may be the deliberate outcome of cooperation and may even have the same compliance record as traditional hard law.[15] The EU Treaties offer input for positivist lawyers and conform with their preference for legal interpretation and doctrinal rigour. Economists care more for what underlies the emergence of law—the rationale and motivation for cooperation and the mechanics ensuring stability of legal commitment (eg compliance through endogenous self-serving compliance or through exogenous compliance pressure). The exploration of incentives and cooperation motives allows a more plausible analysis of compliance with treaties beyond a mere positivist *pacta sunt servanda* approach.

Why do states enter into binding commitments vis-à-vis other states, and in the case of the EU even renounce sovereignty rights that other states retain in the international community? European lawyers are silent on this question but rather refer to the evolving EU integration as an endogenous process determined by political, cultural, and economic drivers. Put differently, lawyers tend to be ignorant towards time, because they do not care about factors *before* the laws enter into force (the motion to self-commit), and they pay limited interest to state motivations *after* entering into force, that is, why certain provisions are complied with, and others are not. Lawyers do care about the legal consequences attached to conduct over time—the decision to defect may give rise to state responsibility—but there is only very narrow discussion of the motives for states' conduct. Motives play out when they are relevant for the subjective dimension of the acting state in order to judge the legality of certain conduct: does an EU member breach market freedoms in pursuit of (good) public policy goals or for (bad) protectionist purposes? Economic analysis is not on search for specific motives, nor does it classify good and bad motivations the same way lawyers do. Rather, economic analysis designs states as rational actors who decide on the basis of a state utility function. An idiosyncratic set of selfish or altruistic motivations and decisions are taken to further these objectives, presumably in pursuit of national welfare. This utility function informs the *why* of cooperation and offers examination of a plethora of motivations.

Unlike lawyers, economists care about the driver of legal commitment and their actual effects, which gives rise to both descriptive and normative dimensions of economic analysis. Descriptively, economists offer rationales for state cooperation. What is going to be developed throughout this Part is that cooperation gains can be produced for EU members in multiple ways: by reciprocal exchange of concessions; internalizing external effects; minimizing various kinds of transactions costs; and producing economies of scale. Rationales for cooperation and the

[15] Goldsmith and Posner (n 1) 90; Kenneth W Abbott and Duncan Snidal, 'Hard and Soft Law in International Governance' (2000) 54 International Organization 421, 421; C Brummer, 'Why Soft Law Dominates International Finance—and Not Trade' (2010) 13 Journal of International Economic Law 623, 630.

corresponding incentives and disincentives to cooperate are a productive insight that economics can offer for legal analysis as they make sense of the stability of the legal commitment, hence for compliance and noncompliance with law; they explain why members retain unanimity in the Council on some matters, while allowing a majority in other instances; they highlight why cooperation may proceed through a differentiated format of enhanced cooperation rather than with full membership. Normatively, in turn, economists may advise whether states should agree at all to centralizing sovereignty in Brussels; to what extent EU members should transfer sovereignty rights from an efficiency perspective; and which competences Member States should retain on a decentralized level.

3

What states and EU institutions care about

Exploring *why* EU members cooperate through legal self-commitment requires us to clarify what states care about. Whose interests do they pursue when seeking cooperation? A plausible default assumption in line with rational choice is that EU Member States have (well-behaved) preferences over various goals; the mainstream view in the economic analysis of international law posits that nations tend to pursue their national economic interests while neglecting the interests of foreign states and actors.[1] This is a plausible default assumption, one that extends microeconomic modelling of individuals as utility maximizers to the level of collective decision-makers.[2] It is also a pragmatic view in the sense that, irrespective of the obvious fact that even if law is not a direct manifestation of private preferences, individual preferences are also manifested through the mechanism of the state, as state preferences.[3]

Side streams of economic research have refined the selfish state preference, by adding transnational public goods concerns (beyond a merely national perspective) into the motivation to create a more global welfare perspective;[4] or by adopting a perspective that emphasizes power-mongering and institutional bias, one that questions benevolent purposes in seeking EU integration.[5] Indeed, state leaders may push European integration in pursuit of elitists goals, defying its presumed unbiased connection with citizens' preferences. In this vein, it is possible that the EU decision-making structure enhances the ability of certain political elites or interest groups to achieve their preferred policies at the expense of the broader populace.[6] Specifically, the public choice literature on international organizations suggests that domestic policy pursues action through the EU when it

[1] Andrew Moravcsik, 'Taking Preferences Seriously: A Liberal Theory of International Politics' (1997) 51 International Organization 513, 481; Kenneth W Abbott, 'Trust but Verify: The Production of Information in Arms Control Treaties and Other International Agreements' (1993) 26 Cornell International Law Journal 1.

[2] Andrew Guzman, *How International Law Works* (Oxford University Press 2008) 17.

[3] Joel P Trachtman, *The Economic Structure of International Law* (Harvard University Press 2008) 37.

[4] Ernst-Ulrich Petersmann and Armin Steinbach, 'Neo-Liberalism, State-Capitalism and Ordo-Liberalism: "Institutional Economics" and "Constitutional Choices" in Multilevel Trade Regulation' (2021) 22 Journal of World Investment & Trade 1.

[5] Roland Vaubel, 'The Public Choice Analysis of European Integration: A Survey' (1994) 10 European Journal of Political Economy 227, 232.

[6] Joel P Trachtman, 'Economics of International Organizations' in Francesco Parisi (ed), *The Oxford Handbook of Law and Economics: Volume 3: Public Law and Legal Institutions* (Oxford University Press 2017) 506.

EU Law and Economics. Armin Steinbach, Oxford University Press. © Oxford University Press 2025.
DOI: 10.1093/9780198920915.003.0003

believes it will achieve its domestic policy goals more effectively, or does so in order to blame the EU for an unpopular domestic policy. Far from being the 'benevolent dictator' that some economic models believe the state to be,[7] delegation of competences from the state to the EU might allow governments to hide their actions or otherwise avoid accountability for their actions.[8] This action may allow states to escape desirable inter-state competition in the supply of public goods. A harmonized minimum wage, for example, may serve to maintain competitiveness for some EU members by preventing undercutting from lower wages elsewhere. Thus, while a realist view on state preferences would emphasize its inclination to power and regulatory capture in defiance of citizens' preferences, the idealist view of state preferences being a pure extension of unbiased aggregated individual preferences does not square well with the rationale of public policy—welfare economics justifies public intervention where markets do not produce efficient results, hence in cases where the outcome of private market decisions are sub-optimal. The very justification of public intervention is that private preferences (of those harmed by the inefficient market outcome) are insufficiently accounted for.[9]

As an analytical starting point, we acknowledge that the peculiar design of EU law is above all the result of deliberate choices of Member States. In focusing on how self-interested states could cooperate, it is logical to ask what role legal commitments could play. Legal commitments, irrespective whether as substantive obligations, procedural frames, or institutionalized bodies, could be reconceptualized and theorized as arrangements that make cooperation more feasible and durable. Our argument is that the EU institutional design, the choice of its core legal principles (such as the principles of conferral or subsidiarity), the competence allocation for its institutions, or the choice of sources of law reflect deliberate choices by those having an institutional and legal choice in the EU—which are, at least in the historically early stage of the EU, foremost the founding Member States. The evolution of the EU involved many Treaty amendments, with each amendment building on the pre-established institutional setup rather than overhauling the EU's architecture. With this path-dependent degree of continuity in the EU's evolution, there remains an institutional learning curve that led through Treaty amendments to deliberate shifts in closer integration. Later and thanks to its supranational guise, the EU itself, through its various institutions and endowed with exclusive competences in some fields, became an autonomous actor, for instance when acting through its institutions by adopting secondary law or through the ECJ as its jurisprudential organ. The EU hence evolved from a 'dependent' variable in which it

[7] Randall G Holcombe, 'Make Economics Policy Relevant Depose the Omniscient Benevolent Dictator' (2012) 17 The Independent Review 165.

[8] Trachtman (n 3) 506.

[9] However, this applies to negative impact on preferences due to allocative inefficiency. Public policy decisions leading to distributional effects that are disliked by some citizens (and thus misaligned with their preferences) are by nature not aligned with all individual preferences.

was merely the outcome of inter-state deliberate choice, to an 'independent' variable by being a state-like actor that exerts autonomous influence on other state actors. This makes the EU different from international organizations which, from a rational choice perspective, are largely viewed only as variables dependent on the interests of Member States.[10] The claim that EU law is the product of the deliberate choice of Member States even holds when one acknowledges that path dependency limits and determines the institutional evolution of the EU.

A distinct question is whose preferences *should* guide the creation of EU law. The insight offered by Arrow's impossibility theorem[11] suggests that organizations have no rationality of their own and that the process of collective decision-making is normatively ambiguous and unstable. EU law and governance establishes several actors on the EU landscape, each of them bound by different institutional interests and restraints and therefore set to pursue different interests. Clearly, rather than assigning the EU as a homogenous rational actor, account must be given to the various Member State and Union actors. Genuine EU institutions that embody EU common interests, such as the Commission and the Parliament, pursue different objectives from the Council that channels Member State concerns. The EU Member States are referred to as the 'masters of the Treaties', propagating a legal sovereignty notion that assigns all power to make agreements and create international organizations, a proposition that considers European countries as the ultimate source of authority.

However, the outcome of cooperation between non-identical preferences of Member States does not simply reflect the preferences of the individual state actors, but rather represents their joint efforts and compromises among their preferred outcomes to improve their equilibrium outcome given the strategic circumstances they face. There are different levels of cooperation at which interaction between states and institutions lead to certain outcomes. At the most basic level, Member States agree in intergovernmental conferences on Treaty commitments; in the Council, state representatives interact and strike compromises when crafting EU secondary law; in the EU Commission, interaction between individual Commissioners and directorates produce outcomes; inter-institutional transactions occur between the Council, Parliament, and the Commission. Each of these actors may have specific objectives, and the pursuit of those goals is led by their beliefs about each other's preferences and the relative costs and benefits of different outcomes.

[10] Barbara Koremenos, Charles Lipson and Duncan Snidal, 'The Rational Design of International Institutions' (2001) 55 International Organization 761.

[11] Kenneth J Arrow, *Kenneth Arrow, Social Choice and Individual Values* (Yale University Press 2012).

4

The logic of barter trade: Rational choice and constitutional economics

Interaction and transaction are at the centre of economics. Rational choice informs us that social and economic interactions are transactions of exchange through which the parties seek cooperation gains.[1] Transposed to state level, a state cooperates to the extent it achieves gains through trading commitments. States do not engage in barter trade on one single market. Rather, several markets are used for different aspects of cooperation. The equivalent of the market is simply the forum where states and EU institutions interact—be it in the Council, at summits of head of states, or in the Trilogue involving the Council, Parliament, and the Commission—to cooperate on particular issues in order to maximize their baskets of preferences. A different way to express this trade is to understand cooperation between EU states as a market for trading jurisdiction, with this trade being equivalent to assigning property rights (see below Chapter 10). Goods or services are not the assets traded on these markets, but rather 'jurisdiction', defined as the allocation of authority, or the institutionalized exercise of power. Market outcomes of international states, or European states on a regional market for jurisdiction, are thus jurisdiction to prescribe, to adjudicate, and to enforce.[2]

The trading of jurisdiction occurs on various markets. First, there is an 'invisible' and tacit market for certain conduct between states that does not explicitly appear in the black letters of EU Treaties but remains within the realm of tacit agreements. One example would be the Treaties' silence of certain basic rules of inter-state conduct, which are laid down in the UN Charter, but not explicitly mentioned in the EU Treaties. Take as an example the principles of non-intervention, the absence of violence in inter-state relations, which rank salient in the UN Charter, but which are not explicitly stipulated in the EU Treaties.[3] The validity of these principles may seem obvious in the EU (and tacitly and reciprocally exchanged), due to the greater homogeneity among its members compared to states at a global level.[4]

[1] Joel P Trachtman, *The Economic Structure of International Law* (Harvard University Press 2008) 10.
[2] ibid.
[3] There are vague references to the Charter of the United Nations in the EU Treaties but mainly to commit the EU in relation to third countries.
[4] One may argue that EU Treaties do implicitly incorporate these fundamental rules of international relations because the UN Charter is binding for EU states as subjects of international law. In terms of norm hierarchy, however, the UN Charter enjoys in many jurisdictions no primacy over domestic constitutions, while the EU Treaties rank above national constitutions.

EU Law and Economics. Armin Steinbach, Oxford University Press. © Oxford University Press 2025.
DOI: 10.1093/9780198920915.003.0004

In serving the needs of states, European law is not different from international law in that it can be understood as an attempt to orchestrate cooperation in the face of potential international externalities.[5] For instance, the strive for safety plays out in economic beneficial terms in international cooperation more generally, defined as a diversion of anarchy in the inter-state relationships in which each state must fear hostilities by its neighbours, forming certainly a key driver at the time when the European Community was born. Security established through a legal order stabilizes expectations and allows states to use scarce resources for more productive purposes than maintaining costly security infrastructure. A basic legal infrastructure increasing security provides then the basis for more cooperative gains, as security produces positive spillovers to many areas of cooperation that would not be attainable if stable expectations were not ensured. What emerged historically as international law building on the 'Westphalian system' in terms of state sovereignty, equality of states, and the prohibition of intervention and aggression has been further extended in the EU through its supranational structure, the supremacy of EU law over national laws, and a legal and institutional architecture which fostered a level of economic intertwining that stabilizes the relationship further. Through supranationality, the development of an autonomous legal order claiming prevalence in its Member States' legal orders, the EU has stabilized expectations on a higher level and reduced the probability of unforeseen hostilities more than on an international law level. In that perspective, cooperation rationales under EU law do not differ fundamentally from international law.

Second, and more relevant for this book, there is an inter-state market in which commitments are exchanged through explicit and formal (as well as informal) constitutional rules, which ultimately shape the EU as an international organization. EU states as self-regarding units and many states interacting in pursuit of self-interest create a market where transactions regarding the exercise or renunciation of authority are traded. As an outcome of this trade, states relinquish autonomy in some areas (and craft corresponding authority by EU institutions) in order to obtain certain expected benefits in return.[6] Third, following Treaty ratification, there are subsequent markets or sub-markets created by the EU Treaties themselves. EU constitutional rules provide rules about how subsequent and subordinate rules, specifically EU secondary law, will be made. On the markets for EU secondary law, institutions, politicians, parties, and even countries compete for political resources of power, ultimately specifying additional commitments within the boundaries of the pre-defined Treaties. Political institutions (the Commission, the Council, the Parliament) interact, each of them pursuing different preferences and objectives. Fourth, and on a level not leading to the adoption of EU law, within the EU

[5] Eric Posner and Alan O Sykes, *Economic Foundations of International Law* (Harvard University Press 2013) 20.

[6] Trachtman (n 1) 10.

institutions, there are sub-markets with individual state representatives interacting with each other to craft agreements that secure individual benefits for the parties concerned.

As rational choice actors, states employ cost-benefit analysis.[7] For instance, the principle of reciprocal and 'mutual recognition' under EU law (see below Chapter 13 b) allows products that are lawfully marketed in one Member State to be sold in other Member States regardless of whether they comply with the national technical rules of those Member States.[8] Likewise, Member States may reciprocally consent to removing domestic obstacles to the internal market through legislative harmonization (Article 114 TFEU). This kind of institutionalized exchange of concessions demonstrates that reciprocal commitments lead to overall welfare gains.[9] In an ideal world in which the state leadership pursues overall welfare interests, cooperation ultimately leads to welfare gains. This does not necessarily entail strict Pareto improvements on the domestic level, as international cooperation typically implies distributional effects leading to disadvantages of some (think for instance of protected industries that suffer from trade liberalizing). Welfare economics lets weak Pareto improvements suffice, allowing for the hypothetical compensation of losers of a transaction by those who gain.

However, the utility-increasing trade of reciprocal state concessions do not entirely capture why EU members commit themselves to a supranational design under which each member may experience situations of inferior bargains. States risk being trumped by majority votes in the Council or foregoing the adoption of unilateral measures in cases where domestic preferences would ask for such measures, for example where a merger between companies would be desirable from a domestic perspective but impossible to attain due to exclusive competence of the EU Commission. Cooperation in the EU does not safeguard gains in each individual transaction—EU policy-making, as well as judicial acts of the ECJ, may conflict with national interests. Losses may even be more frequent than gains. Constitutional economics may make sense of this self-restraining and occasionally self-harming design of rules. Developed by James Buchanan, constitutional economics claims that a fundamental inconsistency exists between the methodological individualism as the classic trademark of the economic approach to social phenomena and the whole concept of a social welfare function. While the traditional focus of economics lies on voluntary market exchanges, constitutional economics extends the 'mutual gains from trade' notion to voluntary cooperation more generally understood, including arrangements for collective action, private and public.[10]

[7] Barbara Koremenos, *The Continent of International Law: Explaining Agreement Design* (Cambridge University Press 2016) 29.

[8] Case C-8/74 *Dassonville* (1974) EU:C:1974:82 837.

[9] Kyle Bagwell and Robert W Staiger, *The Economics of the World Trading System* (The MIT Press 2004).

[10] James M Buchanan and H Geoffrey Brennan, *What Should Economists Do?* (Liberty Fund Inc 1979) 27.

It focuses on the question of how people may realize mutual gains by their voluntary joint commitment to rules, that is, from jointly accepting suitable constraints on their behavioural choices.[11] The difference between welfare economics and constitutional economics perspectives on cooperation is that, under the latter, the benefits that participants can expect from such constitutional commitments are not derived from *specific* anticipated outcomes, but are the overall benefits that result over time from having the continuing process of interaction and cooperation bound by suitable constraints.[12] We can speak of 'enabling constitutionalization' in reference to rules, which allocate authority to produce rules (like the EU Treaties), but do not foresee the outcomes. There is a veil of uncertainty as to the distributive outcome, because the distributive consequences are unknown in advance.[13]

The constitutional economic perspective thus illuminates the peculiar design of the EU's supranational institutionalization. On the market for the trade of jurisdiction, EU members have renounced the exercise of their sovereignty in a number of fields, and the ensuing legislation produced by Union institutions does not guarantee a favourable outcome for any individual EU member. Power has been transmitted to the Commission acting in the Unions' interests, which in many cases conflicts with national interests, and even if EU members retain legislative power through the Council, governments have surrendered the paradigm of the Westphalian international legal order that had meant to pursue cooperation strictly in line with national interests. Under the EU supranational design, there is by no means a mechanism for Member States to ensure gains in every case. Institutionally salient is this through majority voting in the Council, with decisions potentially taken against a country's will. And even where unanimity is the predominant decision mode, EU members depend on the Commission for a legislative act to be initiated, they rely on the Commission and the ECJ to enforce mutually agreed obligations rather than reverting to unilateral enforcement, and they may fear Union institutions interpreting or applying EU law in a fashion that contravenes national interests.

We should thus be wary of treating states like individuals as *homo oeconomii*. In line with Buchanan's diagnosis, non-market collective choices in political arenas cannot be determined from the level of individual human action. Society cannot be treated as if it were a choosing entity the same way as individuals decide on markets—rather, it should be seen with its own value scale, thereby abandoning the individualism of the classic economic paradigm.[14] It remains to be determined in whose name constitutional economics requires EU constitutional arrangements

[11] James M Buchanan, *The Economics and Ethics of Constitutional Order* (University of Michigan Press 1991) 81.

[12] Viktor J Vanberg, 'Market and State: The Perspective of Constitutional Political Economy' (2005) 1 Journal of Institutional Economics 23, 27.

[13] Trachtman (n 1) 256.

[14] James M Buchanan, *Freedom in Constitutional Contract* (Texas A&M University Press 1977) 235.

to be made. For social arrangements to be 'socially beneficial', Buchanan-type constitutional economics perspectives require the arrangements to be *mutually* beneficial, that is, beneficial to all parties involved. Buchanan insists that what may count as 'better' in social matters can ultimately only be judged by the persons involved themselves and that, therefore, the relevant test for what qualifies as a 'good rule' must be seen in the voluntary agreement of the parties involved.[15] To the extent that constitutional economics emphasizes the acceptability of the process that leads to a decision rather than the outcome, it connects to the social psychology literature that points to procedural fairness as what matters for the individual more than the specific outcome.[16] With Buchanan remaining faithful to normative individualism for the determination of what should be considered as 'mutually beneficial', it was Vanberg who extended this concept to be tantamount to 'citizen sovereignty'. It captures that the political process should be institutionally governed by the common interest of citizens. Citizen sovereignty thus entails that 'producers of politics', politicians and government bureaucrats, are responsive to citizens' common interests. This contrasts with the legal Westphalian view that emphasizes state sovereignty and state will as reference points for international law,[17] as well as with the literature that equates state action with the corporate preferences of the states.[18] For constitutional economics it is not the state but rather the citizens' and consumers' preferences that form the benchmark for assessing the efficiency of outcomes.

The constitutional economic emphasis on citizens' preferences easily aligns with the traditional legitimacy proposition of constitutional lawyers that traces public authority neatly back to citizens' votes, albeit with the important difference that Buchanan's concept does not tie public decision to *national* citizens but to *European* citizens. National constitutional law puts the national citizen at the core of democratic analysis, as it is the national citizen who holds domestic politicians accountable.[19] Assessing European integration through the lens of national constitutional law thus tends to emphasize the interests of the rather homogenous group of national citizens, a view that is also at the core of the economic theory of federalism, which emphasizes the alignment of homogenous preferences and the supply of public goods (see below Chapter 10 a).[20] Constitutional economics defies both the narrow national perspective as well as the legal homogeneity proposition

[15] James M Buchanan, *Fiscal Theory and Political Economy: Selected Essays* (University of North Carolina Press 1954) 122.

[16] Lita Furby and others, 'Public Perceptions of Electric Power Transmission Lines' (1988) 8 Journal of Environmental Psychology 19; Thomay Priestley and Gary W Evans, 'Resident Perceptions of a Nearby Electric Transmission-Line' (1996) 16 Journal of Environmental Psychology 65.

[17] Claire Cutler, 'Critical Reflections on the Westphalian Assumptions of International Law and Organization: A Crisis of Legitimacy' (2001) 27 Review of International Studies 133.

[18] Trachtman (n 1) 37.

[19] Andreas Voßkuhle, *Europa, Demokratie, Verfassungsgerichte* (Suhrkamp 2021) 50, 58.

[20] Posner and Sykes (n 5) 15.

referring to cultural communalities. Constitutional economics is not authoritative on which level of regulation public power should be exercised, rather it stipulates that, once one level of jurisdiction is chosen, it must be assessed against the benchmark of the consent of the group of citizens concerned, hence ensuring citizens' sovereignty. European public power must be designed in line with the interest of a European citizen—a construct that has been legally introduced by European citizenship in Article 9 of the TEU. We will revert to this when discussing core legal principles such as subsidiarity (Article 5(3) TEU) and the principle of conferral (Article 5(2) TEU).

5
Reducing transaction costs

Cooperation is attractive only if gains from cooperation remain sufficiently high that exceeding all costs of achieving them has been accounted for—with Williamson's concept of transaction costs serving as a benchmark, not only understood as monetary costs, but also encompassing bargaining costs, ratification costs, political costs, and implementation costs associated with international cooperation.[1] Saving on transactions costs may serve as a stimulus for cooperation, while abundance of transactions costs may hamper cooperation. From theoretical scholarship, we know that multilateral institutions can lower the communication and related transaction costs of continued cooperation.[2] Transactions are the analytical lenses through which cooperation on every level of EU law-making and application plays out: treaty negotiation, the struggle for compromise in the Council to enact an regulation, the ECJ engaging in expansive Treaty interpretation that alienates Member States, the transfer of sensitive competence from Member State to Union level, and administrative implementation of EU secondary law. Any kind of EU cooperation within legal boundaries entails context-specific costs that must be taken into account to understand whether and how cooperation unfolds, with all EU members facing different kinds and magnitudes of transaction costs. These costs feed into a country's cost-benefits analysis, and can thus be the flipside of the cooperative gains discussed above.

The cost perspective allows us to integrate the scholarship researching international organization with respect to why and how they are shaped. Koremenos and others have introduced five categories of variables that determine the design of international organizations: distribution problems; enforcement problems; the number of actors and the asymmetries among them; and uncertainties about

[1] Oliver E Williamson, *The Economic Institutions of Capitalism: Firms, Markets, Relational Contracting* (The Free Press 1985) Transaction costs refer to the costs of reaching an agreement, administering it, and enforcing it. If EU members agree on an EU-wide minimum wage, the costs of bargaining, monitoring, and enforcing the minimum wage are transaction costs, but not the fiscal costs and welfare effects of the minimum wage; for an application to international law, see Armin Steinbach, 'The Trend towards Non-Consensualism in Public International Law: A (Behavioural) Law and Economics Perspective' (2016) 27 European Journal of International Law 643, 643.

[2] Robert O Keohane, *After Hegemony: Cooperation and Discord in the World Political Economy* (Princeton University Press 2005); Duncan Snidal, 'Coordination versus Prisoners' Dilemma: Implications for International Cooperation and Regimes' (1985) 79 American Political Science Review 923; Stephen D Krasner, *International Regimes* (Cornell University Press 1983).

EU Law and Economics. Armin Steinbach, Oxford University Press. © Oxford University Press 2025.
DOI: 10.1093/9780198920915.003.0005

behaviour, the state of the world, and others' preferences.[3] While serving international scholars for the purpose of analysing the design and institutional setup of international organizations, these categories can be assessed from an economic perspective through different costs dimensions.

At the most basic level, *sovereignty costs* increase whenever states cannot choose their national prerogatives and surrender competencies.[4] A Member State that transfers competences to the EU or binds itself in a reciprocal way vis-à-vis other EU members curtails the exercise of policy space and the scope of national sovereignty. When national sovereignty is surrendered permanently, this may cause concern, especially if uncertainty prevails about the future state of the world. Should national currency be given up in exchange for a joint currency, with uncertainty over how stable the currency will be and how the currency group will fare? Which competences should be shifted to the centre, and how comprehensively and irrevocably should they be? Granting the EU exclusive competence, such as in competition law or trade policy, would have irrevocable effects. The subsidiarity principle does not apply in these cases of exclusive competence, Member States would permanently lose their competence to act. In turn, granting the EU shared competence still allows Member States to retain a degree of action that eventually may even prevent the EU from taking certain actions. The sensitivity to sovereignty attached to exclusive EU competences such as trade policy or competition regulation may change over time and depend on the issue area concerned. Think of investment policy: until 2009, international investment policy was the exclusive competence of EU Member States, yet the Lisbon Treaty provided the EU with exclusive competence in the area of 'direct investment'. Concerns were raised regarding the specific EU competence to include an investor-state dispute settlement (ISDS) mechanism in investment treaties with other countries. As political debate became increasingly heated, sovereignty concerns were at the heart of the issue, with these quasi-tribunals restraining public policy-makers perceived as intruding into national domains. Despite the EU's sole competence of direct investment, Member States retained this sensitive area of investor-state dispute settlement and the ECJ confirmed that the EU had no exclusive competence in the ISDS mechanism, the Member States' approval hence being necessary and thus limiting sovereignty costs.

The gradual integration process, its sequential extensions from unanimity to majority voting, and the integration of the intergovernmental mode of cooperation into the Community method exemplify the role of sovereignty costs. Core

[3] Barbara Koremenos, Charles Lipson, and Duncan Snidal, 'The Rational Design of International Institutions' (2001) 55 International Organization 761, 773; Barbara Koremenos, *The Continent of International Law: Explaining Agreement Design* (Cambridge University Press 2016) 37.

[4] See Kenneth W Abbott and Duncan Snidal, 'Hard and Soft Law in International Governance' (2000) 54 International Organization 421, 421; David Epstein and Sharyn O'Halloran, 'Sovereignty and Delegation in International Organizations' (2008) 71 Law and Contemporary Problems 89.

state policy areas—foreign policy, social policy, budgetary control—have been retained by Member States, as sovereignty costs would be too high. In this vein, constitutional courts, such as the German Constitutional Court, emphasized that certain core competences cannot by transferred to Brussels.[5] At the same time, this German landmark judgment shows how unevenly sovereignty costs may be distributed in the EU. Other constitutional courts, such as those in France and Italy, have not expressed similarly strong reservations to the EU integration process.[6] Sovereignty costs associated with further integration steps hence vary across countries. In any event, the choice of voting rules in the Council translates directly into sovereignty costs. Not surprisingly, unanimity remains persistent in sensitive areas where the EU has some (but not comprehensive) competences such as in taxation or foreign policy, while other cases, such as Treaty amendments—or budget-sensitive issues such as the Own Resources Decision under Article 311 TFEU—must be ratified according to Member States' national legal orders and typically require involvement of national parliaments in order to reduce sovereignty and agency costs.

One should emphasize that centralization of policy conduct at the EU level does not in all cases increase sovereignty costs, as centralization can also enhance sovereignty. The widespread criticism of the anti-democratic nature of the EU as a supranationalist construct (hence increasing sovereignty costs) does not account for the perspective that the EU—more than individual Member States—can credibly offer problem-solving for a number of transnational challenges. The control of anti-competitive practices, the environment, energy policy, and asylum and migration all present transnational policy challenges or public goods that could not be equally effectively addressed by Member States.[7]

Using internal market harmonization power increases the power of the EU in global standard setting (the 'Brussels effect').[8] Surrender of sovereignty may also allow the EU to effectively enhance the provision of transnational public goods such as effective climate protection. If EU members are able to forcefully represent their (homogenous) preferences through the EU in negotiations at the World Trade Organization or the United Nations, the position is stronger than that of an individual EU member in the arena of international relations. If the EU is able to commit other international actors to enter into binding agreements to reduce CO2 emissions, this will allow EU members to protect the climate as a public good

[5] BVerfGE 123, 267 *Lissabon* (2009)—Lisbon Treaty.

[6] Alessia-Ottavia Cozzi, 'The Italian Constitutional Court, the Plurality of Legal Orders and Supranational Fundamental Rights: A Discussion in Terms of Interlegality' (2022) 1 European Law Open 606; Jacques Ziller, 'European Union Law in the Jurisprudence of French Supreme Courts: Europe-Friendliness with a French Touch' (2015) 21 European Public Law 765.

[7] Anand Menon and Stephen Weatherill, 'Transnational Legitimacy in a Globalising World: How the European Union Rescues its States' (2008) 31 West European Politics 397, 402.

[8] Anu Bradford, *The Brussels Effect: How the European Union Rules the World* (Oxford University Press 2019).

more effectively. In areas where the EU holds exclusive competences such as petition and trade policy, the EU has successfully leveraged its weight vis-à-vis third countries in externalizing its laws. For example, the EU requests from partners of free trade agreements to adopt competition law in line with its own rules.[9] The bargaining and commitment power of the EU offers policy leverage that individual EU members would not have (anymore) in a globalized and interconnected world. In all these cases the transfer of competence to the EU may actually *reduce* sovereignty costs.

Cost-reducing impacts on sovereignty can also be achieved through Treaty design that mitigates intrusion with sovereignty concerns. To that end, EU Treaty-makers implemented sovereignty-safeguarding devices into the EU Treaty through flexibility clauses.[10] In principle, Treaty reservations are not an acceptable practice under EU law, where Treaty accession means adoption of the *acquis communautaire* (see below Chapter 12 a)). The EU is not a 'pick-and-choose' menu like many international law treaties.[11] Alternatives are intergovernmental approaches and *inter-se* agreements that surpass the institutional structure of the EU and leave Member States free of ECJ judicial control and the leadership of the Commission (see below Chapter 12 b)). Once a Treaty member, the most drastic remedy to constrain sovereignty costs associated with sovereignty is the Treaty escape clause in Article 50 TEU, which allows for exiting the Union if its obligations are perceived as constraining national sovereignty. Treaty-based sovereignty protection as national public policy space allowing interference with EU basic freedoms (eg Article 36 TFEU) or authorization of Member States being allowed stricter rules than are harmonized on the EU level (eg competition law). Flexibility is not only granted for Member States to preserve sovereignty by circumventing the Union institutional architecture but also to push EU integration further. Take Article 352 TFEU as an example of a transformative clause—it allows the EU, following a sovereignty-protecting unanimity vote in the Council, to take appropriate measures (if necessary) to attain one of the objectives set out in the Treaties. More recently, the solidarity clause in Article 122 TFEU offers a good example of a rule maintaining sovereign states' freedom. This provision was at the core of the various EU crises over the past decade. It was invoked to establish financial assistance during the euro debt crisis through the European Financial Stabilisation Mechanism (EFSM);[12] to craft a fund during the migration crisis; it was the legal

[9] Anu Bradford and others, 'The Global Dominance of European Competition Law Over American Antitrust Law' (2019) 16 Journal of Empirical Legal Studies 731.

[10] On the role of flexibility in the design of international organizations, see Koremenos, Lipson, and Snidal (n 3) 773.

[11] Bruno de Witte, 'The Law as Tool and Constraint of Differentiated Integration' in Mark Dawson and Markus Jachtenfuchs (eds), *Autonomy without Collapse in a Better European Union* (Oxford University Press 2022) 63.

[12] Council Regulation (EU) No 407/2010 of 11 May 2010 establishing a European financial stabilisation mechanism [2010] OJ L118/1.

basis for Next Generation EU (NGEU) addressing the hardship of the pandemic,[13] and during the Ukraine crisis it was used for a solidarity contribution from companies benefiting from windfall profits.[14] This provision gives leeway to Member States to set up a solidarity-based financial mechanism without being subject to the scrutiny of the European Parliament. With the vague conditions and legal consequences stipulated in Article 122 TFEU, this provision can be seen as a reservoir of remaining EU Member States' sovereignty power, as it leaves the power to act mainly with the Council and thus in Member States' hands.[15]

Negotiation costs capture both the facilitation of interaction by employing the EU institutional architecture, on one side, and the multiple coordination needs associated with EU decision-making, on the other. These costs may either incentivize or disincentivize EU cooperation. Cooperation may serve to reduce costs, which offers motivation to delegate power from Member States to the EU. Take the case of competition policy, which is an exclusive competence of the EU. If Member States had retained competence of competition policy, they would frequently conclude agreements with other states on the treatment of competition law cases, with each competition authority eager to maximize national welfare. An institutional design that gives the EU Commission power and precedence to deal with (cross-border) competition issues avoids coordination costs that would necessarily occur between national competition authorities. Institutionally, shifting from unanimity to qualified majority voting reduces bargaining costs significantly compared to bilateral agreements outside the EU framework.

In turn, negotiation costs may increase not only with the number of EU members participating or the degree of heterogeneity of preferences, but also according to the complexity of the policy issue concerned. The non-consensual ways of variable integration reflect this fact, as we will discuss below. Take the Schengen Agreement as a case in point, that EU members decided to initiate it outside the EU decision-making structure to overcome a stalemate within the EU institutional structure and to seek integration in a sovereignty-sensitive area.[16] Negotiation costs are particularly salient where the agreement entails distribution problems and strategic interaction. To that purpose, we distinguish coordination problems from the prisoner's dilemma. Coordination problems require states to agree on a standard (eg, for the ease of communication, one agrees to use English as the language of communication for EU air traffic interoperability), with all states benefitting from agreeing on one standard which offers an endogenous incentive to

[13] Council Regulation (EU) 2020/2094 of 14 December 2020 establishing a European Union Recovery Instrument to support the recovery in the aftermath of the COVID-19 crisis [2020] OJ LI433.

[14] Council Regulation (EU) 2022/1854 of 6 October 2022 on an emergency intervention to address high energy prices [2022] OJ LI261/1.

[15] Armin Steinbach and Sebastian Grund, 'Next Generation EU—Auf dem Weg in die Fiskal- und Transferunion?' (2023) Neue Juristische Wochenschrift 425.

[16] Kenneth W Abbott, 'Modern International Relations Theory: A Prospectus for International Lawyers' (1989) 14 Yale Journal of International Law 335, 398.

comply with it. In a prisoner's dilemma, states have different preferred outcomes and an incentive to defect. Where the distributional implications of an agreement are small, bargaining costs will also be relatively small. In situations where the distributional implications are large—think of the design of the EU agricultural policy or, from an institutional perspective, the setup of voting weights in the Council—bargaining costs will likely to be high.[17]

In two contexts, negotiations costs are particularly sizeable. First, strategic behaviour is natural conduct in EU relationships. In economic terms, this means one party has incomplete information regarding other countries' preferences, as strategic behaviour may induce parties not to reveal their preferences. For example, negotiations among eurozone members on fiscal rules may be driven by different motivations. Country A may ask for lenient rules, but Country B does not know whether Country A wants to engage in unproductive fiscal expenditures or whether it seeks to retain leeway for reasonable investments or policy space for stabilization purposes in times of crisis. Similarly, when EU members agree to introduce a carbon-border adjustment mechanism levying non-European imported goods, EU countries may not reveal whether this tool serves to protect its domestic industry or is for genuine climate policy purposes. Second, uncertainty extends to the state of the world.[18] When EU members agree on introducing a financial transaction tax, there is a lack of predictability regarding the effect of the tax on various economic indicators. Limited experience with similar ways of taxation will make it more costly to write complete contracts to deal with every contingency.[19] Introducing a financial transaction tax with only few EU members may have undesirable side-effects due to capital movements between participating and non-participating countries. In all these instances, countries may want to invest both resources and time in improving their knowledge pertaining to other parties' preferences or to reduce the degree of uncertainty about the future state of the world.[20]

Enforcement problems may occur in various guises and cause *enforcement* costs. EU law is, like all law produced by international organizations that lack nation-like enforcement structures, under risk of not being complied with by EU members. This introduces different perspectives from enforcement or managerial theories, which draw on different reasons for why states comply with or disregard rules in international organizations. Managerial theories refer to a nation's capacity or inability to comply.[21] Barriers to enforcement may be technical in nature and refer to difficulties owing to the complexity of the substance and challenges in

[17] James D Fearon, 'Bargaining, Enforcement, and International Cooperation' (1998) 52 International Organization 269.

[18] Koremenos (n 3) 39.

[19] Joel P Trachtman, *The Economic Structure of International Law* (Harvard University Press 2008) 174.

[20] Koremenos, Lipson, and Snidal (n 3) 782.

[21] Abram Chayes and Antonia H Chayes, 'On Compliance' (1993) 47 International Organization 175.

implementation across legal, technical, or institutional dimensions. Lack of bureaucratic institutions or cumbersome legal requirements are examples of enforcement problems. More competent bureaucracies are more likely to implement EU directives without delay, but the domestic structure of decision-making—namely veto players at both the national levels and the sub-national levels—are equally important predictors of delay.[22] Enforcement theories, in line with rationalist and realist approaches, centre on nations' material incentives to comply with or shirk from international law implementation. Enforcement costs depend on the strength of individual actors' incentives to cheat on the agreed rules.[23] One EU member may prefer not to adhere to it because it can do better individually by defecting from the agreed rules. The enforcement problem arises when actors find unilateral non-cooperation so enticing that they sacrifice long-term cooperation. Take, for example, Hungary's persistent violations and non-observance of the rule of law principle, the ensuing persistent back-and-forth in addressing the EU Commission's request, and the continuation of these violations despite the financial sanctions imposed by withholding funds. The gains of non-cooperation may be multifold. When they occur as political gains in the domestic policy arena helping the incumbent government to improve its re-election chances (while accepting overall welfare losses), it is particularly difficult for the EU to influence such gains because sanctions may have a harmful effect not only on the government but also on citizens (eg by withholding funding for EU regions in need as practiced under the budget protection tool[24]).

Closely related are *monitoring costs* occurring when compliance with EU law must be observed or when an institutional structure is established to administer an agreement. The EU Commission as 'guardian of the Treaties' has a genuine monitoring function to the extent that it scrutinizes compliance with EU law and eventually may bring an infringement procedure before the ECJ. On other occasions, additional monitoring bodies may be implemented outside the existing Union structure, such as the EFSM established during the euro crisis to administer financial assistance. The number of participating countries may influence monitoring costs as well as the different monitoring needs of formal and informal formats of cooperation. However, EU law can also be genuinely designed or interpreted (by the ECJ) to reduce monitoring costs. The mobilization of the individual as an enforcer is a case in point. Endowment by the ECJ to invoke EU law directly before national courts decentralizes the monitoring of EU law adherence—individuals detect and tackle national measures incompatible with EU law, which significantly reduces monitoring costs at the EU Commission level. Likewise, innovations of

[22] Katerina Linos, 'How can International Organizations Shape National Welfare States? Evidence from Compliance with European Union Directives' (2007) 40 Comparative Political Studies 547.

[23] Koremenos, Lipson, and Snidal (n 3) 776.

[24] Antonia Baraggia and Matteo Bonelli, 'Linking Money to Values: The New Rule of Law Conditionality Regulation and Its Constitutional Challenges' (2022) 23 German Law Journal 131.

the ECJ, such as liability of EU Member States for incompliance with EU law (the Francovich doctrine[25]), further strengthens the decentralized and cost-reducing monitoring.

*Modification cost*s are highly relevant with regard to adapting current primary or secondary law to new (factual, legal, or political) circumstances, and may vary depending on the binding nature of the agreement (eg by transforming intergovernmental EFSM law into Union law through the modification of Article 136 TFEU). Member States cannot write complete treaties due to a lack of knowledge and punitive bargaining costs. Yet, modification of treaties through its cumbersome procedure for Treaty amendments is likewise costly. A fully fledged treaty change requires a convention involving national parliaments (Article 48(2)–(5) TEU), while Article 48(6) TEU offers a simplified modification leaving the decision to the European Council. EU members may therefore want to install a transformative clause below the level of Treaty amendment, which allows the EU to react flexibly to new challenges or when it uncovers any gaps in the EU Treaty. Article 352 TFEU is an example of a rule that mitigates the modification costs by offering alternatives to formal treaty changes. Modification may occur through different procedural and institutional steps that involve different actors, with the general rule that the more fundamental the modifications are the more EU and national actors must give their consent in order to secure legitimacy.

[25] Joined cases C-6/90 and C-9/90 *Francovich, Bonifaci and others v Italian Republic* (1991) EU:C:1991:428 I05357.

6
Supplying public goods and addressing external effects

One could conceive of a world without the EU, possibly even without international law. In such world of autarky, goods and services would be produced and consumed by people in the same state, and no state would take actions affecting other states' citizens. Likewise, political decisions would be limited to inward-looking effects that do not affect other countries. In such a context, European states would have no incentive to engage in cooperation, less so through binding self-commitment. However, in practice there are multiple relations and interactions between states, companies, and citizens, and the nature of these relationships offers a rationale for cooperation through EU law. In a world of increasing economic, cultural, and social interconnectedness, what were conceived as national public goods have turned into transnational public goods, leaving national states struggling to effectively supply them.[1] EU law then serves the function of ensuring sufficient supply of EU public goods, addressing externalities, and promoting a level of conduct and commitment that serves to achieve cooperation gains from an overall European perspective. The increase in European surplus can then be divided among participating states to make them all better off.[2]

The logic of public goods is well known: with non-rivalry and non-excludability as characteristics of public goods, collective goods such as a clean environment or security are suffering from collective action problems. Free-riding on the climate commitments of others is the rationale behind binding environmental agreements, solving the problem of under-provision of climate efforts. These efforts culminate in EU law and international law, with EU law being the more specific and more binding reduction commitment than the international law climate obligations under the Paris Agreement. However, for the purpose of understanding cooperation on public goods within the EU, we consider the traditional definition of public goods to be too restrictive, as there are other coordination failures that can lead to the under-provision of goods compared to its optimal level that might require public intervention. We adopt a slightly broader definition: a public good

[1] Ernst-Ulrich Petersmann and Armin Steinbach, 'Neo-Liberalism, State-Capitalism and Ordo-Liberalism: "Institutional Economics" and "Constitutional Choices" in Multilevel Trade Regulation' (2021) 22 Journal of World Investment & Trade 1, 1.

[2] Eric Posner and Alan O Sykes, *Economic Foundations of International Law* (Harvard University Press 2013) 13.

EU Law and Economics. Armin Steinbach, Oxford University Press. © Oxford University Press 2025.
DOI: 10.1093/9780198920915.003.0006

is simply defined as a good that is not supplied at an adequate level without public intervention (which could take various forms including direct provision, government expenditure, or regulation) due to coordination problems (not only non-exclusion or non-rivalry, but also, eg, network effects). This broader definition captures further incidences of public good cooperation which do not fall under the narrow definition of public goods: 'pecuniary' externalities (ie externalities that run through prices and do not constitute market failures) can offer a rationale for EU cooperation. Public investment in an EU member producing cross-border spillovers are felt in other EU Member States as well and may require coordination to optimize their effects from an overall EU perspective. Also, we consider 'club goods' to be of relevance (which do not fit the traditional definition because they are not non-exclusionary). Consider the European Economic and Monetary Union (EMU) as a 'club' public good. Price stability in the eurozone and fiscal stability are public goods to which all countries should contribute, while, however, leaving incentives to free-ride on the other countries' efforts of fiscal prudence—a dilemma that the EU seeks to resolve by fiscal rules and credible no-bailout clauses. Hence, even though club public goods would allow for the exclusion of certain members from the club good (recall the debate on 'Grexit'), this may, however, not be a viable economic and political option. Efficient club goods thus require incentivizing club members to contribute to the supply of public goods, with the privatization of the benefits of the club accruing to club members offering a strong incentive to join the club. Again, the euro is an example. Clearly, sharing a common currency on the internal market offers economic benefits. Limiting access to these benefits by requiring that prospective members converge their economies towards viable economic levels reveals a logic of incentivization that ensures the effective supply of public goods.

Supranational cooperation, such as that of the EU, may suffer from being insufficiently cooperative where a 'weakest-link public good' is concerned. Weakest-link cooperation can be traced to Oliver Williamson's transaction theory.[3] He sees vertical integration as a governance response to high asset specificity. In our context, high asset specificity occurs when a Member State makes investments in a good whose value depends on the cooperation of other states. Hence, for a weakest-link public good to generate benefits, all members must invest in the supply of the good—if this does not happen, any state's investment is wasted. In these cases, there is no compensation possible in the sense of a country making additional efforts to compensate for another state's reduced efforts. Take policy areas as diverse as the fight against terrorism in the EU, the fiscal conduct of states in the euro currency zone, or the border control of European states fighting illicit trade. In these cases, the Treaty effort level and the number of EU members are complementary in the

[3] Oliver E Williamson, *The Economic Institutions of Capitalism: Firms, Markets, Relational Contracting* (The Free Press 1985).

sense that both commitment at the Treaty level and commitment to enforcement positively increase the value of the good concerned. Regarding the fight against terrorism, for instance, in an interconnected EU (without internal borders), the lack of compliance of only one EU member may undermine the value of security for all other members. Likewise, in fiscal policy, the economic misconduct of only one country may destabilize the entire euro area irrespective of the performance of other countries; inadequate measures in the area of banking regulation may undermine financial stability through contagious effects on financial markets; and if EU border control is lax in only one Member State, illicit trade may occur to the detriment of other EU states. In all these cases the supply of the public good suffers, for other EU countries cannot compensate for the underperforming state, hence creating a 'weakest-link' public good.

With weakest-link public goods being serious concerns, the value of the early ECJ jurisprudence on primacy of EU law over Member States law becomes evident—it ensures consistent application of EU law in all Member States, and it precludes Member States from applying laws that are potentially harmful to the European public good provision. There is thus an ambivalence from an economic perspective: on one hand, EU law primacy ensures consistent protection of EU public goods preventing Member States from defecting from their commitments. On the other hand, uniform application of EU law overrides divergent Member States' rules, which can be criticized for ignoring diverse preferences by setting rules indistinctively at a central level, hence causing a mismatch between rules and preferences (see Chapter 10 a)).

Unlike 'weakest-link public goods', 'substitute public goods' allow states to compensate for the insufficient efforts of other European states. If European country A lowers its climate ambition and emits more CO2 than it is permitted to under CO2-reduction paths of EU climate law, country B could increase its efforts to compensate for it, as it does not matter from the perspective of climate protection who reduces the CO2 emission. Yet, the core challenge also remains with substitute goods, where a country may have an incentive to invest too little and thus free ride on the efforts of other countries. In addition, the equal commitment of countries A and B may be inefficient if the costs of avoiding CO2 emission is cheaper in one country than in the other (hence favouring a cost-oriented approach to CO2 reduction as implemented through the Emissions Trading Scheme).

Closely related to the provision of public goods, externalities offer a straightforward case for entering into binding EU law commitments. In an interconnected and globalized Europe, the actions in or by one state have implications for the well-being of citizens in other states. In such settings, an international externality occurs. In economic parlance, many of these externalities are non-pecuniary, in that they do not travel through the price system. The initial motivation for establishing the European Community is probably the most obvious example of negative non-pecuniary externalities motivating the forming of the Treaties of Rome. Fears of territorial expansion, (trade) wars, political threats, and unchecked political power motivated the EU founding members to submit to self-commitment through the EU Treaties.

Other externalities are pecuniary, meaning that the effects on others are felt through changes in price. In that regard, the EMU is a field of multiple pecuniary externalities. Soon after the inception of the European Communities, members identified decentralized monetary policies as a source of instability for other EU members, channelled as pecuniary effects through the price system, which led to the establishment of the European Central Bank (ECB): the effects of Germany (or other large EU members) pursuing expansionary fiscal impulses (positive pecuniary externality) felt in neighbouring countries; domestic state aid distorting competition on the internal market and harming competitors from other countries; national banking regulation affecting domestic banks' operations, which in turn feeds through EU capital markets into other countries; and low wage development undercutting the competitiveness of other European countries (negative pecuniary externality), perceived as a 'beggar-thy-neighbor' policy. More recently, the EU debt crisis revealed another form of 'beggar-thy-neighbour' policy that resulted from Member States inflicting financial instability on other euro members through fiscally unsound actions.

The EU has adopted various legal instruments to deal with externalities. Not only has externality been mitigated through treaties and secondary law by way of implementing directives and regulations—for example, prohibition on inflicting harm on other countries; state aid rules precluding negative effects on foreign competitors; regulations curtailing free-riding on other members' efforts in the pursuit of climate goals; and fiscal rules disincentivizing EU members from free-riding on the fiscal solidity of other states. At the level of jurisprudence, the ECJ also engaged in the removal of externalities by ruling that not only are discriminatory measures forbidden (which obviously follows from EU law) but also any measures that could potentially hinder the free trade of goods and services (the so-called Dassonville formula[4]). By eradicating even non-discriminatory barriers to inter-state commerce, the Court abolishes (pecuniary) externalities that regulatory measures impose on other EU members. In other words, the idea of an internal market without barriers incorporates the elimination of externalities of domestic regulation on other states (eg health).

From the perspective of European integration, externalities have been addressed in rather a non-uniform manner. While mitigating the negative external effects from company market power or the distortive effects of state aid has been brought rather early under the EU legal umbrella in the integration process, addressing externalities and free-riding in fiscal affairs became imminent when

[4] Case C-8/74 *Dassonville* (1974) EU:C:1974:82 837.

creating the EMU. Other externality-prone policy fields such as security and defence policies remain in Member States' control and thus are sources of potential externalities (even though cooperation and loyalty requirements apply in these domains). With Article 42(7) TEU obliging its members to act in solidarity when military threats from external actors occur, domestic military expenditure creates positive externalities. A member investing in defence and military capacities increases the overall security for all EU members. In social policies, yet another area of remaining Member State competences, externalities may result from different policy designs, which may create incentives for workers to migrate between EU Member States. Just as with wage policies, social policies can be designed in ways that are perceived as 'beggar-thy-neighbour' policies by other states.

With positive externalities just as relevant for EU regulation as negative externalities, the EU internal market offers an example of *network externalities* at work. Adopting new technological and regulatory standards, more cooperation and participation in the standards increase the value of the standards for all participating countries. By definition, network externalities occur when benefits to all members increase when new members join. International organizations are built on the concept of network externalities. This may be, for example, the case for trade or dispute settlement.[5] The more members that join the EU customs union and the EU internal market, the more efficiency gains are possible. Not only do incumbent EU members benefit from the spread of the network, but network externalities also create incentives for the participation of non-EU states, thereby increasing the potential benefits for both new (and existing) EU members joining the standard (and it ultimately lowers new members' costs to incorporate the growing *acquis communautaire* as a precondition for accession to the EU). The larger the market and the greater the participation in the EU's standards, the higher the EU's global weight in standard setting. Hence, Member States have an incentive to expand standard setting exercises in the EU.

Enforcement costs for goods characterized by network externalities are fairly low, as the risk of defection of Member States or third states by deviating from the agreed standard is unlikely. This is because we are in a coordination game (not in a prisoner dilemma situation), offering an endogenous incentive to comply with standards. The network externality effect may not only promote trade between EU insiders, it may also increase the EU's weight geopolitically, hence strengthening the EU in international organizations and in the international arena more generally. Clearly, the advantages of acceding must be weighed against the costs. Transferring trade policy competence to the EU creates positive network effects for members, but there are sovereignty costs associated with Member States

[5] David Epstein and Sharyn O'Halloran, 'Sovereignty and Delegation in International Organizations' (2008) 71 Law and Contemporary Problems 89; Joel P Trachtman, *The Future of International Law: Global Government* (Cambridge University Press 2013) 28.

losing their autonomous representation at the World Trade Organization (WTO). Dilution of sovereign representation in international organizations (when the EU represents its members) or loss of domestic regulation or standard-setting autonomy add to sovereignty costs. Also, while overall efficiency gains exist with new members joining public goods with network effects, distribution of benefits may vary and affect certain groups of society more than others, which gives rise to internal domestic resistance. More importantly, the EU comprises cooperation across many policy sectors and goods. Some may produce network externalities (trade or financial regulation), while others exhibit weakest-link public goods (eg security, migration). This inconsistency across goods may give rise to diverse patterns of cooperation and to differentiated integration—the Schengen Agreement and euro membership are examples. Treaty opt-outs and opt-ins as well as enhanced cooperation (Article 20 TEU) are governance options under EU law to account for different public goods enshrined in the EU (see below Chapter 12).

7
Leveraging economies of scale

With the EU Member States shifting the level of public power from the national to the supranational level, economics examines the benefits of supranationalization. Economies of scale offer a normative benchmark—tested and widely applied in economic scholarship to federal states[1]—to assess the benefits of allocating policy responsibilities at the centralized level. These benefits must be held against the costs of harmonization that accrue mainly where one-size-fits-all regulation is adopted despite heterogeneity of preferences across the regions.[2] Balancing the benefits from economies of scale with the varying preferences of the citizenry, the optimal degree of centralization should follow one logic: all functions where economies of scale offer compelling benefits should be held at the central level, whereas all functions with high heterogeneity of preferences should be kept at the local level.[3]

Economies of scale are the paradigmatic economic tool offered to assess the subsidiarity principle—the core Treaty principle laid down in Article 5(3) TEU governing the competence allocation between Union and Member States where shared competences are concerned (unlike exclusive EU competence, where the subsidiarity principle does not apply). The legal subsidiarity principle has been notoriously criticized by legal scholarship for not being based on consistent logic, as well as for the perception that Union institutions—the Commission and the ECJ—have interpreted subsidiarity in a fashion that favours centralization.[4] This criticism in legal scholarship has been echoed in the political domain, positing that the alleged lack of subsidiarity is tantamount to an intrusive EU encroaching on Member States' competences.

[1] Gordon Tullock, 'Federalism: Problems of Scale' (1969) 6 Public Choice 19; Jacques LeBoeuf, 'The Economics of Federalism and the Proper Scope of the Federal Commerce Power' (1994) 31 San Diego Law Review 555, 565.

[2] Stephen Weatherill, 'Why Harmonise?' in Takis Tridimas and Paolo Nebbia (eds), *European Union Law for the Twenty-First Century: Rethinking the New Legal Order* (Hart Publishing 2003) 11, 13.

[3] Francesco Parisi and Vincy Fon, *The Economics of Lawmaking* (Oxford University Press 2008) 52.

[4] Catherine Barnard, 'What the Keck? Balancing the Needs of the Single Market with State Regulatory Autonomy' (2012) European Journal of Consumer Law 201; Stephen Weatherill, 'The Limits of Legislative Harmonization Ten Years after Tobacco Advertising: How the Court's Case Law has become a "Drafting Guide"' (2011) 12 German Law Journal 827; Dieter Grimm, *Constitutionalism: Past—Present—Future* (Oxford University Press 2006) 303; Gareth Davies, 'Subsidiarity: The Wrong Idea, in the Wrong Place, at the Wrong Time' (2006) 43 Common Market Law Review 63, 64; Nicholas W Barber, 'Subsidiarity in the Draft Constitution' (2005) 11 European Public Law 197; Peter M Huber, 'Das Kooperationsverhältnis zwischen BVerfG und EuGH in Grundrechtsfragen' (1997) Europäische Zeitschrift für Wirtschaftsrecht 517.

EU Law and Economics. Armin Steinbach, Oxford University Press. © Oxford University Press 2025.
DOI: 10.1093/9780198920915.003.0007

'Economies of scope' can weaken the case for economies of scale. Even if there are economies of scale for some policy functions, there are functional synergies between two governmental functions that create valuable economies of scope. These governmental functions are best carried out jointly at the same level of government, and shifting one of these functions to a centralized level would result in loss of these economies of scope. Hence, only if the benefits of economies of scale outweigh the sum of switching costs plus the cost of the foregone economies of scope, would the subsidiarity test be satisfied and the function should be centralized.[5] The economies of scope that are created by performing two or more functions at the same level of government are generally due to the opportunities for pooling information, sharing organization infrastructure, and internalizing other administrative externalities between two or more governmental functions. Take banking resolution and banking supervision as an example. In the EU, banking resolution and banking supervision have long been subject to variable domestic regimes, but have been revised and to a significant degree supranationalized following the financial crisis. Building on the EU's internal market competence, the EU enacted legislation establishing centralized rules and conditions for re-capitalization of failing banks through the Single Resolution Fund (SRF) and introduced a Single Supervisory Mechanism that shifted the supervision of the most important banks from national to EU level. If these areas—resolution and supervision—were regulated separately, thus split between the decentralized and centralized levels, the economies of scope would be lost as friction between supervision and resolution would occur. The logic unfolding is that there is a case for centralized supervision giving rise to economies of scale, and the resolution of centrally supervised banks should also be handled centrally to achieve economies of scope.

Not only do economies of scale serve to determine the level of governance with reference to the policy issue concerned, but the benchmark also highlights the evolving EU's institutional architecture. This architecture, by incorporating the intimate interaction between Union institutions with each of them performing a quasi-constitutional function to safeguard the institutional balance, has evolved over decades and was modified through various Treaty amendments. The institutional balance rests on the EU Commission acting as the administration or executive, the ECJ as judiciary, and the Council and Parliament as political legislative organs. Economies of scale considerations apply where the EU architecture deviates from Member States' models. For example, the national competition authorities of EU Member States typically act through entities that are separate from national ministries, while this task is institutionally merged with other executive and political branches at the EU Commission, for which institutional economies of scale offer a sound rationale (rather than creating a new agency). Likewise, using

[5] Parisi and Fon (n 3) 60.

the same institutional structure for issues as diverse as agricultural and research policies rather than setting up separate institutions for each issue area is an expression of economies of scale. It would be too costly to build a new institutional setup for each task performed by the EU Commission. There is enough institutional flexibility to account for the specificities of issue areas—the Commission can easily create a new Directorate exploiting economies of scale while allowing institutional specialization, and the Council offers a flexible format which can convene in various compositions with national ministers gathering depending on the issue area.

While the above structure, known as the 'Community method', mimics a quasi-constitutional balance of power, in other policy areas Member States have retained an intergovernmental mode of cooperation (eg in security and defence policies) or have limited the EU's role to that of coordination rather than legislative powers (eg coordination of economic policies, Article 121 TFEU). In these areas, the EU foregoes economies of scale. The fact that the EU lacks geopolitical weight due to its heterogenous representation in the international arena of security and lacks 'one voice' in European external matters is a reflection of untapped economies of scale: geopolitical weight would increase with a more centrally determined foreign policy.[6] Likewise, in the area of EMU, the asymmetry between a centralized monetary policy and decentralized economic and fiscal policies has been identified as a fundamental cause of economic turmoil. While economies of scale have been exploited for monetary policy through a single European central bank, there are increasingly high costs due to economies of scope as described above—economic and fiscal policies should be allocated on the EU level in order to avoid friction between monetary and economic policies. By separating monetary and fiscal policies between the EU and state levels, economies of scope are costly due to the insufficient coordination of monetary and fiscal policies.[7] Consider however that economies of scale (or scope) are only one element of the equation. Fiscal federalism theory requires that a task be performed on a centralized rather than a decentralized level such that an overall assessment of externalities, economies of scale, and preference heterogeneity must be made (see below chapter 10 b)).[8] Even if economies of scale favour centralization, preference heterogeneity among Member States may mitigate against it— 'trade-offs' are the consequences, requiring a weighing of relevant factors.

In some cases, Member States may consider that the economies of scale weigh less than the costs they anticipated from using the established architecture. Take

[6] Stefan Lehne, 'Making EU Foreign Policy Fit for a Geopolitical World' *Carnegie Europe* (14 April 2022).

[7] Martin Feldstein, 'The Political Economy of the European Economic and Monetary Union: Political Sources of an Economic Liability' (1997) 11 Journal of Economic Perspectives 23.

[8] Grégory Claeys and Armin Steinbach, 'A Conceptual Framework for the Identification and Governance of European Public Goods' (2024) Working Paper 14/24, Bruegel.

the example of the ESM as the core instrument for rescuing states in financial distress. It would have been possible to integrate this task into the Commission, given that the Commission is experienced in administering and monitoring financial instruments. Yet Member States considered the Commission insufficiently fit for this task. Instead, they created a new legal entity in Luxembourg that runs the ESM outside the regular institutional setup, albeit established under EU law (Article 136(3) TFEU). One motive might have been that members perceived the Commission as 'too political', implying a risk of politicizing decisions that should be technical, hence making Member States with high financial stakes in the assistance feel insecure and raising political costs to a level that outweighed the economies of scale.

One can also trace economies of scales in the ECJ jurisprudence defending its jurisprudential monopoly to interpret EU law (Article 19 TEU). The ECJ has repeatedly declared that other courts are not allowed to rule on issues that may imply interpretations of Union law. For example, the ECJ denied competing jurisdiction by tribunals established under bilateral investment agreements that EU Member States concluded with third countries.[9] There are two ways of looking at this from an economic perspective. A public choice perspective emphasizes prestige-seeking motivations that cause institutional rivalry leading the ECJ to avail of its Treaty-based authoritative power to forbear competing courts from its jurisdictional space. At the same time, looking at this jurisprudence from an economies of scale perspective, the Court seeks to optimize the economies of scale which the Treaty has granted to the Court by assigning it the sole role of interpreting EU law.[10] Having more than one court dealing with the same issue would create jurisdictional friction, conflicting rulings, and thus increased costs in terms of legal insecurity.

[9] Case C-284/16 *Slovak Republic v Achmea* (2018) EU:C:2018:158.

[10] For a similar reasoning in relation to the WTO agreements, see Andrew Guzman, *How International Law Works* (Oxford University Press 2008) 169.

8
Why cooperation fails

Member States may fail to achieve an agreement on EU law matters. Negotiations over Treaty amendments may collapse in the midst of irreconcilable positions; even if Treaty amendments have been consented to on the state level, national referenda may fail preventing signed Treaties from being ratified, as happened in France and Ireland. On a more frequent basis, EU secondary legislation may fail by lacking unanimity or insufficient votes to attain a qualified majority. Failure in EU cooperation remains ubiquitous where competing equilibria are in play, many actors are involved, and uncertainty prevails. Theoretically, many of these failures are due to obstacles to cooperation. These obstacles were downplayed by early game-theoretic applications emphasizing 2 x 2 games. In these simple games, there is only one point of mutual cooperation, the unattainable Pareto optimum where both sides choose to cooperate rather than defect. In practice, states have a wide range of choices and many possible cooperative outcomes, often with different distributional consequences.[1] This wide range of options available to EU Member States on whether and how to seek cooperation can be explained by the rationales for cooperation discussed above: gains of cooperation may simply not be sufficiently high for all EU members compared to costs, whether such costs are actual or perceived.

To start with, a strong Pareto criterion prevents a Treaty amendment or a secondary legislation with unanimity vote if not every member gains; in many cases this rigid welfare benchmark may be overcome where transfers and side-payments make gains possible to all participating members (weak Pareto criterion). A rational government compares the net payoff with and without European cooperation. If the 'self-help' payoff is higher than the 'cooperation' payoff, it may consider attaining a goal alone. The highest self-help payoff represents the opportunity costs that states face when considering whether to agree to Treaty changes or to engage in secondary legislation. In the case of Brexit, the United Kingdom (UK) (or its relevant state leaders) forecasted self-help payoff as (*ex-ante*) higher than costs associated with continuing to be an EU member, thus withdrawing membership from the EU. Clearly, European states are to different degrees capable of pursuing specific goals in the absence of European cooperation and may derive different net

[1] Barbara Koremenos, Charles Lipson, and Duncan Snidal, 'The Rational Design of International Institutions' (2001) 55 International Organization 761, 765.

EU Law and Economics. Armin Steinbach, Oxford University Press. © Oxford University Press 2025.
DOI: 10.1093/9780198920915.003.0008

benefits from autonomous pursuit of policy objectives. Opportunity costs attached to cooperation in the EU differs across EU members.

Opportunity costs refer to outside options.[2] Some states have better means to achieve given policy objectives without cooperation and they can leverage the threat to act unilaterally to shape the rules. This phenomenon is particularly salient on the global level, where some states can use informal and formal power to design and control international economic institutions.[3] The UN Security Council, with veto powers and the design of multilateral development banks such as the IMF and the World Bank, are illustrative of power biases due to variable outside options. Veto powers have better outside options in all cooperation matters under international law because they control the ability of the Security Council to react on international law matters. Power imbalances are less pronounced in the EU, where the institutional design generally reflects the notion of equality among states, and where it does deviate from this principle—concerning representation in the European Parliament or voting weights in the Council, for example—smaller countries are even favoured relative to larger countries.[4] That said, opportunity costs vary depending on policy issues—take the recent euro crisis which led to creditor states wielding financial power over debtor countries, thus allowing the former to dictate the conditions of cooperation under financial assistance programmes.[5]

Heterogenous distributional effects add to the difficulty in reaching cooperation. There are up to twenty-seven members involved in negotiations, each of them with a variable degree of size, political weight, and financial power, and agreements must be made on how to share both the costs and benefits of cooperation. With each member making its own deliberate cost-benefit analysis, the distributional effects of cooperation may be diverse, which makes side-deals and compensation in other fields necessary for reaching agreements. Think of the multiple failed attempts to set up a central fiscal instrument in the EU (or euro area) that would allow fiscal transfers to countries in need of financial assistance.[6] There are significant redistributional effects with the potential of perpetuating financial flows from some members to others.

[2] Erik Voeten, 'Making Sense of the Design of International Institutions' (2019) 22 Annual Review of Political Science 147, 153.

[3] Randall W Stone, *Controlling Institutions: International Organizations and the Global Economy* (Cambridge University Press 2011).

[4] Jonathan Rodden, 'Strength in Numbers?' (2002) 3 European Union Politics 151.

[5] Deirdre Curtin, 'Challenging Executive Dominance in European Democracy' (2014) 77 Modern Law Review 1; Armin Steinbach, 'EU Economic Governance after the Crisis: Revisiting the Accountability Shift in EU Economic Governance' (2019) 26 Journal of European Public Policy 1354.

[6] Jean-Claude Juncker, 'The Five Presidents' Report: Completing Europe's Economic and Monetary Union' (2012) (hereinafter 'Five Presidents' Report'); Nathaniel G Arnold and others, 'A Central Fiscal Stabilization Capacity for the Euro Area' (2018) Staff Discussion Notes No 2018/003; European Commission, 'A Blueprint for a Deep and Genuine Economic and Monetary Union: Launching a European Debate' (2012).

But irrespective of distributional effects, cooperation may be hampered if absolute losses are perceived by one Member States as inconceivable. From the experience of recent years, it is sovereignty costs which may pose a barrier to cooperation in the EU, notably if sovereignty costs exceed an absolute level, above which these costs cannot be outweighed by other gains. As mentioned above, cooperation through shifting competence to the EU level may cause prohibitive sovereignty costs at least in some Member States, if a core sensitive issue is concerned. Sovereignty costs are determined by national constitutional law. The German Constitutional Court has identified prohibitive sovereignty costs associated with core state policy areas such as certain criminal law matters, social policy, and budgetary control.[7] With the German Constitutional Court determining what is non-transferable to the European level, the German law-makers are barred from independently judging whether they consider the benefits of a transfer of competences exceeds the costs. In these circumstances, it is for citizens only to decide—under a new German constitution—whether to transfer sensitive core-state competences to Brussels. Hence, even if economies of scale may be significant and support EU centralized action, domestic constitutional law may erect prohibitive costs. Take the ESM as an illustration. Setting up the intergovernmental ESM was complicated by a Constitutional requirement seeking to minimize sovereignty costs. Germany's Constitutional Court found that offering loans to other countries would require Germany to condition financial aid in compliance with fiscal and structural reforms that recipient countries would have to accept, as well as requiring a unanimity vote on the disbursement of loans.[8] Unless these conditions were met, sovereignty costs would be unacceptably high, regardless of the overall positive welfare effect achieved through avoiding a break-up of the eurozone. At least for Germany, and to some extent for Poland too,[9] one can therefore conceptualize sovereignty costs as a non-linear costs curve that grows exponentially with additional transfer of competences. The voting rule in the Council can further shift the cost curve, with majority voting driving the costs to higher levels.

Even if cooperation could produce win–win situations, transaction costs for achieving cooperation or for bargaining over compensation deals are sometimes simply too high, with the effect that the sum of cooperation costs and transaction costs exceed EU members' benefits. This slows down EU decision-making where unanimity is required, particularly for Treaty amendments but also where unanimity persists in EU policy-making such as in foreign policy.

[7] BVerfGE 123, 267 *Lissabon* (2009)—Lisbon Treaty.

[8] BVerfGE 132, 195 *European Stability Mechanism (ESM)* (2012).

[9] See the Polish Constitutional Court judgment emphasizing the limitation of more European integration, Case K 18/04, judgment of 7 October 2021. Sára Kiššová, 'Overview of the Doctrine of Ultra Vires from the Perspective of the German Federal Constitutional Court and the Polish Constitutional Court' (2022) 2 Slovak Yearbook of European Union Law 33.

Heterogeneity in preferences, benefits, and costs make EU accession rounds increasingly challenging, because each accession of new EU members make Pareto improvements more difficult to achieve. On one hand, what entices incumbent (as well as acceding) members are the benefits from an enlarged area of common rules, internal market, and geopolitical weight. In addition, some legal instruments are in place that make new EU accessions sufficiently attractive for countries that extend the club advantages of EU membership to other states. Most relevant, by shifting the burden of adaptation onto the shoulders of the acceding states who must adopt the entire *acquis communautaire*, incumbent members are less likely to lose on the existing level of integration. On the other hand, the dilutionary effect of EU expansion and the heterogeneity effect count as costs for incumbent members. They must accept a dilution of voting rights in the Council as the number of members increases. More generally, with heterogeneity increasing through diverging preferences, it becomes harder to agree between states. As long as there were five founding members of the European Community with more or less similar, or at least complementary interests, members were able to agree in substance in the limited fields in which Member States initially dealt with cooperatively. Yet, as the number of members increased, the heterogeneity within the group also rose. New members are qualitatively different for various reasons, be it culturally, economically, or socially. While heterogeneity limits cooperation, issue linkages may generate new opportunities for mutually beneficial arrangements. The EU expanded both in its number of members and in scope and depth of integration, which facilitated agreements because side-deals and compensation in unrelated fields became possible. There is, however, a limit to simply expanding the scope of issue areas, as increased scope comes at higher (bargaining) costs. Strategic behaviour may lead some actors to 'hold up' the agreement to gain additional benefits. The risk of unravelling, whereby failure in one issue may lead to failure in all linked issues, is then greater.[10] Accessions are thus a mixed endeavour: an EU growing in membership increases network and coordination benefits across policy fields for all participating states (incumbent and acceding states), but it also exacerbates diversity and hence makes the landing zone in terms of Treaty rules that satisfy all states' preferences smaller.

High enforcement costs can be an obstacle to cooperation where compliance with EU law is weak. In principle, one of the features distinguishing the EU from international organizations is its effective enforcement structure with infringement procedures and the role of the Commission and the ECJ as enforcers (see below Chapter 14). However, in other areas, enforcement mechanisms are weak and thus invite defection and rule breaches. In the EMU, this has been a perennial issue.[11] The EU debt crisis was (at least partially) caused and exacerbated by a

[10] Koremenos, Lipson, and Snidal (n 1) 786.

[11] Armin Steinbach, *Economic Policy Coordination in the Euro Area* (Taylor & Francis Ltd 2014).

lack of compliance with pre-agreed fiscal rules and led many external observers to question the character of the EU as a supranational role model for other regions.[12] The climax of the sovereign debt crisis led the EU to introduce conditionality as a prerequisite for crisis support in order to improve enforcement. Hence, in cases of fiscal transfer and with a view to mitigating moral hazard concerns, the EU has reverted to conditional financial assistance on the delivery of structural and fiscal reforms as an instrument to safeguard the long-term benefits of EMU membership, which would be at risk if individual EMU members could destabilize the common good by opportunistic behaviour. The ensuing discussion on the break-up of the euro area and 'Grexit' illustrates how cooperation may collapse over insufficient compliance with what is required by law. Put differently, by giving the EU weak enforcement institutions in EMU affairs, EU members decided to accept high enforcement costs in order to minimize sovereignty costs (through strict fiscal surveillance). More than once throughout the history of the EMU, political considerations trumped legal (and economic) rules—the initial entry requirements for states to join the euro were interpreted leniently, and the Stability and Growth Pact was not rigorously enforced. On a conceptual level, as each EU member determines the payoff for non-cooperation as a function of the credibility of sanctions attached to non-compliance, there is a public good dilemma where enforcement costs may be determined by the strength of individual actors' incentives to cheat on agreed rules.[13] Managerial theories of compliance look at it differently.[14] Take the Greek flagrant non-compliance with EU fiscal rules when statistical miscalculations were hiding that actual budget deficits were much higher than publicly reported.[15] Managerial theories would liken data misreporting and institutional shortcomings to the lack of bureaucratic capacity. In any case, as members of the EMU, all countries benefit from a stable currency as club public goods and factual risk-sharing smoothing bonds spread, but for this positive spillover to materialize requires investment in markets' trust through fiscal prudence. In the past, rules failed to constrain disincentives for contributing to the common good of a stable currency.[16]

Despite a restraining set of EU rules, Member States continue to have an incentive to free-ride on the policy efforts of other states. If a Member State is certain that a desired collective action will happen anyway, even without their particular contribution (eg financial stability in the euro area, security efforts in the EU), they have an incentive to leave it to others to deliver the common good. Besides the

[12] Charles Wyplosz, 'Europe's Quest for Fiscal Discipline' (2013) European Economy—Economic Papers 2008–2015 No 498.

[13] Koremenos, Lipson, and Snidal (n 10) 776.

[14] Katerina Linos, 'How Can International Organizations Shape National Welfare States? Evidence from Compliance with European Union Directives' (2007) 40 Comparative Political Studies 547.

[15] Benny Andersen, 'The Crisis in Greece: Missteps and Miscalculations, European Stability Mechanism' (2020) Discussion Paper Series No 9.

[16] Steinbach (n 11).

EMU, foreign policy offers another example. Small Member States may be particularly prone to free-riding. While they participate in decision-making on international developments, they assume barely any responsibility for concrete action, with their societies unprepared to bear the costs and risks of operational engagement. This conduct has been observed in relation to establishing a common financial base for EU military operations. In case of security challenges, for instance in North Africa, it has been left to bigger countries with regional ties to the region to deal with security challenges, while many other states have tended to free-ride on these efforts, contributing little towards setting up an effective EU funding mechanism.[17]

While the unanimity requirement has been a perennial problem for the adoption of EU secondary law, the extended introduction of qualified majority voting has allowed the Union to move from Pareto improvements (unanimity voting) to weaker Pareto and Kaldor-Hicks solutions (qualified majority voting). Depending on the individual case, those countries that are overruled in the Council may face significant costs outweighing the benefits accruing to other EU members, but the level of thresholds for qualified majority voting (55 per cent of Member States vote in favour and support by Member States representing at least 65 per cent of the total EU population) reduces the instances in which an EU act fails to offer any kind of welfare improvement. The two voting thresholds tend to secure that, from an EU-wide perspective, there is at least a possibility that the gains resulting from the enacted secondary law exceed the costs. However, the EU integration process is characterized by making majority voting more frequent, which on one hand is desirable because it makes the impact of national regulatory capture or biased decision-making less far reaching compared to unanimity. On the other hand, however, extending qualified voting reduces the willingness of incumbent EU members to accept new members. With each new member, majority thresholds are harder to achieve and blocking opportunities are reduced, thus creating problems that would not exist under the unanimity requirement.

A complicating factor is that when negotiating Treaty amendments or adopting EU secondary law, each EU country is facing different restraints on the EU level than they are on the domestic level. We recall Putnam's two-level games to make cooperation work.[18] At the EU level, national governments seek to maximize their own ability to satisfy domestic pressures, while minimizing the adverse consequences of foreign developments. When negotiating EU Treaties between

[17] Stefan Lehne, 'Is There Hope for EU Foreign Policy?' (Carnegie Endowment for International Peace 2017).

[18] Robert D Putnam, 'Diplomacy and Domestic Politics: The Logic of Two-Level Games' (1988) 42 International Organization 427, 434; Joel P Trachtman, *The Future of International Law: Global Government* (Cambridge University Press 2013) 43.

state representatives on the inter-state level, bargaining costs matter for finding an agreement that is agreeable to all state leaders. At the national level, domestic groups weigh their interests by pressuring the government to adopt favourable policies, and politicians seek power by crafting alliances with those groups, while complying with domestic legal requirements. Sovereignty costs and implementation costs are a function of the domestic policy constraint.[19] Member States can concede to EU partners only what is domestically feasible, that is, the political costs of implementing the EU deal at home must not be too high. The negotiators of EU law thus need to address the concerns of domestic interest groups and, at the same time, reach an agreement that is acceptable for other EU members. In certain circumstances, greater domestic policy constraints can lead to more bargaining advantages in international negotiations in Brussels. A purely welfarist perspective emphasizes an equilibrium where welfare increasing policies for national states overlap. In a world without public choice, states find compromises and accept second-best solutions (from national perspectives) which may lead to a cooperative equilibrium (even if this is inferior to the optimum as long as it is superior to non-cooperation). However, domestic politics constraints determine possible equilibria.[20] In that sense, greater domestic policy constraints strengthen the position in negotiations on European cooperation because an EU member cannot be expected to violate the domestic policy constraint.[21]

Cooperation is thus prone to failure when domestic political welfare (based on the public choice approach) deviates from actual welfare. The state is a dynamic aggregator with parties, social classes, interest groups, and public opinion as determinants of domestic policy constraints.[22] To appraise the relevance of the domestic policy restraints one should acknowledge that EU Member States may, as posited by rational choice, pursue a welfarist perspective (maximizing national welfare), but at the same time pursue domestic policy welfare. The latter builds on the liberal theory of international relations, which prioritizes the demands of individuals and societal groups over politics.[23] A state's preferences are thus not necessarily rational in their pursuit of maximizing objective welfare, but simply the aggregation of individual preferences by the state's political mechanisms.[24] With domestic policy constraints in mind, cooperation through EU law is generated (by

[19] Katerina Linos, 'A Theory of Diffusion Through Democratic Mechanisms', in Katerina Linos (ed), *The Democratic Foundations of Policy Diffusion: How Health, Family, and Employment Laws Spread Across Countries* (Oxford University Press 2013).

[20] Anne van Aaken and Joel P Trachtman, 'Political Economy of International Law: Towards a Holistic Model of State Behavior' in Alberta Fabricotti (ed), *Political Economy of International Law: A European Perspective* (Edward Elgar 2016) 9.

[21] Trachtman (n 18) 46.

[22] Putnam (n 18) 432.

[23] Andrew Moravcsik, 'Taking Preferences Seriously: A Liberal Theory of International Politics' (1997) 51 International Organization 513, 516.

[24] Trachtman (n 18) 42.

crafting EU Treaties or making EU secondary law)—in line with Putnam—when there is sufficient overlap between equilibria in Brussels and those in members' capitals. Moreover, one should consider the interaction between the welfarist (rational choice) rationale for cooperation and the domestic policy rationale. The very function of cooperation on the EU level is to create outcomes that enhance domestic welfare—either by increasing domestic objective welfare or improving domestic policy outcomes. In other words, cooperation on the EU level widens the scope of possible domestic equilibria that are superior to those available in the absence of EU law. While increases in objective welfare (based on the cooperation rationales discussed above) are desirable, public choice informs us that governments may also make EU laws for the sole purpose of generating domestic policy welfare (even when going against a welfarist benchmark). EU law may be produced in order to satisfy domestic political preferences stabilizing the position of the acting government in the domestic context, irrespective of actual welfare. EU law is effective from that perspective if it changes domestic politics (by stabilizing the incumbent position). An important factor countervailing solutions favouring domestic policy welfare over objective welfare is the use of qualified majority voting as the predominant decision mode in the Council. This decision mode reduces the number of countries and occasions in which domestic policy welfare trumps the objective welfare function of EU law.

In many cases, this two-level requirement does not play out in a prohibitive manner: a government may agree to concessions on the EU level when the adoption of an EU directive or regulation is at stake. Despite domestic policy resistance, the government may consider other types of benefits to be sufficiently high in the interest of overall welfare gains. What weighs in is that domestic policy costs often materialize with certain time-lags, as EU regulations take effect after a delay, for example when EU directives require Member States to take implementing measures. The effect of such time-lags is that governments may blur their accountability for an EU decision to which they agreed in the Council. The time-lag between a Member State's responsible action (eg the adoption of a directive in the Council) and the materialization of political costs (domestic implementation) allows national politicians to externalize some of the costs that would otherwise hinder the agreement on an EU level—this somehow relaxes the constraint under Putnam's two-level game. In other cases, however, the domestic policy level may be an insurmountable requirement of the two-level game. Take EU Treaty amendments under Article 48 TEU requiring not only an accord between EU governments but also ratification, with the negative referenda in France and The Netherlands offering a case in point. Governments were able to come to an accord on the European level (hence on one of Putnam's two levels), but the solution found at EU level did not overlap with the range of acceptable solutions under the domestic policy constraint. Since the referenda were indispensable for the EU Treaty amendments to enter into force, the domestic policy constraint was prohibitive and ultimately hindered the entering into force of the EU Constitutional Treaty.

There is evidence to suggest that information provided to ordinary persons that a policy is required by international law shifts opinion in favour of that policy.[25] Member States can thus facilitate the implementation of EU directives by adequately communicating to their constituents that compliance with EU law is required. A different logic with similar effect unfolds when governments use the delegation of governance tasks to third parties in order to avoid blame once policies become contested.[26] Member States' governments can benefit by attributing unpopular decisions to EU requirements. Legislating unpopular domestic laws that implement binding EU directives can lead to a blame game at the expense of the EU, while proving highly useful for enabling national politicians to keep political costs with EU compliance low.

Domestic policy constraint may interact with a welfarist perspective in the particular case of externalities, which as discussed above provide a strong rationale for (European) cooperation. However, the domestic policy situation may be such that voters have an interest in externalizing costs by imposing them on other countries. This may lead to an equilibrium in which the desirability of cooperation is independent of the magnitude of spillovers. The rationale—as modelled by Loeper—is that cross-border cooperation (in the EU) requires the policy-makers of one Member State to provide more public goods—and thus its voters to pay higher taxes. Therefore, the higher the externality, the higher the costs of cooperation on the voters of that particular Member State. This puts re-election at risk because voters will prefer lower taxes in combination with higher externalities undermining the cooperative regime.[27]

Uncertainty may hinder cooperation, not only where benefits or costs are hard to predict but also where EU members are reluctant to disclose information that could make them more vulnerable. Uncertainty is reduced through institutions, notably the EU Commission and the ECJ acting as bodies that disclose information from Member States (see below Chapter 20 a)). Involving neutral brokers representing Community interests (or a neutral Member State's interest like the President of the Council) can enhance certainty and facilitate information-sharing.

There may also be behavioural economic factors at work that undermine scope for cooperation. Psychologists and economists have constantly investigated the systematic heuristics and biases contradicting the rationality assumption, in order to establish a more realistic model of human behaviour.[28] While European law has

[25] Adam Chilton and Katerina Linos, 'Preferences and Compliance with International Law' (2021) 22 Theoretical Inquiries in Law 247.

[26] Tim Heinkelmann-Wild and others, 'Blame Shifting and Blame Obfuscation: The Blame Avoidance Effects of Delegation in the European Union' (2023) 62 European Journal of Political Research 221.

[27] Antoine Loeper, 'Cross-Border Externalities and Cooperation among Representative Democracies' (2017) 91 European Economic Review 180.

[28] See, in particular, Daniel Kahneman and Amos Tversky, 'Prospect Theory: An Analysis of Decision under Risk' (1979) 47 Econometrica 263; Gerd Gigerenzer and Daniel G Goldstein, 'Reasoning the Fast and Frugal Way: Models of Bounded Rationality' (1996) 103 Psychological Review 650.

yet to be systematically analysed via behavioural economics,[29] some behavioural economic insight may be intuitive, in particular where it may impede cooperation. Loss aversion may play a role where EU cooperation is associated with risks and losses rather than with potential and opportunities.[30] Risks can become salient, creating sentiments of losses. If a country's state leaders are subject to heuristics, this may bias an objective cost-benefit analysis, and perceived losses may lead them to reject an agreement that would increase overall welfare.[31] As discussed, sovereignty costs are crucial for a rational country to decide whether it agrees to surrender competences to the EU or not. If a country suffers from a strong bias by overemphasizing the loss, this will compound sovereignty costs and hence entail a reduced willingness of the country to enter into the agreement. Loss aversion may well be used as a tool of political manipulation. As 'framing' plays an important role in political communication, politicians may try to generate loss aversion in their constituency in the pursuit of their political agenda, a propagandistic technique that populist parties frequently employ. For instance, fostering fear of *losing* one's own currency to trigger resistance or opposing the Schengen Agreement in order not to *lose* control over borders are among the issues that can easily be framed to trigger behavioural economic insight. Framing may also play out in the internal market context, with regulation promoting liberalization of trade within the Community or with external states as an example. Consider the impact of trade concessions, where liberalization can be framed either to impact 'employees' or 'consumers'. While the employee frame would illuminate the risks such as loss of employment due to increasing competition, the consumer perspective highlights the benefits for consumers through lower prices and a greater variety of products.[32]

Yet, loss aversion may also lead to excessive weight being placed on the loss of transferring competences to the EU. Concerns may be multifold: will resources be squandered in bureaucratic excess by the Commission? Are EU institutions likely to transgress their competences, hence undermining the principle of conferral? States view centralization warily, and for the same reasons states are also concerned with maintaining tight control over institutional arrangements so as to minimize agency costs, which, however, is difficult to ensure. There is no mechanism through which individual members could easily tackle a competence breach by the Commission. While the annulment procedure under Article 263 TFEU allows Member States to review EU legislative acts, this possibility runs void if the ECJ is biased towards integration itself (see below Chapter 17). There is a

[29] For international law, see Gregory Shaffer and Tom Ginsburg, 'The Empirical Turn in International Legal Scholarship' (2012) 106 American Journal of International Law 1.

[30] Surveys show that public opinion does not typically align with a country's optimum welfare strategy, see 'Americans on Globalization: A Study of US Public Attitudes' (2000).

[31] Russell B Korobkin and Chris P Guthrie, 'Heuristics and Biases at the Bargaining Table' (2004) 87 Marquette Law Review 795.

[32] Anne van Aaken, 'Behavioral International Law and Economics' (2014) 55 Harvard International Law 421, 457.

mass of literature elaborating on the restrained scrutiny of the ECJ over the EU Commission.[33] From a public choice perspective, both the EU Commission and the ECJ have aligned interests as their importance increases with the scope of EU law. Limited monitoring capacities on the part of Member States and the lack of sanctions for the agent's selfish actions weigh as costs for current EU members and prospective losses for future EU members.

Often, states overvalue the costs of their trade concessions significantly, to the extent that realizing an agreement becomes impossible.[34] Meanwhile, the actors often overestimate the value of their own concessions and underestimate the value of their adversary's commitment during a negotiation. This situation makes bargaining more difficult and can lead to an impasse.[35] It is comparatively more difficult to achieve an agreement when bargaining over the allocation of losses compared to bargaining over the distribution of gains. This often manifests in a permanent struggle over EU Treaty reforms, where the transfer of authority to the EU and perceived losses of sovereignty amount to a bargain over losses, which are clearly identifiable and immediate, while the corresponding gains through integration are vague and uncertain in terms of their actual materialization in the future (eg through future secondary law). Hence, from a behavioural perspective a great deal of information depends on the 'framing' of an agreement. Policy-makers are inclined to be more reluctant when states perceive an agreement rather as loss (eg domestic industries 'losing' market shares), despite overall welfare gains (eg through higher consumer rents). Meanwhile, policy-makers might tend to agree when perception is dominated by profit (eg when accession to EU Treaties is dominated by a narrative of gaining access to EU institutions and markets). Drawing on behavioural economic insight, EU Treaty reforms are more likely to be achieved when the benefits for consumers and exporters are the dominant narrative in public perception influencing the government's choice architecture, as they are among the groups that typically benefit from deeper (economic) integration. In turn, governments whose focus is the protection of the working class (rather than the business sector) may be inclined to underscore the impact on workers in the importing or protected industries.[36]

Further, a status quo bias might also play out. For individual states, consent avoids welfare losses. Consequently, ambitious Treaty reforms—such as the Constitutional Treaty in 2004—which aim to make profound changes to the structure of the EU may not be concluded because of a bias for the status quo.[37] The

[33] Wolf Sauter, 'Proportionality in EU Law: A Balancing Act?' (2013) 15 Cambridge Yearbook of European Legal Studies 439, 450.

[34] van Aaken (n 32) 468.

[35] Jack S Levy, 'Prospect Theory and International Relations: Theoretical Applications and Analytical Problems' (1992) 13 Political Psychology 283, 290.

[36] Bruce E Moon, *Dilemmas of International Trade* (Routledge 2018) 29.

[37] van Aaken (n 32) 457.

status quo bias may be particularly relevant where potential benefits are uncertain giving rise to ambiguity aversion. While traditional fields of EU Treaty reforms (eg enhancing internal markets and removing barriers to trade) allow *ex-ante* quantification of costs and benefits, future effects in other areas are far less certain (eg social policy coordination, institutional changes to decision-making rule in Council, and lifting the EU Treaties to become a 'Constitution'). Major Treaty changes implying institutional changes aiming to overhaul the current practice and engender unprecedented substantive obligations and even threaten national cultural roots by introducing an EU flag or anthem are prone to failure due to ambiguity and loss aversion. However, the effects of aversion can be diminished by avoiding salient reference points. Consider the differences between the failed EU Constitutional Treaty and the successful Lisbon Treaty. The latter avoided being considered a constitution and hence removed all constitution-like features from the reform agenda (eg explicit supremacy of EU over national law; EU symbols such as a flag or anthem; relabelling EU 'regulations' as 'laws'). However, in substance the Lisbon Treaty maintained many of the core ideas of the Constitutional Treaty, in particular the institutional (eg revised decision-making in the Council; a permanent European Council president) as well as substantive changes (eg abolishing the EU's so-called three-pillar structure). The EU's evolution from a failed constitution to the accepted Lisbon Treaty was hence effective in responding to patterns of loss and ambiguity aversion.

PART III
HOW TO COOPERATE UNDER EU LAW

Introduction to Part III

There are many legal variations of cooperation across EU members, with a differing scope of participation, variable bindingness of commitments, and customized degree of centralization. The Treaties foresee, for example, enhanced cooperation and multispeed integration; they provide for opt-outs in Treaty commitments; in some areas, the EU reverts to soft law rather than hard law; some EU competences are allocated to Brussels as exclusive competences, while others are subject to a subsidiarity test to which the economic analysis offers interpretative guidance. With this variability and diversity in form, participation, and scope of commitments under EU law, the focus of this chapter lies on the design of EU law. Having established the core rationales for *why* EU members seek to commit to binding law, we may further explore *how* cooperation under EU law may unfold.

We may draw from the arsenal of economic methods introduced in the Introduction and from the basic rationales for entering into EU cooperation, as discussed in Chapter 1, to explore different design features of EU law. For example, federalism theory inspires the legal principle of conferral, with citizens' preferences and economies of scale as analytical benchmarks; public good theory underpins the subsidiarity principle; contract theory identifies where EU law provides for exception and escape clauses; transaction costs analysis informs phenomena of hard law and soft law under EU law; game theory makes predictions about compliance with EU law and informs the enforcement institutions with the roles of the EU Commission and the ECJ. Likewise, we will benefit from the analysis of Chapter 1 on the rationales of cooperation, in order to understand why EU members choose a specific Treaty design the way they do in light of their individual government objectives and payoff function, the spillovers of policy actions.

Given the focus of this Part on the general arrangements tailored in EU law, that is, the basic principles stipulating the legal framework of EU Treaties, we should recall that the EU is a self-conscious product of its Member States—illustrated by the fact that EU members are the 'Masters of the Treaties', even if the production of EU secondary law is a product of multiple actors combining EU institutions and

Member States.[1] The conceptual departure of this book has been to characterize the EU as an institutional arrangement that Member States pursued through 'rational design'. While the EU is present in the international arena as an independent state-like actor interacting with other countries and hence shaping international law through its own actions, the EU is at its origin an international organization itself. It did not emerge from the same idea of Westphalian sovereignty as an exogenous and standalone actor like the nations that today form the EU. Rather, the EU has been shaped by its Member States. We can thus accept both constructivist and rational choice perspectives on the EU. Constructivists emphasize the pivotal role of international institutions in spreading global norms. In this vein, the EU propagates international agreements or even other international institutions.[2] A constructivist standpoint hence views the EU as an 'independent' variable in international relations, acknowledging that the EU shapes both the EU's actions directed towards the internal EU as well as its external relationship—our analysis accepts this perspective in particular when examining how EU secondary law is made or enforced, with genuine Union institutions (the Commission, the Council, and the ECJ) acting autonomously. However, through the rational choice perspective—as well as emanations of rational choice that relax rationality assumptions such as behavioural economics or institutional economics—which offers us analytical tools to understand the specific design that Member States gave to the EU as a 'dependent variable'—we are thus concerned with understanding the choices that Member States, the 'masters of the Treaties', made in the primary law governing the institutional architecture of the EU.[3]

Disciplines have shown different interests in the study of international organizations. Lawyers traditionally focus on substantive and institutional issues regarding the exercise of competences of international organization, the interpretation of substantive rights and obligations, and the accountability of their authority.[4] Scholarship in international relations has offered systematic accounts of the wide range of design features that characterize international institutions.[5] Our economic analysis seeks to integrate both legal and international relations approaches. Drawing from a legal perspective, our analysis builds on the normative content of primary law decisions—the way lawyers give interpretation to core principles such as subsidiarity or the principle of conferral. We need the positivist reference point

[1] Karen J Alter, 'Who Are the "Masters of the Treaty"? European Governments and the European Court of Justice' (1998) 53 International Organization 121.

[2] Alec Stone Sweet and Wayne Sandholtz, 'European integration and Supranational Governance' (1997) 4 Journal of European Public Policy 297; Thomas Risse, 'Neofunctionalism, European Identity, and the Puzzles of European Integration' (2005) 12 Journal of European Public Policy 291.

[3] Barbara Koremenos, Charles Lipson, and Duncan Snidal, 'The Rational Design of International Institutions' (2001) 55 International Organization 761, 766.

[4] Anne Peters, 'International Organizations and International Law' in *The Oxford Handbook of International Organizations* (Oxford University Press 2017).

[5] Erik Voeten, 'Making Sense of the Design of International Institutions' (2019) 22 Annual Review of Political Science 147, 153.

in order to explore this positivism with an economic eye. From international relations we draw its focus on institutional design—inquiring why Member States in some policy areas have variable membership compared to others,[6] why some areas are governed by hard law while others by soft law,[7] and why states take recourse to escape clauses.[8]

In this perspective, we seek to explain how EU states construct and shape EU institutions to advance their goals. Rational choice posits that the *how* of EU cooperation is the result of rational, purposive interactions among states and EU institutions in an attempt to pursue the cooperation gains laid out in Chapter 1. But we should also account for distributive rational approaches arguing that institutional design is the by-product of purposive attempts by powerful actors to structure interactions in their favour.[9] Unlike strict rational choice approaches, the distributive approach acknowledges suboptimal outcomes due to the fact that powerful states design institutions to advance their interests rather than to achieve socially desirable outcomes.[10] While the veto voting in the UN Security Council is an obvious example from the international law arena, it appears at least debatable whether the qualified majority voting rule in the Council is inefficiently biased in favour of large countries because the size of their population allows three of them to block any decision taken by a qualified majority;[11] or that the narrow fiscal discipline focus of economic policy coordination is due to German power-wielding to the detriment of efficient stabilization policies.[12] Distributional rationalist considerations emphasize here that power asymmetries between members lead to variable opportunity costs of EU cooperation, leaving some states with better outside options than others.[13] States with better outside options will have more leverage in tweaking EU cooperation to their own preferences.

[6] Judith Kelley, 'International Actors on the Domestic Scene: Membership Conditionality and Socialization by International Institutions' (2004) 58 International Organization 425.

[7] Abraham L Newman and Elliot Posner, *Voluntary Disruptions: International Soft Law, Finance, and Power* (Oxford University Press 2018); Anne van Aaken, 'Effectuating Public International Law through Market Mechanisms?' (2009) 165 Journal of Institutional and Theoretical Economics 33.

[8] B Peter Rosendorff and Helen V Milner, 'The Optimal Design of International Trade Institutions: Uncertainty and Escape' (2001) 55 International Organization 829 (arguing that states design trade institutions to have optimal escape clauses that are neither so cheap that they can be used with impunity nor so expensive that states can never deviate from their obligations without abandoning an institution altogether).

[9] Terry M Moe, 'Political Institutions: The Neglected Side of the Story' (1990) 6 Journal of Law, Economics, and Organization 213, 213; James D Fearon, 'Bargaining, Enforcement, and International Cooperation' (1998) 52 International Organization 269.

[10] Voeten (n 5) 149.

[11] Scopelliti (n 2) 180.

[12] Shawn Donnelly, *Power Politics, Banking Union and EMU: Adjusting Europe to Germany* (Taylor & Francis Ltd 2018) 180.

[13] Lloyd Gruber, *Ruling the World: Power Politics and the Rise of Supranational Institutions* (Princeton University Press 2000); Phillip Y Lipscy, 'Explaining Institutional Change: Policy Areas, Outside Options, and the Bretton Woods Institutions' (2015) 59 American Journal of Political Science 341.

9
Membership of EU Treaties

Lawyers, political scientists, and economists have adopted different analytical angles on the issue of membership of international organizations. Lawyers take membership as an independent variable and focus on members' rights and obligations under the agreement, how membership translates into procedural decision-making, and what the effects are of membership in terms of legally binding constraints on policy scope.[1] Scholars of international relations have fruitfully distinguished between the independent variable, 'number', and the dependent variable, 'membership'. Number is defined as an exogenous feature of the issue context, let's say that the number of countries potentially eligible to join the EU would be confined to the European continent. Among the potentially participating states, the interest of actors varies as does their relative power in a specific issue and their preference for joining the EU. These scholars distinguish numbers from membership to the extent that the latter is an endogenous design choice made in the course of establishing, changing, and/or operating the institution.[2] Pertaining to the EU, this implies that the rules governing who becomes a member and participates in cooperation may vary with the enlargement of the EU and the specific issue area concerned.

We look at the EU as an organization that has evolved in terms of its membership and its scope, with the EU membership shaped by the objectives set by the incumbent EU members. Specifically, we want to better understand how founding or incumbent EU members design and determine membership to the EU Treaties and what the implications of the rules of membership are for the substantive commitment level of EU Treaties. Put differently, the conditions under which new members can join an international treaty such as the EU determines how rational states design the Treaty text in order to maximize their payoff from the agreement. To that end, we can draw on the work of economic scholars on international organization and the distinction between closed Treaties and semi-open Treaties[3]—a

[1] Gerd Droesse, *Membership in International Organizations: Paradigms of Membership Structures, Legal Implications of Membership and the Concept of International Organization* (TMC Asser Press 2020).

[2] Barbara Koremenos, Charles Lipson, and Duncan Snidal, 'The Rational Design of International Institutions' (2001) 55 International Organization 761, 777.

[3] Francesco Parisi and Vincy Fon, *The Economics of Lawmaking* (Oxford University Press 2008) 52, 215.

EU Law and Economics. Armin Steinbach, Oxford University Press. © Oxford University Press 2025.
DOI: 10.1093/9780198920915.003.0009

distinction between incumbent members and acceding members with respect to their willingness to commit to a new EU agreement.

Closed Treaties require consent by all signatory states for an applicant's accession. This ensures that incumbent parties approve changes in membership, so that their rights and obligations are not disturbed without their consent.[4] Closed Treaties subscribe to the notion of strict Pareto improvement. This contrasts with *semi-open* and *open* Treaties, the former leaving admission in the hands of a majority of the signatory states while the latter does not require any vote from incumbent Treaty signatories. Think of the WTO as an example of a semi-open agreement, where accession of new members only needs to gain the approval of two thirds of the WTO membership, hence allowing certain incumbent members to be overruled.

For the EU, there are elements of *closed* Treaties and *semi-open* Treaties engraved in the Treaty architecture. The EU is foremost a closed Treaty: while all European states may ask to become members (Article 49(1) TEU), the Council decides by unanimity and after an absolute majority of votes in the European Parliament. Accession Treaties must be ratified by all EU members in line with their constitutional requirements. For new members, the EU Treaty is 'closed'.[5] If another country aspires to join the EU, and provided the enhanced participation generates benefits for all incumbent states and the new Member State has preferences sufficiently aligned with those of existing EU membership, the incumbent EU members will welcome accession, as more states joining the EU increases the benefits from EU Treaty participation without modifying Treaty content. Conversely, in a closed treaty scenario such as the EU, if an incumbent member faces a reduced payoff as result of a new round of accession, that state has the power to veto the proposed expansion. Any EU incumbent views an application of a new EU member by first calculating whether an additional member in the Treaty is beneficial.

Hence the general design of the EU Treaties reflects a standard Westphalian approach in the sense that it gives a strong position to existing EU members. Not only do they retain veto rights to accession, but there is also, at least in principle, no renegotiation of the Treaty to which new members accede. This latter feature is particularly salient in the EU as the requirement is that new entrants align their legal systems with the EU *acquis communautaire*, hence shifting the burden of adaptation to the new members. The disadvantages of a possible mismatch of preferences of new and old members' citizens thus do not affect the level of commitment of incumbents, at least not for existing legal commitments (though this may be different

[4] Joseph Gabriel Starke, *Introduction to International Law* (Butterworths 1989).

[5] Below the threshold of Treaty amendments, the EU may decide to enhance its arsenal of instruments through invoking transformative clauses, such as Article 352 TFEU, which does not require ratification and domestic decision, while leaving the unanimity requirement in the Council unchanged.

for future EU legislation, as more preference heterogeneity leads to more difficult and costly negotiations and possible future mismatch of rules and preferences).

While in principle EU Treaties are closed treaties requiring unanimous approval by the EU states as the 'masters of the Treaties', there are elements of semi-open and even open features of Treaty design under EU law. EU membership combines both elements. For new countries to join the EU, majority in the Parliament suffices (semi-open), while unanimity is required in the Council (closed). In addition, differentiated integration within the EU legal framework highlights how semi-open sub-Treaties are integrated into the European Treaties. Consider two examples of integrated semi-openness in an otherwise closed EU Treaty. One is membership in the euro area. According to Article 139 TFEU, there are Member States for which the Council has not yet decided that they meet the criteria for adopting the euro—for these countries, certain rules such as the fiscal surveillance do not apply (Article 139(2) TFEU). The procedure for adopting the euro leads through a qualified-majority vote of the Council, after consulting the European Parliament and after discussion in the European Council and based on a proposal of the Commission (Article 140(2) TFEU). The main decision of EU members on whether integration of new euro members is possible is thus one that is semi-open through a qualified majority vote, as no veto is possible.[6] Since EU members are only by way of derogation not members of the eurozone, their accession to the euro is generally kept open and feasible. Majority voting ensures that this is semi-open, as no unanimity requirement exists.

Another example of combining closed and semi-open membership under EU law is differentiated integration through 'enhanced cooperation' (Article 329 TFEU). Enhanced cooperation initiatives can start on the request of at least nine Member States. Introduced with the purpose of offering an area for experimentation with a range of flexibility regimes, enhanced cooperation allows an agreement within the EU Treaty, one that has semi-open and open elements. Launching enhanced cooperation requires qualified majority voting in the Council and hence cannot be blocked by vetoes, corresponding to a semi-open Treaty. Once enhanced cooperation is established, other EU members are free to join (Article 331 TFEU)—no member of 'enhanced cooperation' can block the participation of new EU members, as acceding members only need to strike a deal with the EU Commission in order to join the enhanced cooperation.

Whether closed or (semi-)open Treaties are concerned bears relevance for how states are going to *design* the Treaty texts. Regarding the design of the EU Treaty, incumbent members do not need to anticipate future accessions, because their veto rights on future accessions secures that at any point of EU enlargement, a revision of Treaty norms can be vetoed. In turn, regarding open Treaties, Parisi and

[6] Only the fixing of the rate at which the euro should be substituted for the currency of the Member State is decided unanimously, Article 140(3) TFEU.

Fon have shown that when a Treaty is left open (ie when it is predicated on future accessions of new members), the initial treaty content is set optimally on the basis of the incumbent states' expectation of Treaty enlargement.[7] Hence, drafting semi-open Treaty sections would have to anticipate a growing (and potentially more heterogenous) membership. The rational Treaty designer anticipates growing heterogeneity of preferences between participating states and thus designs rules in a way that minimizes negative repercussions. Looking at the euro membership as an example, incumbent euro members would be well advised to specify upfront in the initial Treaty the precise conditions under which accession to the euro for new members is possible. It is straightforward that euro members have a strong economic interest in predetermining these conditions, as the eurozone has weakest-link public good character (see above Chapter 6) and thus bears the risk of free-riding and negative spillovers. Consequently and unsurprisingly, the path to euro adoption is well-defined, with Article 140 TFEU enumerating the 'high degree of sustainable convergence by reference to the fulfilment of criteria', which are further specified in Protocol 13 of the TFEU, with even permissible inflation and budget deficit threshold numerically defined.[8] The high degree of up-front and Treaty-based specification of entry requirements is in line with the above mentioned logic—in a semi-open Treaty, the participating countries should anticipate future accessions by choosing a Treaty design that ensures the alignment of future Treaty participants with the principles and goals of the Treaty founders. By contrast, the closed sections of EU Treaties do not make such high specification necessary, as the veto principle allows incumbent members to decide ad-hoc whether they consider accession beneficial. Accordingly, accession requirements to the EU are only vaguely referred to under Article 49 TEU, by mentioning the necessary respect of the values referred to in Article 2 TEU.[9]

(EU) Treaty formation and amendment further depend on the payoff structure for incumbent and acceding members. In general, from the perspective of the incumbent EU members, accession of new members causes a different kind of potential costs which incumbents seek to minimize. Granting conditional access to the EU is in line with rational choice suggesting that restrictive membership is necessary due to uncertainty about the acceding member's preferences.[10] The negotiation process of accession with new members can be understood as a procedure for revealing private information about the applicant's preferences. The incumbent EU members do not want new members who free-ride on public goods provided

[7] Parisi and Fon (n 3).

[8] The fiscal surveillance procedure as well as economic policy coordination governance, which are explicitly mentioned in Article 139(2)(a) and (b) TFEU will kick in once a new member enters the common currency area.

[9] The admission criteria were also absent in earlier Treaty versions and were then laid down at the June 1993 European Council in Copenhagen.

[10] Barbara Koremenos, *The Continent of International Law: Explaining Agreement Design* (Cambridge University Press 2016).

across the Union (eg legal stability, solidarity, security), but instead they seek to take on members who contribute to the public goods and comply with the *acquis communautaire*. Adoption of the *acquis communautaire* is a costly signal ensuring an equilibrium where only those who share certain characteristics are included.[11] By forcing acceding EU members to undertake concessions and bear significant adjustment costs, they increase the likelihood that the applicant will be a compliant and cooperative EU member. While this serves to reduce one source of costs for incumbent states associated with new accessions, there are significant institutional costs due to the dilution of voting power and influence on policy outcomes. Each round of accession requires negotiations about the redesigning of the institutional representation in order to balance the influence of current and new EU members. Hence, potential benefits of increased EU Treaty participation and deeper Treaty content must be balanced, from the perspective of the EU incumbent, against the costs of diluted power. With each accession, much depends on the marginal benefits and costs—whether gains from increased participation outweigh dilution of influence. Connected to dilution of voting power, future adoption of secondary law through EU institutions may come at a higher price with extended membership—the risk of being overruled in the Council increases sovereignty costs, and heterogenous preferences raise negotiation costs, all of which must be factored in by a rational incumbent before giving approval to new members.[12]

Importantly, opportunity costs of countries vary. Variable opportunity costs signify that countries may be able to pursue gains from cooperation outside the EU to different degrees. Variable opportunity costs invite the insight of distributive rationalist approaches, which argue that what matters is that some states have better outside options than others.[13] According to this logic, states with a greater ability to achieve their preferred outcomes without cooperation can leverage the threat to act unilaterally to shape multilateral institutional rules; on the international level, the United States has used both its informal and formal power to design and control international (economic) institutions. This would suggest that on the EU level, powerful states skew voting rules in their favour. However, the Lisbon Treaty rules modifying qualified majority voting led to a decrease in the total power of larger countries, while the total power of smaller states increased, which supports the existing phenomenon of smaller countries being overrepresented in EU institutions.[14] At least regarding the voting structure of the EU, larger incumbent

[11] Koremenos, Lipson, and Snidal (n 2) 784.

[12] Mareike Kleine, *Informal Governance in the European Union: How Governments Make International Organizations Work* (Cornell University Press 2013) 54.

[13] Lloyd Gruber, *Ruling the World: Power Politics and the Rise of Supranational Institutions* (Princeton University Press 2000); Phillip Y Lipscy, 'Explaining Institutional Change: Policy Areas, Outside Options, and the Bretton Woods Institutions' (2015) 59 American Journal of Political Science 341.

[14] Alessandro Scopelliti, 'The Political Decision-Making Process in the Council of the European Union Under the New Definition of a Qualified Majority' (2008) 73 Il Politico 180.

countries have not translated their comparative low opportunity costs into relative advantages over smaller acceding states.

EU enlargement happens when benefits for incumbent and acceding members are significant, where the general rationales for cooperation apply (Part II). Enlargement may be particularly plausible where policy areas are characterized by coordination games and network effects, that is, in situations where benefits increase for all members as the number of participants grows (eg joint product standards on the EU internal market).[15] Also, admitting a new EU member may create additional value-enhancing opportunities for all states, for example through stimulating economic growth or stabilizing external relationships.[16] In turn, with weakest-link public goods the situation is more ambivalent. In principle, cooperation in weakest-link public goods declines with the number of states, as the cost of monitoring increases and the probability of a weakest link rises. If new EU members undertake insufficient efforts to combat illicit trade or to secure border protection, this lowers the payoff for all other members. In these cases, either cooperation fails, or alternatively, there is plausibility for centralization of the weakest-link good in order to ensure minimum enforcement, provided that the EU is sufficiently prepared to ensure a consistent level of protection for these goods. One example is the EU Schengen Agreement: as border protection is a weakest-link public good, several Eastern European countries have not been able to join this element of the EU Treaties. Incumbent countries request a high level of border protection to ensure that the benefits of removing internal border controls are not undermined by some members. Euro membership is another illustrative example: new members must subject themselves to convergence criteria and EU fiscal rules requiring solidity of national budgets. A common currency has features of a weakest-link public good, as a critically unstable country may cause repercussions for all other members.

[15] Sébastien Dupuch, Hugues Jennequin, and El Mouhoud Mouhoub, 'EU Enlargement: What Does it Change for the European Economic Geography?' (2004) 91 Revue de l'OFCE, Presses de Sciences-Po 241; Paolo Cecchini, *The European Challenge 1992: The Benefits of a Single Market: European Challenge—Benefits of a Single Community* (Gower Publishing Ltd 1998).

[16] Arjan M Lejour, Vladimir Solanic, and Paul JG Tang, 'EU Accession and Income Growth: An Empirical Approach' (2009) 16 Transition Studies Review 127.

10
Centralization

The objectives for pursuing cooperation within the EU, laid out in Part I, refer to the motivation of *inter*jurisdictional efficiency.[1] Interjurisdictional efficiency seeks to determine the best allocation of resources among different jurisdictions. Interjurisdictional efficiency is achieved when the public policies offered by the government satisfy the collective demands of citizens at the lowest cost.[2] Interjurisdictional efficiency addresses the foundational problem and rationale for the EU—it acknowledges the legal Westphalian system of relationships between European sovereign states. There are multiple motives for cooperation as a result of interjurisdictional (in)efficiencies, such as externalities either between individuals in one state and individuals in another or between public policies. These externalities can either be channelled through prices (and amount to market failure) or, if reflected in prices, they can be felt as spillovers in neighbouring states (and amount to 'beggar-thy-neighbour' policies).[3] Hence, interjurisdictional *in*efficiencies arise if Member States produce decentralized spillovers which are likely to ignore the overall economic costs or benefits which will lead them to over- or underprovide the activity.

In this chapter, we are concerned with *intra*jurisdictional efficiency. In theory, it concerns the choice of public policy satisfying the collective demand within a given jurisdiction in a way that ensures citizens' willingness to pay for those activities. Intrajurisdictional efficiency addresses the question whether public activities are pursued either at the EU level or at Member State level. In general terms, the EU should set the public policy if the benefits-to-cost ratio is more favourable compared to when Member States pursue the policy individually. Intrajurisdictional efficiency strategies may aim at reducing bargaining and transaction costs or establish institutions to reveal and disseminate information that would not be available in a setting of bilateral interaction between EU Member States, such as the EU Commission and the ECJ. Likewise, centralization can facilitate the enforcement

[1] Frank H Easterbrook, 'Federalism and European Business Law' (1994) 14 International Review of Law and Economics 125, 129; Alan O Sykes, 'Externalities in Open Economy Antitrust and Their Implications for International Competition Policy Competition, Free Markets, and the Law-Symposium on Law and Public Policy-1999' (1999) 23 Harvard Journal of Law and Public Policy 89.

[2] Robert P Inman and Daniel L Rubinfeld, 'Rethinking Federalism' (1997) 11 Journal of Economic Perspectives 43; Charles M Tiebout, 'A Pure Theory of Local Expenditures' (1956) 64 Journal of Political Economy 416.

[3] Hendrik Spruyt, 'Institutional Selection in International Relations: State Anarchy as Order' (1994) 48 International Organization 527.

EU Law and Economics. Armin Steinbach, Oxford University Press. © Oxford University Press 2025.
DOI: 10.1093/9780198920915.003.0010

of agreements: when bilateral or regional cooperation relies on decentralized enforcement, there is a perennial risk of undercompliance because the costs of enforcement deter the enforcing party, unlike with a neutral enforcer (such as the EU Commission and the ECJ) who mutualizes the costs of enforcement, giving rise to a second-order collective action problem (see below Chapter 14).

The intrajurisdictional question of *whether* and *how* to centralize within the EU revolves around two core legal provisions in the EU Treaty—the *principle of conferral* and the *principle of subsidiarity*. While the principle of conferral governs the limits of EU competences, the use of those competences is governed by the principle of subsidiarity. The principle of conferral embodies the deep Westphalian international law idea that the EU's competences are voluntarily conferred on it by its Member States and that the EU must remain within these borders—the EU is treated as a 'dependent variable', crafted in line with the preferences of Member States as 'masters of the Treaties' or as 'independent variables'.

The legal EU jargon of 'competences' is a key term which encapsulates the degree to which Union institutions or Member States can exercise authority in a given policy area. With competences being nothing more than authority, we may leverage Trachtman's property right analogy applied to international law. In this vein, European law may be understood in terms of reciprocal restraints on state autonomy, and therefore as transactions regarding the exercise of jurisdiction. This lends itself to the argument that jurisdiction is analogous to property in a private context. Jurisdiction gives states the power to rule on activities and assets, while property gives individuals the right to control certain assets.[4] Both jurisdiction and property rights are constructed by law to encompass certain rights, and both jurisdiction and property rights are transferable.

The property rights theory offers insights into the EU's nature as an international organization to which members have surrendered certain sovereign functions (ie their power to exercise jurisdiction). One may inquire whether and to what extent centralization—a transfer of jurisdiction—should occur. The theory of property rights suggests an initial vesting of rights in favour of those who are likely to value them most, in order to minimize transaction costs.[5] Let's assume two states, one which pursues domestic regulation for domestic policy reasons, but which creates a negative effect on another country. The property rights strategy would ask from a normative perspective which country would value the right to regulate most, and to this country sole authority should be given. Speaking of a jurisdiction having a value is alien to legal jargon, but it connects to an economic effect orientation. Societies positively value the pursuit of public values, but they negatively value being adversely affected (eg through negative policy spillovers.)

[4] Joel P Trachtman, *The Economic Structure of International Law* (Harvard University Press 2008) 72, 31.

[5] Richard A Posner, *The Economics of Justice* (Harvard University Press 1983).

Hence, the value a government attaches to jurisdiction is proportionate to the benefits it can obtain through regulation, or through avoidance of the application of another state's regulation.[6]

In such situations, the property rights theory would suggest that jurisdiction should be allocated to the country that would be chosen in negotiation between countries in the absence of any transaction costs. An inefficient allocation would be one where all negative or positive effects of a country's regulation would materialize in another country. In turn, if mixed effects occur (or if the regulating country values the domestic policy positively while the affected country negatively), the dispersion of jurisdiction among all affected jurisdictions would be the optimal solution.[7] In this case, the appropriate entity for exercising prescriptive jurisdiction may not be a national government but an international organization—such as the EU.

In practice, it is clearly difficult to determine how much a country values the right to regulate or how it perceives foreign policies as costs. This suggests that the authority to allocate property rights should be given to the entity who is able to analyse costs and benefits, and to initiate appropriate re-allocative transactions.[8] From this perspective, in the context of multiple countries such as in the EU, a neutral entity is positioned to act as broker and agent to collect information and to assess cross-border comparisons of costs and benefits. This logic is indeed enshrined in the EU's shared competence principle (Article 5(3) TEU) —it paves the way for two alternative allocations of jurisdiction. Either Member States remain competent in cases where the acting state pursues a policy (one to which it attaches positive value). As long as the state manages to achieve the policy objective by acting alone, the jurisdiction remains with the Member State. Or, the single state does not achieve the policy objective effectively—either because it causes harm to another state (negative externality), or because it remains insufficiently implemented. In these cases, the EU monitors the overall effects within the EU and assumes competence to act.

a) Principal of conferral: which role for the EU and Member States?

Inquiring into the principle of conferral laid down in Article 5(1) TEU from an economic perspective can unfold in two dimensions. First, the principle of conferral can be understood as an allocation device in the sense that it stabilizes a certain competence distribution between the EU and Member States—this distribution

[6] Trachtman (n 4) 41.
[7] ibid 42.
[8] Guido Calabresi, *The Costs of Accidents: Legal and Economic Analysis* (Yale University Press 1970).

can be efficient or inefficient from an intrajurisdictional perspective. The principle of conferral is thus inextricably linked to the question of whether a competence should be dealt with at Member State or EU level. The principle of conferral enshrines the notion of *Kompetenz-Kompetenz*, positing that it is Member States who decide on the scope of surrendering competences to the EU.[9] This positivist-legal approach can be contrasted with an economic view as to how the competence allocation between the centre and the decentralized entities, that is, between the EU and Member States, *should* be designed (irrespective of its positivist allocation). This question leads us to federalism theory, which offers insight into the relationship between the EU and its Member States.[10] In this context, 'homogeneity' has been a term widely used by lawyers, political scientists, and economists in order to make inferences on the optimal distribution of competences between the centre and its members.[11] Cultural homogeneity has been discussed as a prerequisite for statehood and was seen as a barrier to more EU centralization,[12] while homogeneity of preferences captures the economic yardstick to determine the optimal level of regulation.[13] Moreover, lawyers take recourse to 'legitimacy', and political scientists have distinguished between input and output legitimacy to justify public authority, a distinction that one can capture with the outcome focus of welfare economics versus the process orientation of constitutional economics.[14]

While the first question concerns the role of the principle of conferral in making the optimal distribution of powers, we can also ask a second question—whether the principle of conferral is effectively applied and respected within the existing allocation of competences in the EU. This second perspective accounts for the judicial innovations crafted by the ECJ, propelling a dynamic ushering of EU law into doctrinal inventions such as 'implied powers' or *effet utile* which can be understood as legal techniques undermining the principle of conferral.[15] The first question

[9] Erin Delaney, 'Managing in a Federal System without an "Ultimate Arbiter": Kompetenz in the EU and the Ante-Bellum United States' (2005) 15 Regional & Federal Studies 225.

[10] Wallace E Oates, 'On the Evolution of Fiscal Federalism: Theory and Institutions' (2008) 61 National Tax Journal 313.

[11] Matthias Mahlmann, 'Constitutional Identity and the Politics of Homogeneity' (2005) 6 German Law Journal 307; Oliver Mader, 'Enforcement of EU Values as a Political Endeavour: Constitutional Pluralism and Value Homogeneity in Times of Persistent Challenges to the Rule of Law' (2019) 11 Hague Journal on the Rule of Law 133.

[12] Stephen Weatherill, 'Why Harmonise?' in Takis Tridimas and Paolo Nebbia (eds), *European Union Law for the Twenty-First Century: Rethinking the New Legal Order* (Hart Publishing 2003) 11, 13; Stelio Mangiameli, 'The European Union and the Identity of Member States' (2013) No 369 L'Europe en Formation 151.

[13] Wallace E Oates, *Fiscal Federalism* (Harcourt Brace Jovanovich 1972).

[14] Viktor J Vanberg, 'Market and State: The Perspective of Constitutional Political Economy' (2005) 1 Journal of Institutional Economics 23, 28.

[15] Carl Lebeck, 'Implied Powers beyond Functional Integration—The Flexibility Clause in the Revised EU Treaties' (2007) 17 Journal of Transnational Law & Policy 303; Elio Maciariello, 'EU Agencies and the Issue of Delegation: Conferral, Implied Powers and the State of Exception' (2019) 4 European Papers 723; Urška Šadl, 'The Role of Effet Utile in Preserving the Continuity and Authority of European Union Law : Evidence from the Citation Web of the Pre-Accession Case Law of the Court of Justice of the EU' (2015) 8 European Journal of Legal Studies 18.

can be boiled down to asking whether public policy action is better placed at the EU level or at the decentralized Member States level. The second question asks whether and how the principle of conferral should be adhered to—through a strict or flexible interpretation.

Federalism theory: decentralization as the optimal solution?

The principle of conferral can be explored by asking whether there should be many individual EU members acting separately instead of one single EU entity. The theory of system competition anchored in institutional economics offers an answer. Charles Tiebout offered a model describing fiscal competition between many independent local governments.[16] The Tiebout model is an extension of the purely competitive market model with complete information. Governmental or interjurisdictional competition follows the logic of efficient private market competition and builds on similarly strong assumptions, but the basic insight from theories of federalism is that jurisdiction over a problem should be allocated to the lowest level of government capable of internalizing the relevant externalities.[17] At the centre of this is the idea that states compete for citizens as mobile resources. The rationale for decentralized individual or member states is that they can better accommodate the specific preferences of their citizens and thus provide better public service offers ('race to the best fit').[18] It reasons that the state supplies public goods at specific tax prices and uses this 'product' to compete with other states for citizens.

With the focus on individuals' preferences, from the Tiebout perspective, the world of competitive governments will allow for the analogy of a marketplace in which individuals move among local jurisdictions to select the public goods and public services combination that they most desire. By definition, citizens can choose their preferred legal regime in the same way consumers choose among competing products. Under certain assumptions—such as frictionless legal competition, institutional rules such as mutual recognition—there will be a competitive legal equilibrium maximizing aggregate welfare.

From a political economic perspective, competition is intended to foster legal diversity in order to be an effective constraint on public policy-makers who are not inclined to act in benevolent ways. Just as competition on the supply side reduces the margin and promotes quality, the competitive environment in jurisdictional markets disciplines the law-maker's discretion. In order to maximize

[16] Tiebout (n 2).

[17] Inman and Rubinfeld (n 2).

[18] David Christoph Ehmke, *Institutional Congruence the Riddle of Leviathan and Hydra*, vol 16 (Nomos Verlagsgesellschaft 2018) 38.

pro-competitive pressure, transaction costs should be minimized in order to facilitate citizens' choices. The resulting hypothesis is that law gives states an incentive to compete by providing efficient legal rules.[19] It follows from this political economic logic that decentralized solutions that leave competences at Member State level, are all the more appropriate the more heterogeneous regional preferences are.[20] Since individual needs are different due to culture, ethnicity, history, and the state of the economy, decentralized solutions can better design suitable public goods, that is, tailoring their supply to individual preferences.[21]

The more diverse the preferences *between* regions and the more homogeneously they are distributed *within* regions, the more advantageous the competition between EU members is, and the more disadvantageous Europeanization is.[22] However, this theory does not fare well in the practical realities of the EU. The Tiebout framework posits a number of strong assumptions, one of which is mobility of households among jurisdictions at no cost, or that businesses can easily choose the jurisdiction that offers the tax-expenditure-regulation package that it most prefers.[23] Yet mobility costs remain high in the EU, despite the free movement of persons and employees stimulating mobility.[24] The euro crisis triggered some, though limited, south–north migration, yet considerable barriers to the 'exit' remain (eg language, recognition of professional qualification). Also, a (too) strong assumption of the Tiebout model is the perfectly elastic supply of public goods in EU Member States, one that assumes each state to be capable of replicating all of the attractive economic features of its competitors. The idea of 'inefficient politicians' being driven out of the market through election ignores the realities of political economics. In addition, information presuming households, citizens, and businesses to be fully informed about the fiscal and regulatory policies of each jurisdiction, appears an overly ambitious theorical assumption. Households and businesses are often ill-informed—it is difficult for them to ascertain the implications of regulations, tax rules, and public activities, let alone to make a comparison with other EU Member States given regulatory idiosyncrasies in EU Member States.

[19] Francesco Parisi and Vincy Fon, *The Economics of Lawmaking* (Oxford University Press 2008) 52, 7.

[20] Stephen Weatherill, 'Protecting the Internal Market from the Charter' in Sybe de Vries, Ulf Bernitz, and Stephen Weatherill (eds), *The EU Charter of Fundamental Rights as a Binding Instrument: Five Years Old and Growing* (Hart Publishing 2016) 151.

[21] Robin Boadway and Anwar Shah, *Fiscal Federalism: Principles and Practice of Multiorder Governance* (Cambridge University Press 2009) 35.

[22] Charles B Blankart, Föderalismus in Deutschland und in Europa (Nomos Verlagsgesellschaft 2007) 59.

[23] Tiebout (n 2); William W Bratton and Joseph A McCahery, 'The New Economics of Jurisdictional Competition: Devolutionary the New Economics of Jurisdictional Competition: Devolutionary Federalism in a Second-Best World Federalism in a Second-Best World' (1997) 86 Georgetown Law Journal 201.

[24] In the US, moving between states is mostly job motivated and not due to a more attractive public service environment, Frank H Easterbrook, 'Antitrust and the Economics of Federalism' (1983) 26 Journal of Law and Economics 23.

Individuals and businesses face high costs in resolving this lack of comparability and undertaking a cost-benefit calculus. Adding to this, while system competition may be efficient from an allocation perspective, it has cross-regional distributional effects through 'beggar-thy-neighbor' policies. EU countries can try to entice international market shares away from other EU members for their industries by reducing wages and thus increasing their current account surplus, which impairs the relative competitiveness of other countries.[25] In the worst case scenario, this may cause a harmful 'race to the bottom', when social and environmental standards are dismantled.[26] Overall, this can lead to suboptimal competition for society as a whole.[27]

'Homogeneity' of what: preferences or public space?

But even if one acknowledges federalism theory's plea for decentralized Member State competences, the theory builds on a notion of preferences orientation that may be contested from legal and political science perspectives. Economics, law, and political science converge at a pivotal juncture of EU governance research, that is, determining what jurisdictional level—local, regional, national, or EU-wide—public authority should be exercised. Homogeneity and heterogeneity are both terms that have inspired economic, legal, and political scholarship and they may entail commonalities, but also divergences.

Take the economic relevance of heterogeneity of preferences for the provision of public goods. Unlike private goods, public goods are hard to adjust to diverse preferences. Since all public goods are non-rivalrous, citizens must accept the same set of public good characteristics, whether they align with their preferences or not. Naturally, when the EU regulates a heterogeneous group of citizens with different norms, values, and habits, we are more likely to observe the emergence of disagreements over public goods and policies, such as how security should be supplied or what the preferences for environmental protection concern.[28] The EU has not strictly followed this rationale of aligning homogeneity (heterogeneity) of preferences with harmonization (decentralization) of laws: harmonization

[25] Palma Polyak, 'The Silent Losers of Germany's Export Surpluses. How Current Account Imbalances Are Exacerbated by the Misrepresentation of Their Domestic Costs' (2024) 22 Comparative European Politics 31.

[26] Catherine Barnard, 'Social Dumping Revisited: Lessons from Delaware' (2000) 25 European Law Review 57 (arguing against the 'race to the bottom' as a European problem at least in the area of social policies).

[27] Albert Breton, 'The Existence and Stability of Interjurisdictional Competition' in Daphne A Kenyon and John Kincaid (eds), *Competition among States and Local Governments* (The Urban Institute Press 1991); Robert P Inman and Daniel L Rubinfeld, 'Economics of Federalism' in Francesco Parisi (ed), *Oxford Handbook of Law and Economics* (Oxford University Press 2017) 90.

[28] Enrico Spolaore, 'The Economic Approach to Political Borders' (2022) CESifo Working Paper No 10165.

and centralization have occurred in areas where heterogeneity of preferences is predominant (such as consumer protection or agricultural policy) whereas other areas characterized by strong externalities or economies of scale have remained in the Member States domain (such as defence and environmental protection).[29]

From a legal perspective, whether homogeneity of citizens is a necessary precondition for a normative order has been an explicit and implicit subject in constitutional and European law.[30] Its explicit and most radical version is offered by Carl Schmitt who stipulated that a normative order without a homogenous society remains precarious. More subtle and recent, this notion of homogeneity persists in the interpretation of the principle of democracy advanced in the German Constitutional Court.[31] Consequently, democratic self-governance is only possible within the framework of a 'demos', and the political community must be confined to a nation-state.[32] This view has resonated in the legal literature for quite some time—the lack of a European 'demos', expressed through a sense of common citizenship or an EU-wide identity—has been seen as an obstacle to further European integration.[33] Lawyers have controversially discussed the issue of identity and whether a European identity exists and how it relates to the Treaties' commitment to 'respect the equality of Member States before the Treaties as well as their national identities' (Article 4(2) TEU). Whether a European demos is a necessary precondition for more EU integration, and whether a collective 'We' as Europeans should exist or should be a prerequisite at all, is controversially discussed.[34] Likewise, the need for a minimum political unity on the basis of homogeneity, publicity, legitimacy, or a shared set of values is viewed controversially.[35] Supporters for requiring homogeneity as a necessary underpinning for EU integration point at the lack of a common language, underrepresented European media, and the lack of a European public preventing a deliberative and interacting European society from emerging.[36] More relaxed views accept a de-territorialized

[29] Weatherill (n 12) 11; Parisi and Fon (n 19) 8.

[30] Nancy Christine Staudt, Barry Friedman, and Lee Epstein, 'On the Role of Ideological Homogeneity in Generating Consequential Constitutional Decisions' (2008) 10 University of Pennsylvania Journal of Constitutional Law 361; Volker Roeben, 'A Concept of Shared Principles and the Constitutional Homogeneity in Europe: The Case of Subsidiarity' (2021) 4 Cardozo International & Comparative Law Review 903.

[31] BVerfGE 89, 155, 186 *Maastricht* (1993).

[32] Michael Zürn, 'Democratic Governance beyond the Nation-State' (2000) 6 European Journal of International Relations 183, 191.

[33] Joseph HH Weiler, 'The State "über alles" Demos, Telos and the German Maastricht Decision' (1995) Jean Monnet Working Papers 1995/19; Dieter Grimm, 'Does Europe Need a Constitution?' (1995) 1 European Law Journal 282.

[34] Anand Menon and Stephen Weatherill, 'Transnational Legitimacy in a Globalising World: How the European Union Rescues its States' (2008) 31 West European Politics 397, 400.

[35] Armin von Bogdandy, *Strukturwandel des Öffentlichen Rechts: Entstehung und Demokratisierung der Europäischen Gesellschaft* (Suhrkamp Verlag 2022) 176; Charles Taylor, *Wieviel Gemeinschaft braucht die Demokratie? Aufsätze zur praktischen Philosophie* (Suhrkamp Verlag 2019) 273; Joseph HH Weiler, 'The Transformation of Europe' (1991) 100 Yale Law Journal 2403.

[36] Peter Mair, *Ruling the Void: The Hollowing of Western Democracy* (Verso 2013); BVerfGE 97, 350 *Euro* (1998) [98].

notion of identity, advancing 'demoi-cracy' rather than 'democracy' in light of various peoples united within the EU, or pointing to EU citizenship as a source of de-territorialized identity.[37]

Claiming homogeneity as a prerequisite undermines the EU's capacity as a normative order. With societal homogeneity persisting only on a national level, the German Constitutional Court has insisted on the need to preserve areas that must remain outside the scope of European unification.

Member States would need to remain autonomous in the formation of economic, cultural, and social life. This extends in particular to areas governed by fundamental rights—the private sphere of citizens or the domain of social security. It also extends to political decisions with close connections to culture, history, and language—among which the German Constitutional Court considers citizenship; the civil and military monopoly on the use of force; revenue and expenditure, including external financing; and all elements of encroachment that are decisive for the realization of fundamental rights. This is particularly true for intensive encroachments on fundamental rights, such as deprivation of liberty in the administration of criminal law or institutional placements.[38] Additional sensitive fields are the fundamental fiscal decisions on public revenue and public expenditure, with the latter being particularly motivated, inter alia, by social policy considerations.[39] Budget sovereignty is considered a core function of parliamentary sovereignty rights and Member States' parliaments, as budget sovereignty is the place of conceptual political decisions on the connection of economic burdens and privileges granted by the state. This right would be compromised if it were substantially transferred to the EU.

Hence, constitutional areas of sovereign sensibility are among those issue areas that are hostile to being shifted. Legally, the main concern is one of democratic legitimacy, though deeply rooted in the notion of nations. If the EU gained the authority to perform these functions, the level of democratic legitimization would not be commensurate with the extent and the weight of the supranational power of rule in light of the differences in cultural values between states. As long as the EU does not offer the same quality of democratic legitimacy, the argument goes, with administrative and legislative decisions traceable to an act of democratic delegation by citizens, national constitutional courts will raise national constitutional law as a barrier to further integration. For sure, this varies across Member States. National constitutional courts have shown variable degrees of openness to European integration, with the Italian Constitutional Court and the German Constitutional

[37] Kalypso Nicolaïdis, 'The New Constitution as European "Democracy"?' (2004) 7 Critical Review of International Social and Political Philosophy 76; von Bogdandy (n 35) 237.

[38] BVerfGE 123, 267 *Lissabon* (2009)—Lisbon Treaty, para 249.

[39] ibid 252.

Court engaging in a critical dialogue with the Luxembourg Court.[40] Cultural, political, and legal costs occur in Member States in idiosyncratic fashions as functions of national particularities.

Whereas for some lawyers, the 'demos' is a homogenous group along criteria such as a shared public space and media, economists explore it with reference to preference homogeneity and the social contract theory as developed by the Virginia School[41] and the theory of clubs.[42] In this sense, the question is whether the EU is a space of common political 'demos' or an economic 'club'.[43] The legal concerns resonate particularly in the constitutional economic analysis. Through this analytical lens, there should be a congruence between the allocation of political authority and the geography of common interests. This mechanism ensures an optimal alignment between preferences of citizens and public policies. This calls for a flexible mechanism that makes the authority of political authority responsive to citizens' common interests.[44] Put differently, one can translate the concept of cultural homogeneity into an optimum legal area (or 'club'), defined as a group of citizens that is submitted to the same public policy agency enforcing a legal order for which net benefits are maximized.[45]

Heterogeneity is also relevant to the principal–agent theory. Consider that the EU Member States are heterogenous principals who have engaged the Union institutions as agents. A mismatch between the principal's interests and the agent's action necessarily engenders efficiency losses or agency costs, leading to heterogeneity costs.[46] By extension, the larger the population of EU citizens, the larger the costs that result from the EU adopting public policies that satisfy some but not all citizens. These policies impose costs on non-beneficiaries. Certainly, these losses may be outweighed by other benefits and costs that must be taken into account: economies of scale or associated transaction costs may tip the balance in favour of or against centralized public power (see below Chapter 10 b)). Hence, while (constitutional) lawyers refer to homogeneity as a defining feature of a state,

[40] Giuseppe Martinico and Giorgio Repetto, 'Fundamental Rights and Constitutional Duels in Europe: An Italian Perspective on Case 269/2017 of the Italian Constitutional Court and Its Aftermath' (2019) 15 European Constitutional Law Review 731, 732.

[41] James M Buchanan, *The Limits of Liberty: Between Anarchy and Leviathan* (University of Chicago Press 1977).

[42] Larry Allen, Ryan C Amacher, and Robert D Tollison, 'The Economic Theory of Clubs: A Geometric Exposition' (1974) 29 Public Finance = Finances publiques 386; Todd Sandler and John Tschirhart, 'The Economic Theory of Clubs: An Evaluative Survey' (1980) 18 Journal of Economic Literature 1481.

[43] Dieter Schmidtchen, Alexander R Neunzig, and Hans-Jörg Schmidt-Trenz, 'One Market, One Law: EU Enlargement in Light of the Economic Theory of Optimal Legal Areas' (2001) CSLE Discussion Paper, No 2001-03.

[44] Vanberg (n 14).

[45] Schmidtchen, Neunzig, and Schmidt-Trenz (n 43).

[46] Eric Posner and Alan O Sykes, *Economic Foundations of International Law* (Harvard University Press 2013) 16.

economists use it as yardstick to assess the optimal level of regulation—legitimacy versus efficiency.

If fiscal federalism theory militates against EU centralization when differences in preferences between regions are significant, another way for the EU to deal with this divergence would be through redistribution and compensation. The theoretical underpinning for this is offered by Alesina and Spolaore. When voters with political preferences that are 'distant' from the central government (let's say, the EU) pay taxes based on their income and not on their preferences (ie when there are no 'preference-based' compensations), this will lead citizens to prefer fragmentation rather than centralization at the EU level.[47] Therefore, appropriate compensation and side-payments may change voters' calculation and affect the choice of regulatory level (centralized or decentralized). In other words, preference-based transfers could compensate regions that would otherwise prefer to be governed decentrally. Then, everyone (or, at least, a large enough majority) could potentially be better off in the unified and centrally governed EU. The problem is that transfers based on preferences overlook differences in income or wealth, which makes transfers politically costly to implement. Moreover, existing EU transfers are income-based, with the EU Structural Funds as the most obvious examples, which are determined based on the GDP performance of the recipient regions. Similarly, EU-debt funded funds such as the NGEU funds are redistributed based on economic performance, not preference-based. Thus, the existing income-based fund architecture of the EU does not ensure that the EU is an efficient central regulator.[48]

Legitimacy as legal and economic category

So far, we have assumed the individual as our normative benchmark as to whether to allocate competence at Member State or EU level. Normative individualism enshrined in economic models also extends to the choice of jurisdictional level—public goods should be aligned with citizens' preferences. However, this benchmark is far from obvious. There are three possible benchmarks for preference alignment—states, the citizen as a *national* citizen, or the citizen as a *European* citizen. First is the state, 'master of the Treaties' and rational choice actor in inter-state relationships, operating within a Westphalian legal order? Second, does the national citizen align with the constitutional law perception, drawing on the proposition that ultimate legitimacy of the EU is channelled through national states? Third, could the European citizen be the core of legitimacy pursuant to Article 20 TFEU emanating from an autonomous EU?

[47] Alberto Alesina and Enrico Spolaore, *The Size of Nations* (The MIT Press 2005).
[48] Spolaore (n 28) 7.

Identifying the reference subject for assessing preference heterogeneity is of relevance in understanding the character of the EU from both legal and economic perspectives. Let us recall that the principle of conferral is the Treaty-based device underscoring that, despite the EU's supranational character and its largely undisputed autonomous legal order, the EU is not a sovereign state.[49] The endeavour of establishing a European constitution that would have brought the EU close to a European state has failed.[50] EU members remain the principals of the EU as an agent. In turn, the EU States themselves draw their *internal* legitimacy on the basis of democratic principles through citizens' sovereignty, with domestic public authority established through elections.[51] Once the sovereign has delegated power to their representatives (agents), constitutional law justifies the authoritative validity of enacted law by reference to a state will, crafted by elected (parliamentary) agents, a will that prevails and is enforceable. This is the *internal* constitutional dimension that characterizes both the justification of public power (through elections) and its application (through emanations of legislative and administrative actions representing state will). There is thus a dual benchmark: from a citizens' legitimacy perspective, the benchmark is an aggregated form of citizens' preferences, while from a state power perspective, it is the preferences of law-makers and administrative agencies that set the standard.

The internal sourcing of legitimacy is to be distinguished from legitimacy of binding law in external relationships to other states. International lawyers apply a Westphalian concept of state sovereignty. This corresponds to the rational choice literature of law and economics, as set out in the cooperation motives analysed in Chapter 2 above, as they presume a rational state (without referencing the will of citizens).[52] In this sense, the rational choice perspective in international law is one of a private law character viewing states as transactional parties. It is a horizontal relationship between states as equal parties, a concept that stands in contrast to the hierarchical nature of constitutional law between bodies forming state will that is enforceable in relation to citizens. Under international law, the state is the traditional source of preferences—state consensus gives international law legitimacy and its binding character. This traditional notion of state sovereignty aligns better with states as the benchmark for preferences than citizens' preferences. These two benchmarks converge under the assumption of a benevolent law-maker, one that makes actual state agents' preferences match with aggregated citizens' preferences.

[49] Jean-Marc Ferry, *La Question de l'État Européen* (Gallimard 2000) 277.

[50] Armin von Bogdandy, 'The Prospect of a European Republic: What European Citizens Are Voting On' (2005) 42 Common Market Law Review 913.

[51] Dieter Grimm, *Sovereignty: The Origin and Future of a Political and Legal Concept* (Columbia University Press 2015) 106.

[52] Jack L Goldsmith and Eric A Posner, *The Limits of International Law* (Oxford University Press 2006) 23, 83.

Many economic models assume that law-makers are benevolent and efficiently aggregating citizens' preferences.[53]

Between these poles—citizens' legitimacy and state will—the EU offers a hybrid model, no longer anchored in international law alone due to its autonomous character, but not yet a state. This hybridity is institutionalized in the role of the Council, in which Member States sit as 'masters of the Treaties' and as producers of state will; through the European Parliament as the most direct producer of European citizens (representing European citizenship in line with Article 20 TFEU); and through national parliaments as indirect suppliers of national citizens' will.

Another relevant distinction inviting legal versus economic insight is between *input* and *output* legitimacy, introduced by political scientists.[54] The traditional constitutional law view is one of input legitimacy, emanating from the democratic principle enshrined both in domestic constitutional as well as EU law—the government *by* the people, in the words of Abraham Lincoln, propagates that citizens elect the leaders who enact public policies while expressing their will. Input legitimacy goes to the core of representative democracies and stipulates certain requirements and expectations on the characteristics of representation, such as free, fair, and open elections, as well as associated fundamental freedoms.[55]

However, citizens' preferences in economic perspectives are not exactly input legitimacy. Standard welfare economics refers to preferred outcomes of public policy decisions. Welfare economics claims to be able to measure 'improvement' directly in terms of the welfare attributes of outcomes. The standard notion of the efficiency of market outcomes is transaction-based and reflects outcomes of market exchanges. While economic welfare thus follows the maximization paradigm and outcome-orientation, input legitimacy is process-oriented. The latter represents the exercise of collective self-government—it does not specify the outcome of self-governance but determines how the process of self-governance must be designed in order to ensure government responsiveness to people's preferences. The focus of input legitimacy is on tying public policy decisions back to the sovereigns' decision. Input legitimacy requires certain *ex-ante* predications to be met, which is not the same as requiring the outcome of decision-making to be aligned with preferences.

Input legitimacy in the EU has been considered a perennial deficit[56]—because of its contrast to Member States' regimes of input legitimacy, in which elections

[53] Randall G Holcombe, 'Make Economics Policy Relevant Depose the Omniscient Benevolent Dictator' (2012) 17 The Independent Review 165.

[54] Fritz W Scharpf, 'Economic Integration, Democracy and the Welfare State' (1997) 4 Journal of European Public Policy 18.

[55] Vivien A Schmidt, *Europe's Crisis of Legitimacy: Governing by Rules and Ruling by Numbers in the Eurozone* (Oxford University Press 2020).

[56] Ben Crum and Stefano Merlo, 'Democratic Legitimacy in the Post-Crisis EMU' (2020) 42 Journal of European Integration 399.

directly feed into the composition of governments and state leadership. The lack of input legitimacy has widely been criticized by lawyers and has led them to request that the EU should not further expand its competences.[57] Others have emphasized the poor performance in terms of output legitimacy.[58] The process of supranationalization led to a shift of governmental power from the politized national level, which was deeply rooted and connected to national citizens, to the technocratic EU level that defines itself through technocratic resolution of its competences.[59] The merit of depolitization was seen in its ability to ensure better governance *for* the people without significant effects on governance *by* and *of* the people.[60]

Input legitimacy may find its economic corollary in what constitutional economics has described as *citizens' sovereignty*. Constitutional economics suggests a normative design of these constitutions, as initially coined by William H. Hutt[61] and elaborated by Viktor Vanberg[62]: an economic constitution that enhances consumer sovereignty, and a political constitution that enhances citizen sovereignty. While consumer sovereignty builds on the proposition that non-discriminatory market competition and internalized externalities generate welfare maximizing outcomes, citizen sovereignty looks at the collective arrangements in the political arenas, allowing formation of political will through 'cooperative ventures for mutual advantage'.[63] In a manner similar to consumer sovereignty, citizen sovereignty places the individual at the heart of a democratic polity, in whose common interests the polity should be operated. Accordingly, the political process should be institutionally framed in a manner that makes citizens' common interests its principal controlling force.[64] In other words, citizen sovereignty requires that political institutions, domestic politicians, and bureaucracies as well as international organizations are made most responsive to citizens' common interests—a requirement echoed by input legitimacy. Institutions, decision-making processes, fundamental rights protections, and adjudication must be implemented and respected in ways that maximize the prospect of the political process working to the mutual advantage of all citizens.[65]

[57] Simon Hix and Andreas Follesdal, 'Why is There a Democratic Deficit in the EU? A Response to Majone and Moravcsik' (2006) 44 Journal of Common Market Studies 533; Dieter Grimm, Europa ja - aber welches? Zur Verfassung der europäischen Demokratie. (CH Beck 2016) 29.

[58] Giandomenico Majone, *Europe as the Would-Be World Power: The EU at Fifty* (Cambridge University Press 2009) 10.

[59] James Ferguson, *The Anti-Politics Machine: Development, Depoliticization, and Bureaucratic Power in Lesotho* (University of Minnesota Press 1994).

[60] Schmidt (n 55) 69.

[61] William H Hutt, *Plan for Reconstruction: A Project for Victory in War and Peace* (Kegan Paul 1943) 215.

[62] Vanberg (n 14) 37.

[63] John Rawls, *A Theory of Justice* (Harvard University Press 1971) 84.

[64] Vanberg (n 14) 42.

[65] ibid.

In turn, welfare economics' focus on outcomes can be likened with *output legitimacy*. Assessing whether policy decisions are adopted in line with citizens preferences is predicated on whether the policy outcome matches what citizens want. Output legitimacy focuses on whether public policies actually serve the common good in line with the community norms. Output legitimacy is empirically assessable: the extent to which the outcomes of a governing authority's policies are effective in solving the polity's problems and objectives.[66] Some scholars have argued that the EU's lack of input legitimacy could be compensated by its performance in output legitimacy. While the EU's policy-making through non-majoritarian institutions was criticized from an input legitimacy perspective, their comparative positive record in producing effective policies has been appreciated.[67] Others have emphasized the benefits of the checks and balances in the EU's multiple veto system to ensure appropriate outcomes.[68] There is no empirical proof that EU decisions actually satisfy citizens' preferences. One could draw on surveys highlighting the level of satisfaction with EU policies or participation in elections for the EU parliament, or refer to the perception of individual events taking place at the EU level—such as protests in France and elsewhere against the Commission's initial services directive or the protests of farmers on the streets of Brussels.[69]

In conclusion, the legal and political science concepts revolving around homogeneity and legitimacy can be likened with economic concepts in different ways. Some lawyers refer to homogeneity of citizens as reference points for which and how many competences can be shifted to the EU level—according to some, only if there is a sufficient European identity, a sense of 'peoples-hood', an identity predicating on people's shared sense of belonging to a political community and acceptance of European practices. Economists in turn have used homogeneity of preferences as a concept for determining the scope of centralization versus decentralization. Economics also connects to the long-standing academic discourse on capturing the EU's identity by reference to input and output legitimacy. The economic perspective may vary in this respect. On one hand, an institutional economic perspective of *process*-orientation can be likened with input legitimacy by focusing on citizens being able to articulate their preferences to public policy-makers. On the other hand, welfare economics, unlike constitutional economics, is concerned with specific *outcomes*.[70] To the extent that constitutional economics emphasizes the acceptability of the process that leads to a decision rather than the

[66] Schmidt (n 55) 32.

[67] Giandomenico Majone, 'Nonmajoritarian Institutions and the Limits of Democratic Governance: A Political Transaction-Cost Approach' (2001) 157 Journal of Institutional and Theoretical Economics 57.

[68] Andrew Moravcsik, 'In Defence of the Democratic Deficit: Reassessing Legitimacy in the EU' (2002) 40 Journal of Common Market Studies 603.

[69] Schmidt (n 55) 61.

[70] Vanberg (n 14) 27.

outcome, it connects to input legitimacy, while standard welfare economics with its outcome orientation can be likened with output legitimacy.

effet utile and 'implied powers'

We can further ask whether the principle of conferral is effectively applied and respected within the existing allocation of competences under EU Treaties. This perspective invites an economic eye to the dynamic enshrined in jurisdictional innovations developed by the ECJ such as 'implied powers' or *effet utile*, both of which can be understood as legal techniques innovated by the Court without approval from the 'master of the Treaties'. More generally, a competence shift in the EU can be the result of a creeping erosion of competences.[71] It is then not the deliberate rational choice of EU members to transfer a set of public policies to the EU, but it is Union institutions that use the Treaty-based transferred competences to expand them informally through Treaty interpretation, which practically amounts to creeping Treaty amendments (though without complying with the substantive requirements for amendments). In theory, such an interpretation would amount to a breach of the Treaty duty and violate the principle of conferral, but if that breach is condoned or even committed by the 'custodians of the treaties' (the Commission and the ECJ), the Member States have limited recourse, particularly if both the executive and the judiciary of the EU agree on an extensive interpretation of EU law. When it is easy to circumvent the Treaty-based distribution of competences by way of interpretation and Treaty application, the *Kompetenz-Kompetenz* as a stronghold of national sovereignty loses its function of protecting the sovereignty of the Member States.[72]

The implied powers doctrine states that a principal competence expressly conferred on the EU must include those powers without which the principal competency cannot reasonably and expediently be exercised.[73] This doctrine can operate in a narrow or broad manner, depending on whether an authority is deemed 'necessary' or only 'reasonably necessary' for the exercise of the expressly conferred powers.[74] Closely conceptually related to this is the *effet utile* interpretation of the ECJ, according to which the Treaty-based competence should be interpreted teleologically, with the aim of fully developing the meaning of the provision or of achieving its 'full effectiveness'. The ECJ thus interprets the limited competence

[71] Stephen Weatherill, 'Protecting the Internal Market from the Charter' in Sybe de Vries, Ulf Bernitz and S Weatherill (eds.), *The EU Charter of Fundamental Rights as a Binding Instrument: Five Years Old and Growing* (Hart Publishing 2016), 133.

[72] Grimm (n 57) 112.

[73] Piet Eeckhout, 'The Doctrine of Implied Powers' in *EU External Relations Law* (Oxford University Press 2011).

[74] Trevor C Hartley, *The Foundations of European Community Law: An Introduction to the Constitutional and Administrative Law of the European Community* (Clarendon Press 1994) 110.

according to the principle of *effet utile* in such a way that all conceivable Union powers can be fully exploited.[75]

Typically, under international law, courts that are established by Member States interpret the rules that were designed by Member States according to the will of Member States. This corresponds with a rational choice perspective—Members have no interest in an international organization turning against the will of the founders. Interpreting an agreement between states with reference to the historical and actual will of Member States ensures that international law is applied in line with the preferences of those who crafted it. Some even argue that only the *original* agreement to the constitution matters.[76]

Rational choice suggests that states creating an international agreement do so on the premise of retaining their full national sovereignty, even if they partially bind themselves to decisions of the international organizations they create (eg accepting compulsory WTO dispute settlement rulings). Likewise, and in line with the Westphalian logic of international law, conventional legal interpretation focuses on the will of the state, its agents, interpreted by reference to, for example documents drafted by government representatives.[77] If the adjudicative bodies deviate from the founding states' intention, we speak of a principal agent issue, with bargaining costs (predefining rules to limit deviation by adjudicative bodies) to be balanced with agency costs (caused by deviation of the courts as agent). From the early days of the European integration process, the ECJ established that EU law does not form part of regular international law, nor is EU law dependent on national acts. Rather, the EU evolved independently from its national origins and an autonomous legal order emerged, a supranational construct that stands on its own feet, an institutional organization *sui generis*.[78] Consequently, the ECJ considered itself as not bound by conventional ways of interpreting EU law that would have subjected the interpretation of EU law to the will of the Member States and, in particular, respecting Member States' national sovereignty.

While a legal originalist interpretation of law partners with a rational choice perspective, the narrow focus on state perspective contrasts with a constitutional economic perspective, which is more concerned with the importance of *ongoing* agreement of citizens with the legal arrangement rather than the issue of *original* agreement. We recall that constitutional economics posits 'citizen sovereignty' and a procedural responsiveness of public policy choices to *current* members of society.[79] The constitutional economic tenets state that it is the voluntary agreement

[75] Michael Potacs, 'Effet utile als Auslegungsgrundsatz' (2009) 44 Europarecht 465.

[76] Adrian Vermeule, *Common Good Constitutionalism: Recovering the Classical Legal Tradition* (Polity 2022) 91.

[77] Grimm (n 57) 46.

[78] William Phelan, 'What is Sui Generis about the European Union? Costly International Cooperation in a Self-Contained Regime' (2012) 14 International Studies Review 367.

[79] Vanberg (n 14).

of all members to the constitution that provides legitimacy. It is concerned with the *ongoing* voluntary acceptance of members' citizens by its *current* members. Legitimacy to the constitution is drawn from the consent of the current democratic polity, not from some original agreement that may or may not have existed at the founding of the polity. Constitutional economics hence turns the 'original intent' legal interpretation upside down. Consequently, as Vivien Schmidt puts it, 'if a constitution is no longer generally accepted by its current members, it can surely not be considered more legitimate than a constitutional arrangement that may have been imposed originally by outside force or by decree, but that in its current operation is met by general approval within the respective constituency'.[80]

With constitutional economics militating against legal interpretations attaching value to originality in interpretation and rigidity of Treaty application, it may even raise doubts as to whether the 'principle of conferral' effectively preserves the original allocation of competences. Constitutional economics looks favourably at an 'implied power' legal interpretation, one that dynamically adapts to evolving circumstances. To the extent that EU members consider a competence to be enshrined in a competence of the EU Treaty, even if not explicitly mentioned, they express their consent by practice—a sufficient indication for constitutional economists to assume this constitutes an arrangement of 'mutual gains'. However, in practice it has been Union institutions—the Commission and the ECJ—who have been invoking extensive interpretations of EU competences—not Member States.[81] One should accept mutual gains and consent with extensive Treaty interpretations only if they have been approved (unanimously) in the Council.

Clearly, the supporters of literal interpretation and 'original intent' have a point when arguing that the initial Treaty was subject to (parliamentarian) approval, unlike the 'implied power' interpretation. The claim that current members of society are more relevant than the will of original members lacks empirical support because there is no active choice of current members, as no parliamentary approval nor referendum vote is exercised in relation to 'implied power' interpretation, while tacit acknowledgment of ECJ jurisprudence can hardly be taken as deliberate approval. Policy actions of specific EU policy decisions have never been brought to the citizen's choice. Citizens' choices form the basic idea of 'competitive federalism' (see above Chapter 4), yet Treaty amendments or implied powers are limited to Member States' consent articulated through the Council rather than direct approval by citizens through elections or referenda.

[80] Schmidt (n 55).

[81] Aurelien Portuese, 'Principle of Proportionality as Principle of Economic Efficiency' (2013) 19 European Law Journal 612, 631; Gareth Davies, 'Subsidiarity: The Wrong Idea, in the Wrong Place, at the Wrong Time' (2006) 43 Common Market Law Review 63, 64; Martin Nettesheim, 'Grundrechtliche Prüfungsdichte durch den EuGH' (1995) Europäische Zeitschrift für Wirtschaftsrecht 106.

b) Subsidiarity principle

Article 5(1), sentence 2 and (3) TEU enshrines the principle of subsidiarity. From an economic perspective the principle of subsidiarity is a core element in a theory of system competition or fiscal federalism. Taking fiscal federalism as a benchmark, the subsidiarity principle can be economically operationalized with reference to externalities, economies of scale, and heterogeneity of preferences. Legally, it is a principle governing the exercise of competences and as such protects Member States from intrusive exercise of Union power. It precludes Union action when a matter can be effectively dealt with by the Member States at national, regional, or local level, and empowers the Union to exercise its powers when the objectives of a proposed measure are not sufficiently satisfied by the Member States.[82]

The subsidiarity test under EU law evolves in two steps. First, the policy action concerned must be one of shared competence between the Union and Member States. In the second step, the effectiveness test applies inquiring whether the policy action 'cannot be sufficiently achieved by the Member States'. Concerning the nature of the competence, when the EU holds exclusive competences, or if the competence, in line with the principle of conferral, remains with the Member States, the subsidiarity test does not apply. The exclusive responsibilities of the EU (Article 3 TFEU) include customs policy, monetary policy, competition rules, and the common trade policy. Shared competence (Article 2(2) TFEU) includes, for example, internal market rules, agriculture, and environmental policies.

The Treaty-based limitation of subsidiarity to shared (and not exclusive) competence is not compelling from an economic perspective, because the considerations offered by the theory of system competition or fiscal federalism apply irrespective of the (artificial) legal delineation. Surely the competences accorded exclusively to the EU are those where economies of scale (customs administration), reduced transaction costs (internal market), or avoidance of negative externalities (single monetary policy) are rather intuitive. However, exclusive competences are carved into the Treaties without exception, which is not convincing for each and every case. Take as an example how euro members (exclusive competence) would have fared through the euro crisis with individual currencies, allowing them flexibility to devalue or appreciate their currencies, and thus facilitate economic adjustment. While hypothetical in nature, it is not obvious that a single currency in all circumstances is the adequate regime—Treaty-based exclusive competence may not always meet the economic subsidiarity test.

[82] On the economics of subsidiarity, see Roger van den Bergh, 'The Subsidiarity Principle in European Community Law: Some Insights from Law and Economics' (1994) 1 Maastricht Journal of European and Comparative Law 337; on the legal contours of subsidiarity, seed Alan Dashwood, 'The Relationship between the Member States and the European Union/European Community' (2004) 41 Common Market Law Review 355, 356.

The first prong of the subsidiarity test—does the issue concerned fall under shared competence?—is a purely legal exploration, one that applies competence delineation techniques based on Treaty-based competence allocation. EU lawyers typically assess the objective of the policy instrument in order to identify the corresponding competence.[83] What matters for the ECJ in order to determine which competence is relevant is the objective pursued by EU legislators which motivates the use of a Treaty-based instrument.[84] The objective pursued may be controversial at times—think of the German Bundesverfassungsgericht questioning the ECB's objective to pursue monetary policy. The Bundesverfassungsgericht considered ECB bond purchasing to be driven by economic policy objectives (Member States' competence), not monetary policy (EU competence).[85]

The second and core element of the test can be conceptualized as *cost-benefit analysis* informing whether the optimal level of allocation of a given shared competence lies at the Member State or EU level.[86] If these conditions are met, the EU may pursue policies at the central level. Lawyers tend not to engage in a rigid economic assessment of costs and benefits. Rather they apply common sense reasoning by vaguely offering an account of how different considerations might support either EU or Member States competences.[87] A more rigid economic approach is to characterize the benefits of centralization as the possibility of exploiting positive externalities, avoiding negative externalities, or leveraging economies of scale in the central allocation of policy responsibilities—on one side. On the other side, it would principally account for the costs of harmonization, as those are associated with overruling heterogeneity of preferences. Balancing the benefits with the varying preferences of the citizenry, the optimal degree of centralization should ensue: all functions where positive effects are dominant should be held at the central level, whereas all functions where high heterogeneity of preferences exceed the benefits should be kept at the local level.[88]

[83] Sionaidh Douglas-Scott, *Constitutional Law of the European Union* (Longman Pearson Publishers 2002) 261; Stephen Weatherill, 'The Limits of Legislative Harmonization Ten Years after Tobacco Advertising: How the Court's Case Law has become a "Drafting Guide"' (2011) 12 German Law Journal 827.

[84] Case C-370/12 *Pringle* (2012) EU:C:2012:756 [53]; Case C-62/14 *Gauweiler and others v Deutscher Bundestag* (2015) EU:C:2015:400 [46].

[85] BVerfGE 154, 17, 119 *PSPP* (2020); following Case C-493/17 *Heinrich Weiss and others* (2018) EU:C:2018:1000.

[86] Jacques Pelkmans, 'Testing for Subsidiarity', Bruges European Economic Policy (BEEP) Briefing 13/2006 (2006).

[87] Gracia Vara Arribas, 'Subsidiarity and EU Added Value: The Difficulty of Evaluating a Legal Principle in a Pragmatic Way' (2020) 3 European Court of Auditors Journal 30.

[88] Parisi and Fon (n 19); Weatherill (n 12) 13.

(Dis-)economies of scale

Relevant economic categories for operationalizing the subsidiarity principle are economies of scale, diseconomies of scales, and economies of scope. Economies of scale are discernible from the logic of the Tiebout model, which states that decentralized provision of public goods is preferred where relatively small populations are sufficient for the efficient provision of the service. But federalism theory and its preference for small governance units does not square well with other government services, where economies of scale allow for cost-efficiency when centralizing the provision of the public good. Examples include national defence, electricity, and telecommunication networks; transnational infrastructure; monetary policy; research; and pandemic health action. Because of economies of scale (in addition to externalities), these goods and services can more efficiently be provided to large populations. Centralization may enhance efficiency.[89]

However, some policy functions may be associated with *dis*economies of scale at the central level. This concept captures the idea that there are some things that are best done at the Member State level. There are different kind of costs that occasion the transfer of competences; not all are genuinely economic in nature. Political theory points at values of economic and procedural fairness, democratic participation, and the protection of personal rights and liberties. Regarding democratic participation, there is extensive literature dealing with the question of which level government activities should be placed in order to maximize the impact of constituents on actual decision-making. Giving more local self-governance increases participation and thus increases chances that public policies align with local preferences, which is the ultimate objective from an economic perspective.[90] If overlapping jurisdictions exist, people with control over policy may adopt measures that affect other people who have no control over policy, and this may engender a transfer of wealth from the group with less control to the group in control.[91] For example, citizens in subregion A may wish to be offered a different set of public policies than in subregion B. Their needs on infrastructure, security, and consumer protection may diverge. Offering one-size-fits-both services leaves citizens in both regions partially unsatisfied, as they have to bear costs for services offered to others.

Government 'by the people' is thus not only a core idea of democratic governance applicable to states in their entirety, but also offers an economic rationale for lower-than-federal-level governance. This concern is inherent in the sceptical views of legal and political science scholarship that lament the lack of EU

[89] Inman and Rubinfeld (n 27) 88; Alberto Alesina, Ignazio Angeloni and Ludger Schuknecht, 'What Does the European Union Do?' (2005) 123 Public Choice 275, 53.

[90] Robert Alan Dahl and Edward R Tufte, *Size and Democracy* (Stanford University Press 1973).

[91] Posner and Sykes (n 46) 15.

democratic legitimacy.[92] A recurrent argument is that supranational decision-making in Brussels decouples decision-making and legitimacy, with the double source of legitimacy from Member State representation in the Council and the representation in the European Parliament as directly elected body offering insufficient say to European citizens. Conceptually, this argument builds on the idea of citizens as a nationally determined group, as discussed above. A European 'demos' does not exist in that perspective, and as long as debates in media and public discourse remain predominantly national, European decision-makers will remain notoriously deficient in terms of democratic legitimacy. This view is prominently represented, as mentioned, in the German Constitutional Court and in parts of legal scholarship. It serves as a counterargument opposing the transfer of competences that are particularly reliant on democratic input.[93] This view connects easily to emphasizing the value of participation at a sub-federal level.

Diseconomies of scale also provoke the following question: which competences are non-amenable and should remain at Member State level? One could argue that the protection of personal rights and liberties should remain decentrally protected. Isaiah Berlin refers to 'negative rights', such as physical integrity, which should be secured well at local level through local police and local jurisdiction. The logic is that certain rights are best protected by local jurisdictions coupled with the free choice of citizens as to their place of residence.[94] A connected view is the 'transfer barrier' that the German Constitutional Court erected as a red line for giving up national competencies. In this logic, the realization of fundamental rights, above all as regards intensive encroachments on fundamental rights such as the deprivation of liberty in the administration of criminal law, touches core democratic affairs. As a general rule, intensive encroachments on fundamental rights have to be based on national parliamentary decisions and should remain a prerogative of national parliaments to which citizens participate through election. Similarly, the French Constitutional Council stated that changes to the European Treaties in the sense of further competence transfers may be acceptable provided that they do not undermine the essential conditions for the exercise of national sovereignty. Among these 'essential conditions' are the fundamental rights and liberties of nationals.[95] With the sensitivity of the relationship between legitimacy and fundamental rights being so high, decentralized participation thus ensures democratic safeguarding of fundamental rights. While this is convincing for negative rights, one may argue the contrary in relation to positive rights such as equal access to education, healthcare,

[92] Grimm (n 57) 117; Crum and Merlo (n 85).

[93] Joseph HH Weiler, 'Does Europe Need a Constitution? Demos, Telos and the German Maastricht Decision' (1995) 1 European Law Journal 219.

[94] Isaiah Berlin, *Four Essays on Liberty* (Oxford University Press 1969).

[95] Peter van Elsuwege, 'The EU Constitution, National Constitutions and Sovereignty: An Assessment of a "European Constitutional Order"' (2004) 29 European Law Review 741, 746 with reference to the decision on 9 April 1992, Conseil Constitutionnel, décision No 92-308 DC.

and perhaps a safe physical environment. Equal access to achieve one's full potential will be best protected within democratic federalism with responsibility assigned to a strong central government.

Framing the legal concerns within our economic framework, one could say that there are *switching costs* associated with the transfer from Member States to the EU level. These costs, primarily political and social, vary depending on the nature of the competence concerned. Hence, Member States cannot ignore the barriers erected by constitutional courts blocking the transfer of sovereign rights. Pushing integration further may cause diseconomies of scale to the extent that the cost-benefit assessment under the subsidiarity principle turns negative.

Another source of diseconomies of scale may result from vanishing *rules competition*. The inclusion of rules competition as consideration for the subsidiarity principle militates against centralization. The logic is that rule competition (or interjurisdictional competition) serves as a discovery tool to identify regulatory paths of cost minimization that would remain untapped under the harmonization of rules.[96] Unlike centralization, rules competition is not about harmonization of rules, but rather rules sharing. Rules competition leads ultimately to superior rules, because better rules in one Member State are imitated in countries with inferior rules. Consequently, successful and effective rules employed in one Member State have a higher chance of being adopted by other Member States by means of legal transplantation or by application of choice-of-law rules. In these cases, it is not centralization, but rather Member States' legislation that prevails. One may thus identify an additional diseconomy of scale of full centralization at the EU level given by the disappearance of virtuous rules competition, which could provide ways to minimize the costs of regulation at the local level but also, by extension, at the EU level. Rules competition thus makes it more difficult for a proposed centralization to pass the subsidiarity test. Applying a dynamic efficiency, that is, one that incorporates the cost advantages of rules competition through dynamic interaction between Member States, will add diseconomies of scale at central level. Incorporating the dynamic effect of rules competition in the subsidiarity test offers a factor that counterbalances the centralization push of the subsidiarity principle.

Economies of scope

While the rationale behind (dis)economies of scale is intuitive and well-researched, economies of scope must be taken into account as well. Economies of scope refer to the added value of concentrating the combination of two or more policies at the same level of government (federal or subfederal). This is because creating and

[96] Gerhard Wagner, 'The Economics of Harmonisation: The Case of Contract Law' (2002) 3 *ERA Forum* 77, 79; Weatherill (n 12) 13.

enforcing two or more policies together costs less than doing so at different levels. Shifting one or more policy responsibilities to the central level, while keeping other functions at the local level, implies that costs of those policy responsibilities left at the local level will be greater initially. Intuitively, if policies use the same institutional infrastructure and thus share the fixed costs, they can deliver their performance at lower overall costs. Institutional techniques to untap scope economies are, for example, pooling information, sharing organizational infrastructure, or internalizing other administrative externalities between two or more governmental functions. Take financial regulation and banking supervision as one example. In the EU, financial regulation is based on international market competence outlined in Article 114 TFEU, whereas the centralization of banking supervision by establishing a single supervisory mechanism was built on the basis of Article 127(6) TFEU. Though based on different competences, there are obvious links between both areas with financial stability secured through the Single Supervisory Mechanism (SSM) which feeds positively into an effective financial regulation, and vice versa. There are merits to having both of these competences at the same level of public authority. Similarly, one could argue that banking and insurance sectors should be jointly regulated in order to share common costs. Enforcement of both sectors can be done more efficiently and at lower costs. By employing the same entity for both tasks, spillovers between both sectors can be internalized in an efficient manner. Within one given policy area, it is likely that centralized policy responsibilities will yield some economies of scope.[97]

There is however a dynamic component to economies of scope, one that causes the subsidiarity principle to favour centralization. This dynamic process is path-dependent and, once started, may lead to strong centralization even in policy areas where local preferences are quite heterogenous (and should thus remain at a decentralized level). This process is rooted in the economies of scope just described.

When most policy functions are delivered at the central level, centralization is less likely to pass the subsidiarity test compared to a situation when more functions are allocated at the central level and forgone economies of scope at the local level are relatively small.[98] In the long run, the dynamic causes subsidiarity to become a self-defeating principle leading to path-dependent centralization: once a critical number of functions have been centralized, further centralization is often unavoidable.

The drivers of this development are switching costs, which decrease as the number of functions allocated at central level increase. This is particularly problematic if the economies of scope concern policy areas which are not necessarily governed by the subsidiarity principle. As mentioned, subsidiarity does not apply to exclusive competence under EU law, only to shared competence. If the Treaty

[97] Parisi and Fon (n 19) 53.
[98] ibid 62.

designer chooses to centralize one policy area by assigning it as a Union exclusive competence, this undermines the effectiveness of the subsidiarity test regarding the other policy area with which the exclusive competence exhibits economies of scope. As soon as a Member State renders some policy enforcement functions to the EU level, starting with, for instance, exclusive monetary policy, it may be easier (and less politically, administratively, and economically burdensome) to transfer other functions to the EU as well. Specifically, once monetary policy is centralized, it will then make sense to address financial stability through banking supervision in European hands too—the development in this area confirms this observation, with banking supervision following the centralization of monetary policy. Switching costs associated with transferring banking supervision from national to EU supervisors are then lower, because it helps align monetary policy and financial stability (incorporating policy spillover) and also makes use of the existing institutional infrastructure (economies of scope). The logic of switching costs decreasing as the number of functions allocated at the central level increase thus describes the phenomenon of a self-defeating principle. This logic may extend to other fields as well—with the EU accorded exclusive competence for customs affairs (Article 3(1)(a) TFEU), this may create economies of scope to pull border control competences to the central level.

This dynamic perspective, propelled by economies of scope, thus points to the subsidiarity principle's double-edged sword: on one side, with the dynamic described it accelerates the process of centralization. On the other hand, it fails to perform its (legal) function to safeguard against complete centralization. Subsidiarity does not manage to slow down the process of centralization, as is intended by EU Member States. There is a risk of excessive centralization, especially over time, and with a growing number of centralized tasks it becomes an increasingly weaker instrument safeguarding decentralized competence. One could argue that this is echoed in the debate in legal and political science literature on the expansion of subsidiarity, which is mostly critical of the Union encroaching on Member States' spheres of competence.[99]

We thus see the effect of the subsidiarity principle on centralization possible in two directions: one promoting centralization due to economies of scale at the EU level in conjunction with declining economies of scope at the Member States level. However, with regard to the constitutional law situation in Member States that prohibits or complicates the transfer of certain core state competences to the EU, it is more realistic to accept certain diseconomies of scale. These diseconomies of scale are akin to non-linear effects of declining switching costs. Switching costs decline with lower economies of scope at the Member State level,

[99] Stephen Weatherill, 'The Limits of Legislative Harmonization Ten Years after Tobacco Advertising: How the Court's Case Law has become a "Drafting Guide"' (2011) 12 German Law Journal 844; Davies (n 81) 64.

but diseconomies of scale at EU level rise with increasing transfer of competences from Member State to the EU level. There are thus opposing effects triggered under the subsidiarity principle that depend on the size and sign of economies of scope and diseconomies of scale.

Diseconomies of scale may also occur in the guise of agency costs as a result of reduced control powers of citizens. Transferring competences to supranational levels leads to a loss of citizens' control options. The legitimacy problem of weaker citizen control power can thus be structured as a cost problem, with the citizen as a principal controlling their agent. By transferring competencies from the domestic to the central level, an additional layer of public authority is added to the principal–agent relationship, with both the national government and the Council (or EU legislator) as agents. This multilevel governance (citizen–states–EU) increases the distance between the voter (principal) and the decision-maker (agent), as the traditional chain of legitimacy between voter and government is extended through the decision-making processes in the Council. This raises the probability that citizens' preferences will lose weight in the EU's decisions, hence causing agency costs. In order to reduce agency costs, institutional arrangements should be put in place to ensure that the principal's control and oversight options are maintained under the EU's multilevel public authority. Put differently, an effective subsidiarity check should account for control options from the point of view of citizens.

Switching costs may vary across countries. While the competence may be well placed at the EU level overall, individual EU members may benefit to varying degrees. The cost-benefit analysis enshrined in the subsidiarity test gains complexity if one considers that several Member States (not only one) are concerned, and when accounting for different voting rules (either majority voting or unanimity). This realistically mirrors the EU case: if the EU Commission seeks to exercise its shared competence and invokes the subsidiarity principle to favour of centralization, Member States must give their qualified, weighted agreements (or in some cases even unanimity in the Council). However, satisfaction of the centralization test for the entire EU does not imply satisfaction of the test at the local level of each Member State. Rather, the benefits of centralized EU action must be higher than the combined switching costs. It may well be that switching costs in Member State A are much higher than in Member State B, for example because the political sensitivities of surrendering a competence to EU level are different. If the decision in the Council must be made on a unanimity basis, both Member States must agree, and for each individually, switching costs must be lower than the country-specific benefits from centralizing the policy. This Pareto test is difficult to pass. More easily, by contrast, majority voting does not require all Member States to be better off with the task centralized at EU level. For the qualified majority vote to pass, there must be a critical number of countries whose country-specific benefits are greater than their country-specific costs (while from a general welfare perspective, it is collective welfare that must be positive).

How is it possible to implement subsidiarity in a weak Pareto fashion, that is, one that accounts for the diverse cost structure among EU Member States and, at the same time, reduces the agency costs that result from citizens being deprived of control of the EU as their agent? An implementation of this principle is guaranteed by the fact that the national parliaments, can assert a violation in accordance with Article 5(3), subpara 2 TEU. As part of an 'early warning system', the national parliaments can explain in a reasoned statement within eight weeks of the submission of a draft legislative act why they consider the draft to be incompatible with the principle of subsidiarity. In addition, it is provided that in Member States with two-chamber parliaments, each of these chambers can raise a subsidiarity objection or subsidiarity action against legal acts of the Union. In principle, this effectuation mechanism can serve as an institutional arrangement in the service of the economic approach: the subsidiarity mechanism is responsive to the variable switching costs, in particular to local political and cultural costs associated with transferring competences. As the organs genuinely legitimized by the electorate, national parliaments will have a special interest in safeguarding the control options at the central level. In this way, the costs borne by the citizen due to loss of control can be minimized. In practice, however, the control mechanism has weaknesses.[100] First, the necessary cooperation between the national parliaments is lacking. Given the eight-week deadline, many parliaments seem overwhelmed by the task of preparing reasoned statements and voting with other parliaments. Secondly, there is great heterogeneity in the interpretation of the concept of subsidiarity—too often national sensitivities and peculiarities decide on the interpretation of the principle of subsidiarity. Thirdly, the instrument lacks power—the European Commission is not obliged to amend a legislative proposal as a consequence of a complaint about subsidiarity.

[100] Ian Cooper, 'National Parliaments in the Democratic Politics of the EU: The Subsidiarity Early Warning Mechanism, 2009–2017' (2019) 17 Comparative European Politics 919; Jacob Öberg, 'Subsidiarity as a Limit to the Exercise of EU Competences' (2017) 36 Yearbook of European Law 391.

11
Flexibility

The principle of conferral laid down in Article 5 TEU is the core legal tenet of the Treaties maintaining sovereignty of its members over the design and evolution of the EU and to safeguard their role as 'masters of the Treaties'. The principle of conferral of powers stipulates that the European legislative bodies always require an explicit assignment of powers in the Treaties—to which only sovereign states are signatory parties. There is an economic ambivalence enshrined in this rule. On one side, adhering to this principle ensures that preferences of EU members as principals of the EU (as agent) are being observed. Agency costs are limited by making sure that the EU does not transgress its competences and by adhering to the initially agreed level of Treaty commitment. EU actions and deployment of EU Treaty-based competences are held in line with Member States preferences. On the other hand, rigid adherence to the Treaties' norms risks being insufficiently aligned with the external environment. Circumstances change and EU norms may become inadequate for dealing with external dynamics. As inherently incomplete contracts, the EU Treaties did not anticipate all future state-contingencies that EU countries (if they had known them initially) would have incorporated in the Treaties.

In order to prevent the principle of conferral from making the Treaty entirely static, there is a need for flexibility. Self-commitment for the future poses challenges if new circumstances arise. Factual uncertainties, political changes, and economic shocks are among the many factors that determine an EU member's preferred course of policy action. Rigid rules reduce the legally permissible scope of action, which may leave a country facing restraint on actions that a flexible rule would not impose. EU members would like to retain flexibility as a matter of state contingencies, allowing them to pursue certain measures depending on the state of the economy.

As 'masters of the Treaties', EU states have the freedom to design the Treaties according to the prospective need for flexibility. Choices of flexible rule design are made in relation to the institutional design of legal governance and by crafting individual Treaty provisions offering leeway. On the level of institutional choice, Member States determine their scope of flexibility depending on whether they are subject to full scrutiny, either through the administrative power of the European Commission (eg under competition law) or the judicial scrutiny of the ECJ. They introduce institutional flexibility by, for example, precluding the Court to exercise adjudicative power (eg under fiscal surveillance, Article 126 TFEU); stipulating

EU Law and Economics. Armin Steinbach, Oxford University Press. © Oxford University Press 2025.
DOI: 10.1093/9780198920915.003.0011

EU exclusive competence that restricts the scope of action of Member States (eg in trade issues); and using the freedoms granted under international law that surpass the constraints of the EU community methods (eg through intergovernmental cooperation[1]).

The degree of flexibility marks a significant difference between international law and European law. Soft law, vagueness, and reduced enforcement are recurrent patterns of international law.[2] International law dispute resolution rarely binds in the same ways as the sanction-based adjudication under EU law, and a 'quasi-executive' like the EU Commission is unparalleled in international law. Finally, Treaty reservations are a lot more common in international law than under EU law.[3] The legal literature has addressed flexibility of law through the lens of systemically analysing the contrast to the more rigid types of law in terms of bindingness, decision-making, and the sources of law employed.[4] In turn, economic approaches to flexibility have asked *why* states retain flexibility through Treaty design in relation to international law, even if each state has an interest that all countries commit to and comply with a certain substantive standard.[5] One straightforward answer is that states seek to retain scope for uncooperative and unilateral scopes of action, even if this flexibility comes at the cost of other Treaty members being lax in their commitments too, through reciprocity of commitments, which engenders lowering the overall gains from cooperation. The reciprocity principle governing international law thus poses a barrier to too much flexibility in the agreement.

Beyond this rather intuitive case, parties may also prefer flexibility when they anticipate significant costs associated with a breach that a country is likely to make in the future (eg for domestic political reasons). Since these violation costs could undermine the cooperative gains on a more permanent basis, under international law a country may choose a less rigid commitment as a Treaty provision in the first place, even if this means foregoing the benefits of rigid application of

[1] Sandrino Smeets, Alenka Jaschke, and Derek Beach, 'The Role of the EU Institutions in Establishing the European Stability Mechanism: Institutional Leadership under a Veil of Intergovernmentalism' (2019) 57 Journal of Common Market Studies 675; Sandrino Smeets and Derek Beach, '"It Takes Three to Tango": New Inter-Institutional Dynamics in Managing Major Crisis Reform' (2022) 29 Journal of European Public Policy 1414.

[2] Chris Brummer, 'Why Soft Law Dominates International Finance—and Not Trade' (2010) 13 Journal of International Economic Law 623, 630; Michael Reisman, 'The Concept and Functions of Soft Law in International Politics' in Emmanuel G Bello and Prince Bola A Ajibola (eds), *Essays in Honour of Judge Taslim Olawale Elias* (Brill 1992) 135.

[3] Andrew Guzman, *How International Law Works* (Oxford University Press 2008) 22, 33, 71, 119, 183; However, Koremenos' empirical account highlights that reservations are a lot more common in human rights agreements than in economics agreements, Barbara Koremenos, *The Continent of International Law: Explaining Agreement Design* (Cambridge University Press 2016) 3.

[4] CM Chinkin, 'The Challenge of Soft Law: Development and Change in International Law' (1989) 38 International and Comparative Law Quarterly 850; Michael Hahn, 'Interesting Times: Soft Law in International Economic Governance' in Manjiao Chi, Marc Bungenberg, and Andrea K Bjorklund (eds), *Asian Yearbook of International Economic Law 2022* (Springer 2022).

[5] Alan O Sykes, 'The Economics of Public International Law' (2004) John M Olin Program in Law and Economics Working Paper No 216.

international law.[6] This is likely to be different under EU law, which has, though flexibility exists, committed to a comparatively stricter regime with a more compelling enforcement mechanism in place. One obvious difference justifying more need for flexibility at the international law level than at the EU law level is that preferences of EU members are more homogenous than at the global level which makes exception and escape clauses less (often) necessary.[7] Also, costs of retaliation are relevant: under international law, there is no centralized sanctioning entity that would either bear or mutualize the costs of retaliation between Treaty members, but sanctions are imposed largely through bilateral relationships and therefore also impose costs on the sanctioning party (not only on the sanctioned party)—rational sanctioning parties may want to avoid these costs and thus choose more flexibility in the Treaty design in the first place.[8] Note that even under the comparatively advanced WTO dispute settlement mechanism, retaliation occurs bilaterally between the parties concerned, not through centralized sanctions. By contrast, in the EU there is an enforcement mechanism (put in place by the Commission and the ECJ) that assumes the costs of retaliation at the central level, hence Treaty parties face lower costs of enforcing rigid Treaty provisions compared to the predominantly bilateral sanction structure of international law.

a) Exceptions and escapes clauses

Focusing on specific forms of flexibility, Treaty designers must choose whether to craft vague Treaty language that gives leeway for discretion. Alternatively, the Treaty may foresee explicit flexibility clauses. Depending on the need for flexibility, *adaptive* or *transformative* clauses can be integrated into the Treaties.[9] Adaptivity captures the notion of allowing flexibility *within* the existing agreement in order to allow for efficient non-application of the rules. Adaptive clauses exemplify flexibility by allowing members to respond to unanticipated political events, economic shocks, and special domestic circumstances while preserving existing institutional arrangements. Sticking strictly to the Treaty commitment in this case would incur high compliance costs if an efficient decision would be non-compliance, while blatantly breaching the rules would incur violation costs associated with disrespecting the binding agreement with detrimental long-term effects on the credibility of the rules.

[6] Guzman (n 3) 135.

[7] This is also in line with regional cooperation being generally more likely to succeed than at the global level, Armin Steinbach, 'The Trend towards Non-Consensualism in Public International Law: A (Behavioural) Law and Economics Perspective' (2016) 27 European Journal of International Law 643.

[8] Guzman (n 3) 140.

[9] Barbara Koremenos, Charles Lipson, and Duncan Snidal, 'The Rational Design of International Institutions' (2001) 55 International Organization 761, 773.

Under these circumstances, adaptive clauses thus reduce the overall level of compliance by allowing deviations from the desired commitment level to take place in a lawful manner so as not to force a Treaty member to violate the rules. Adaptive clauses reduce the total costs incurred in the event of non-compliance with the substantive Treaty commitment. In other words, if compliance costs are so high that parties would breach the Treaty regardless of whether an escape clause exists, having an escape clause is better than not having one.[10] However, from an economic perspective, adaptive clauses should be activated only in cases where it is efficient for a state to deviate from their obligations, and not, for example, give in to lobbying pressure by interested parties.[11]

We can further differentiate between types of adaptive clauses, specifically between *exception* and *escape* clauses. Exception clauses introduce flexibility to allow hard-pressed states to avoid the full burden of their Treaty obligations on a decentralized basis. Within existing Treaty boundaries, unilateral invocations of flexibility, such as exception clauses, can be costly but necessary for countries to retain a positive payoff of commitment to EU rules. Situations may arise in which the benefits of domestic regulation curtailing EU law commitments may be high. In such situations a government may want to pursue restrictive measures. To allow such discretion, states may converge on accepting certain motives that reflect high-cost domestic concerns that could allow restrictive measures. To that end, EU members agreed to accept measures that were 'justified on grounds of public morality, public policy or public security' (Article 36 TFEU). This provision is an exception clause allowing Member States to deviate from their internal market obligations. It is sensible to allow these exceptions (under the restrictions mentioned) as they can lead to efficient results. Take for example the import of an unsafe product—the efficiency question is whether the overall costs of allowing the import are smaller than the benefits of an import ban. The exclusion of such a product would normally be worth more to an importing state than the sale of an unsafe product would be to an exporting state.[12] Hence, the existence of this escape clause increases the value of the internal market provisions in the Treaty.

Likewise, take the exception ground to protect 'order and security'—if risks occur to life and health, a negative externality would be attached to the imported good that the bearer of the basic freedom inflicts on the society as a whole. In such a case, the exception clause allows an efficiency assessment, since the costs to society are higher than the benefits of the individual service provider. Furthermore, Article 36 TFEU requires that prohibitions based on the grounds numerated in this provision must not be 'a means of arbitrary discrimination or a disguised

[10] Guzman (n 3) 152.

[11] Alan O Sykes, 'Protectionism as a Safeguard: A Positive Analysis of the GATT Escape Clause with Normative Speculations' (1991) 58 University of Chicago Law School 255.

[12] Guzman (n 3) 151.

restriction on trade between Member States'. These impermissible trade restrictions would enhance the costs by further imposing unnecessary costs on trading partners. Note that a crucial institutional device is that the authority to determine what constitutes a justifiable ground for a Treaty exception must not lie with the state invoking the measure. Giving too much discretion to the state would invite abuse and protectionism[13]—in order to allow for objective and neutral legal assessment (ideally coinciding with an economic efficiency analysis), the EU Commission and the ECJ as representatives of Union interests must specify the terms and scrutinize states' interpretations of the legal exception. Particularly, the independent ECJ has a pivotal role in defining the conditions, given that public choice literature suggests that exception clauses are prone to regulatory capture with rent-seeking efforts focusing on invoking exception for distributive purposes.

Exception clauses should be distinguished from escape clauses, the latter being a frequent instrument used by international organizations. Activation of escape clauses may lift obligations under the international Treaty on a temporary basis, while exception clauses offer punctual justification of Treaty violations. Take international trade agreements as an example. Trade agreements incorporate escape clauses (known as 'safeguards'[14]) allowing states to enter into agreements they might not otherwise accept because of unforeseeable contingencies. Escape clauses indicate a lower degree of homogeneity in preferences between Treaty parties than is necessary for exception clauses. No EU Member State could temporarily lift the freedom of movement in its entirety. While EU Member States may escape the Treaty commitments altogether by taking recourse to Article 50 TEU, paving the way for exiting the Union if the Union's obligations are perceived as infringing on sovereignty issues, EU Member States have accepted a higher level of reciprocal commitment by not allowing general escape clauses comparable to international law. While preferences may diverge between EU members depending on the issue area concerned, they do not fall back behind a minimum level of commitment. EU Member States have an incentive to invoke this flexibility in specific cases, but most take into consideration the reciprocal effect meaning that other members may invoke the exception as well.

b) Transformative clauses

While event-based adaptivity clauses separate the outlying cases from the ordinary course of policy action, there are transformative clauses that allow the EU to

[13] On the controversy on the right to self-determine security concerns under WTO rules, see Roger P Alford, 'The Self-Judging WTO Security Exception' (2011) Utah Law Review 697.

[14] Krzysztof J Pelc, 'Seeking Escape: The Use of Escape Clauses in International Trade Agreements' (2009) 53 International Studies Quarterly 349.

respond to new policy challenges. Transformative clauses appear in the EU Treaties in different guises, but they respond to the same need. EU states are confronted with uncertainty about the future state of the world.[15] This causes a dilemma when entering into EU Treaties: becoming locked into an institution may lead to unanticipated costs or adverse distributional consequences when the environment changes in the future. This dilemma may lead states to refrain from joining the EU at all, if uncertainty is high and anticipated benefits are low. Risk-averse states, in particular, will avoid committing themselves to rigid institutions.[16] Assuming that gains from cooperation by committing to the EU Treaties are sufficiently high, how would states ensure that the EU has sufficient flexibility to adapt to changing conditions, while maintaining the will of EU members as the decisive reference point? One avenue is Treaty changes. Over time, Members have adapted to changing circumstances through Treaty changes including those made by the Maastricht, Amsterdam, Nice, and Lisbon Treaties. Treaty amendments are suitable when internal flexibility of the Treaty is insufficient to deal with a changed environment. For example, the enlargement of the EU by acceding new members or acquiring one single currency was not possible through internal flexibility. However, external flexibility through Treaty amendments has a downside. Renegotiation of Treaty terms is costly in terms of negotiation expenses, and it also invites strategic bargaining where states may 'hold up' the cooperation in an effort to increase their own gains from the renegotiated Treaty terms.

EU law offers a number of transformative clauses. Take Article 352 TFEU as an example of a transformative clause—it allows the EU to take appropriate measures, if necessary, to attain one of the objectives set out in the Treaties. It is 'designed to fill the gap where no specific provisions of the Treaty confer on the Community institutions express or implied powers to act, if such powers appear none the less to be necessary to enable the Community to carry out its functions with a view to attaining one of the objectives laid down by the Treaty'.[17] Where the EU holds competence in one issue area, it should be flexible enough to extend its competence to issues that have sufficient links to this core competence. Take the EU's competence for competition law as one example. The Treaty norms initially provided insufficient control over conduct that is incompatible with undistorted competition envisaged in the Treaty, and therefore through Article 352 TFEU, EU powers of action were extended with regard to concentrations.[18] An economically sound approach taking account of the fact that cross-border implications of mergers should not be dealt with at the decentralized Member States level due to policy spillovers.

[15] Koremenos (n 3) 39.

[16] Koremenos, Lipson, and Snidal (n 9) 793.

[17] *Opinion 2/94—Accession of the Community to the European Convention for the Protection of Human Rights and Fundamental Freedoms* (1996) I–01759 [29].

[18] Council Regulation (EC) No 139/2004 of 20 January 2004 on the control of concentrations between undertakings (the EC Merger Regulation) [2004] OJ L24/1, para 7.

Using transformative clauses may thus be aligned with allocative efficiency considerations under the legal constraint that new EU tasks remain within the boundaries of granted competences (complying with the principle of conferral).

There are multiple other provisions in the EU Treaty that allow Member States space to bypass the Union's constraints in order to develop the EU in a transformative way. The solidarity clause in Article 122 TFEU has played an important role in developing macroeconomic tools that produced welfare gains for the entire EU through means that were not explicitly foreseen by the Treaties. This legal provision was employed to furnish financial assistance during the pandemic to establish a risk-sharing instrument that permitted a coordinated macroeconomic response to the pandemic crisis (NGEU).[19] The crisis-induced transformative character of this provision has been criticized for transgressing the competences accorded to the EU. In addition, it is not only Treaty provisions that offer suitable clauses granting space for exceptions and transformations of existing arrangements. The Commission and the Court play an important role too, especially in extending the scope of transformative EU competences. As mentioned before, *effet utile* or 'implied powers' are doctrinal innovations pushed by Union institutions to enhance flexibility within existing rules, hence giving an interpretation to EU law that ensures the greatest possible effect of EU law in Member States' legal orders (see above Chapter 10 a)). With interests between Union institutions and Member States diverging on the desirable outreach of EU law into Member States' legal orders, public choice insight informs us that flexibility enshrined in legal rules can be subject to misuse. Not only do individual states have incentives to free-ride on an agreement by self-serving interpretations of flexibility clauses, but Union institutions can do the same. Driven by Community interest and the desire for prestige, the EU Commission and the ECJ have frequently been accused of being biased in favour of Community interests.[20] From that perspective, the relevance and practical use of flexibility clauses and judicial doctrines under EU law must be viewed from a public choice angle (see below Part IV).

c) Soft law

The choice between hard law and soft law is one through which Treaty designers must balance a trade-off between rigidity and flexibility.[21] The emergence and

[19] Council Regulation (EU) 2020/2094 of 14 December 2020 establishing a European Union Recovery Instrument to support the recovery in the aftermath of the COVID-19 crisis [2020] OJ LI433.

[20] Gareth Davies, 'Subsidiarity: The Wrong Idea, in the Wrong Place, at the Wrong Time' (2006) 43 Common Market Law Review 63, 64; Nicholas W Barber, 'Subsidiarity in the Draft Constitution' (2005) 11 European Public Law 197.

[21] Francis Snyder, 'The Effectiveness of European Community Law: Institutions, Processes, Tools and Techniques' (1993) 56 Modern Law Review 19, 54.

characteristics of informal institutions and soft law-making in global governance—as well as the pressure they exert on the traditional modes of cooperation—have long been analysed with regard to international law[22] as well as EU law.[23] Soft law generally captures rules of conduct which, in principle, have no legally binding force but which nevertheless may have legal implications and compliance pull.[24]

On a theoretical level, the most extreme form of soft law cooperation in terms of reduced binding character and formality could be seen in the renouncing of an explicit agreement completely. Legal obligations may be self-enforcing in the sense that parties may not consider it necessary to agree on a formalized commitment. More generally, whether an issue is dealt with through soft or hard law, a written or oral agreement, or agreed at all, depends on the issue at stake. In a coordination game, in which EU members share a common interest in not pursuing certain conduct, hence in which there are only benefits and no costs, and where defection is not attractive, there may be no need to specify an obligation in formal law, but it could be arranged tacitly or through soft law. This may explain why certain fundamental obligations in inter-state conduct are found in public international law, in which the international community is more heterogenous and interests among states are less aligned than in the EU, but not in EU law. The EU Treaties are less explicit than international law on core rules such as the non-intervention principle, the principle of non-violation, and the equality of sovereign states. Lawyers may argue technically that these core principles are enshrined in the EU Treaty through Article 3(5) TEU and other provisions, but their lack of salience and explicitness may also be explained with reference to these obligations being of such a self-enforcing and obvious nature that EU members have not considered elaborating them in the Treaties—they are tacitly presumed to form the basis of cooperation.

Other comparative patterns of soft law (and the corresponding absence of hard law) support the view that international law relies more heavily on soft law than EU law does. International soft climate law contrasts with European hard climate law—under international law, states fear the free-riding of other countries to an extent that it undermines accepting binding rules or because countries outside Europe (especially developing countries) consider costs of CO2 reduction as too harmful to their economies to enter into an ambitious reduction path; under EU law, states accept binding reduction commitments because free-riding within the EU is less probable due to rigid monitoring, possibly also with a view to reaping first-runner gains from technological advances in climate technologies seizing global market shares. Competition law is another example of soft international law and hard EU law: antitrust rules at the international level are limited to informal

22 See, eg, Kenneth W Abbott and Duncan Snidal, 'Hard and Soft Law in International Governance' (2000) 54 International Organization 421.

23 Mareike Kleine, *Informal Governance in the European Union: How Governments Make International Organizations Work* (Cornell University Press 2013) 54.

24 Snyder (n 21); Guzman (n 3) 142.

exchanges between antitrust authorities short of binding substantive and procedural rules and largely decentralized.[25] There is no cooperation although global welfare would be enhanced under a uniform standard of antitrust governance ensuring a worldwide level playing field curbing monopoly rents and competitive biases. However, several issues related to jurisdictional and sovereignty claims may comprise a fundamental reason not to surrender national competences. Moreover, the uncertainty surrounding the design of a universal standard of antitrust governance and the scope of discretionary practice of national authorities form another barrier. All these factors translate into significant sovereignty and monitoring costs, thus rendering hard-law consensualism an unattractive option.[26] At the EU level, the contrary is the case—Member States have rendered their antitrust competences and passed them to the EU, motivated by welfare gains—even if in singular cases national champions and even national welfare may suffer. Besides greater homogeneity in national antitrust practices, it is the absence of a hegemonic mode of action which is embodied in the extraterritorial action of antitrust agencies, leading international power players such as the United States to be reluctant to relinquish their hegemonic position in economic governance, as losing extraterritorial outreach of their unilateral competition policies would be costly.[27]

While less frequent than under international law, soft law has nevertheless been a popular mode of governance throughout European integration. Provided in the Treaties under Article 288(5) TFEU, the advantages of EU soft law as being fast, flexible, easy to issue, and thus able to adapt to rapid evolutions and changes in policies, contrast with important legitimacy drawbacks, as soft law is hardly justiciable, and its legal effects are blurred.[28] Since the 1990s, there seems to be a growing preference for procedural frameworks over substantive prescriptions, with different forms of coordination emerging in fields such as social and economic policy, employment, the environment, education, and research. The open method of coordination (OMC) has become a frequent mode of coordination favouring new forms of soft governance.[29]

From an economic perspective, we are interested in identifying the conditions under which governments prefer soft laws to the formal hard ones, and vice versa.[30] It is true that from a rational choice perspective, a binary distinction between

[25] Steinbach (n 7).

[26] Yane Svetiev, 'The Limits of Informal International Law: Enforcement, Norm-Generation and Learning in the International Competition Network' in Joost Pauwelyn, Ramses Wessel, and Jan Wouters (eds), *Informal International Lawmaking* (Oxford University Press 2012).

[27] Charles P Kindleberger, 'Dominance and Leadership in the International Economy: Exploitation, Public Goods, and Free Rides' (1981) 25 International Studies Quarterly 242.

[28] Snyder (n 21) 54.

[29] Burkard Eberlein and Dieter Kerwer, 'Theorising the New Modes of European Union Governance' (2002) 6 European Integration online Papers.

[30] From the perspective of international relations, see, eg, Armin Schafer, 'Resolving Deadlock: Why International Organisations Introduce Soft Law' (2006) 12 European Law Journal 194; From an economic perspective, see Stefan Voigt, 'The Economics of Informal International Law—An Empirical

'binding' law and 'non-binding' law does not make sense, because both are chosen by states to facilitate cooperation and both impose some costs on a non-compliant party through the enforcement modes of reputation, retaliation, and reciprocity.[31] A great amount of work has emphasized the functionality of informality, notably the flexibility it offers to parties implying lower sovereignty costs as well as its ability to integrate a broader range of actors and stakeholders than would be possible under formal approaches.[32] Indeed, soft law often emerges in areas where sovereignty costs are high and serves to avoid (even higher) costs implied in formal and binding cooperation in these issue areas, which explains for instance the different degree of softness in competition policy cooperation under international and EU law mentioned above. Also, while informality and soft law are conceptually different, they often coincide. For example, where domestic political costs associated with EU legislation are high, Member States may seek informal ways of decision-making at the EU level.[33] By contrast, hard law is more restrictive as it generates reliance and often exerts (though not always) a greater compliance pull.[34] Hence, formal law restrains policy spaces more significantly than informal conduct which allows for a broader range of conduct and cooperation mechanisms.[35] It is not only sovereignty costs that are higher when hard law entails the countries' acceptance of an external authority over political decisions (eg the Commission and the Council sanctioning an EU member for non-compliance with fiscal rules).[36] Soft law also incurs comparatively less negotiation costs as it offers flexibility and speed both in the conclusion and the endorsement of non-binding guidelines.[37] Accordingly, flexibility due to the changing nature of circumstances may be a valid concern implying the desire for low modification costs.[38]

Therefore, if states prefer greater adaptability in an agreement, they may take recourse to soft terms in order to make rights and obligations under an agreement more flexible. For example, coordination of national economic policies on the basis of Broad Economic Policy Guidelines (Article 121 TFEU) or the practice of EU

Assessment' in Thomas Eger, Stefan Oeter, and Stefan Voigt (eds), *The Economics of Informal International Law* (Mohr Siebeck 2011) 33.

[31] Guzman (n 3) 160.

[32] Charles Lipson, 'Why Are Some International Agreements Informal?' (1991) 45 International Organization 495, 495.

[33] Kleine (n 23).

[34] Dinah L Shelton, 'Introduction' in Dinah L Shelton (ed), *Commitment and Compliance: The Role of Non-Binding Norms in Commitment and Compliance: The Role of Non-Binding Norms in the International Legal System* (Oxford University Press 2000) 8.

[35] Brummer (n 2) 632.

[36] Michael C Dorf, 'Dynamic Incorporation of Foreign Law' (2008) 157 University of Pennsylvania Law Review 103, 133.

[37] Jacob Gersen and Eric A Posner, 'Soft Law: Lessons from Congressional Practice Soft Law: Lessons from Congressional Practice' (2008) 61 Stanford Law Review 573, 589.

[38] Janet Koven Levit, 'A Bottom-Up Approach to International Lawmaking: The Tale of Three Trade Finance Instruments' (2005) 30 Yale Journal of International Law 125, 179.

employment policy based on Commission guidelines (Article 148(2) TFEU) leave Member States with ample flexibility and only require them to take these guidelines into account. The OMC is the dominant governance mode in these areas, with accountability being more horizontal than vertical, meaning that Member States are required to take seriously, and to answer the preferences, objections, and counter-proposals of other governments.[39] This kind of adaptability is most practical where parties to an agreement are faced not only with high sovereignty costs but also with significant uncertainty over factual future developments and where, in economic terms, the cost-benefit balance of the agreement remains to some extent unpredictable. Member States can identify the effects of rules and guidelines in practice by avoiding formal legality in assessing their benefits.[40] In this event, soft law offers strategies for learning processes, in which parties can eventually resolve their problems.[41]

Taber has pointed at instances where EU hard law has been softened to give more manoeuvring space to policy-makers. Some instruments of environmental policy have shifted from the traditional approach based on the setting of uniform, legally binding norms to a less coercive and more flexible approach.[42] For instance, the Directive on Integrative Pollution Prevention and Control, enacted in 1996, introduced soft, non-binding targets and a strong procedural component through the delegation of policy formulation to participatory, co-regulatory networks, in a field where legally binding emission limit values on air, land, and water used to be applied to several industrial sectors.[43] Clearly, informal law typically provides the executive branch with more space.[44] In particular, informal laws with a lower profile are more strictly monitored by the government bureaucracies that negotiate and implement the agreements and are less exposed to intrusion by other agencies or parliamentary bodies. Hence, recommendations, benchmarking, and best practices are based on the desire of participants to agree, through collective deliberation, on procedural norms, forms of regulation, and shared political objectives, while preserving a diversity of solutions and local measures.

Finally, the reputational costs of informal law are comparatively low. Consider that non-compliance with EU hard law typically triggers scrutiny by the Commission and eventually leads to infringement procedures. Since

[39] Fabien Terpan, 'Soft Law in the European Union—the Changing Nature of EU Law' (2015) 21 European Law Journal 68, 81.

[40] Abbott and Snidal (n 151) 442.

[41] Brummer (n 2) 633.

[42] Katharina Holzinger, Christoph Knill, and Ansgar Schäfer, 'Rhetoric and Reality? "New Governance" in EU Environmental Policy' (2006) 12 European Law Journal 403.

[43] Terpan (n 39) 90.

[44] See also Andrew T Guzman, 'The Consent Problem in International Law' (2012) 52 Virginia Journal of International Law 747, 763 (comparing the international sphere with the domestic setting in which power is shared between legislation and administration. Given that the administration, not the legislator, domestically deals with all issues, not all issues at the international level can be managed with international agreements).

non-compliance with hard law may degrade an EU member's reputation, the formation of soft law may be preferable. The soft application of EU fiscal rules with a politically dominated procedure that must be abided by before sanctions can be imposed incorporates the logic of soft or flexible logic and keeps reputational losses of non-compliance with rules low. In turn, even non-compliance with soft law can lead to a loss of reputational capital. The threat of such loss promotes compliance, although it cannot guarantee it. Whether it succeeds depends on the immediate gains obtained from breaking an agreement, the lost stream of future benefits, and the rate of discount applied to that stream, as well as the anticipated reputational costs from specific violations. Hence, reputation can contribute to Treaty self-enforcement.[45]

Our economic perspective invites us to classify soft law into *soft laws* and *soft application*. EU soft law may unfold in combinations of two dimensions by distinction between obligation and enforcement—soft law may occur as a combination of hard obligation/soft enforcement (eg the Stability and Growth Pact), hard law/no enforcement (eg some aspects of the CFSP), or soft obligation/hard enforcement (eg macroeconomic imbalance procedure).[46] The Stability and Growth Pact (SGP) is an example of hard rules, softly implemented. From a legal perspective, the SGP has been problematic as it contradicts *pacta sunt servanda*; it is a practice of searching for loopholes in the rules, and attempting to bend legal rules for political purposes. From an economic perspective, the SGP illustrates how descriptive and normative rule design diverges. There is a sound economic reason for countries to prefer soft fiscal arrangements, while the long-term moral hazard effects of softness are detrimental. In terms of rule design, the soft character initially offered the only fiscal rule commitment level that ensured a sufficiently high number of EU member participation. The soft law character provides—at least for some EU members—the optimal combination of benefits of cooperation (gains through low refinancing costs in normal times and unionized currency promoting trade and welfare) and costs of cooperation (through constrained fiscal policies).

We referred above to the relevant game-theoretic literature which suggests that the more the heterogenous preference levels are among participants, the more high-cost countries (in terms of implementation costs) are able to lower the commitment level of the agreement. Economic and fiscal governance is an area that traditionally has been characterized by diverse cultures entailing high-cost (in terms of compliance costs) and low-cost countries, with the role of government intervention, competition, and independence of fiscal and monetary authorities varying significantly. This asymmetry feeds into diverse preferences and hence cost-benefit ratios of fiscal rules. With high-cost countries more likely to influence the level of commitment of fiscal rules, this situation leaves low-cost

[45] Lipson (n 32) 501.
[46] Terpan (n 39) 77.

countries (such as Germany and frugal states), countries with traditions of balanced budgetary policies who started the fiscal cooperation at low debt levels, far from their optimal level of commitment. In turn, while the heterogeneity of preferences may explain *descriptively* why SGP rules have been designed with flexibility, the detrimental macroeconomic effect of lax rules (combined with unionized monetary policy) shows that *normatively* the commitment level has not been set at an efficient level (or has not been enforced efficiently using the no-bailout clause in Article 125 TFEU).

Soft fiscal rules induced free-riding,[47] bailout expectations,[48] and an incompatible combination of decentralized fiscal policies with centralized monetary policies.[49] In *ex-post* perspectives, following the euro sovereign debt crisis, the bailout of distressed states inflicted high adjustment costs on states that were already high-cost due to, inter alia, the high domestic policy costs of fiscal prudence. Confronted with either extremely high political or social costs associated with leaving the euro, the countries entered into an unfavourable tradeoff vis-à-vis stable countries' financial support in return for painful structural reforms. The conditionality-based financial assistance turned previously soft fiscal rules into hard fiscal governance, as recipient countries were obliged to conduct fiscal prudence rigidly. One could say that strict conditionality tied to financial assistance, safeguarded through interference with core domestic policy issues by creditor states, are offsetting the gains of flexible fiscal regimes that high-cost countries enjoyed until the euro crisis broke out.

d) Incomplete or overcomplete EU Treaties

Are EU Treaties complete contracts? In a complete contract, the contracting parties are fully informed and agree on the allocation of all risks that may arise during the execution of the contract before the contract is concluded. They can foresee and regulate all future state contingencies. This 'Pareto-efficient complete contingent contract'[50] is the contract that parties would write if there were no imperfections such as unpredictability, transaction costs, bounded rationality, and enforcement costs. Such treaties would establish risks, rights, and responsibilities in every conceivable state of the world. The context of the contract would be free from market failures, unforeseen events, and opportunistic behaviour. In this counterfactual

[47] Armin Steinbach, *Economic Policy Coordination in the Euro Area* (Taylor & Francis Ltd 2014).

[48] Eric Mengus, 'Asset Purchase Bailouts and Endogenous Implicit Guarantees' (2023) 142 Journal of International Economics 103737.

[49] Dermot Hodson, 'The EMU Paradox: Centralization and Decentralization in EU Macroeconomic Policy' in Jeremy Richardson (ed), *Constructing a Policy-Making State?* (Oxford University Press 2012).

[50] Steven Shavell, 'Damage Measures for Breach of Contract' (1980) 11 The Bell Journal of Economics 466, 467.

situation, parties would maximize their *ex-ante* commitment since there are no insurance or security issues.

Unfortunately, we do not live in this Panglossian world. Parties can only conclude incomplete contracts. Complete contracts that take all uncertainties into account do not exist and would also result in exorbitant contracting costs. Contracts would be incomplete in the sense that they would fail to differentiate between states of the world that optimally call for different obligations.[51] Therefore, states determine rules to be applied by bureaucracies, accepting dispute settlement to clarify interpretation.

However, constitutions, as treaties, are distinct to the extent that, by definition, they do not intend to be too specific. Typically, drafting a constitution is an incomplete exercise in the sense that constitutions do not aim to address all contingencies and solutions to them. Constitutions are thus thin, often restricted to the bare minimum of state organization and fundamental rights. This maintains leeway in the political sphere to fill the space left by the constitution with actions by the regular law-maker.

Constitutional deferral refers to the practice whereby only core principles and rules are put into constitutions, many of them governing how decisions are to be made, such as rights and procedural rules which serve to limit agency problems of government or facilitate the pre-commitment necessary for politics to operate.[52] Constitutions are 'framework documents', and limiting constitutional text to core constitutional arrangements is an established constitutional theory paradigm.[53]

The EU Treaties function as constitutions in practice. From a legal hierarchy perspective, EU Treaties rank above Member States' constitutions. However, the TEU with 55 provisions and the TFEU with 358 provisions are not the limited, basic set of rules that are typically found in constitutions as deliberately incomplete sets of rules. The EU Treaties offer an excess supply of rules that in a national context would normally be under the disposition of the law-maker. It has been argued that only the TEU should enjoy constitutional status, while downgrading the entire TFEU to the status of ordinary law that could more easily be amended.[54] Indeed, piling up norms in the Treaties raises exclusion costs significantly because it leverages the role of the European Commission and the ECJ in the application and interpretation of the constitutionally cemented rules. It is their interpretation of the rich set of constitutional rules through which they can trump and remove what they perceive as Member States' barriers to EU law. Constitutionalization

[51] Robert E Scott and Paul B Stephan, *The Limits of Leviathan* (Cambridge University Press 2006) 76.

[52] Tom Ginsburg, 'Locking in Democracy: Constitutions, Commitment, and International Law' (2006) 38 New York University Journal of International Law and Politics 707, 710.

[53] Martin Loughlin, 'The Silences of Constitutions' (2018) 16 International Journal of Constitutional Law 922.

[54] Dieter Grimm, *Europa ja—aber welches? Zur Verfassung der europäischen Demokratie* (CH Beck 2016) 27.

means depoliticization and intrusion of EU law into Member States' legal orders.[55] Directly legitimized bodies, such as governments, national, and European parliaments, are marginalized because they must accept the excess supply of constitutional rules as given and permanent, as they can be amended only at very high transactions costs.

'Overcomplete' contracts can be problematic. The more rules are cemented through constitutionalization, the less feasible their adaption to changing external circumstances, the higher the risk of allocative inefficiency as the rules cannot be adapted given that Treaty amendments are extremely cumbersome. Ultimately, the overburdening of the constitutional EU Treaties raises both error costs and decision costs. Decision costs, such as Treaty formation and amendment, are plagued by inflexibility, and require a large amount of negotiation and coordination in order to agree on the text. Take as an example the excessively detailed description of how to assess whether Member States abide by fiscal rules set out in Articles 121 and 126 TFEU. In addition, there are high error costs due to the inflexibility caused by carving in constitutional stone rules that would be better placed at the more volatile disposition of the regular law-maker. When inflexibility of rules meets with a dynamic factual setting and requires rules to be aligned to respond effectively to a new regulatory environment, the rigidity of rules causes error costs. Finally, constitutional rules are not only hard to amend, but they may also give large discretionary space to the Commission and the ECJ, which cannot be reviewed and modified by the ordinary law-maker. The consequences are high agency costs—the EU administrative and judiciary bodies can exploit the constitutionally granted leeway without fearing the risk of the normative benchmark being modified to constrain them.

[55] Graziella Romeo, 'What's Wrong with Depoliticization?' (2022) 1 European Law Open 168; Dieter Grimm, *Constitutionalism: Past—Present—Future* (Oxford University Press 2006) 303; Giandomenico Majone, *Dilemmas of European Integration: The Ambiguities and Pitfalls of Integration by Stealth* (Oxford University Press 2005).

12
Non-consensual EU law

Synchronized integration is the norm for EU integration. It reflects that all EU members share the same rights and obligations under the Treaties and that future integration builds on the participation of all EU members. The lesson from international law and relations is that symmetric cooperation is no more than an ideal, one that emphasizes the (welfare) gains of multilateralism. Unilateralism has been a widely discussed (and often lamented) phenomenon in international politics,[1] where it is defined as 'to opt out of a multilateral framework (whether existing or proposed) or to act alone in addressing a particular global or regional challenge rather than choosing to participate in collective action'.[2]

While the EU itself is a form of regional cooperation, and thus proof of non-multilateralism from a global perspective, we want to understand better how and why within the EU uneven or non-multilateral integration occurs. Specifically, we can explore the incentive structure that guides EU members to engage in differentiated integration (as opposed to a unified integration speed). We are not concerned in this chapter with issues of lawfulness and the legal boundaries of non-consensualism, which has been a fruitful topic of law-only analysis.[3] We will explore the underlying motives to understand why—and under what circumstances—uneven integration takes place.[4] The economic perspective on non-consensualism varies depending on the economic method. The rational choice theory focuses on cost-benefit considerations and game-theoretic considerations as the main drivers of non-consensualism—they offer tools to highlight the incentive structure depending on whether Treaty cooperation takes place between symmetric or asymmetric states (in terms of preferences or power). In turn, drawing from behavioural economics offers a powerful tool to reveal heuristics at

[1] S Forman, 'Foreword' in David M Malone and Yuen Foong Khong (eds), *Unilateralism and U.S. Foreign Policy: International Perspectives* (Lynne Rienner 2003); J Lehman, 'Unilateralism in International Law: A United States-European Symposium' (2000) 11 European Journal of International Law 1.

[2] David M Malone and Yuen Foong Khong, 'Unilateralism and U.S. Foreign Policy: International Perspectives' in David M Malone and Yuen Foong Khong (eds), *Unilateralism and U.S. Foreign Policy: International Perspectives* (Lynne Rienner 2003) 3; Similarly, Monica Hakimi, 'Unfriendly Unilateralism' (2014) 55 Harvard International Law Journal 105, 111.

[3] Duncan B Hollis, 'Why State Consent Still Matters—Non-State Actors, Treaties, and the Changing Sources of International Law' (2005) 23 Berkeley Journal of International Law 137.

[4] James C Hathaway, 'America, Defender of Democratic Legitimacy?' (2000) 11 European Journal of International Law 121, 123.

EU Law and Economics. Armin Steinbach, Oxford University Press. © Oxford University Press 2025.
DOI: 10.1093/9780198920915.003.0012

work when states determine their policy course, which is relevant for differentiated integration.

On a theoretical level, non-consensualism for our purposes captures the difference between the number of states and membership, in our case between EU states and those who actually participate in integration while being EU members. As Keremone and others emphasize, the number of states refers to the exogenous feature of the policy issue concerned.[5] The number of states refers to the set of states interested in participating in cooperation. In many, not all, issue areas, the natural default would be to consider cooperation among all EU members. By being EU members, there is a presumption that all members will participate in the full integration programme of the Treaties as well as in enhanced cooperation. However, we discuss various forms of non-consensualism, that is, where EU members do not consent to the same pace of integration. This can be determined through EU primary law by way of Treaty opt-outs; it can occur through Treaty-based variability in integration, notably through 'enhanced cooperation' between a subgroup of EU members as 'a last resort' when cooperation is not feasible among the EU as a whole (Article 20 TEU); variable pace can also be channelled through *inter-se* agreements sidelining EU law with EU members acting in their traditional international law sovereignty outside of the supranational architecture; and differentiation finally is a common feature during crises, with the euro crisis as an illustrative example of variable forms of cooperation. Our hypothesis is that non-consensualism varies according to multiple factors, mostly due to interests, preferences, variable gains associated with cooperation, but also due to relative power between EU members enabling powerful countries to craft agreements in their favour. These differences in terms of preferences, implementation, and power imbalances determine the degree of asymmetry between parties, a relevant factor in the game-theoretic analysis of parties to cooperation.

a) EU Treaty opt-out

In the context of international agreements, the practice of Treaty reservations is widespread under international law.[6] By contrast, the founding Treaty of Rome foresaw few special protocols and derogations for individual countries. It was only the Treaty of Maastricht that gave differentiated integration—that is, the adoption of EU norms that do not bind all EU members—a Treaty basis. It introduced the innovation of allowing some Member States not to fully participate in the Economic

[5] Barbara Koremenos, Charles Lipson and Duncan Snidal, 'The Rational Design of International Institutions' (2001) 55 International Organization 761, 777.

[6] Eric Neumayer, 'Qualified Ratification: Explaining Reservations to International Human Rights Treaties' (2007) 36 Journal of Legal Studies 397; John King Gamble, 'Reservations to Multilateral Treaties: A Macroscopic View of State Practice' (1980) 74 American Journal of International Law 372.

and Monetary Union. Opt-outs were granted to the UK and Denmark, but these were intended as only temporary exceptions.[7] Likewise, Ireland and Denmark invoked exceptions in the domain of core state powers in Justice and Home Affairs, releasing these states from the binding effect of some but not all EU policies, such as the directives defining the rights of asylum seekers.[8]

Original signatory states crafting a new Treaty often face substantial costs in the process of Treaty negotiation and drafting whereas the costs of accession to an existing Treaty can be ambiguous: accession to an existing Treaty may incur less bargaining costs (in the EU because the *acquis communautaire* is not negotiable upon accession), while the sovereignty costs of the acceding state may be substantial due to the indispensable requirement of implementing the *acquis communautaire* into domestic law, that is, incorporating the entire body of EU law. Acceding states are not able to submit reservations to the vast amount of pre-established written and unwritten rules. Potentially, transitional applications of the *acquis communautaire* through an agreed timetable have been granted but the general principle is that no discriminatory membership in the EU is permitted.

The few special protocols and derogations for single countries introduced with the EEC Treaty notwithstanding,[9] opt-outs do exist but are scarce. This contrasts with the practice under international law: Article 21 of the Vienna Convention is the international law metric on how content and participation of Treaties can deviate from the principle of equal content applicable to all signatories. Reservations to a Treaty at the time of accession or ratification create multiple bilateral implications and transform the international agreement between the reserving state and non-reserving states. The reservation reduces the commitment level of the Treaty to the level agreed to by these two states. The economic perspective on these flexibility-increasing Treaty elements is mixed. It has been argued that reservations, just as exit clauses and escape clauses, increase states' willingness to enter into agreements.[10] However, an increase in one state's willingness to enter an agreement corresponds to a decrease in the value of the agreement to the other party accepting the reservation, lowering that party's incentive to join the agreement.

The law and economics literature has devoted attention to Article 21 of the Vienna Convention, and some of this analysis is of interest to the EU. It was shown that Article 21 tilts the balance in favour of high-cost and low-benefit states who can take advantage of the reciprocity mechanism. High-costs refer to Treaty

[7] Thomas Beukers and Marijn van der Sluis, 'Differentiated Integration from the Perspective of Non-Euro Area Member States' in Thomas Beukers, Bruno de Witte, and Claire Kilpatrick (eds), *Constitutional Change through Euro-Crisis Law* (Cambridge University Press 2017) 14.

[8] Bruno de Witte, 'The Law as Tool and Constraint of Differentiated Integration', in Mark Dawson and Markus Jachtenfuchs (eds), *Autonomy without Collapse in a Better European Union* (Oxford University Press 2022).

[9] Dominik Hanf, 'Flexibility Clauses in the Founding Treaties, from Rome to Nice' in Bruno de Witte, Dominik Hanf, and Ellen Vos (eds), *The Many Faces of Differentiation in EU Law* (Intersentia 2001).

[10] Laurence R Helfer, 'Exiting Treaties' (2005) 91 Virginia Law Review 1579.

implementation and compliance costs and low-benefits to the gains from fulfilment of the international obligations—poorer or developing states often face a high-cost and low-benefit combination.[11] In line with that literature, poorer countries with high implementation costs have a comparatively strong position in multilateral Treaty-setting, because they can ask for cost-reducing side concessions (provided that power imbalances are not at play).[12] The practice of international Treaty law suggests that international agreements accommodate this situation by implementing various levels of Treaty obligations: for example, under WTO law, developing countries enjoy a preferential scheme; under climate change agreements, developed countries must undertake greater climate change mitigation efforts and offer side-payments to less developed countries; and under the Montreal Protocol on Ozone-Depleting Substances, developed countries had to subsidize the developing countries' compliance costs.

One plausible explanation for the absence of treaty reservations as common features under EU law may be the higher homogeneity among members in the EU compared to the level of international treaty law. The theory suggests that the more symmetric countries are in terms of preferences, costs, and implementation, the more similar a country's payoff function of cooperation is. As a result, there is less need for reservations and they are more likely to align at the same level of Treaty obligations.[13] In the game-theoretic perspective, opt-out strategies under EU law, as well as reservations under international Treaty law, imply the same strategic behaviour. During Treaty negotiation, in general, rational states anticipate that other states may potentially draw on Article 21 of the Vienna Convention, and by doing so lower the content level of the Treaty. This provision leads to matching reservations through reciprocity. The reciprocity mechanism in Treaty reservations disincentivizes strategic unilateral reservations, because they would engender mutual losses for all states involved, which is not a dominant strategy given a country's payoff function. With reciprocity prevailing, each state would only lower their Treaty commitment leading to an overall inferior outcome for all parties. Hence, in the case of *symmetric* states with homogenous interests, full Treaty commitment becomes the equilibrium strategy for both states.[14] The matching effects of Treaty reservations furthers levels of Treaty ratification that are higher than those that they would otherwise adopt in a Nash equilibrium.[15]

[11] Francesco Parisi and Vincy Fon, *The Economics of Lawmaking* (Oxford University Press 2008) 52, 268.

[12] This contrasts with bilateral Treaty settings such as bilateral investment treaties, in which power imbalances between larger and smaller states are significant, see Deborah L Swenson, 'Why Do Developing Countries Sign BITs?' in Karl P Sauvant and Lisa E Sachs (eds), *The Effect of Treaties on Foreign Direct Investment* (Oxford University Press New York 2009).

[13] Andrew T Guzman, 'The Consent Problem in International Law' (2012) 52 Virginia Journal of International Law 747; Parisi and Fon (n 11) 246.

[14] Jack L Goldsmith and Eric A Posner, *The Limits of International Law* (Oxford University Press 2006) 23, 243.

[15] Parisi and Fon (n 11) 245.

In turn, incentives to request Treaty reservations are different when participating states are different. The reciprocity-based matching-reservation mechanism does not work when states face *asymmetric* incentives. Asymmetry—that is, diverse preferences, different implementation costs, significant power imbalances—invites unilateral reservations. Asymmetry implies heterogeneity causing states to have different cost-benefit ratios from Treaty implementation. The difference in Treaty bargaining among symmetric states is that asymmetry of states leads to different payoff functions which feeds into varying preferences for levels of Treaty ratification. The commitment level under the Treaty is determined by the marginal benefit under matching reservations and the marginal cost at full ratification. Heterogeneity in payoff functions may, for example, play out in the EU when some acceding Eastern European members find it difficult to comply with the high rule-of-law standards in the EU, which imply costly domestic policy changes. Asymmetry may also be caused by power imbalances, where powerful countries can more impose their preferences, because their outside options are simply wider, and they can pursue their objectives through unilateral action or intergovernmental agreements outside of EU law.

Importantly, asymmetry causes a lower Treaty content level, and it is the highest-cost states, the ones for whom Treaty implementation is particularly costly, who are responsible for this. Parisi and Fon have shown that the highest-costs states, unlike average-cost states, do not need to accept undesired reservations from other states. Through the reciprocity logic of Article 21 of the Vienna Convention, the highest-cost states effectively determine the Treaty commitment level and attain their optimal Treaty terms in all bilateral Treaty relations with other states.[16] This bears consequences for the preferred mode of cooperation. While some multilateral approaches introduce flexibility through differentiation (eg WTO rules), the trend towards regionalization and bilateralization highlights that Treaty membership is increasingly sought among homogenous states. Non-multilateralism means the downsizing of participation towards greater homogeneity in payoff functions (and thus higher Treaty commitment levels). In turn, the reciprocity mechanism under Article 21 of the Vienna Convention ensures the social optimum only in cases where the members face homogenous payoff functions, or when all states prefer full ratification.

What implications can we draw from this literature for the EU? The core 'Westphalian' legal premises of reciprocity and sovereign rights to cooperate are the same principles undergirding both EU and international law. The logic of Article 21 of the Vienna Convention also applies to the EU, yet reservations are empirically more widespread in international law. This difference appears largely as a result of asymmetry—for example, diverse preferences or differences in costs

[16] ibid 265.

of compliance with the agreement. With greater homogeneity across the EU in terms of economic performance and cultural proximity, there is less likelihood for opt-outs to occur. However, cases exist where discrepancies are insurmountable and lead to opt-outs. The UK abstention from social policies, laid down in a social protocol attached to the TEU and prompted by the dogmatically partisan view of the British Conservative government reflected deeply divergent views on social matters.[17] Similarly, currency matters concern core sovereign issues and the UK and Danish opt-out can be interpreted as emphasizing the fundamental division between the euro-area and non-euro-area Member States as reflected in both the institutional and substantive norms of EMU constitutional law. Likewise, Justice and Home Affairs is widely viewed as the domain of core state powers.

A further particularity of the EU compared to the wider international community is the EU's ability to bridge heterogeneity in one Treaty area by cross-compensation. From an economic perspective, there may be an effective side-payment mechanism in place in the EU that would not be available for field-specific international agreements. 'Side-payments' allow Member States to account for a cross-subsidization of treaties by offering concessions to a reluctant state in an area other than the one from which the country wishes to opt-out. Compensatory side-payments may level out heterogenous preferences or may compensate high-cost states. The availability of side-payments as an instrument for levelling out a country's different payoff function in relation to one area of cooperation (eg EU agricultural policy, internal market obligations) highlights a difference between EU law and international law: international agreements are in most cases made for specific subject areas (eg international trade, climate mitigation, and human rights). Their subject-specificity limits the scope for side-payments. Side-payments may exist in some areas—think of the WTO 'single undertaking' approach allowing cross-sectoral side-payments—but for international agreements they are typically not only limited in substance but also institutionally, because international organizations rarely deviate from the one-country-one-vote principle in terms of voting rights or member representation. This is different in the EU: the scope of policy fields in the EU is much larger and gives leeway to the coupling of unrelated concessions as side-payments. For example, a special protocol attached to Ireland's accession to the EU ensures that it will benefit from financial transfers, while Finland was granted favourable treatment under the European Regional Development Fund in order to provide support for its Arctic agricultural region.[18] In addition, the EU, as a supranational construct, is built on an institutional architecture that accommodates structural differences between EU members. One obvious example of institutionally favouring high-cost smaller states

[17] Françoise de La Serre and Helen Wallace, 'Flexibility and Enhanced Cooperation in the European Union: Placebo Rather than Panacea?' (1997) Research and Policy, Papers No 2, 9.
[18] Ibid.

over larger states is the allocation of voting rights in the Council and the allocation of seats in the European Parliament, which are biased in favour of smaller EU members.[19] High-cost countries can be enticed into the EU, despite heterogeneity, through structural advantages in the decision-making architecture. What is scarce under international Treaty law—the availability of side-payments as a mechanism for smoothing the heterogeneity of preferences and levelling out differences between high-cost and low-cost states—is plenty in a European Union that allows side deals and concessions across a wide portfolio of issue areas.

From a behavioural economics perspective, we can further say that 'ambiguity aversion' can be used to explain why opt-outs are chosen, especially when a rational choice analysis suggests that an equilibrium should favour multilateral cooperation due to cooperation gains. This is because actors are ambiguity-averse when probabilities cannot be easily predicted, hence they prefer known outcomes over unknown ones. The degree of uncertainty in EMU matters during the crafting of the Maastricht Treaty was considerable, and the sovereignty costs for the UK were high, as it was asked to abandon a stable currency. While opting-out from the common currency upheld heterogeneity and higher transaction costs due to currency exchanges, any substantial change (going beyond informal exchanges) would create uncertainty about the applicable concept of price stability; hence, the effect of loss aversion is exacerbated. This loss aversion may play out differently in other situations. While Germany feared the threat of losing a stable and dominant currency, side-payments in other fields of EU integration (eg an extended internal market and fiscal rules) attenuated this effect.

b) Differentiating integration

Treaty opt-outs are one form of non-consensualism, but with the Amsterdam, Nice, and Lisbon conferences, the prospect of enlargement with a large number of new states engendered a broader debate on differentiated or 'multi-speed' integration. At the end of the nineties, a general conviction among EU members emerged that the Treaty framework should be further developed in order to allow for 'institutional flexibility' or 'closer cooperation'. The Nice Treaty text allowed for what was now named 'enhanced cooperation' to be launched by a qualified majority vote in the Council, except in common foreign and security policy. However, it was only with the adoption of the Lisbon Treaty that a formal framework for variable geometry through the enhanced cooperation mechanism was established.[20]

[19] Jonathan Rodden, 'Strength in Numbers?' (2002) 3 European Union Politics 151.

[20] Daniela A Kroll and Dirk Leuffen, 'Enhanced Cooperation in Practice. An Analysis of Differentiated Integration in EU Secondary Law' (2015) 22 Journal of European Public Policy 353.

Enhanced cooperation has been implemented five times to date; it is rare but feasible. The first instance concerned the regulation of transnational divorces. The second was the creation of a new EU patent system, agreed following a controversy in which Italy and Spain opposed EU-wide participation due to disagreement over the language regime. The third instance concerned the twin regulations on judicial cooperation in matters of matrimonial property and registered partnership property. The fourth was the financial transaction tax, which obtained Council approval for enhanced cooperation (but was never put in effect). The fifth instance saw twenty-two Member States supporting the creation of the European Public Prosecutors Office.

While enhanced cooperation takes place *within* the EU legal order, there are outside options available to EU members by resorting to international law agreements sidelining the EU institutional structure. Traditionally, legal scholarship has looked with mistrust on (bilateral) treaties between Member States, perceiving them as possible threats to the EU legal order, at least when they addressed issues that formed part of or were related to the EU legal order, applied to some (not all) Member States ('partial agreements'), and did not use the EU institutions.[21] However, Member States resorting to international agreements outside the EU legal order is in itself nothing new.[22] Past *inter se* agreements include instruments such as the Schengen framework or the Prüm Convention, in the area of justice and home affairs, and the Social Policy Agreement. In these cases, a group of Member States decided to push integration further through an instrument of international law.[23] In a sense, one could say that this form of flexibility has existed since the early days of the European integration process. Hundreds of bilateral and multilateral international treaties have been concluded between Member States of the European Union since the 1950s in areas such as tax law, environmental protection, defence, culture, and education. They typically occur in areas in which the European Union has no law-making competence at all, but also occur in areas in which the EU possesses shared law-making competences, where a set of Member States prefer to use their 'share' to conclude an agreement among themselves rather than acting within the framework of the European Union.

These *inter se* agreements become a true alternative form of variable geometry when they serve the purpose of allowing a group of Member States to move European integration forward in the face of opposition from other Member States. More recently, *inter se* agreements between Member States reflect a general trend of intergovernmentalism, propelled by the euro crisis.[24] While a number

[21] Steve Peers, 'Towards a New Form of EU Law? The Use of EU Institutions Outside the EU Legal Framework' (2013) 9 European Constitutional Law Review 37, 40.

[22] See also Bruno de Witte, 'Using International Law in the Euro Crisis: Causes and Consequences' (2013) Arena Working Paper No 4.

[23] Alicia Hinarejos, *The Euro Area Crisis in Constitutional Perspective* (Oxford University Press 2015) 90.

[24] ibid 111; Kenneth A Armstrong, *Governing Social Inclusion* (Oxford University Press 2010) 67.

of reforms to the architecture of EMU have been carried out in the framework of EU law, the Member States have decided to act to a large extent outside the EU legal order, tightening budgetary constraints, establishing new mechanisms of financial stability, and setting up a framework for economic adjustment for countries in fiscal trouble. This has been done notably through the Treaties establishing the European Financial Stability Facility (EFSF) and the European Stability Mechanism (ESM), both of which (like the stability Treaty) aim to supplement the EU law measures on EMU.[25] There was controversy surrounding these 'peripherical agreements', particularly regarding the role of intergovernmentalism as the driving force behind them.[26] This strategy is consistent with an intergovernmental model for the management of the euro crisis, which has stressed the centrality of national governments (in the European Council) and their freedom to act through agreements outside EU law, rather than the centrality of the EU institutional machinery and the potential of EU law to address the crisis.[27] However, the limits of intergovernmentalism in managing the euro crisis effectively and legitimately have been repeatedly emphasized.[28]

Our inquiry aims to explain the use of differentiated integration. Scholars in the international relations[29] and international law[30] literature have emphasized that reducing complexity is a rationale to explain non-multilateralism in international relations. Similar considerations apply for differentiated integration in the European Union. From an economic perspective, the act of abandoning full participation of EU members in favour of 'enhanced cooperation' or even extra-EU intergovernmental approaches responds to the state's individual benefits and costs involved in the bargaining process. In order to achieve welfare gains through cooperation, a welfare improvement requires parties to negotiate on how to compensate for losses by balancing out the gains and losses incurred by different parties. With the increasing number of participating states, the transaction costs on determining a compensation solution increase, impeding compensation solutions. Exempting those states who have a payoff function that does not allow sufficient

[25] Steve Peers, 'Towards a New Form of EU Law? The Use of EU Institutions Outside the EU Legal Framework' (2013) 9 European Constitutional Law Review 37, 39; Fabian Amtenbrink and Menelaos Markakis, 'Never Waste a Good Crisis On the Emergent EU Fiscal Capacity' in Alicia Hinarejos and Robert Schütze (eds), *EU Fiscal Federalism* (Oxford University Press 2023), 183.

[26] Bruno de Witte, 'Using International Law in the Euro Crisis: Causes and Consequences' (2013) Arena Working Paper No 4.

[27] Federico Fabbrini, *Economic Governance in Europe* (Oxford University Press 2016) 110. See also Michele Messina, 'Strengthening Economic Governance of the European Union through Enhanced Cooperation: A Still Possible, but Already Missed, Opportunity' (2014) 39 European Law Review 404, 404.

[28] Edoardo Chiti and Pedro Gustavo Teixeira, 'The Constitutional Implications of the European Responses to the Financial and Public Debt Crisis' (2013) 50 Common Market Law Review 683, 683.

[29] James A Caporaso, 'International Relations Theory and Multilateralism: The Search for Foundations' (1992) 46 International Organization 599, 611.

[30] Andrew Guzman and Beth A Simmons, 'To Settle or Empanel? An Empirical Analysis of Litigation and Settlement at the World Trade Organization' (2002) 31 Journal of Legal Studies 205.

matches with the group of states pursuing closer integration facilitates an agreement. Accordingly, 'enhanced cooperation' allows for varied membership enabling like-minded states to work together separately from a more heterogenous group.

Differentiation can likewise be suitable for dealing with the sensitivity of a given policy subject. The integration of core state powers—such as defence, interior, monetary, and fiscal policies—has led to durable differentiated integration. Distributional and sovereignty concerns have been particularly salient drivers of variable geometry in the EMU (euro membership, ESM, and the Fiscal Compact).[31] In this sense, differentiation serves to overcome the incompatibility of heterogeneity of preferences and unanimity in decision-making, as collective decisions become infeasible unless qualified majority voting prevails.[32] The Schengen experience is still referred to as another model offering an example of both the potential of such agreements to overcome a blockage within the Union's decision-making system, and the possibility for their later re-integration within the EU legal system.

With the pooling of homogenous preferences leading to multispeed integration, negotiations and compensations can more easily be bartered in differentiated settings. As illustrated above with Treaty opt-outs, asymmetric countries as parties to the Treaty bear the risk of Treaty reservations, leading to a lower commitment level to the Treaty content. This supports the idea that countries with more aligned policy preferences are likely to agree on more ambitious Treaty commitments. On this basis, one may, though with an element of speculation, classify past instances of differentiated integration: 'enhanced cooperation' in transnational divorces was only possible between eighteen EU members because some countries had concerns that this law would lead to the recognition of same-sex marriages as well-registered partnerships, in countries where they do not exist—clearly a culturally sensitive issue involving high political costs. Enhanced cooperation on patents was supported by near-to-full membership of twenty-five members, while cooperation on the European prosecutor concerned the sensitive issue of criminal law, a core sovereignty issue. In turn, the *inter se* agreements on EMU affairs are more illustrative of the very heterogenous effects of the sovereign debt crisis on euro members. In any case, in all these areas, like-minded countries have agreed to differentiated but higher Treaty commitments and were thus able to achieve equilibria that were easier to attain than a full membership agreement. It is not surprising that, while the initial EEC Treaty with six founding members contained some protocols, it

[31] Frank Schimmelfennig and Thomas Winzen, *Ever Looser Union?* (Oxford University Press 2020); Philipp Genschel, Markus Jachtenfuchs, and Marta Migliorati, 'Differentiated Integration as Symbolic Politics? Constitutional Differentiation and Policy Reintegration in Core State Powers' (2023) 24 European Union Politics 81.

[32] Philipp Genschel and Markus Jachtenfuchs, 'Introduction: Beyond Market Regulation. Analysing the European Integration of Core State Powers' in Philipp Genschel and Markus Jachtenfuchs (eds), *Beyond the Regulatory Polity?* (Oxford University Press 2013).

was only in the aftermath of Maastricht and with ensuing rounds of accessions, that heterogeneity in the EU raised inevitably to a level where enhanced cooperation and *inter se* agreements became more frequent.

Differentiation is often also the outcome even if overall welfare gains would propagate an agreement with full membership. As discussed above, failure to reach undifferentiated integration may be multifold, even if less prevalent in the EU compared to international law. The positive correlation of bargaining costs and number of participants is straightforward, as is the correlation between bargaining and length of an agreement;[33] heterogeneity leads to divergent preferences that engender different payoff structures, which may be hard to reconcile through compensation in unrelated policy fields (even in the EU[34]); the complexity of a matter may increase bargaining costs to a level exceeding cooperation gains;[35] but the opportunity costs of pursuing 'enhanced cooperation' (compared to full participation) are not too high as any non-participating EU member is able to join the cooperation at any stage (Article 331 TFEU). More generally, in order for European cooperation to be successful, the outcome of two games must overlap—within the logic of Putnam's two-level game involving complexity. At the national level, domestic groups pursue their interests by pressuring the government to adopt favourable policies, and politicians seek power by constructing coalitions among those groups. At the international level, national governments seek to maximize their own ability to satisfy domestic pressures, while minimizing the adverse consequences of foreign developments.[36] The negotiators thus need to address the concerns of domestic interest groups and, at the same time, reach an agreement that is acceptable for the parties to the international Treaty. As every EU Member State government has to cope with a different domestic policy situation, the success of full participation of all EU members is far from obvious.

To this one may add behavioural economic idiosyncrasies in domestic policy contexts. Consider that behavioural economics adopts a perspective emphasizing that 'framing' of the policy decision is important. This means that individuals may exist in a framework as employees, not as consumers (as suggested by economists to capture consumer rents); or as national citizens with selfish interests, not as Europeans with a common interest; or as 'netpayers', not viewing the positive spillovers from EU transfers for the EU as a whole. Framed accordingly, loss aversion may play an important role, given that some groups may lose from policy changes while the benefits are distributed more broadly. Loss aversion plays out forcefully

[33] James D Fearon, 'Bargaining, Enforcement, and International Cooperation' (1998) 52 International Organization 269.

[34] Joel P Trachtman, *The Economic Structure of International Law* (Harvard University Press 2008) 72, 187.

[35] Eric Posner and Alan O Sykes, *Economic Foundations of International Law* (Harvard University Press 2013) 23.

[36] Robert D Putnam, 'Diplomacy and Domestic Politics: The Logic of Two-Level Games' (1988) 42 International Organization 427, 434.

when entire nations are framed as losers—in relation to differentiated integration, take for example the dogmatically partisan view of the British Conservative government during a pre-electoral period which led to the categorical refusal of the Major government to accept any social provisions in the TEU.[37] This led to the British opt-out on social policies. Differentiated integration may be triggered by powerful national policy groups making national idiosyncrasies salient, giving rise to loss aversions.

Differentiated integration concerning weakest-link public goods may follow a different economic rationale. Take the Schengen Agreement that abolished internal borders in the EU. Security in this case is a weakest-link public good because it is only ensured if all states participate at sufficiently high commitment levels. If one country fails to contribute, it threatens the value of the public good for all other countries. Why has Schengen been concluded as a differentiated agreement (first outside EU law as an *inter se* agreement, then integrated in the EU framework)? If cooperation depends on an equilibrium of universal compliance, it may be appropriate to exclude states that are relatively impatient and therefore less reliable in maintaining a sufficient level of compliance with the agreement.[38] The Schengen Agreement excludes countries with external borders that are exposed to a risk of uncontrolled migration (Ireland, Croatia, Romania, Bulgaria, and Cyprus). Uncertainty regarding the preferences and abilities of some members to contribute to the good suggests that it might be wise to exclude them.[39] Cooperation in weakest-link public goods declines with the number of states, as the cost of monitoring increases and the probability of a weakest link rises. It is thus not rational to organize Schengen across all EU members as long as some countries have limited enforcement and compliance capacities.

Like Schengen, the introduction of the euro has limited membership, as the stability of the common currency area is maintained only by the compliance of all states, with one country defecting potentially causing significant negative spillover for the currency stability as public good—as the euro crisis and the case of Greece has shown. Given the risks for the public good, current members of the currency must ensure that new members have a sufficiently credible level of future compliance. Entry conditions to euro membership are thus parameters that signal sufficient commitment and minimize risk of spillovers: stable price levels, sound public finances, exchange rate stability, and stable long-term interest rates. Both Schengen and euro membership are hence organized as club goods—benefits are excludable, thus facilitating cooperative equilibrium.[40] As stability of the common currency

[37] de la Serre and Wallace (n 17) 9.

[38] Joel P Trachtman, 'Economics of International Organizations' in Francesco Parisi (ed), *The Oxford Handbook of Law and Economics: Volume 3: Public Law and Legal Institutions*, vol 1 (Oxford University Press 2017) 520.

[39] Barbara Koremenos, Charles Lipson, and Duncan Snidal, 'The Rational Design of International Institutions' (2001) 55 International Organization 761.

[40] James M Buchanan, 'An Economic Theory of Clubs' (1965) 32 Economica 1.

has a weakest-link public good character, participating states set high conditionality thresholds in order to ensure a sufficient degree of alignment in preferences and commitment to maintaining currency stability—differentiated integration is the consequence of selective entry requirements for joining the club.

In sum, reservations and differentiation exist under EU law, though it is much less widespread than under international law. A core explanation for this difference likely lies in greater homogeneity, less asymmetry between European states. This may have multiple roots: a shared set of values, greater similarity in socioeconomic conditions and implementation costs, and lower power imbalances. Under these conditions, the reciprocity logic under Article 21 of the Vienna Convention also applies in the European context, widening the range of mutually agreeable levels of Treaty ratification. Occasionally, differentiated integration remains the preferred mode of cooperation as a way of pooling homogenous preferences leading to multispeed integration, helping to overcome high negotiation costs or lack of side-payments that would ensure cross-policy compensation of policy-specific losses.

13
Legislative choices

Rational legislation has been a fertile topic of research for legal theorists,[1] constitutional lawyers,[2] economic scholars,[3] and political scientists.[4] This scholarship has produced a plethora of normative benchmarks as to what characterizes rational legislation, such as consistency, legitimacy, efficiency, and effectiveness. For the purpose of this analysis, we are interested in the legislative techniques for determining the legislative competences in multilevel governance of the EU, as the ongoing process of unification of many areas of law poses the question of choice among alternative legislative instruments. By building on the above discussion of the optimal level of allocating competences between the EU and Member States, safeguarded in primary law through the principles of conferral and subsidiarity, the process of EU integration has engendered different legal instruments for the EU to use to implement EU law. Specifically, primary law lays out the instruments at hand for the EU to legislate, with regulations and directives as the main tools for rule-setting in the EU. In turn, the principle of 'mutual recognition' was developed initially as ECJ adjudication and was later reinforced through legislation, which determined the extent to which Member States must accept in their legal orders the application of regulatory choice by other Member States. The underlying notion of rules competition is one that accepts certain legislative diversity and as such differs from harmonization as a legislative technique.

[1] Luc J Wintgens, 'Rationality in Legislation—Legal Theory as Legisprudence: An Introduction' in Luc J Wintgens (ed), *Legisprudence: A New Theoretical Approach to Legislation* (Hart Publishing 2002) 1; A Daniel Oliver-Lalana, 'Legitimacy through Rationality: Parliamentary Argumentation as Rational Justification of Laws' in Luc J Wintgens (ed), *The Theory and Practice of Legislation* (Routledge 2005) 248.

[2] Kaarlo Tuori, 'Legislation Between Politics and Law "in LJ Wintgens"' in Luc J Wintgens (ed), *Legisprudence: A New Theoretical Approach to Legislation* (Hart Publishing 2002) 105; Susan Rose-Ackerman, Stefanie Egidy, and James Fowkes, *Due Process of Lawmaking: The United States, South Africa, Germany, and the European Union* (Cambridge University Press 2015) 17.

[3] Gerd Gigerenzer, *Bounded Rationality: The Adaptive Toolbox* (The MIT Press 2002); See also Herbert A Simon, *Reason in Human Affairs* (Stanford University Press 1983) 19. On the legislator's bounded rationality, see Luc J Wintgens, 'The Rational Legislator Revisited. Bounded Rationality and Legisprudence' in Luc J Wintgens and A Daniel Oliver-Lalana (eds), *The Rationality and Justification of Legislation: Essays in Legisprudence* (Springer 2013) 14.

[4] Dennis C Mueller, *Public Choice II* (Cambridge University Press 1989) 1; David Mayhew, *Congress: The Electoral Connection* (Yale University Press 2004).

EU Law and Economics. Armin Steinbach, Oxford University Press. © Oxford University Press 2025.
DOI: 10.1093/9780198920915.003.0013

a) Directives versus regulations

EU secondary law offers legislative choice mainly between regulations and directives. Legal scholarship has focused on descriptive accounts of systematic proliferation, bindingness, and legal consequences attached to these instruments. However, with lawyers typically not being concerned with the *why* of certain legal choices (see above Chapter 1), legal scholarship has not provided an analytical approach to explain why Union institutions employ a given legal instrument in different circumstances.[5]

Both regulations and directives are binding with the key differences being that the former is 'binding, as to the result to be achieved, . . . but shall leave to the national authorities the choice of form and methods', whereas the latter 'shall be binding in its entirety and directly applicable in all Member States' (Article 288 TFEU). Directives allow Member States some leeway in how they implement them into domestic law, while regulations are directly applicable without further Member State contribution. The EU Treaties either prescribe which instrument can be used in pursuit of a given policy objective, or in other cases the Commission's discretionary legislative choice is bound by the principles of subsidiarity and proportionality (Article 296 TFEU).

Exploring the legislative choice, we can draw from theoretical and empirical law and economic scholarship. The theoretical strand allows us to connect our inquiry to the debate concerning the choice between 'standards' and 'rules'—a well explored distinction in the law and economics literature.[6] Drawing from that literature, we can conceptualize the law-maker as making investment decisions which come at present law-making costs but generate benefits in the future. A cost-benefit analysis helps evaluate the optimal degree of specificity in laws and the capability of rules and standards to deal with uncertainty. *Rules* are specific legal commands: they offer a clear benchmark to distinguish legal from illegal behaviour. *Standards* are criteria and principles, they are vague and unclear, giving guidance to the judiciary and administration.[7] A standard is a legal criterion that rule enforcers or adjudicators use to judge actions under particular circumstances. Being open-ended, they allow administrators and adjudicators to make fact-specific determinations and often entail discretion.[8] The principal choice between

[5] Jürgen Bast, 'On the Grammar of EU Law: Legal Instruments' (2003) Jean Monnet Working Paper 9/03; Annegret Engel, *The Choice of Legal Basis for Acts of the European Union: Competence Overlaps, Institutional Preferences, and Legal Basis Litigation* (Springer 2018).

[6] Louis Kaplow, 'General Characteristics of Rules', *Encyclopedia of Law and Economics* (National Bureau of Economic Research 1997); Cass R Sunstein, 'Problems with Rules' (1995) 83 California Law Review 953; Hans-Bernd Schaefer, 'Legal Rules and Standards' in Charles K Rowley and Friedrich Schneider (eds), *The Encyclopedia of Public Choice* (Springer 2004) 671.

[7] Louis Kaplow, 'Rules Versus Standards: An Economic Analysis' (1992) 42 Duke Law Journal 557.

[8] Francesco Parisi and Vincy Fon, *The Economics of Lawmaking* (Oxford University Press 2008) 10; Joel P Trachtman, *The Economic Structure of International Law* (Harvard University Press 2008) 51.

rules and standards is determined by the magnitude of the costs associated with the formulation and enforcement of legal norms. Designing specific rules is costly because the optimal design requires the acquisition of information, while the costs of well-designed rules may be preferable to larger operating costs caused by sub-optimal rules later.[9] Rules and standards can be understood as two poles between which the degree of precision of laws may vary. In this dichotomy, EU directives resemble standards, while regulations share the characteristics of rules. With EU directives as equivalent to standards, the implementing Member State, as well as the adjudicating ECJ, enjoy considerable leeway. With EU regulations equivalent to rules, conversely to standards, they prevent Member States and adjudicators from accounting for specific circumstances and curtailing discretionary spaces for national administrations as regulations are directly applicable in Member States' legal orders. When choosing between rules and standards, the legislator must consider when, and at what cost, the rules and standards should be applied to specific situations. Rules (EU directives) tend be suitable to promote certainty and consistency, and to seize judicial economies by minimizing the need to account for case-specific circumstances;[10] standards (EU regulations) give more accuracy in implementation to circumstances, prevent obsolescence of rules, and allow for dynamic adaptation, though they reduce predictability and consistency.[11]

Empirical work has shown that in roughly half of the cases, the Commission makes a discretionary and autonomous decision over the choice of the legal instrument, and by implication, the amount of discretion it grants to Member States to decide on the ways and means to reach a certain policy goal by choosing a directive rather than a regulation.[12] Empirical studies further highlight the factors guiding the Commission's legal instrument choice. One predictable factor is the legacy of prior decisions. The Commission tends to abide by its previous practice. Once it chooses a specific instrument in a given policy area, it will most likely continue using this instrument even if the entire instrument is being replaced. This is in line with a 'historical institutionalism' perspective (see above Chapter 1), one that highlights the stickiness of institutional choices.[13] Pre-existing institutions shape the constraints and opportunities for institutional creation. Moreover, there is a rational choice factor weighing in: the initial choice of either a regulation or a directive influences the expectations of the Member States on the future trajectory of EU law. Stabilizing expectations reduces uncertainty. Replacing regulations with directives would reduce legal certainty and would also increase monitoring costs

[9] Parisi and Fon (n 8) 272.

[10] Kathleen Sullivan, 'The Justices of Rules and Standards' (1992) 106 Harvard Law Review 22.

[11] Kaplow (n 7); Isaac Ehrlich and Richard A Posner, 'An Economic Analysis of Legal Rulemaking' (1974) 3 Journal of Legal Studies 257.

[12] Steffen Hurka and Yves Steinebach, 'Legal Instrument Choice in the European Union' (2021) 59 Journal of Common Market Studies 278.

[13] Paul Pierson, 'Increasing Returns, Path Dependence, and the Study of Politics' (2000) 94 American Political Science Review 251.

on the side of the Commission. In turn, repealing directives by implementing regulations implies switching and implementation costs due to the need to agree on uniform legal standards that would overrule existing national provisions.

Second, the political science literature suggests that there is an indication that the legislative choice is driven by ideological bias in the Commission and the Council. Intuitively, increasing euroscepticism should have led the Commission to offer Member States more leeway in implementing EU legislation. Higher sovereignty costs (as reflected by increased euroscepticism) should lead the Union institutions to favour the directive as the instrument giving more leeway to Member States. Contrary to this, however, it has been observed that the Commission has intensified its use of regulations, hence further minimizing Member States' flexibility.[14] This may be driven by the Commission's genuine desire to preserve the uniform application of EU law across Member States, which naturally considers uneven application of EU law as a threat to the functioning of the internal market,[15] as Member States may be inclined to use leeway to pursue greater legal heterogeneity and to bypass legal constraints to seek rents during implementation.[16]

More generally, the Commission's tendency to respond to euroscepticism with a more uniform and harmonized choice of legislation is also supported by a similar stance adopted by the ECJ. It has been argued that the ECJ tends to adopt an activist approach towards EU directives.[17] The ECJ has continuously narrowed the legislative scope available to Member States in the implementation of directives. In the event of non-fulfilment or poor fulfilment of the implementation obligation, the ECJ has often allowed for directives' direct application within Member States (insofar as their wording allows this). This can be seen as an invitation to the Commission to formulate directives in even more detail. In turn, there have been no ECJ decisions overturning a directive for being too intrusive with Member States' scope of manoeuvre. Moreover, the ECJ obliges national courts to interpret national law in line with directives, even if not yet implemented in domestic law. Finally, if a directive is not implemented in a timely manner or is not implemented satisfactorily, the ECJ can impose fines and require damages from the Member State.

There is a public choice plausibility to the Commission's preference for regulations despite Member States' euroscepticism and to the ECJ turning directives into 'quasi-regulations' through narrowing or even eliminating Member States' leeway. These stances flow directly from the payoff functions of the Commission

[14] Hurka and Steinebach (n 12).

[15] European Parliament and Council, 'Regulation (EU) 2016/679 of the European Parliament and of the Council of 27 April 2016 on the Protection of Natural Persons with Regard to the Processing of Personal Data and on the Free Movement of Such Data, and Repealing Directive 95/46/EC (General Data Protection Regulation)' (2016) 5.

[16] Parisi and Fon (n 8) 23.

[17] D Starr-Deelen and B Deelen, 'The European Court of Justice as a Federator' (1996) 26 Publius: The Journal of Federalism 81, 18.

and the ECJ. Both institutions benefit from the uniform and direct application of EU law, hence precluding Member States diversity in application. As the ECJ holds the monopoly in interpreting EU laws, an extensively applied directive enhances the scope of jurisdiction of the ECJ, just as it extends the Commission's outreach in Member States' legal orders. From a normative perspective, this militates not only against the legally defined order of competence (giving rise to agency costs). An extensive use of regulations may also create allocative inefficiencies where one-size-fits-all legislation fails to account for national prerogatives, circumstances, and preferences. Directives are suitable where national legal systems are heterogenous and where preference diversity exists (other than pertaining to the objectives of the legislative act). In these situations, regulations or 'regulation-like directives' restraining Member States' scope of implementation lead to inefficient harmonization.

b) Mutual recognition

Federalism theory supports the notion of regulatory competition.[18] It predicts favourable outcomes in terms of satisfaction of citizens preferences that result from states competing for the most apt rules.[19] 'Mutual recognition' reinforces this kind of interjurisdictional competition, while harmonization of rules undermines competition. The principle of mutual recognition has been increasingly advocated in the EU starting from the mid-1980s. According to this principle, rules implemented in one Member State must also be lawful in all other Member States.[20] The ECJ applied the principle of mutual recognition for the first time in the cases of *Dassonville*[21] and *Cassis de Dijon*.[22] The *Cassis-de-Dijon* principle corresponds to a market opening mechanism as it requires recognition of foreign regulations. A Member State must allow a product lawfully produced and marketed in another Member State into its own market, unless a prohibition of this product is justified by mandatory requirements, such as health and safety protection. Member States cannot apply regulations to EU goods imported from other EU members if the latter has regulations in place, the objective or effect of which is equivalent to that of the importing country. Only when the regulatory objective or effect are

[18] Gerhard Wagner, 'The Economics of Harmonisation: The Case of Contract Law' (2002) 3 ERA Forum 77, 79; Joel P Trachtman, 'Regulatory Competition and Regulatory Jurisdiction' (2000) 3 Journal of International Economic Law 331.

[19] Bruno S Frey and Alois Stutzer, 'The Role of Direct Democracy and Federalism in Local Power' (2004) Working Paper No 209.

[20] Parisi and Fon (n 8) 54.

[21] Case C-8/74 *Dassonville* (1974) EU:C:1974:82 837.

[22] Case C-120/78 *Rewe-Zentral AG v Bundesmonopolverwaltung für Branntwein* (1979) EU:C:1979:42 0649.

not equivalent can intra-EU trade be restricted.[23] The presumption behind mutual recognition is that all Member States care for their citizens and cannot be assumed to produce (for instance) unsafe or unhealthy products, merely because technical specifications differ.

Hence the principle of mutual recognition plays a pivotal role in the internal market since it ensures free movement of goods (and services) without making it necessary to harmonize national legislation.[24] With a more diverse range of goods and services thus recognized in each Member State, a broader variety of consumer preferences can be satisfied than under harmonized rules. In economic terms, mutual recognition reduces the cost of regulation across states. With competition fostered through recognition of the different regulatory approaches, the overall level of costs is reduced because states aim to deliver the public policy function of regulation at the minimum available cost. Member States minimize their political, constitutional, and cultural costs associated with regulation, while still enjoying the benefit of the regulation being recognized in other Member States. Mutual recognition can be reconciled with constrained forms of harmonization. If harmonization is minimized to the 'essential requirements' of health, safety, environmental, or consumer protection, each Member State remains free to set the desirable level of regulation. Member States are free to regulate more strictly, but mutual recognition (and thus free movement) applies.

The idea of rules competition pushes the equilibrium towards efficiency if certain conditions are met: production factors must be sufficiently mobile to move to cost-efficient jurisdiction, and, likewise, citizens should be responsive in moving to jurisdictions offering regulations aligned with their optimal preferences (eg in terms of product safety). However, rules competition has a Darwinian element, as ineffective or inferior rules are supposed to phase out as they are driven out of the market by superior rules. With rules and jurisdictions more generally being in constant competition across the EU, only the fittest rule survives. While competition between standards may represent a useful deregulation boost in the area of technical standards when consumer protection is secure, the 'competitive forces' become questionable in the area of product-related health, environmental, and consumer protection standards. In the context of economic and social affairs, rules competition gives rise to concerns of a 'race to the bottom', which may lead to losses to overall welfare.[25]

[23] Jacques Pelkmans, 'Mutual Recognition in Goods and Services: An Economic Perspective' in Fiorella Kostoris Padoa Schioppa (ed), *The Principles of Mutual Recognition in the European Integration Process* (Palgrave Macmillan 2005).

[24] Daniel C Esty and Geradin Damien, *Regulatory Competition and Economic Integration. Comparative Perspectives* (Oxford University Press 2001).

[25] Albert Breton, 'The Existence and Stability of Interjurisdictional Competition' in Daphne A Kenyon and John Kincaid (eds), *Competition among States and Local Governments* (The Urban Institute Press 1991) 43. He points at the instability of a 'race to the bottom', 'unless, in the language of international relations "realists", a hegemonic power undertook to prevent the debacle'. ibid 51–52; Catherine Barnard, 'Social Dumping Revisited: Lessons from Delaware' (2000) 25 European Law

The probability of a regulatory downward spiral is minimized under the assumption that, in accordance with the principle of mutual recognition, the product must be offered to consumers at least in accordance with the rules applicable in the country of origin and that mutual recognition requires an *equivalence* test.[26] Only when objectives or effects of regulations in different countries are considered equivalent can the principle of mutual recognition apply. This slows down the race to the bottom. If a state applies lower health and social standards to give its producers an advantage, the equivalency test would fail. When non-equivalence of national regulations leaves mutual recognition unapplicable, the EU can decide to harmonize national legislative provisions in order to ensure free movement of goods and services. The information and enforcement costs caused by the application of the equivalence test therefore reduce the advantage of mutual recognition compared to central harmonization.

c) Harmonization

The EU's competence to harmonize the internal market (Article 114 TFEU) is at odds with the principle of mutual recognition fostering rules competition—unification precludes competition.[27] As discussed above, federalism theory supports harmonization of laws across EU members in situations where homogeneity of preferences prevails (see above Chapter 10 b)). Under these circumstances there will be a welfare-optimal match between the bundle of collective goods supplied through public policy and citizens' preferences. By default, mutual recognition is the preferred mode of regulation because it accommodates a wider range of public policies, hence allowing a better match with diverse preferences, and, from a dynamic efficiency perspective, it serves as a continuous learning process to make sure that laws adapt to changing external circumstances. Adaptability and learning processes are more likely under competition than where all differences have been levelled out in favour of only one legislative option.

With the principle of mutual recognition thus prevailing as the default approach, harmonization is suggested when there is no prior equivalence between objectives of national regulation. Otherwise mutual recognition should apply (see above Chapter 13 b)). The competitive environment created by mutual recognition can be softened through harmonization of minimum standards. This may be justified not only where homogeneity of certain basic preferences suggests so, but

Review 57 (showing the limited plausibility of the 'race to the bottom' argument for social policies in the EU).

[26] Trachtman (n 8) 62.

[27] Gerhard Wagner (n 18) 81.

there may also be externalities, economies of scale, economies of scope at stake.[28] Harmonization is preceded by an EU legislative process to determine which uniform EU minimum quality requirements a product or service must have. In the legislative process, the interests between high-standard providers and low-standard providers must be weighed up. If the high standard prevails, low-standard suppliers will be kept out of the market. As a consequence, the range of product quality is narrowing, and competition is decreasing. If, for example, fireworks from countries with lower safety standards are excluded from the market by EU-wide minimum standards, the preferences of risk-inclined consumers can no longer be served.

The advantage of legal harmonization lies in the transaction cost savings. Uniform legal provisions (or even uniform legal orders) ensure, for example, that cross-border contractual relations are facilitated. Information costs associated with determining the applicable rules are significantly reduced. By contrast, costs arise from negotiating uniform standards, and their implementation, monitoring as well as administrative and judicial enforcement with EU-wide standards across domestic legal orders. Uniform legal standards may in some cases further unleash positive network externalities in the EU; in particular where the value of a product or service increases as more people use it, a wide roll-out of uniform EU standards may create positive effects. For instance, the harmonization of technical and product standards is a straightforward case leveraging the EU market size and giving both EU members as well as third countries an incentive to employ EU standards as network effects are at work.

Harmonization as an alignment process can also be seen where the division of competences between EU and Member States is shifted to an EU-only competence. Consider that homogenous preferences between states may not only justify harmonized laws (in line with federalism theory). With identical preferences and costs of negotiation and drafting, and the same gains from cooperation, Member States may renounce their right of regulation and agree to exclusive EU competence. For example, convergence of interests and preferences in external economic affairs facilitated a Lisbon Treaty reform which expanded EU trade and investment competences. The external dimension of trade affairs has for a long time been an exclusive competence of the EU, while leaving space for Member States pertaining to the field of investment policy. However, the ECJ interpreted the rules such that parallel competences of members and the Union should be excluded in favour of uniform EU standards, because it viewed that members would, for the purpose of

[28] Emanuela Carbonara, Barbara Luppi, and Francesco Parisi, 'Self-Defeating Subsidiarity: An Economic Analysis' (2008) Minnesota Legal Studies Research Paper 1; Joel P Trachtman, 'Economics of International Organizations' in Francesco Parisi (ed), *The Oxford Handbook of Law and Economics: Volume 3: Public Law and Legal Institutions*, vol 1 (Oxford University Press 2017) 58.

'satisfying their own interests', undermine the Union's interests, which is another example of the ECJ urging uniform application of rules (see above Chapter 13 a)).[29]

Since the Treaty changes brought by Lisbon, Article 3(1)(e) TFEU stipulates in conjunction with Article 207(1) TFEU, a comprehensive competence of the common commercial policy. Trade policy is unionized, and Members align on uniform positions when representing their interests before the WTO. Divergences in Member States' policy preferences must be balanced through the internal decision-making procedure between the European Commission in interaction with members' governments. EU-internal homogeneity in preferences regarding trade issues sharply contrasts with heterogeneity in the global context. Therefore, while the impasse on global trade negotiations may be associated with the resistance of a few countries to agree on trade concessions, the sheer number of negotiating countries has exacerbated the bargaining process despite some groupings of like-minded states facilitating negotiations. Needless to say that with each round of EU accessions, the degree of homogeneity of preferences declines. It is plausible to argue that the expansion of the EU is negatively correlated with homogeneity and thus reduces the economic desirability of harmonization.

[29] *Opinion of the Court of 11 November 1975 Opinion given pursuant to Article 228 (1) of the EEC Treaty* (1975) EU:C:1975:145 01355, 1363.

14
Enforcement

Treaties must be enforceable in order to secure gains from cooperation. Enforcement problems occur when actors have incentives to defect from cooperation while others cooperate, notably when free-riding on the cooperation efforts of others is optimal.[1] EU Member States operate in a game-theoretic setting under the constraints of EU law by reaping the highest cooperation gains possible. In a repeated game setting, if reciprocity is the main channel of enforcement, a decentralized mechanism without central adjudication may create a cooperative outcome (it requires that concessions in the agreement are of reciprocal nature). But if reciprocity does not stabilize compliance and when states are uncertain about others' behaviour, they cannot achieve the same mutually beneficial outcomes.[2] Within the leeway offered under EU rules, Member States may be competing for cooperation gains under EU rules creating uncertainty about the conduct of other states.

How precisely enforcement should be designed in the EU depends on the kind of game-theoretic situation at stake. Where the issue area has the characteristics of a coordination problem, in which states have no incentive to defect, there is little need for punishment (see above Chapter 6). In such cases, there is no distributional problem with the agreement in the sense that parties' gains are competitive and mutually exclusive depending on the content of the agreement.[3] Take the coordination of air traffic as an example—all EU Member States have an incentive to coordinate air traffic for safety purposes and efficient management. There is no incentive to defect. A monitoring mechanism may be necessary, but interests are aligned. Similarly, standard-setting in the EU internal market may be another example where preferences are aligned, and sanction-based enforcement is not necessary. While controversies may arise about the standard definitions, particularly which country's standard serves as the role model, all countries benefit from the EU's global weight in standard setting, as illustrated by the 'Brussels effect'.[4] Given the network effects of wider participation, EU members reap benefits from positive

[1] Barbara Koremenos, *The Continent of International Law: Explaining Agreement Design* (Cambridge University Press 2016) 32.

[2] David Kreps, *A Course in Microeconomic Theory* (Princeton University Press 1990).

[3] Barbara Koremenos, Charles Lipson, and Duncan Snidal, 'The Rational Design of International Institutions' (2001) 55 International Organization 761, 775.

[4] Anu Bradford, *The Brussels Effect: How the European Union Rules the World* (Oxford University Press 2019).

EU Law and Economics. Armin Steinbach, Oxford University Press. © Oxford University Press 2025.
DOI: 10.1093/9780198920915.003.0014

network externalities by agreeing to common standards. Free-riding is less of a problem.

By contrast, there may be issue areas prone to prisoner's dilemmas, for which a rule, a detecting agency, and an enforcement agency may be useful. In these situations, the defection of EU members is the most dominant and least efficient strategy. The role of EU law changes the payoffs towards making cooperation the dominant strategy. Domestic commitment problems or time-inconsistency problems are additional destabilizers of cooperation. These occur in situations where the payoffs of cooperation change over time leading actors to deviate from their previously optimal plans.[5] Credible enforcement devices may thus serve as a 'lock-in' tool for certain obligations, thereby enhancing their credibility and stability.[6]

International law, from an economic perspective, has been seen as offering three enforcement channels: *reputation, retaliation, and reciprocity*.[7] Reputation plays out in the EU, with violation of EU rules disclosed and outlawed by the European community. Reciprocity plays out saliently in the international law arena which is short of independent enforcement mechanisms and has inspired economic analysis, though it is less important in the EU as an enforcement mechanism.[8] Reciprocity builds on the Vienna Convention providing that 'a material breach of a bilateral treaty by one of the parties entitles the other to invoke the breach as a ground for terminating the treaty or suspending its operation in whole or in part'. If one country breaches its commitment, another country will revoke its own concessions, with the WTO trade rules incorporating this logic in an exemplary way. This mechanism does not work in the EU, however. There is no legal ground for a reciprocal withdrawal of concessions towards another EU member in response to violations of EU rules. If an EU member breaches its obligations, let's say France discriminating against German imports, the mechanism in the EU is not for Germany to revoke its non-discrimination obligation towards French products but for the Commission to step in, pursue an infringement procedure, and ultimately bring the case before the Court of Justice, at the end of which sanctions can be imposed on France, without reciprocal withdrawal of concessions being in the arsenal of sanctions.

Retaliation is the main channel for enforcement in the EU. The EU offers a unique enforcement architecture making it distinct from the multiple enforcement issues appearing under international law. Take two paradigmatic enforcement

[5] Koremenos (n 1) 33.

[6] Andrew Moravcsik, 'The Origins of Human Rights Regimes: Democratic Delegation in Postwar Europe' (2000) 54 International Organization 217, 220.

[7] However, compliance also decisively depends on the domestic policy context, Joel P Trachtman, *The Economic Structure of International Law* (Harvard University Press 2008) 21; Katerina Linos, 'How Can International Organizations Shape National Welfare States? Evidence from Compliance with European Union Directives' (2007) 40 Comparative Political Studies 547.

[8] Pär Hallström, 'The European Union—From Reciprocity to Loyalty' (1999) 39 Scandinavian Studies in Law 79.

issues under international law: Treaties can be self-enforceable if there is a sufficient threat that defection of one country will trigger retaliation by other states to the agreement. This is most obvious in treaties offering reciprocal concessions, such as those in international trade. In these cases, withdrawal of concessions offers an incentive scheme for parties to comply with the agreement.[9] This differs from universal treaties usually sponsored by the United Nations, of which human rights treaties offer a paradigmatic example of enforcement issues. To start with, human rights treaties reflect a great variation of Member States' commitments due to a diverse array of reservations and declarations that produce a scattered degree of bindingness across parties. Since these treaties are not based on reciprocal concessions but concern the rights of third-party individuals, they lack enforceability.[10]

If the EU had the laws it has but no detection agency (the Commission) and no adjudication agency (the ECJ), payoff from unilateral defection of EU members could in many cases be greater than from mutual cooperation. Self-enforcing cooperation would be at risk. In these situations, the delegation of power to an adjudicating third party serves to enforce mutually beneficial agreements. This does not mean that EU states would have easily given their consent to the enforcement architecture of the EU—the Commission and the ECJ. As the limited availability of administrative enforcement agencies and third-party adjudication in international law demonstrates, there are sensible sovereignty issues limiting states' preparedness to delegate strong coercive capacities to international organizations (see above Chapter 5). Clearly, the capacities of the Commission and the ECJ impose reputational costs on states violating EU law.[11] In most cases states comply with the decisions of the Commission and the Council (eg decisions in state aid or competition cases) or with the legally binding judgments of the ECJ. The value of these institutions is underscored by the literature showing the advantages of strengthening centralized arrangements by a central authority that has the ability to impose sanctions. The wide-reaching information, administrative, and adjudicative powers of Union institutions are likely to detect non-compliant conduct by Member States and thus increase contributions to cooperation, as it increases the value of cooperation for all parties.[12] Importantly, the effect is not only one of compliance *ex post* with the sanctioning decision of the EU institutions. Rather, there is an *ex-ante* chilling effect on defecting behaviour.

It is important to understand why retaliation as an enforcement device works much better under EU law than international law. The peculiar retaliation in the

[9] Robert E Scott and Paul B Stephan, 'Self-Enforcing International Agreements and the Limits of Coercion' (2004) Wisconsin Law Review 551; Beth Simmons, 'Treaty Compliance and Violation' (2010) 13 Annual Review of Political Science 273.

[10] Eric A Posner, 'Human Reciprocity' (2010) John M Olin Program in Law and Economics Working Paper No 537; Emilie M Hafner-Burton and Kiyoteru Tsutsui, 'Human Rights in a Globalizing World: The Paradox of Empty Promises' (2005) 110 American Journal of Sociology 1373.

[11] Koremenos, Lipson and Snidal (n 3) 790.

[12] ibid.

EU responds to a second order collective action problem. Enforcement can only be expected if the benefit of sanctioning the breach of the law exceeds the costs of sanctioning. If a public good is at stake, then there is an incentive for every state to wait for another state to bear the costs of the sanction ('sanctioners' dilemma').[13] The sanctioning country that punishes the country violating international law offers a public good—punishment is almost invariably costly to the punisher, while the benefits of punishment are spread across all members. Enforcement of public goods remains notoriously undersupplied as long as costs of sanctioning are privatized—in the case of this second-order collective action problem, defectors will not be adequately punished. There may be a single country that has a particular interest in punishing the violating country or in deterring third states from breaching international law as a general preventive measure.[14] This country may potentially be a hegemonic power, a country sufficiently large relative to the others that it receives a substantial portion of the benefits from the public good, larger than the entire cost of providing it.[15] In the absence of such a hegemonic provider of the public good, in order to overcome the second-order collective action dilemma, countries should establish an international organization as a third party to carry out punishment and to provide a credible threat of punishment, therefore resulting in an equilibrium of compliance.[16]

The enforcement structure, consisting of the EU Commission as the administrative and detective agency as well as the ECJ as the adjudicating body, is specifically designed to overcome the second-order collective action dilemma. The obligations and sanctions imposed by the Commission (if confirmed by the Court) are owed by the violating Member State to the EU as a whole. Procedurally, this is anchored in Article 259 TFEU—infringements by one Member State cannot only be brought by the Commission but by every Member State, irrespective of whether the violation occurs in the bilateral relationship between the violator and the country directly affected by the breach. This differs fundamentally from the standard under international law in which adjudication is brought by the damaged party only (eg under WTO law).[17] Obligations under EU law thus apply in relation to the entire EU community. This implies that the costs of retaliation are not borne by one

[13] Leslie Johns, 'The Design of Enforcement: Collective Action and the Enforcement of International Law' (2019) 31 Journal of Theoretical Politics 543; Douglas D Heckathorn, 'Collective Action and the Second-Order Free-Rider Problem' (1989) 1 Rationality and Society 78.

[14] Alexander Thompson, 'Coercive Enforcement of International Law' in Jeffrey L Dunoff and Mark A Pollack (eds), *Interdisciplinary Perspectives on International Law and International Relations* (Cambridge University Press 2012) 503.

[15] Duncan Snidal, 'The Limits of Hegemonic Stability Theory' (1985) 39 International Organization 579, 581.

[16] Trachtman (n 7) 519.

[17] Narrow exceptions are *erga omnes* obligations owed to the entire international community, see Christian J Tams, 'Erga Omnes Enforcement Rights and Competing Enforcement Mechanisms' in Christian J Tams (ed), *Enforcing Obligations Erga Omnes in International Law* (Cambridge University Press 2005).

individual Member State but by all Member States because sanctions are imposed on behalf of the whole EU and may lead to the withdrawal of the violator's rights vis-à-vis the entire community (eg monetary fines going to the budget of the EU or the loss of voting rights in the Council).

While under international economic law, small countries often refrain from bringing litigation against large states because they fear that retaliation, such as withdrawing trade concessions could harm their own interests (thus undermining the effectiveness of the trade rules), in the EU the costs of retaliation are centralized and spread across all members. In the EU's centralized arrangement, the Commission (supported by the ECJ) is a 'director' serving as a third-party enforcer who in effect issues a judgement on the deviant player, a sentence that will then be carried out by rational players.[18] As the EU centralizes the provision of information, its value increases with the growing number of Member States. If violation of EU obligations occurs on a bilateral basis (eg by erecting border barriers between two EU neighbours), multilateral cooperation allows an equilibrium where non-cooperation is punished by all other EU members, not just the one that was directly harmed.

But not only can the Commission investigate and find misconduct and impose fines and other sanctions. EU law mobilizes individuals to enforce EU law. EU regulations are directly effective and can be invoked by individuals to invalidate contrary Member State law and give rise to monetary damages. A domestic-law-like judicial system that is entitled to render binding judgments lays the foundation for liability claims of individuals and ultimately inflicting monetary sanctions. Through a system of conditionality, the EU has established effective tools to create incentives for states to comply in areas that would otherwise suffer implementation issues, such as conditional access to financial funds tied to compliance with standards of rule of law or financial assistance conditioned on fiscal prudence. Hence, enforcement costs do not weigh on the retaliating party alone, as the EU Commission distributes these costs of retaliation offering a greater incentive for Member States to actually pursue action against a non-compliant country. For example, if Germany hinders commerce with Luxembourg, under an international law agreement such as the WTO, Luxembourg would be advised not to retaliate against Germany since retaliation would be costly to its own economy, or even worse, it might fear further counterreactions from its big neighbour. Hence, in a decentralized non-EU setting, the reciprocity-based, self-enforcing cooperation would be at risk, as (smaller) states would refrain from sanctioning the defection of larger states. In such contexts, states may find it optimal to delegate power to a third party to adjudicate and enforce mutually beneficial agreements. Within the EU setup, it is the Commission as surveillance operator who is able to bring an

[18] Randall L Calvert, 'The Rational Choice Theory of Institutions: Implications for Design' in David L Weimer (ed), *Institutional Design* (Springer 1995).

infringement procedure on behalf of the Community interest and pursue withdrawal and possible remedies to offset damages, making retaliation more effective overall.

This does not mean that enforcement of EU law is consistently centralized—in fact, in their domestic legal orders Member States are the predominant enforcers of EU law. With regulations directly applicable in Member States' legal orders, EU law can be enforced by national authorities and courts. The EU relies on decentralized enforcement arrangements through national authorities being bound by EU law that enjoys supremacy over national law. It is only when the interpretation of EU law is in doubt or Member States' conduct under suspicion of breaching EU law, that the ECJ will step in as enforcer.

PART IV

WHO COOPERATES UNDER EU LAW

Introduction to Part IV

Lastly, we examine the actors who cooperate under EU law. This discussion will draw in part on conventional legal assessments of institutional architecture while considering the subdivision of competencies among EU institutions. Economists are particularly interested in the legal powers conferred upon EU institutions because their assessment can shed valuable light on institutional behaviour. By way of example, legal analysis reveals that the ECJ holds a position of considerable significance, as it has independent and authoritative competences to interpret EU law. Drawing on this insight, an economist could seek to conduct a political-economic assessment of the Court's inclination to confirm the primacy of EU law over Member State law, or to illuminate Court opposition to jurisdictional competition with Member State courts.[1] Principal–agent theory can illuminate why the *de facto* exercise of competences may diverge from the *de jure* provisions of the Treaties, such that institutions develop their own agendas that are misaligned with the interests of their principals—namely, Member States or EU citizens.

To effectively explore *who* acts within the EU, we must first consider the factors that impact and shape institutional preferences, rather than assuming these preferences are an exogenous 'given', as one does in rational choice theory.[2] As discussed in Chapter 1, the simplistic presumption that institutions unfailingly pursue the formal objectives for which they were established may be significantly flawed. Both realists and constructivists have challenged the view that the institutions invariably serve their founding purposes, albeit from different perspectives. Realists tend to see EU institutions as mere agents of state power, and assert that stronger countries exert control over the EU, preventing it from becoming fully autonomous actor. Constructivists, by contrast, acknowledge an autonomous role for the EU when it

[1] Dimitry Vladimirovich Kochenov, and Nikos Lavranos, 'Achmea versus the Rule of Law: CJEU's Dogmatic Dismissal of Investors' Rights in Backsliding Member States of the European Union' (2022) 14 Hague Journal on the Rule of Law 195.

[2] Barbara Koremenos, *The Continent of International Law: Explaining Agreement Design* (Cambridge University Press 2016) 12.

comes to producing and disseminating norms.[3] Ultimately, depending on the analytical perspective taken, we find agency attributed to Member States (in line with rational choice theory), hegemonic Member State actors (realists), or the EU institutions themselves (constructivists). Rational choice and realist approaches are hard to reconcile with the constructivist view that preferences depend on context, and in particular on existing political, legal, and institutional arrangements.[4] A further problem with the state-focused rational choice perspective is that it does not entertain the possibility of a dynamic relationship between the EU and Member States, with EU institutions potentially influencing the preferences of Member States.[5] Insofar as Union institutions such as the ECJ or the Commission pursue their own interests and also shape Member State preferences, Member States can hardly be considered exogenous factors and the sole source of preferences. Precisely this insight is proffered by the constructivists, who note the replication of the EU's supranational architecture in integration processes around the globe.[6]

While rational choice perspectives have been further refined by public choice theory (in part by relaxing the view that state preferences are necessarily benevolent or welfare maximizing), constructivist perspectives require the examination of how Treaty institutions were established and vested with rights and obligations. Constructivist and public choice theories align insofar as they endogenize the decisions of international organizations, seeing them as more than a mere aggregation of the preferences of Member States (the putative 'masters of the Treaties'). This is supported by the positivist perspective that views EU institutions not as vehicles for the expression of Member State will, but rather as invested with *Kompetenz-Kompetenz*—that is, with an ability to determine the scope of their own powers. Formally, Member States can influence the legislative process of the EU Commission and Parliament through the EU Council. However, the Treaties recognize the independence of Union institutions (the Commission, the ECJ, the ECB) and enshrine a 'separation of powers' principle by invoking the need for 'institutional balance' among Union institutions. Thus, while EU institutions may have initially reflected Member State preferences at their inception, they have since acquired significantly expanded autonomy. This, in turn, implies a need to relax the 'state-only' notion of Treaty formation that underlies the realist approach.

The view that EU institutions are an 'exogenous variable', and mere extensions of Member State will is difficult to sustain in light of empirical evidence for the

[3] Barbara Koremenos, Charles Lipson, and Duncan Snidal, 'The Rational Design of International Institutions' (2001) 55 International Organization 761, 768.

[4] Oren Bar-Gill and Chaim Fershtman, 'Law and Preferences' (2004) 20 Journal of Law, Economics, & Organization 331.

[5] Joel P Trachtman, *The Economic Structure of International Law* (Harvard University Press 2008) 19.

[6] Tanja A Börzel and Thomas Risse, 'From Europeanisation to Diffusion: Introduction' (2012) 35 West European Politics 1.

'endogenous' character of the EU, as Union institutions regularly shape policy outcomes in a (quasi)autonomous fashion. Principal–agent analysis provides an important conceptual tool for understanding how the preferences of Union institutions may diverge from that of Member States and/or their electorates. Legal analysis can clarify the scope of action that EU institutions enjoy, while the discipline of economics provides a means of analysing incentives. In this way, the two disciplines offer complementary perspectives regarding how EU institutions exercise their Treaty-based mandates. In the most basic sense, *agency costs* occur when states delegate authority to a (supranational) organization, as is evident from principal–agent models.[7] EU institutions can be conceptualized as agents that have been commissioned to act on behalf of Member States (the 'principals'). EU Member States appoint agents to perform functions that they cannot fulfil themselves (or cannot fulfil as efficiently). This understanding of the mandate enjoyed by EU institutions is in accordance with the functionalist interpretation of EU law that is native to legal analysis. Specifically, this strand of thinking characterizes EU institutions as 'special-purpose associations of functional integration'.[8] As agency theory crucially suggests, agents pursue utility functions that deviate from that of their principal. A complicating factor is that there are multiple principal–agent relationships within the EU. Besides the fundamental principal–agent relationship between Member States and the EU, or, alternatively, between the citizenry and the EU,[9] we find principal–agent relations between political authorities in Member States and supranational EU bodies (eg the ECJ, the ECB, and the European Commission).[10] In addition to carrying out Treaty-based functions, the members of the Commission, the ECB, and the ECJ are not directly elected (ie they are 'non-majoritarian'), and their decisions in most cases cannot be appealed.[11]

[7] Kenneth W Abbott and Duncan Snidal, 'Why States Act through Formal International Organizations' (1998) 42 Journal of Conflict Resolution 3; Michael J Tierney and others, *Delegation and Agency in International Organizations* (Cambridge University Press 2006); Mark A Pollack, 'Delegation, Agency, and Agenda Setting in the European Community' (1997) 51 International Organization 99.

[8] Hans Peter Ipsen, 'Der deutsche Jurist und das europäische Gemeinschaftsrecht', *Verhandlungen des 43. Deutschen Juristentages* (1994) 15.

[9] Tom Delreux and Johan Adriaensen, 'Principal–Agent Analysis and the European Union', *Oxford Research Encyclopedia of Politics* (Oxford University Press 2019).

[10] Fabio Franchino, 'Efficiency or Credibility? Testing the Two Logics of Delegation to the European Commission' (2002) 9 Journal of European Public Policy 677; Hussein Kassim and Anand Menon, 'The Principal-Agent Approach and the Study of the European Union: Promise Unfulfilled?' (2003) 10 Journal of European Public Policy 121.

[11] Mark Thatcher, Alec Stone Sweet, and Bernardo Rangoni, 'Reversing Delegation? Politicization, De-delegation, and Non-majoritarian Institutions' (2023) 36 Governance 5; Fabrizio Gilardi, *Delegation in the Regulatory State* (Edward Elgar Publishing 2008); Mark Thatcher and Alec Stone Sweet, 'Theory and Practice of Delegation to Non-Majoritarian Institutions' (2002) 25 West European Politics 1.

15
The European Council and Council of Ministers

The concepts of sovereignty and legitimacy have featured prominently in discussions concerning the 'autonomization' of the EU as an agent.[1] In the Westphalian tradition, states alone enjoy unfettered sovereignty, and any transfer of this sovereignty should be ascribable to the deliberate will of the state. By contrast, 'constitutional pluralism' expresses the notion of 'shared sovereignty'. In the European context, the sharing of sovereignty between EU institutions and Member States can culminate in mutually exclusive claims to decision-making authority.[2] To some degree, the autonomy of EU institutions from Member State preferences has been a deliberate 'design feature' of the EU's institutional architecture from the very beginning, one that has only become more accentuated over time. To be sure, insofar as the European Commission and Parliament pursue genuine community interests, they are pursuing interests which, virtually by definition, may be at cross-purposes with the preferences of individual Member States. With a view to the principal–agent problem, suffice it to say that even though the EU has gained an unprecedented range of powers and organizational capacity, for various reasons it cannot (yet) be viewed as a federal state. Indeed, the EU is properly conceived in its present form not as a sovereign state but rather as an international organization with supranational authority. From a traditional legal perspective, the powers invested in EU institutions have been conferred by Member States, and it flows from this conferral that EU institutions enjoy their legitimacy. From an economic perspective, voter preferences are revealed in elections, and governments are formed in order to give expression to majority preferences. This national root of EU legitimacy holds so long as Member States retain their legislative *Kompetenz-Kompetenz*—that is, 'competence over competence', or, in the present case, the power to determine the scope of the mandate fulfilled by EU institutions. This makes Member States the 'masters of the Treaties'. From this perspective, the

[1] Dieter Grimm, *Sovereignty: The Origin and Future of a Political and Legal Concept* (Columbia University Press 2015) 106, 107.

[2] Neil Walker, 'The Idea of Constitutional Pluralism' (2002) 65 Modern Law Review 317; Catherine Richmond, 'Preserving the Identity Crisis: Autonomy, System and Sovereignty in European Law' (1997) 16 Law and Philosophy 377.

EU Law and Economics. Armin Steinbach, Oxford University Press. © Oxford University Press 2025.
DOI: 10.1093/9780198920915.003.0015

EU has no right of self-determination with a view to its purpose, powers, or institutional arrangements, as such questions fall under the purview of the Member States.

A different perspective emerges if we consider governments and citizens as two distinct subjects of legitimacy under international law. European integration has slowly moved away from the Westphalian logic towards a hybrid legitimacy model in which legitimacy is drawn from state representatives and from citizens. At the beginning of the European project, the Westphalian model was of decisive importance. According to this model, heads of state were the primary source of legitimacy in EU rule-making, with citizens only playing a secondary role in establishing legitimacy, through the decision-making of the head of states. However, the individual has subsequently emerged as the source from which legitimacy stems. A first step was taken in this regard with the ECJ granting individuals the power to directly invoke fundamental rights and freedoms. A second important step right was the establishment of the directly elected European Parliament. However, representational asymmetries persist both in the Council and in the Parliament, as representation on the Council deviates from the one-country, one-vote principle, while representation in the Parliament deviates from the one-citizen, one-vote principle. While the one-country, one-vote principle is the Westphalian benchmark of international law, the one-citizen, one-vote principle is based on democratic theory.

The realist, rational-choice conception of international organizations predicts that any asymmetry in the control of international organizations will increase given growing asymmetry amongst the entities that confer authority.[3] This perspective sets aside the legal understanding of Westphalian sovereignty and reasons that a country's control over an international organization depends on its importance for that organization. Game theory lends plausibility to this notion by highlighting that payoff functions determine the importance of an actor in a coalition. When some members contribute more to an organization than others (eg because they contribute greater resources, or because they are pivotal to that organization's performance), they are likely to exert greater managerial influence. In this regard, it is worth noting that the EU is supposed to finance its activities wholly from its 'own resources' (Article 311 TFEU). To this end, Member States contribute an equal share of GDP to EU coffers, which in absolute terms results in very unequal contributions from different Member States.

Are the power asymmetries that would be predicted by game theory evident in Member States' influence over the EU Council and Parliament? At a formal level, the Westphalian notion of equality among sovereign states has served to check the influence exerted by individual state actors, particularly when unanimity voting is required. The principle of equality among sovereigns recedes to the background,

[3] Barbara Koremenos, Charles Lipson, and Duncan Snidal, 'The Rational Design of International Institutions' (2001) 55 International Organization 761, 792.

however, on issues that require qualified majority voting, as more populace countries have more voting rights. It is here that we find an asymmetry between contributors that can give rise to the aforementioned game-theory dynamics, although the contributor asymmetries in the EU Council are less pronounced than they are in other international organizations such as the IMF, which accords voting weights in proportion to a member's share of global GDP.[4] By contrast, parliamentary decision-making is protective of smaller states, thus reducing the game-theory dynamic, as smaller states are 'overrepresented' (in terms of population) compared to larger ones.[5]

If one acknowledges that the one-country, one-vote principle is the traditional legitimacy standard in international law, then the Council's decision-making practice can be assessed with reference to the cost of adopting EU secondary law. In this connection, the EU has been moving towards an increasing reliance on qualified majority voting, rather than unanimity voting. The law-making mechanisms used by the Council should be chosen to minimize the transaction costs incurred when rendering collective decisions. This cost minimization problem involves the evaluation of two different costs: (i) direct costs of decision-making, such as the costs of reaching a majority consensus in a political context by means of bargaining and a search for compromises; and (ii) indirect or agency costs, such as the cost imposed on a minority group by the rules chosen by a majority coalition, which implies that some principals (eg an EU member or its citizens) are overruled and must accept an outcome that runs counter to their preferences.[6] As public choice theory has shown in the case of political decision-making, the direct and indirect costs of law-making are negatively correlated.[7] This can be vividly illustrated by considering the extreme cases of unanimity and dictatorship in a voting context. Under unanimous voting, there are no agency costs, because every member has veto power and can prevent undesirable choices. In the case of dictatorship, the mirror opposite of unanimity, the agency costs are very high, because the dictator can make decisions without consulting the preferences of the populace, and can thus pass all costs of policy/preference misalignment to the citizenry. The direct costs of law-making are the lowest under a dictatorship, however, as there is no need to reach consensus or engage in political bargaining.[8] In the EU, decision-making costs pull in two directions: under unanimity requirements, the decisive

[4] In a similar vein, one may see the UN Security Council's veto powers as a result not only of these countries' political weight but also their contribution to world's peace.

[5] Jonathan Rodden, 'Strength in Numbers?' (2002) 3 European Union Politics 151.

[6] Francesco Parisi and Vincy Fon, *The Economics of Lawmaking* (Oxford University Press 2008) 272; parts of the theoretical economic literature assume a benevolent government, meaning that elected political agents pursue politics in line with voters' preferences—an idealized view that has been contested from public choice and behavioural economic perspectives. Lack of benevolence gives rise to agency costs.

[7] James Buchanan and Gordon Tullock, *The Calculus of Consent* (University of Michigan Press 1969).

[8] Parisi and Fon (n 17) 52, 274.

role of Member State representation on the Council lowers the external costs. At the same time, unanimity comes with high direct costs, because significant bargaining is required to achieve unanimity. By contrast, qualified majority voting situations, such as that used in EU legislation, can result in higher agency costs, because decisions may be adopted in some cases against the will of Member States, while also generating lower direct costs, as not all members need to be ultimately satisfied. Hence, the more qualified majority voting serves as a basis for EU law-making, the higher the likelihood of policy that contravenes the preferences of certain segments of the population, thus generating significant agency costs, at least in some Member States.

Importantly, this finding is related to a basic insight in fiscal federalism that relies on preference heterogeneity as a core criterion for assessing whether the provision of public goods should be take place in a centralized or decentralized manner. Unanimity voting is viewed as a suitable voting mechanism when preferences are highly heterogeneous and spillovers between jurisdictions are significant. By contrast, qualified majority voting is seen as more appropriate when preferences are homogenous and spillovers between jurisdictions are insignificant. In addition, with a growing number of participants, the space for agreeable solutions under unanimity rules shrinks. This insight renders the shift towards qualified majority voting in the EU more understandable, as it has been closely tied to the accession of new Member States. Until the Lisbon Treaty entered into force, it was even possible for a majority vote to be achieved by a minority of the EU population. However, since Lisbon, a 'double majority' has been required, that is, a majority of Member States (55 per cent) along with a majority of the EU's population (65 per cent).

While rational choice theory elucidates the divergent transaction and agency costs that must be considered when selecting voting rules, legal scholars consider these costs in terms of political legitimacy, which shifts the focus to the preferences of the citizenry. From this perspective, elected national governments are the true vehicles for the expression of popular will, and the democratic sovereignty may not be adequately safeguarded when governments can be outvoted in the Council. Furthermore, these impairments to sovereignty may not be adequately compensated by the representation afforded in the European Parliament.

Constitutional economics offers a different perspective, furnishing a forceful argument for why majority voting should be preferred over unanimity voting arrangements. Citizens must agree to constitutional rules if they are based on 'mutual advantage and voluntary agreement'. With Vanberg, a distinction can be made between voluntary agreement as the ultimate *legitimizing principle* for political action and unanimity as a *decision rule* in practical politics. This perspective acknowledges the difficulties associated with unanimity voting, difficulties that invite strategic behaviour and impede the efficient functioning of an institution. A distinction is thus made between the *constitutional* and *sub-constitutional* rules. Unanimity voting may be plausible for constitutional rules, for example changes to the TEU and TFEU. By contrast, less-than-unanimity rules should be implemented at the sub-constitutional level, for example for all matters of EU secondary law. From this perspective, it is the voluntary agreement at the constitutional level that legitimizes non-unanimity as the mode of decision-making at the sub-constitutional level.[9]

[9] Viktor J Vanberg, 'Market and State: The Perspective of Constitutional Political Economy' (2005) 1 Journal of Institutional Economics 23, 44.

16
The European Parliament

In theory, the preference revelation process during European Parliament elections and the preference formation process within the Parliament works the same way as those under national constitutions. In this way, policy formation can be viewed as a process by which the heterogeneous preferences of law-makers become reconciled and aggregated into law. In the setting of the nation-state, political parties play an intermediate role, connecting imperfectly informed citizens to the politicians who ultimately serve in parliament.[1] From this perspective, political parties allow voter preferences to be articulated and translated into political will. This allows elected officials to act as credible agents of the popular will.

This model of representative democracy faces challenges when applied to the European Parliament. First of all, European Parliament decisions will tend to have higher agency costs, due to greater limitations on the expression of public preferences. This is attributable in part to the fact that European elections are not truly 'Europeanized': voters do not vote for supranational parties as such, but rather for political blocks based on similarities between platforms. This is problematic from both a legal and economics perspective. Legally, the chain of legitimacy that runs from voters through political parties to the parliament is significantly diluted.[2] And economically, parties in the European Parliament only partially fulfil their intermediate function of aggregating public preferences.

By law, EU parliamentarians serve European citizens. Article 10(2) TFEU stipulates that 'citizens are directly represented at Union level in the European Parliament'. Yet public choice analysis exposes significant factual deviation from this normative ideal. EU parliamentarians serve more than one principal. Specifically, parliamentarians must be loyal to the *national* parties who nominate them to the electoral lists. Unlike national parties, the political groups within the European Parliament are based on similar political orientations, but these groups do not engage directly with the electorate, and have no accountability to the individual voter (who has cast their vote for a national party). At the same time, EU parliamentarians are beholden to voters, due to their desire for re-election. However, the connection to the voter is not to a 'European' one (as Article 10(2) TFEU

[1] John R Petrocik, *Party Coalitions: Realignment and the Decline of the New Deal Party System* (Chicago University Press 1981).
[2] Dieter Grimm, *Europa ja—aber welches? Zur Verfassung der europäischen Demokratie* (CH Beck 2016) 29, 139.

EU Law and Economics. Armin Steinbach, Oxford University Press. © Oxford University Press 2025.
DOI: 10.1093/9780198920915.003.0016

presumes). There is no 'supranational voter'; accordingly, the 'national voter' remains the primary source of legitimacy from a political-economy perspective. The problems associated with this lack of a proper European dimension to parliamentary elections is further exacerbated by the weakness of the political groups in the European Parliament vis-à-vis the Commission; in the national setting the executive branch's dependence on parliament is much more pronounced.

Crucially, Europe lacks a pan-European public that could facilitate preference formation among poorly informed voters and thus enable meaningful electoral control over political representatives at the EU level. Pan-European forums for policy debate are conspicuously lacking; rather, discourse is fragmented into various national contexts, and public opinion largely coalesces around issues of national concern. Accordingly, the German Constitutional Court has observed that 'the public perception of factual issues and of political leaders remains connected to a considerable extent to patterns of identification related to the nation-state, language, history and culture'.[3] The process of political preference formation and articulation thus remains fragmented across national domains.[4] This is highly apparent on a practical level, as there is no body of public opinion to which, say, Spanish and Finnish citizens can equally contribute; there is no common forum for dialogue. This hinders information dissemination and preference formation on issues decided in Brussels. It also increases citizens' agency costs, because European parliamentary decisions are not subjected to the same scrutiny as decisions at national levels. Statements emanating from the European Parliament in Brussels and Strasbourg are also generally lost in the noise of national conversation. Yet what should we infer from voter preoccupation and identification with the parochial context of the nation? The German Constitutional Court has argued that this represents grounds for limiting the transfer of sovereign rights to the EU level. While this line of argument has been criticized as 'ethno-cultural'[5] and has fuelled debate regarding the existence of a European 'demos',[6] it nevertheless shows a parallel to the theory of fiscal federalism: in the absence of a sufficient degree of preference homogeneity, public goods should be provided at the local rather than at the federal level. From an economic perspective, this ensures local policies that are genuinely reflective of local preferences.

Seats in the European Parliament are assigned based on national quotas, which are not proportional to population size. The principle of one man, one vote—a fundamental tenet of national constitutions and their election laws—is thus

[3] BVerfGE 123, 267 *Lissabon* (2009)—Lisbon Treaty, para 251.

[4] Joseph HH Weiler, *The Constitution of Europe: 'Do the New Clothes Have an Emperor?' And Other essays on European Integration* (Cambridge University Press 1999) 350.

[5] Anneli Albi and Peter van Elsuwege, 'EU Constitution, National Constitutions and Sovereignty: An Assessment of a "European Constitutional Order"' (2004) 29 European Law Review 741, 757.

[6] Dieter Grimm, 'Does Europe Need a Constitution?' (1995) 1 European Law Journal 295; Marlies Desomer and Koen Lenaerts, 'New Models of Constitution-Making in Europe: The Quest for Legitimacy' (2002) 39 Common Market Law Review 1217, 1252.

contravened, which necessarily undermines preference aggregation. This representational arrangement also creates divergent agency costs between Member States. Citizens from some countries—such as Germany—have less weight than citizens from smaller states. This representational discrepancy ultimately led the German Constitutional Court to view the European Parliament not as a representative of European citizens (as is foreseen by Article 10(2) TEU), but rather as a representative of the Member State collectives.[7]

Given the deficits in the democratic legitimacy enjoyed by the European Parliament that result from this unequal weighing of European voters, strengthening the European Parliament vis-à-vis the Council by expanding the decision rights accorded to the Parliament would be unlikely to produce the efficiency gains that have been touted by advocates of such a reform. The Council is a vehicle for the expression of preferences held by national governments, and thus indirectly for the preferences of Member State citizens. However, this 'chain of legitimacy' has been weakened by two developments. First, as mentioned, there has been a gradual shift from unanimity to qualified majority voting in the Council, leading to an increase in outvoted preferences and associated agency costs. Second, the shift to qualified majority voting has been accompanied by expanded powers for the European Parliament due to the widened scope of the ordinary legislation procedure (Article 294 TFEU). This has put the Parliament on an equal footing with the Council. However, the combination of weakening the Council while strengthening the Parliament does not necessarily lead to a net increase in legitimacy, for the legitimacy gains from a strengthened Parliament are offset by the legitimacy losses incurred as countries are more frequently outvoted.

[7] BVerfGE 123, 267 *Lissabon* (2009)—Lisbon Treaty, para 284.

17
The European Court of Justice

All modern democracies delegate substantial authority to unelected bureaucrats. The legal literature discusses the *independence* of EU institutions in terms of a 'separation of powers' and an 'expertise-based subdivision competences' while also recognizing the legitimacy concerns associated with the delegation of power to institutions that enjoy a degree of independence.[1] Such legitimacy concerns, while not trivial for the Council and Parliament, become considerably more fraught when we turn our attention to non-majoritarian EU institutions such as the ECB and ECJ.

Economics offers a rationale for certain features of delegation to non-majoritarian institutions. In particular, a principal may benefit from deliberately providing a considerable degree of independence to an agent, insofar as this agent is able to pursue policies to which the principal could not credibly commit. Furthermore, the delegation of authority can generate efficiency gains, thanks to task specialization.[2] However, these benefits are not entirely free of costs.

Adjudicative bodies play an important role in resolving principal–agent concerns.[3] International courts solve 'commitment problems'. Specifically, when a country has committed to comply with an agreement, it may have an incentive to defect from these commitments, either because the payoff of defection is favourable or because it has the option of free-riding on other members' commitments. Creating non-majoritarian institutions such as courts or central banks limits the time-inconsistency problem by granting these institutions independence from the principals' monitoring or control.[4]

The role of the ECJ is ambivalent from a principal–agent perspective. On one hand, the purpose of the Court is to act as a check on the Council and the Commission. Specifically, the ECJ is tasked with ensuring observation of the law in the interpretation and application of the Treaties, as per Article 19(1), sentence 2 TEU. The judicial review performed by the Court helps to compensate for weaknesses in democratic control over the Council and the Commission. Judicial review introduces a mechanism for *ex-post* accountability that may be inadequately fulfilled by elections. Indeed, the cost of holding the Council and the Commission

[1] Allan Rosas, 'Separation of Powers in the European Union' (2007) 41 International Lawyer 1033.
[2] Mark A Pollack, *The Engines of European Integration* (Oxford University Press 2003).
[3] Robert Cooter and Michael Gilbert, *Public Law and Economics* (Oxford University Press 2022) 474.
[4] Giandomenico Majone, 'Two Logics of Delegation' (2001) 2 European Union Politics 103.

EU Law and Economics. Armin Steinbach, Oxford University Press. © Oxford University Press 2025.
DOI: 10.1093/9780198920915.003.0017

to account is high—for both institutions are only accountable to the European Parliament to a limited extent, and difficulties in demonstrating legal standing prevent direct lawsuits by members of the public. To address this lack of supervision, the Council and the Commission are subject to comprehensive judicial oversight that aims to hold them to Treaty obligations. Accordingly, the presumption is that the ECJ will act to safeguard the interests of the Treaty-makers (ie the Member States).

On the other hand, decades of jurisprudence that have encouraged European integration suggest that the ECJ itself has tended to support 'innovative' legal interpretations that stretch (or, for some, transgress) the writ of the Treaties. Based on a 'dynamic' reading of the law, the Court has often adopted interpretations that have led to an expansion of EU law at the expense of national law. ECJ decisions have also shifted competencies away from Member States. Examples include seminal decisions that established the primacy of EU law over national law; the 'implied powers' doctrine; and the *effet utile* approach. Accordingly, the ECJ has been dubbed an 'engine of integration'. Alternatively, lawyers have referred to this as a process of 'constitutionalization' by which EU law has gained features that are native to genuine constitutions.[5] In the words of Eric Stein: 'Tucked away in the fairyland Duchy of Luxembourg and blessed, until recently, with benign neglect by the powers that be and the mass media, the Court of Justice of the European Communities has fashioned a constitutional framework for a federal-type structure in Europe.'[6] This process of 'constitutionalization' has been significantly driven by the ECJ's early judgments on the primacy of EU law in combination with the ruling that EU law has direct effect on national legal regimes. Yet notably, this process was not foreseen by the founding Member States, nor is it a natural consequence of the EU Treaties. In fact, the original function of the Court was to safeguard the interests of Member States in relation to the High Authority (the predecessor to the European Commission). In line with traditional Westphalian logic, which sees the state as the proper unit for the formation of the collective will, adjudicative powers were vested in the ECJ to ensure conformance of the High Authority decisions with Member State preferences.[7]

From an economic perspective, ECJ-driven 'constitutionalization' has driven up agency costs by weakening the ability of Member State citizens to control

[5] Gerard Conway, 'Recovering a Separation of Powers in the European Union' (2011) 17 European Law Journal, 304, 313; Carolyn Moser and Berthold Rittberger, 'The CJEU and EU (de-) Constitutionalization: Unpacking Jurisprudential Responses' (2022) 20 International Journal of Constitutional Law 1038; Anne Peters, 'The Constitutionalisation of the European Union—Without the Constitutional Treaty' in Sonja Puntscher Riekmann and Wolfgang Wessels (eds), *The Making of a European Constitution* (VS Verlag für Sozialwissenschaften 2006).

[6] Eric Stein, 'Lawyers, Judges, and the Making of a Transnational Constitution' (1981) 75 American Journal of International Law 1, 1.

[7] Anne Boerger-de Smedt, 'La Cour de Justice Dans Les Négociations Du Traité de Paris Instituant La CECA' (2008) 14 Journal of European Integration History 7, 13.

European institutions. Put differently, the increased competences of Union institutions (induced without Treaty changes) mean there is a higher risk that the bundle of collective goods offered on the supply side by EU institutions will diverge from the demand-side preferences of citizens. The ECJ's relaxed interpretation of the subsidiarity principle, which has led to a 'creeping' expansion of Commission competences at the expense of Member States, has understandably provoked pointed criticism.[8] As explained above, the subsidiarity principle should be read—like fiscal federalism—as a legal principle that can be informed by economic criteria (ie external costs, economies of scale, preference heterogeneity). It is easy to see how a European Court that enjoys autonomy from Member State preferences could potentially attach little importance to these criteria and favour a more lenient interpretation of the subsidiarity principle.[9] Since the original purpose of the subsidiarity principle was to preserve authority in the hands of Member States, the principal–agent problem posed by ECJ autonomy clearly accrues to the detriment of the Member States. This may ultimately conflict with the legal safeguard to ensure the EU remains bound by the will of the Members States—the legal principle of conferral—as well as with the primary law requirement that the Union must respect the national identity of the Member States (Article 4(2) TEU).[10]

For some scholars, the Court's early seminal judgments have also encouraged 'de-democratization' by creating a de-coupling of the EU institutions from the preferences of Europe's citizens. This reading asserts that once the Court had established primacy and direct effect, the jurisprudence required to establish and promote the common market no longer relied on parliamentary authority. Direct effect and primacy empowered the ECJ and the Commission to pursue the liberalization of the common market, without the need for legislative input. With the primacy of EU law, the Commission and the ECJ could suspend national law that, in their view, was inconsistent with economic freedoms. Further market integration could thus be achieved via judicial decision, reducing the need for parliamentary action. The ECJ continued on the road of expansive interpretation by transforming prohibitions regarding discrimination into general prohibitions regarding Member State regulation.[11] Member States were thus increasingly prevented from adopting their own standards of product safety or consumer protection.

[8] Sacha Garben, 'Restating the Problem of Competence Creep, Tackling Harmonisation by Stealth and Reinstat-Ing the Legislator' in Sacha Garben and Inge Govaere (eds), *The Division of Competences between the EU and the Member States: Reflections on the Past, the Present and the Future* (Hart Publishing 2017).

[9] Stephen Weatherill, 'Protecting the Internal Market from the Charter' in Sybe de Vries, Ulf Bernitz, and S Weatherill (eds), *The EU Charter of Fundamental Rights as a Binding Instrument: Five Years Old and Growing* (Hart Publishing 2016), 135.

[10] Clive Barnett, 'Culture, Policy, and Subsidiarity in the European Union: From Symbolic Identity to the Governmentalisation of Culture' (2001) 20 Political Geography 405.

[11] Jan Zglinski, 'The End of Negative Market Integration: 60 Years of Free Movement of Goods Litigation in the EU (1961–2020)' (2024) 31 Journal of European Public Policy 633.

Upon closer examination, the jurisprudence establishing a direct effect (allowing economic actors to disregard Member State law, by invoking economic freedoms) and the supremacy of EU law (over that of Member States) may have an economic justification if two conditions are met: first, on the issue in question there must be an environment of relative preference homogeneity across the Union, such that EU law overriding Member State law allows closer alignment with the popular preferences; and second, there must be a general preference for the assurance of individual economic freedoms that takes precedence over interventions motivated by public policy concerns, because it is typically individuals (companies or citizens) who invoke EU law in order to override public policies adopted under Member States' law. However, the fulfilment of both of these conditions is unlikely given the persistent heterogeneity that has been observed across the EU with a view to policy preferences.[12] Insofar as this conclusion is correct, the constitutionalization that has been propelled by the Court brings a substantial risk of mismatch between legislation and popular preferences, thus creating significant agency costs for Member States and citizens. Member States never formally consented to such extensive constitutionalization, nor did they anticipate it. At the same time, democratic restraints exercised by the citizenry have been diluted due to the shift in competencies to supranational level, notwithstanding the potential gains in other areas (eg individual economic rights).

One counterargument that partially shields the ECJ from criticism is that the EU legislator could at any time act to ensure a closer match between popular preferences and applicable law by simply adopting legislation that would bind the ECJ and thus overrule the 'negative integration' induced by lawsuits and accelerated by the ECJ due to its enforcement of basic freedoms. Acting in this way, the legislator could counterbalance the negative integration bias that has resulted from plaintiffs invoking economic freedoms to escape the restraints of public policy measures. It is true that, under domestic constitutional law, the institutional balance between the ECJ and the EU legislator follows the general constitutional law principle that legislators may adopt legislation that is binding upon the ECJ (unless incompatible with primary law). By harmonizing Member States' law or adopting regulatory measures in pursuit of public policy goals, the legislator could pursue 'positive integration' that offsets the economic freedom bias.

Yet crucially, such an approach would do little to reduce agency costs. First, positive integration (eg harmonization of secondary EU law by imposing minimum standards) is much harder to put in place than negative integration (in terms of invalidating Member State measures by legal verdict) due to voting requirements in EU legislative bodies. In this way, the EU Parliament, as a vehicle for democratic will formation at the EU level, proves to be an unwieldy instrument, due to

[12] Jana Paasch, 'Revisiting Policy Preferences and Capacities in the EU: Multi-level Policy Implementation in the Subnational Authorities' (2022) 60 Journal of Common Market Studies 783.

the difficulties of consensus formation. Second, ECJ jurisprudence has been discriminatory in its review of statute legality, for the Court adopts strict legal stances when Member State law is at issue, but is lenient in relation to Union law. While some see a bias that favours Union institutions and thus promotes integration,[13] others view it as a tendency to strengthen the European political process, because leniency towards the Union legislator strengthens the legislator's choice, while supressing Member States' policy measures reduces heterogeneity and the fragmentation of Member States preferences.[14] In theory, this may favour the preferences of EU citizens (which are upheld in principle by the EU Parliament). Indeed, the Treaty of Lisbon introduced Article 10(2) TEU, which asserts that citizens are directly represented at Union level in the European Parliament. However, this discriminatory bias undermines the role of Member State citizens as a source of legitimacy (as discussed above), weakening their voice as expressed through national parliaments and national representation in the EU Council.

The principal–agent perspective also invites us to explore the Court's discretionary space.[15] The starting point in this regard is the observation that judicial leeway may be checked by the ability of the legislature to correct the court or to provide it with guidelines for interpretation. The more difficult it is to enact new laws, the wider the Court's room for manoeuvre. This in turn depends on institutional issues, including in particular consensus requirements and the specific institutions involved. Various scholars have observed that the Council is not an effective counterweight to the ECJ. Although the Council represents the interests of Member States, it does not represent common EU interests. The decision-making process in the Council is not, as in national parliaments, based on 'preference maximizing negotiation', but rather on 'deliberative supranationalism', as in international associations.[16] The voting requirement in the Council is decisive in this regard: the Court of Justice has a great deal of leeway in policy areas in which there is a unanimity requirement for legislation in the Council, because in these cases, given the heterogeneity of Member State interests, it is difficult to provide the Court of Justice with specific interpretation specifications through secondary law. Conversely, when qualified majority voting is required, the Court has less leeway because it is easier to contain its actions, which face a higher risk of being corrected by the legislator. But even qualified majorities are difficult to achieve, especially for the purpose of correcting case law, a significant hurdle compounded by the fact

[13] Gunnar Beck, *The Legal Reasoning of the Court of Justice of the EU* (Hart Publishing 2013) 318.

[14] Armin von Bogdandy, *Strukturwandel des öffentlichen Rechts: Entstehung und Demokratisierung der Europäischen Gesellschaft* (Suhrkamp Verlag 2022) 176, 332.

[15] Stefan Voigt, 'Spielräume Des EuGH—Eine Ökonomische Analyse' in Peter Behrens, Thomas Eger, and Hans-Bernd Schäfer (eds), *Ökonomische Analyse des Europarechts* (Mohr Siebeck 2012) 37.

[16] Mark Rhinard, 'The Crisisification of Policy-making in the European Union' (2019) 57 Journal of Common Market Studies 616, 626.

that the Council, when passing secondary law, is dependent on initiatives from the Commission.

Compared to the domestic context where decisions regarding legislation only require a simple majority, the ECJ is assumed to enjoy greater decision-making powers than national courts. Also, the more difficult it is for law-makers to change the law, the lower the risk faced by the Court of being corrected. This is, as mentioned above, the case in the EU, in part because EU primary law is nearly impossible to change due to unanimity and ratification requirements. However, in addition, the magnitude of norms having quasi-constitutional character (the 55 norms of TEU and 358 of TFEU) goes well beyond the typical scope of basic rules enshrined in national constitutions, which are generally limited to fundamental rules regarding state organization and individual rights. This combination reduces the risk of ECJ being constrained by legislators. Adding to this is the increasing number of EU Member States that bring different legal cultures into the application of the law, so that the preferred interpretation from the point of view of the nation-states has become more heterogeneous. This also has the effect of expanding judicial discretion in the justification of decisions.

While this analysis highlights the incentives within the institutional framework for the ECJ to be expansionary in its jurisprudence, there is also a reinforcing public choice determinant at work. Courts are not different from bureaucratic bodies, and inherently seek to enlarge their prestige and power.[17] While the ECJ has remained within the procedural boundaries foreseen in the EU Treaties, it has been able to enlarge its influence and authority over time through interpretative innovations such as EU law primacy, direct effect, *effet utile*, and implied powers. Accordingly, the ECJ now enjoys significantly expanded powers, while Member States have seen a corresponding diminishment in their authority. By stipulating that only the ECJ can give authentic interpretation to EU law, the ECJ has shifted the balance of power between the EU and its Member States. Indeed, the ECJ has frequently intruded directly into Member States' legal orders, overruling the decisions of national parliaments and governments. This has led to a decisive weakening of the legislative authority exercised at the national level.

Viewed through the lens of economics, this constellation of limited constraint on the ECJ in conjunction with a political economy of judicial expansionism presents a mixed picture. The augmentation of ECJ autonomy has exacerbated principle–agent issues in relation to Member States. While EU legislation is at least partly under the control of Member States (via the Council), Member States have no influence over the interpretation of EU primary and secondary law. In response to this development, the German Constitutional Court has sought to undertake intensified monitoring of the ECJ, grounding this effort in a line of

[17] William A Niskanen, *Bureaucracy and Representative Government* (Routledge 2017); Public choice in courts.

jurisprudence originally developed in the 1970s. By ruling that Germany can accept EU supremacy only so long as basic principles of the German constitution are safeguarded, the German Constitutional Court has sought to 'cap' agency costs, while at the same time signalling acceptance of a certain level of these costs.[18] The German Constitutional Court's 'European law-friendly' line of interpretation thus shows acceptance for the partial emancipation of the ECJ from its principals,[19] yet not without stressing the view that the authority of EU law is derived from Member States.[20]

An alternate principal–agent perspective would be to consider citizens rather than governments as the true principals. From this perspective, citizens are the ultimate source of legitimacy, and government policy should reflect the preferences of the citizenry. Against this backdrop, a remarkable development is that the constitutionalization that has been driven by the ECJ has resulted in the enshrinement of the direct effect principle, an innovation that has allowed individual holders of rights to invoke EU law in national courts. The direct effect principle empowers EU citizens to pursue negative integration that may be viewed as aligning EU law with the preferences of *individual* citizens, but this comes at the expense of an imposition upon Member States' public policy choices, which reflect *collective* preferences. What is more, there are significant hurdles to reversing this negative integration through positive integration by way of secondary legislation, due to the need for consensus formation. The decisions of national parliaments and governments reflect the will of national societies. Individuals may maximize their personal benefits by invoking EU law directly; however, this is achieved to the detriment of national public policy, which is overridden by individual plaintiffs.

While the European Union relies on cooperation between the ECJ and national constitutional courts, there are obvious rivalries between the two. The judicial expansion pursued by the ECJ comes at the expense of national courts, which must cede authority in their interpretation of national law. In more recent years, the gradually increasing encroachment of EU law into national sovereignty has triggered fiercer resistance by national authorities, including in particular by the German Constitutional Court, which has emerged as the primary opponent of ECJ impingement upon national legal orders.[21] The conflict between the courts reached fever pitch during the European sovereign debt crisis as the ECB implemented new fiscal policy measures. German Constitutional Court criticism

[18] On the Solange jurisprudence, see Peter Hilpold, 'So Long Solange? The PSPP Judgment of the German Constitutional Court and the Conflict between the German and the European "Popular Spirit"' (2021) 23 Cambridge Yearbook of European Legal Studies 159.

[19] Dieter Grimm, Mattias Wendel, and Tobias Reinbacher, 'European Constitutionalism and the German Basic Law', *National Constitutions in European and Global Governance: Democracy, Rights, the Rule of Law* (TMC Asser Press 2019).

[20] BVerfG, *Judgment of the Second Senate of 6 December 2022*—2 BvR 547/21, paras 126, 166.

[21] Teresa Violante, 'Bring Back the Politics: The PSPP Ruling in Its Institutional Context' (2020) 21 German Law Journal 1045.

focused in no small part on the legality of the ECB's direct purchase of sovereign debt from crisis-wracked states as part of the Outright Monetary Transactions (OMT) programme.[22] From a game-theory perspective, the conflict between the German Constitutional Court and the ECJ resembles the 'battle of the sexes' game, where one player holds a first-mover advantage.[23] In this classic two-person asymmetric game, the payoff matrices do not align after transposition. The game seeks to quantify the preferences prevalent in a male/female couple who match traditional stereotypes, with the male preferring to attend a boxing match, and the female preferring to go to the opera. Although both players want to coordinate their choices, there is a conflict component because the preferred activities are non-compatible. There are two Nash equilibria: either both go to the opera, or both go to the football game.[24]

Similarly, in the confrontation between the ECJ and the German Constitutional Court, both players had a different preferred outcome—the ECJ wished to confirm that the OMT programme was legally permissible, while the German Constitutional Court deemed the OMT programme to be a violation of the ECB mandate. In the case of conflicting judgments (ie legality versus OMT as illegal), both courts experienced a lower payoff due to their blunt disagreement. Since the ECJ holds the first-mover advantage, given its rendering of a preliminary judgment, the equilibrium in the game is the decision of the first player (ie the ECJ's assessment), with the second player (the German Constitutional Court) 'following' the first mover in order to avoid a payoff that is even smaller (ie open disagreement between the courts, which is worse than reluctantly accepting the ECJ's reasoning). This game-theory scenario explains why the Constitutional Court might have an incentive to accede to the ECJ's assessment despite an initial preference to rule the OMT programme illegal. A few years later, the German Constitutional Court issued a decision regarding a similar monetary policy measure known as the Public Sector Purchase Programme (PSPP). In this case, however, instead of accepting the ECJ's judgment (with grumbling reluctance), the German Constitutional Court found the ECB to have exceeded its monetary policy mandate and to have encroached upon the Member States' responsibilities. In addition, the German Constitutional Court found the ECJ to have exceeded its jurisdiction—that is, to have acted *ultra vires* ('beyond its powers').[25] The implication of this finding—namely, that EU law

[22] Armin Steinbach, 'The Trend towards Non-Consensualism in Public International Law: A (Behavioural) Law and Economics Perspective' (2016) 27 European Journal of International Law 643, 668.

[23] Ramón Alonso-Sanz, 'On a Three-Parameter Quantum Battle of the Sexes Cellular Automaton' (2013) 12 Quantum Information Processing 1835; for a rational choice perspective see Niels Petersen, 'Karlsruhe's Lochner Moment? A Rational Choice Perspective on the German Federal Constitutional Court's Relationship to the CJEU After the PSPP Decision' (2020) 21 German Law Journal 995.

[24] BVerfGE 142, 123 *OMT-Programm* (2016); Paul P Craig and Menelaos Markakis, 'Gauweiler and the Legality of Outright Monetary Transactions' (2016) 41 European Law Review 4, 21.

[25] BVerfGE 154 *PSPP* (2020), paras 1–237.

as interpreted by the ECJ could be incompatible with the German legal order—prompted a significant legal and political debate. Returning to the game-theory perspective, it would appear the German Constitutional Court found the agency costs of assenting to the ECJ's decision too high in this case, making it preferable to rule against the decision rather than consent to it.

18
The European Central Bank

Much like the ECJ, the ECB has been endowed with considerable autonomy to fulfil a very specific (technical) task.[1] And also like the ECJ, the scope of authority exercised by the ECB has evolved beyond the mandate initially envisaged by the EU Treaties as originally ratified. Under Articles 127–133 TFEU, the Member States delegated authority for monetary policy to the ECB. Later, the ECB was granted authority for banking supervision as part of secondary law.[2] During financial crises, the ECB has acted as a lender of last resort, both in relation to commercial banks as well as to euro sovereigns, as underscored by Draghi's famous declaration that the ECB would 'do whatever it takes' to preserve the euro. More recently, the ECB has proclaimed it will support the fight against climate change and the implementation of the European Green Deal, invoking Article 127(1), sentence 2 TFEU, which stipulates that the ECB 'should support the general economic policies in the Union'.[3]

Unsurprisingly, these extensions of the ECB mandate (including in particular its large-scale asset purchase programmes) have come under heavy criticism. The drastic measures taken by the ECB to ensure the financial stability of the eurozone during the sovereign debt crisis faced particularly sharp condemnation as blatant violations of the ECB's monetary policy mandate.[4] Yet the ECB's independence shields it from *ex-ante* and *ex-post* control.[5] The decision to grant extensive leeway for the ECB's activities stems in part from the experience of the 1970s, when monetary policy at the Member State level was often subject to the authority

[1] Giandomenico Majone, 'Two Logics of Delegation' (2001) 2 European Union Politics 103; Giandomenico Majone, 'Nonmajoritarian Institutions and the Limits of Democratic Governance: A Political Transaction-Cost Approach' (2001) 157 Journal of Institutional and Theoretical Economics 57; Dermot Hodson, 'Reforming EU Economic Governance: A View from (and on) the Principal-Agent Approach' (2009) 7 Comparative European Politics 455; Philipp Genschel and Tobias Tesche, 'Supranational Agents as De-Commitment Devices: The ECB During the Eurozone Crisis' (2020) Amsterdam Center for European Studies Research Paper No 2020/02.

[2] David Howarth and Lucia Quaglia, *The Political Economy of European Banking Union* (Oxford University Press 2016).

[3] Chiara Zilioli and Michael Ioannidis, 'Climate Change and the Mandate of the ECB: Potential and Limits of Monetary Contribution to European Green Policies' (2022) 59 Common Market Law Review 363.

[4] Georgios Psaroudakis, 'The Scope for Financial Stability Considerations in the Fulfilment of the Mandate of the ECB/Eurosystem' (2018) 4 Journal of Financial Regulation 119.

[5] Fabian Amtenbrink and Rosa M Lastra, 'Securing Democratic Accountability of Financial Regulatory Agencies—A Theoretical Framework' in Richard V de Mulder (ed), *Mitigating Risk in the Context of Safety and Security—How Relevant is a rational Approach?* (Erasmus School of Law 2009) 115.

EU Law and Economics. Armin Steinbach, Oxford University Press. © Oxford University Press 2025.
DOI: 10.1093/9780198920915.003.0018

of national finance ministries. At that time, monetary policy was misused for fiscal policy purposes, and this exacerbated harmful inflationary tendencies. Furthermore, in economic theory, an independent monetary policy authority is considered a prerequisite for maximizing macroeconomic welfare.[6] An extensive literature in political economy predicts that commitment problems will induce governments to pursue output and employment maximization even at the expense of higher inflation or a loss of monetary policy credibility. Such fiscal policy misuse can be averted through monetary policy independence. However, from a principal–agent perspective, this entails minimal supervision by governments or the citizenry.[7]

The massive expansion of ECB power as part of the sovereign debt crisis, which entailed ECB intervention into non-monetary parameters such as Member State solvency, has exacerbated concerns related to ECB oversight and control. The problem is not just that responsibility for economic policy is supposed to lie in the hands of Member States. From a principal–agent perspective, central bank officials should seek to minimize monetary policy spillovers to policy domains over which they have no authority. Also, according to federalism theory, there are justifications for leaving economic policy in the hands of Member States, in order to allow public policies to reflect regionally heterogeneous preferences. This entails the need to contain spillovers from fiscal policy, for example through fiscal policy supervision.[8] The weak accountability mechanisms to which the ECB is subject further bolsters the view that ECB competences should be interpreted restrictively.[9] Indeed, the European Parliament and European heads of state have a limited ability to influence the ECB; the ECJ subjects ECB action to a reduced level of scrutiny; and the ECB enjoys considerable autonomy in determining monetary policy.[10] All of these factors, combined with the *de facto* expansion of ECB competencies witnessed in recent years, suggest a need to implement safeguards that minimize control costs.

For some observers, there are grounds to suspect a quasi-conspiratorial collaboration between the ECJ and ECB, which they believe has been detrimental to Member States. The ECJ been harshly criticized for shielding Union institutions

[6] Kenneth Rogoff, 'The Optimal Degree of Commitment to an Intermediate Monetary Target' (1985) 100 Quarterly Journal of Economics 1169.

[7] Rosa María Lastra, *International Financial and Monetary Law* (Oxford University Press 2015) 76; Paul Tucker, *Unelected Power: The Quest for Legitimacy in Central Banking* (Princeton University Press 2020) 147

[8] Charles M Tiebout, 'A Pure Theory of Local Expenditures' (1956) 64 Journal of Political Economy 416.

[9] BVerfGE 154 *PSPP* (2020), para 143.

[10] Adina Akbib and Mark Dawson, 'From Procedural to Substantive Accountability in EMU Governance' in Mark Dawson (ed), *Substantive Accountability in Europe's New Economic Governance* (Cambridge University Press 2023) 19, 20.

from judicial scrutiny while clearly applying more stringent standards to Member States.[11] Indeed, in 2018 the ECJ was sharply criticized for the leniency with which it scrutinized ECB policy, a dispute that led to a major clash with the German Constitutional Court.[12] From a political economy perspective, one can argue that there are incentives for the ECJ, the ECB, and the Commission to coordinate their actions to achieve greater autonomy from their principals, that is, Member States. The Commission relies extensively on its monopoly power to initiate legislation in the face of a European Parliament that has been persistently seeking to expand its legislative powers. The expanding legal scope of EU law has increasingly marginalized Member States' legal orders, which has empowered the ECJ as the arbiter of EU law. With the desire to acquire additional power and prestige as a recognized motive in institutional decision-making, this reading of ECB, ECJ, and Commission collaboration is not without merit. To be sure, there are legal barriers to excessively self-interested behaviour on the part of EU institutions. The conferral of power principle set forth in Article 5 TEU is the core provision that aims at aligning agents' actions with principals' interests, as it stipulates that Union institutions must act within the Treaty's boundaries. Accordingly, agency costs may arise when institutions transgress the principle of conferral.

[11] Martin Nettesheim, 'Grundrechtliche Prüfungsdichte durch den EuGH' (1995) Europäische Zeitschrift für Wirtschaftsrecht 106, 107; Georg M Berrisch, 'Zum "Bananen"-Urteil des EuGH vom 5.10.1994' (1994) Europarecht 461, 466.

[12] Case C-493/17 *Heinrich Weiss and Others* (2018) EU:C:2018:1000.

19
The European Commission

The principal–agent perspective is also relevant for assessing the activities of the European Commission. In accordance with Article 17(3), subpara 3, sentence 1 TEU, the European Commission is 'completely independent' when carrying out its work. In addition, the Commission has sole responsibility for proposing legislation (Article 289(3) TFEU), and is tasked with monitoring compliance with primary and secondary Union law as the 'guardian of Union law' (Article 17(1), sentence 2 TEU).

With a view to costs incurred by Member States as principals in order to ensure compliance by the Commission as agent, one relevant question is how the legislative agenda can be controlled and by whom. This is relevant because 'agenda-setting power' is a major determinant of which policy options are ultimately pursued. 'Positive agenda power' refers to the authority to decide which issues are introduced to the legislative agenda, while 'negative agenda power' refers to the power to protect the status quo and keep issues from being considered.[1] In the EU, the Commission has positive agenda power due to its near monopoly control over the proposal of new legislation. Yet it also has negative agenda power, as it can refuse to entertain legislative initiatives. The Council, in turn, is indispensable for adopting legislative proposal, yet it cannot prevent the Commission from launching a legislative proposal or subsequently vetoing a proposal. This makes the Commission an incredibly powerful actor when it comes to shaping the political agenda. Thus, while formal power rests with the Commission, there are informal mechanisms at work that allow Council representatives (particularly from large Member States) to influence positive and negative agenda power. As the Commission knows that approval from the Council is required for the successful adoption of legislative proposals, some agenda-setting power is held by the Council. This, in turn, means lower agency costs. Agency costs are also lowered when unanimity is required on the Council, as this ensures that national governments cannot be overruled.

However, given that the Commission is largely exempt from political control by the electorate when exercising its functions, agency costs are inevitably

[1] Kenneth A Shepsle and Barry R Weingast, 'The Institutional Foundations of Committee Power' (1987) 81 American Political Science Review 85; Gary W Cox and Mathew D McCubbins, 'The Institutional Determinants of Economic Policy Outcomes' in Stephan Haggard and Mathew D Mccubbins (eds), *Presidents, Parliaments, and Policy* (Cambridge University Press 2001).

EU Law and Economics. Armin Steinbach, Oxford University Press. © Oxford University Press 2025.
DOI: 10.1093/9780198920915.003.0019

incurred. It is precisely this lack of control that drives agency costs. While the Treaty of Lisbon made European Parliament approval necessary for the appointment of the Commission President (Article 17(7), sentences 2 and 3 TEU), two institutional obstacles stand in the way of effective political control by the principal. First, a motion of no confidence is only possible against the Commission as a whole, not against the individual president of the Commission or individual Commissioners. Targeted accountability that allows the principal to sanction individual conduct that violates the boundaries of the principal–agent relationship is thus not possible. As a result, the political costs and consequences of dismissing the Commission as a whole through a vote of no confidence are likely to be prohibitively high, making this sanction mechanism unsuitable as a remedy for principal–agent inconsistencies. Secondly, as we discussed, the European Parliament itself suffers from insufficient legitimacy, and induces high control costs for its principals. With the Commission legally accountable (although in a limited fashion) to the European Parliament, the agency costs induced by the Parliament exacerbate the agency costs for the Commission, because citizens are the main principals to the European Parliament (as per Article 10(2) TEU).

Thirdly, there is no genuine 'European public' that could exercise effective pressure on the Commission and thus hold it accountable. While it is certainly conceivable that a broad public consensus could arise regarding the need to sanction the Commission, as noted previously, the absence of homogeneous preferences across the EU prevents the emergence of a 'European public' that could act as a general check on the Commission. To be sure, political parties make an important contribution to Union integration and to development of a shared European political awareness, as foreseen by Article 10(4) TEU. However, the European parties are in practice rather loose associations that lack the mobilization potential enjoyed by national parties.[2] As discussed previously, European elections are not truly 'Europeanized', nor do they aggregate the will of the citizenry in Member States in a consistent fashion. Also, preference formation within the Parliament suffers from a 'mobilization bias' where certain preferences are systematically overrepresented compared to others. The vast majority of groups that exert lobbying pressure in Brussels represent private-sector interests, and in many cases the lobbying efforts are focused on rent-seeking. In light of the foregoing, a crucial concern is that if the citizenry as a principal lacks an effective means of control due to structural circumstances, there is a risk that the cost advantages achieved through centralization will not be passed on to citizens.

In this way, institutional constraints must be considered when it comes to assessing agency costs. In this connection, a distinction must be drawn between the Commissioners (and elected political officials) and the Commission's bureaucrats.

[2] Simon Hix, 'Parties at the European Level', *Political Parties in Advanced Industrial Democracies* (Oxford University Press 2002).

Given the Commission's monopoly over the introduction of legislation, the political orientation of decision-makers in the Commission is a significant factor. Empirical studies have explored whether Commission officials have a preference for deeper European integration and whether a pro-integrationist attitude is emerging due to 'consensus bias' effects. These studies conclude that among non-elected bureaucrats, there is considerable variation in attitudes towards European integration.[3] While civil servants who were previously active in the bureaucracies of large nation-states tend to favour subsidiarity rather than further centralization, civil servants who come from smaller Member States tend to support more robust integration.[4] This finding aligns with the realist view that sees smaller states as the primary beneficiaries of commitments that restrain the power of larger states. Accordingly, these studies find no empirical support for the view that the Commission's civil service has a clear bias in favour of supranationalism.[5]

Thus, while the Commission's civil service exhibits divergent attitudes towards integration, a different picture emerges with regards to political commissioners. Formally, the Commission members are independent, not bound by instructions, and committed to the good of the Community (Article 245 TFEU). Empirical examination of the party orientation of appointed commissioners finds that in two-thirds of cases, the commissioners have the same party membership as the governments nominating them. During the appointment process, Member State governments will take a candidate's political loyalty into account.[6] Accordingly, this selection process can lead to consistency between the preferences of Commission members and Member States, despite the formal independence of the former. This creates a potential point of discord with the Treaty-based normative requirement that Commission members are to serve the general interests of the Union (as stipulated by Article 17(1) TFEU).

[3] Liesbet Hooghe, 'Images of Europe: Orientations to European Integration among Senior Officials of the Commission' (1999) 29 British Journal of Political Science 345, 364.

[4] Liesbet Hooghe, 'Supranational Activists or Intergovernmental Agents? Explaining the Orientations of Senior Commission Officials Toward European Integration' (1999) 32 Comparative Political Studies 435, 459.

[5] Arndt Wonka, 'Die Europäische Kommission in EU-Entscheidungsprozessen, in: Die Politische Ökonomie Des EU-Entscheidungsprozesses' in Torsten Selck and Tim Veen (eds), *Die politische Ökonomie des EU-Entscheidungsprozesses* (VS Verlag 2008) 121.

[6] Robert Thomson, 'National Actors in International Organizations' (2008) 41 Comparative Political Studies 169; Arndt Wonka, 'Technocratic and Independent? The Appointment of European Commissioners and Its Policy Implications' (2007) 14 Journal of European Public Policy 169; George Ross, *Jacques Delors and European Integration* (Oxford University Press 1995) 57.

20
Adjudication

a) Why international courts at all?

Lawyers view adjudication as an important tool for ensuring checks and balances between the legislative, executive, and judicial branches.[1] As discussed in Chapter 17, the principal–agent perspective is one valuable analytical angle for assessing the delegation of adjudicative power to the Court. For realists, international courts have the limited function of reducing informational asymmetries. Such courts often act as agents of the state, and (powerful) states will seek to influence international courts by threatening to challenge or ignore rulings. Courts may resolve conflicts by offering an interpretation of the agreement and by producing information about the dispute at stake. Hence, courts provide information that reduces the decision-making costs of states involved in a conflict. Specifically in the EU, there is a need for a mechanism to reveal information held privately by Member States and Union institutions concerning factual circumstances, preferences, and legal interpretations. Centralized information can reduce uncertainty about the behaviour of relevant actors to make cooperation more effective. A law merchant model suggests that adjudication can serve as a repository of information about the past performance of traders. This actor makes the information available to prospective partners, thereby creating a reputational bond that facilitates current transactions.[2]

Let us consider the EU internal market and its basic freedoms as an example. EU members may try to obtain advantages that are either justified (in their view) from a legal perspective or merely difficult to oppose due to lack of factual clarity. For example, Member States may claim that the conditions of a 'security exception' under Article 36 TFEU are met in order to erect barriers to the free movement of goods and thus protect their domestic market from imports. In these cases, there is a need for an institution not only to enforce the rules, but also to establish and monitor facts and clarify standards. Both the EU Commission and the ECJ have specific roles with a view to clarifying the factual circumstances of a case and associated

[1] Paul Craig, 'Institutions, Power, and Institutional Balance' in Paul Craig and Gráinne de Búrca (eds), *The Evolution of EU Law* (Oxford University Press 2021) 46.

[2] Barbara Koremenos, Charles Lipson, and Duncan Snidal, 'The Rational Design of International Institutions' (2001) 55 International Organization 761, 788; Paul R Milgrom, Douglass C North, and Barry R Weingast, 'The Role of Institutions in the Revival of Trade: The Law Merchant, Private Judges, and the Champagne Fairs' (1990) 2 Economics & Politics 1, 19.

EU Law and Economics. Armin Steinbach, Oxford University Press. © Oxford University Press 2025.
DOI: 10.1093/9780198920915.003.0020

legal obligations. In this regard, informational asymmetries are invariably present, for each state has knowledge about certain facts and about its own specific interests that other states do not have. For example, an EU member may adopt a food safety standard for all marketed goods that another EU member finds to be in violation of the Treaty. The state knows how much it values the safety standards, but lacks information concerning how the other state values its opposition. Each state has a legal opinion concerning the interpretation of the Treaties, and each state may have evidence concerning whether the safety standards are justified by empirical research.

In the absence of adjudication, neither state has an incentive to reveal the relevant information it possesses. With adjudication, contentious claims can be resolved through fact finding and legal interpretation. In the EU, both the Commission and the ECJ are vested with adjudicational functions. The Commission is a primary information provider; it assesses Member State compliance, investigates cases of alleged non-compliance, and in some cases may make administrative decision (eg to enforce competition law). The ECJ, by contrast, serves as the judicial branch of the EU, issuing authoritative decisions regarding the interpretation of EU law in order to settle disputes. By issuing judgments, the ECJ interprets the conduct of other Member States. This reduces uncertainty for the Commission and Member States regarding each other's motivations and preferences. More specifically, ECJ judgments may illuminate whether instances of non-compliance are intentional and merit retaliatory action. This, in turn, provides a legal basis for the Commission to engage in retaliatory measures (eg assessment of fines, withholding of funds). In this sense, adjudication plays a crucial informational role, letting Member States know when and why policy preferences are unlawful. However, for this informational role to work properly, the facts and circumstances of a case must be observable and verifiable. If this condition is not fulfilled, states will avoid adjudication.[3]

Institutionalists view the informational function of adjudication as insufficient. They see courts acting as trustees, not representatives (agents), and as trustees they enjoy a degree of political autonomy to serve the public interest. Courts reduce policy ambiguities, stabilize policy outcomes, and discipline the authorities that exercise public powers.[4] In an international context, courts increase the credibility of the commitments that states make to each other. In particular, the existence of an international court augments the likelihood that a state will comply with its obligations in situations where compliance brings short-term disadvantages but long-term benefits.

Ultimately, why do states establish courts that may restrict their freedom of action and force them to uphold their commitments? Empirical research suggests

[3] Robert E Scott and Paul B Stephan, *The Limits of Leviathan* (Cambridge University Press 2006) 147.

[4] Karen J Alter, 'The Multiple Roles of International Courts and Tribunals' in Jeffrey L Dunoff and Mark A Pollack (eds), *Interdisciplinary Perspectives on International Law and International Relations* (Cambridge University Press 2012) 345.

that institutions are better able to resolve conflict when they establish binding dispute resolution mechanisms. This is because courts provide both private and public goods. From an economic point of view, the court's function is not limited to the settlement of bilateral disputes in individual cases (which represents a private good). Rather, litigation also creates a public good by contributing to peaceful dispute resolution, by stabilizing expectations regarding compliance, and by furthering the development of international law by monitoring judgment compliance.[5] Accordingly, international adjudication provides a mechanism for ensuring that dispute resolution contributes to general welfare.

Adjudication also helps to address the problems associated with the potential incompleteness of international agreements. As international agreements may be underspecified, the delegation of authority to interpret agreements lowers initial negotiation costs, as not all eventualities need to be formally addressed. By entrusting the ECJ to interpret EU law, EU members are able to design the EU Treaties with greater efficiency. In particular, this allows avoidance of costs that would arise given the need to anticipate all future contingencies within Member States. Under-specification and incompleteness are in fact inescapable given the goal of striking an effective balance between rigidity and flexibility in Treaty design. We discussed earlier that constitutional texts are typically under-specified and that the comprehensive body of provisions laid down in the TEU and the TFEU have been perceived as an 'overcomplete contract' (see Chapter 11 d) above). To be sure, from an efficiency perspective, both over-specification and under-specification may be inefficient. Over-specification entails inadequate flexibility for addressing state-level contingencies, while under-specification carries the risk of inadequately detailed provisions for ruling on the specific circumstances under dispute. Especially in dynamic regulatory domains, standards are preferred over rules, while specificity is advantageous to rule out policy designs that are, prima facie, inefficient (such as discrimination or a general curtailment of business between private parties, as addressed under Article 34 TFEU). When designing the rules, states must balance rigidity, state contingency, and discretion. Amongst these parameters, rigidity limits the scope of adjudication. However, rigidity may lead to inefficient judicial outcomes by causing market actors to generate inefficient results or creating adverse incentives. Hence, state contingency and discretion are captured in the Treaties by unspecified standards (rather than rules), with authority to render judgment on disputes concerning their application accorded to the ECJ.

In the case of prohibitions to quantitative restrictions on imports and exports, Treaty-enshrined state contingencies must be accounted for in two respects. First, not all possible trade-restrictive measures and situations are foreseeable at

[5] Sara McLaughlin Mitchell and Paul R Hensel, 'International Institutions and Compliance with Agreements' (2007) 51 American Journal of Political Science 721.

the moment of contract negotiation. Quantitative restrictions represent one such measure: the prohibition of 'all measures having equivalent effect' captures the prohibition of other distortive measures, irrespective of the formal nature of the instrument. Second, in order to avoid inefficient rigidity, rules must allow states to pursue certain measures depending on the state of their economies. Built-in flexibility such as the exception clause in Article 36 TFEU allows leeway to pursue measures 'justified on grounds of public morality, public policy or public security'. As argued above, it is sensible to allow these exceptions (under the restriction mentioned) because they lead to efficient results. Consider the import of an unsafe product, for example: the efficiency question concerns whether the overall costs of allowing the import are smaller than the benefits of an import ban. The exclusion of such products will normally be worth more to an importing state than the sale of such a product will be to an exporting state.[6] Hence, the existence of this escape clause increases the value of the internal market provisions in the Treaty. Likewise, consider the need to protect 'order and security' as grounds for an exception. If risks occur to life and health, a negative externality is attached to the imported good that the person invoking the basic freedom inflicts on society as a whole. In such cases, the escape clause allows an efficiency assessment, since the costs to society are typically higher than the benefits that accrue to the individual service provider. Importantly, the authority to determine what constitutes justifiable grounds for Treaty exception must not lie with the state invoking the measure. Giving too much discretion to that state would induce abuse and protectionism. In order to ensure an objective and neutral legal assessment (ideally coinciding with an economic efficiency analysis), the ECJ—safeguarded by its independence—must therefore scrutinize the states' interpretation of legal exceptions.

b) Efficient breaches of EU law

Balancing rigidity and flexibility through adjudication in order to arrive at efficient solutions must be distinguished from deliberate breaches of international agreements. For lawyers, *pacta sunt servanda* is the bedrock of the customary international law of treaties—yet this maxim does not apply to economic assessment. For the economist, violations of international agreements may be desirable. Efficient breaches of the EU Treaties provide an excellent example of the difference between a purely legal approach (which stresses rule compliance as a matter of principle) and economic assessment (which is concerned with obtaining efficient outcomes). The ECJ is strictly bound to verify legal compliance. While the interpretative approaches open to the ECJ provide little scope for 'effect-oriented

[6] Andrew Guzman, *How International Law Works* (Oxford University Press 2008) 151.

jurisprudence',[7] situations may arise in which the pre-defined rules are inadequate for addressing novel circumstances, particularly when built-in flexibility is insufficient and strict rule adherence would create undesirable inefficiencies.

'Efficient breach of contract' refers to situations in which a party voluntarily breaches a contract and accepts the requirement to pay damages when an even greater economic loss would have been incurred by contract compliance.[8] For a lawyer, breach of contract based on efficiency considerations would be an impermissible violation of *pacta sunt servanda*, unless there are positively defined exception clauses that can be invoked. From an economic perspective, the costs and benefits that accrue from a breach are crucial. The liquidity measures undertaken by the ECB during the European sovereign debt crisis provide an example in this regard. A legal interpretation based on a strict reading of the Treaties may have found that asset purchasing measures to support crisis-wracked countries were in violation of the no-bailout clause contained in Article 125 TFEU.[9] From this perspective, the decision to offer assistance could then be seen as an efficient breach of contract, insofar as the denial of support would have meant a break-up of the eurozone and catastrophic welfare losses.[10]

Similarly, in other situations it may be more efficient for a Member State to breach the rules and pay damages rather than to comply. Consider by way of example the track record of compliance with deficit rules in the eurozone.[11] According to fiscal rules, Member States are required to keep their annual budget deficits below 3 per cent and public debt levels below 60 per cent of GDP. Not least, given checkered compliance with these rules, we must assume that states view it as preferable in certain circumstances to breach these rules in favour of more expansionary fiscal policies, rather than risk economic downturns.[12] In such cases, if the EU Commission strictly enforces the rules, it may forego the efficiency gains associated with a more flexible stance. France and Germany temporarily violated the Stability and Growth Pact in 2003 by taking advantage of their power in the Council. Both countries sought flexibility and relief from the fiscal rules, which

[7] Armin Steinbach, 'Effect-Based Analysis in the Court's Jurisprudence on the Euro Crisis' (2017) 42 European Law Review 255.

[8] Wenqing Liao, *The Application of the Theory of Efficient Breach in Contract Law: A Comparative Law and Economics Perspective* (Intersentia 2015); Melvin A Eisenberg, *Foundational Principles of Contract Law* (Oxford University Press 2018).

[9] Jeffery Atik, 'From "No Bailout" to the European Stability Mechanism' (2016) 39 Fordham International Law Journal 1201, 1215.

[10] However, some economists claimed Greece's exit from the eurozone would have been the preferable economic scenario. Nikitas-Spiros Koutsoukis and Spyros A Roukanas, 'The GrExit Paradox' (2014) 9 Procedia Economics and Finance 24.

[11] Martin Larch, Janis Malzubris, and Stefano Santacroce, 'Numerical Compliance with EU Fiscal Rules: Facts and Figures from a New Database' (2023) 58 Intereconomics 32.

[12] Christoph Paetz and Sebastian Watzka, 'The Macroeconomic Effects of Re-Applying the EU Fiscal Rules: Returning to the Status Quo Ante or Moving to Expenditure Rules?' (2023) 264 National Institute Economic Review 59.

ultimately culminated in an ECJ verdict.[13] One could argue that this breach was beneficial insofar as it allowed France and Germany to cushion the impact of negative economic trends. If this is true, fiscal rigidity would have been an inefficient solution, not least given the low level of economic risk posed by slightly higher public debt levels.[14] Sanctioning Germany and France in these cases would only have generated increased economic costs. From this perspective, enforcing the fiscal rules would have been economically inefficient.

However, this does not account for the dynamic knock-on effects that even singular breaches may have on efficiency. From a dynamic efficiency perspective, the toleration of non-compliance may create a moral hazard that encourages other countries to follow suit. This may culminate in an overall relaxation of the rules. And, indeed, it has been argued that the repeated non-compliance with fiscal rules observed over the last decade was crucially enabled by the 'bad example' of French and German behaviour in the early 2000s. In a repeated fiscal game, defection of one party may trigger defection by other parties in subsequent games. Although such dynamic interrelationships are difficult to identify and predict, they must be taken into account when considering efficient breaches of EU law.

There are further limits to efficient breaches of international treaties. Guzman has argued that WTO rules should not be enforced with sanctions when states adopt WTO-incompatible measures in the pursuit of legitimate interests that are not recognized by WTO bodies. The EU beef hormone case provides an interesting example of this tension. The WTO dispute settlement body found the EU import regime to be in violation of WTO rules. Yet it was argued that sanctions should not be imposed, as the EU would continue to uphold the measure, convinced of its legitimacy and legality.[15] In this case, sanctions would be 'welfare inferior', as they would not lead to legal compliance (thus making them ineffective). Yet making this a general rule would have far-reaching effects. By way of example, should Hungary be exempted from rule-of-law sanctions because the Hungarian government already faces high domestic political costs for pursuing policies that disrespect the rule of law? If the Hungarian majority supports such measures and wishes to subject their judiciary to political control, ignoring their will would occasion high political costs (possibly even higher than the costs of a partially politicized judiciary). Here, as well, dynamic efficiency effects must be taken into account. The positivist

[13] Wolfgang Ringe, 'COVID-19 and European banks: no time for lawyers' in C Gortsos and Wolf-Georg Ringe (eds), *Pandemic Crisis and Financial Stability* (European Banking Institute 2020) 57; Dimitrios Doukas, 'The Frailty of the Stability and Growth Pact and the European Court of Justice: Much Ado about Nothing?' (2005) 32 Legal Issues of Economic Integration 293.

[14] A similar argument of efficient breaches of WTO in light of high domestic political costs has been put forward by Alan O Sykes, 'Protectionism as a Safeguard: A Positive Analysis of the GATT Escape Clause with Normative Speculations' (1991) 58 University of Chicago Law School 255. He argues that the GATT escape clause requirements may capture circumstances in which trade obligations are likely to impose large political costs on the importing state and violation is likely to impose small costs on the exporting state.

[15] Guzman (n 6) 152.

lawyers' exhortation that we must respect *pacta sunt servanda* regardless of efficiency considerations may be important to consider from a long-term perspective, as the weakening of *pacta sunt servanda* may change the strategic behaviour of parties. A key concern in this regard is that non-enforcement can expand the scope of permissible actions, making the conduct of parties less predictable.

c) Judicial authority: leeway and constraints

If delegation of the power to adjudicate serves to ensure compliance with the Treaty commitments, how do we explain the ECJ's judicial innovations, which some observers have characterized as judicial activism? The ECJ's early landmark judgments on the direct effect and primacy of EU law have been a particular target of criticism, and have paved the way for the development of further doctrinal innovations by the Court, including implied powers and *effet utile*, which have promoted legal interpretations that give EU law the greatest possible effect. Posner's work on judicial behaviour may offer a model for explaining an assertive ECJ eager to employ judicial innovation.[16] The EU judiciary, like Member State judiciaries, is designed to protect judicial autonomy. In principle, ECJ judges are independent, both materially and politically. Yet, despite this insulation of European Court judges from political interference, their actions can be determined, in line with *Posner*, as a function of income, leisure, and judicial voting. While income and leisure are standard criteria that motivate suppliers of labour, additional determinants present among bureaucrats are the positive utility of a good reputation, relevance, and prestige. This public choice insight modifies the legalistic view that judges are strictly guided by their obligation to apply rather than create law. It posits that practical reality is incompatible with the notion of the judge as a neutral arbiter of statutory provisions.[17] From this perspective, the personal interests and ideological perspectives of the judge may play an important role in their interpretation of the law, not least when legal provisions lack completeness. In EU law, various Treaty-based objectives, rights, and obligations are vaguely defined, meaning there may be significant leeway for non-legal considerations to influence a judge's decisions.

While judges are typically independent when carrying out their tasks, we can distinguish three prominent factors that constrain a judge's discretion in interpreting law. The first is specificity of the legal matter at issue and relevant precedent. The wealth of past judgments on an issue is a crucial constraint because it can create

[16] Richard A Posner, 'Judicial Behavior and Performance: An Economic Approach Judicial Behavior and Performance: An Economic Approach' (2005) 32 Florida State University Law Review 1259.

[17] Lee Epstein and Nicholas W Waterbury, 'Judicial Behavior' in William Thompson (ed), *Oxford Research Encyclopedia of Politics* (Oxford University Press 2020).

'path dependence' that guides future decision-making. What can we draw from the law and economics literature on judicial path dependence? In addition to the doctrine of precedence, two important principles that guide the development and application of case law are *stare decisis* and *jurisprudence constante*.[18] The former, originating from common law traditions, requires adherence to past legal precedent. *Jurisprudence constante*, by contrast, is more lenient, requiring the judge to follow a consistent line in judicial decisions. While precedent traditionally plays a greater role in common law systems, in civil law systems (including EU law), case law is relegated to the rank of a secondary legal source.[19] The Treaties are the only guiding law in the EU, and judges are strictly obliged to apply statutory law. Article 19(1) TEU stipulates that the ECJ must 'ensure that in the interpretation and application of the Treaties the law is observed', and Article 19(3) TEU reiterates that the ECJ must act in accordance with the Treaties. Generally, the role of precedents in the EU, as well as under civil law, can be described as follows: the higher the specificity of the applicable law as well as the level of uniformity in past precedents, the greater the persuasive force of case law. In this regard, we must consider the historic variations in the degree of constraint imposed on ECJ judges through EU primary law and precedents. During the early years of the ECJ, when the ECJ passed its path-breaking jurisprudence on supremacy and direct effect, two issues came together: the limited specificity of the initial European Community Treaties, as well as the lack of an established line of jurisprudence. Regarding the former, the Treaty of Rome establishing the European Community contained 248 provisions, while the consecutive Treaty changes have brought this up to 358 articles (TFEU) and 55 articles (TEU). Probably more importantly, the Treaty provisions were rather vague and did not contain specific individual rights but rather objectives, competence norms, and state obligations.

With a vague statutory law and a small, though growing body of case law, there was no jurisprudence constraint—that is, there was no line of established judgments that would have significantly limited the discretion of the ECJ. The landmark cases of *van Gend en Loos* and *Costa v Enel* paved the way for a gradual expansion of directly applicable EU laws that granted individual rights.[20] While individual rights were literally absent in the Treaty of Rome, it was the notion of direct effect that the ECJ read into state obligations, such that individuals were empowered to invoke state obligations as directly effective rights against the state. With the emergence of the Francovich jurisprudence establishing state liability for the non-transposition of EU directives, the Court further mobilized the economic interest of individuals in order to exert pressure on EU states to comply with EU

[18] Francesco Parisi and Vincy Fon, *The Economics of Lawmaking* (Oxford University Press 2008) 78.

[19] On the role of precedents, see Thomas Lundmark, D Neil MacCormick, and Robert S Summers, 'Interpreting Precedents: A Comparative Study' (1997) 46 American Journal of Comparative Law 211.

[20] Case C-26/62 *Van Gend en Loos v Administratie der Belastingen* (1963) EU:C:1963:1.

law.[21] From a historical perspective, the ECJ initially enjoyed greater discretion than it currently does, given the comprehensive Treaties as well as a dense body of ECJ precedents. More recently, the Court has privileged general references to 'established case law' and extensive citation over substantive reasoning when dealing with precedents. This is driven in part by a desire to convey an impression of systematic coherence in the evolution of case law.[22]

A second source of constraint on ECJ judges comes from the fact that judges are subject to a hierarchical system of appellate review, and are incentivized to avoid reversals by higher courts. This factor is particularly relevant with regard to the ECJ, as the Court, like the highest supreme courts at national levels, is not subject to judicial review. Being bound exclusively by the EU Treaties but not by judicial review affords judges significant discretion in their interpretation of EU law. Particularly in its early years, as the ECJ rendered its landmark judgments that encouraged the constitutionalization of EU law, it was not subject to serious external constraints. Only later, after the German Constitutional Court's *Solange I* judgment of 1974, did national constitutional courts begin to act as a check on ECJ jurisprudence.[23] In the *Solange I* judgment, the German Constitutional Court challenged the legality of the *Van Gend en Loos* decision, thus questioning the primacy of EC law.[24] After this judgment, a number of constitutional lawyers became vocal opponents of EC law primacy, highlighting the 'structural incoherence' between EU law and German national constitutional law. Ever since this landmark decision, the relationship between the ECJ and the German Constitutional Court has been marked periodically by bitter clashes (despite interludes of congenial relations). The *PSPP* judgment of 2020 signalled the start of a new period of tension between the courts. Such conflict creates challenges for ECJ judges, who must realize that, while their decisions are not formally reversible, there is a risk that the ECJ will lose legitimacy among those who are supposed to follow its judgments. It is against this backdrop that we must accord plausibility to Posner's remarks that judges are political actors who are motivated by professional ethics and concern for their reputation, but also the desire of 'getting on' and playing the 'judicial game'.[25]

Third, dissatisfaction of law-makers with a judgment can give rise to a change in law in order to modify the normative constraints for the court. Considering that

[21] Luigi Malferrari, 'The Functional Representation of the Individual's Interests Before the EC Courts: The Evolution of the Remedies System and the Pluralistic Deficit in the EC' (2005) 12 Indiana Journal of Global Legal Studies 667. See also Joel P Trachtman, *The Economic Structure of International Law* (Harvard University Press 2008) 520.

[22] Marc A Jacob, *Precedents and Case-Based Reasoning in the European Court of Justice: Unfinished Business* (Cambridge University Press 2014).

[23] BVerfGE 73, 339 *Solange II* (1986)

[24] Peter Hilpold, 'So Long Solange? The PSPP Judgment of the German Constitutional Court and the Conflict between the German and the European "Popular Spirit"' (2021) 23 Cambridge Yearbook of European Legal Studies 159.

[25] Richard A Posner, 'The Role of the Judge in the Twenty-First Century the Role of the Judge in the Twenty-First Century' (2006) 86 Boston University Law Review 1049.

ECJ judges are constrained by the possibility that their decisions will be repealed by legislation, the judicial discretion enjoyed by the ECJ can be assessed through the lens of game theory. Building on the public choice principle, judges are just one additional player in a wider institutional interaction with other officials. Assuming that judges pursue their own political and individual preferences with a view to the political order (possibly even concerning the outcomes of specific cases), then judges can satisfy their preferences within the boundaries of statutory laws and established methods of interpretation.[26] While judges are constrained by the countervailing power of legislators, whether and to what extent judges exploit 'judicial space' depends on the likelihood of provoking legislative repeal. Drawing on game theory, one can suppose that judges will take more advantage of their discretional authority if the legislative repeal of their decisions is less likely (and vice versa). A prudent judge pursues their own political preferences only to the extent that legislative repeal can be avoided.[27] This finding has a connection to the literature on domestic bureaucracy. International bureaucrats are given more discretion when the issue requires more specialized technical and scientific knowledge, but the complexity of legal interpretation may also be seen as a form of specialized knowledge. If bureaucrats, like judges, pursue their own policy goals, governments will continue to confer adjudicative power only as long as the advantages that are associated with reduced uncertainty and rule-making exceed the dissatisfaction that governments suffer from misalignment with these policy goals. The Polish government's and constitutional court's refusal to accept the rulings of the ECJ (in a flagrant violation of EU law) demonstrates this logic. They claim that European judges have interpreted EU rules in a way that is no longer compatible with the Polish constitution.[28]

[26] Rahul Hemrajani and Tony Hobert, 'The Effects of Decision Fatigue on Judicial Behavior: A Study of Arkansas Traffic Court Outcomes' (2024) Journal of Law and Courts 1.

[27] Dieter Schmidtchen, Alexander R Neunzig, and Hans-Jörg Schmidt-Trenz, 'One Market, One Law: EU Enlargement in Light of the Economic Theory of Optimal Legal Areas' (2001) CSLE Discussion Paper, No 2001-03, 109.

[28] Marta Lasek-Markey, 'Poland's Constitutional Tribunal on the Status of EU Law: The Polish Government Got All the Answers It Needed from a Court It Controls' (*European Law Blog*, 21 October 2021). See also Erik Voeten, 'Making Sense of the Design of International Institutions' (2019) 22 Annual Review of Political Science 147, 151.

PART V

WHAT TO COOPERATE ON IN THE EU

Introduction to Part V

The *why*, *how*, and *who* have highlighted the juxtaposition and alignment of legal and economic perspectives. The analytical *why* has revealed how to look at the Member States' motivation to use the EU to maximize their respective payoff function; how legal principles and core Treaty decisions can be made sense of through an economic eye; who acts as a Union institution, including an explanation of their actions. This leads us to look at some substantive fields of EU competences more closely. Clearly, economic analysis varies in its ability to offer insights for the study of EU law and policies. The connection is most obvious where the law explicitly asks for the import of economic insight into the normative legal analysis. Competition law has probably been the most popular field for blending law and economic scholarship.[1] This is, for one, because the emergence of antitrust law was a direct response to economic phenomena. The call for a level playing field between competitors and the containment of monopolistic power has been at the core of economic traditions as diverse as the German ordoliberalism,[2] the Brandeis movement,[3] and the (late) Chicago school.[4] It is not surprising that competition concepts have influenced the practical application and interpretation of EU laws—such as using economics to define geographical and substantive markets, determine the substitutability of goods, and evaluate whether mergers lead

[1] See only Anu Bradford and others, 'The Global Dominance of European Competition Law Over American Antitrust Law' (2019) 16 Journal of Empirical Legal Studies 731; Anu Bradford, Robert J. Jackson Jr. and Jonathon Zytnick, 'Is EU Merger Control Used for Protectionism? An Empirical Analysis' (2018) 15 Journal of Empirical Legal Studies 165; Damien Geradin, Anne Layne-Farrar and Nicolas Petit, *EU Competition Law and Economics* (Oxford University Press 2012).

[2] Peter Behrens, 'The Ordoliberal Concept of "Abuse" of a Dominant Position and Its Impact on Article 102 TFEU' in Fabiana Di Porto and Rupprecht Podszun (eds), *Abusive Practices in Competition Law* (Edward Elgar Publishing 2018).

[3] Manuel Wörsdörfer, 'Louis D. Brandeis and the New Brandeis Movement: Parallels and Differences' (2023) 68 The Antitrust Bulletin 440.

[4] Richard A Posner, 'The Chicago School of Antitrust Analysis' (1979) 127 University of Pennsylvania Law Review 925.

to efficiencies or innovation.[5] Thousands of competition cases have allowed the Commission and the Court to refine both the legal rules as well the import of economic concepts, with industrial economics probably being the most important disciplinary contribution to the practice of competition law.[6] But the abundance of scholarship in this area raises the question of whether other fields of EU substantive law have been under-analysed from an economic perspective.

Specifically, we look at elements of EU law where the role of economics has either been (implicitly or explicitly) denied by legal scholars or where it simply has not gained sufficient salience in highlighting the added value of an economic perspective. First, the question of *European public goods* is an essential one, because it offers normative guidance on which public good (and the corresponding competence) should be supplied at the Union or at the Member State level, a question that has too often been accepted by lawyers as an exogenous political decision. Lawyers employ techniques to determine the assignment of competences *within* the EU legal framework, but the law is silent on the more fundamental question predating positive Treaty allocation of at what level—between the Union and Member States—public goods *ought* to be provided (this silence can be likened with the limited interest of lawyers in the *why* of EU cooperation. It turns out that economics has a lot to say, and a normative framework to offer, for the question of the optimal level of public goods supply. In turn, EU law is vocal when it comes to the governance of these public goods, that is, the question of what legal and institutional framework one should design for the European public good in order to account for the economic normative suggestion on public good provision. From that perspective, law and economics generate, taken together, new insight on *why* and *what* to supply as an EU public good (and what should remain a Member State public good) as well as *how* this provision of public goods should be put in place.

Second, probably no substantive law field has served as constantly as the core motivation of deepening EU integration as the *internal market*. Given that the EU was initially launched as a market-enhancing and economy-stabilizing project, the emergence of the 'market citizen' was an inevitable consequence.[7] It relied on (and was basically propelled by) the ECJ which transformed the EU from an obligation-centric order requesting Member States to establish a common market to an individual-centric perpetuum mobile that leveraged individuals (first as economic agents, later as EU citizens) to pursue their rights with a view to invalidating what they perceived as unjustified barriers to the exercise of common market freedoms. While ECJ jurisprudence on market freedoms has consistently

[5] Geradin, Layne-Farrar, and Petit (n 1).

[6] Oliver Budzinski, 'Modern Industrial Economics and Competition Policy: Open Problems and Possible Limits' (2009) IME Working Paper, No 93.

[7] Hans Peter Ipsen and Gert Nicolaysen, 'Haager Kongreß für Europarecht und Bericht über die aktuelle Entwicklung des Gemeinschaftsrechts' (1964) Neue Juristische Wochenschrift 339, 340.

expanded, law and economics have rarely joined forces. *Cum grano salis*, lawyers seek doctrinal soundness and systematic comparison between the fundamental freedoms, while economists have abstracted from individual freedoms and discuss the outcome of exercising fundamental freedoms ushering into economic integration supporting macroeconomic functions such as the EU Capital Union,[8] intra-EU mobility,[9] and the growth effects of eradicating barriers to commerce and trade.[10] We seek to integrate legal and economic perspectives to better understand the function of individual freedoms as pillars of internal market integration; specifically, how the law governing basic freedoms has evolved in an economically sound way (or has not) and how, if possible, legal interpretation could be guided to that effect.

Third and finally, the economic approach should be tested on what has possibly been the most controversial, yet certainly evolving, substantive law area in recent years. Crisis after crisis has shattered the tenets of the Economic and Monetary Union, with the banking crisis and sovereign debt crisis revealing architectural deficiencies. Core legal premises of the EMU—notably the bailout prohibition as well as the ban on monetary financing—have been applied and interpreted by (the German constitutional and the European) courts in a heterogenous, often conflicting fashion. Again, lawyers and economists tended to speak past each other. Before the onset of crises, lawyers paid little attention to the imbalance between fiscal, economic, and monetary institutional architecture enshrined in the Treaties which they accepted as an exogenous (political and economic) choice of Treaty-makers. Lawyers were abruptly confronted with the reality that, during crises, their preference for doctrinal purity and systematic coherence ran into conflict with an economic reality (and economic scholarship) that called for exceptions and leniency in the interpretation of rules.[11] Lawyers could not find this flexibility in the Treaties, some even saw the canon of interpretation methods as incompatible with non-conventional economic measures. This led some 'pure' lawyers to suspect that the credibility of the legal order as whole was at stake.[12] It is against this backdrop of disciplinary alienation that we explore how rules

[8] Ashok Vir Bhatia and others, 'A Capital Market Union for Europe' (2019) Staff Discussion Notes No 2019/007.

[9] Timo Baas, 'The Macroeconomic Impact of Intra-EU Migration on the German Economy. Gefälligkeitsübersetzung: Der makroökonomische Einfluss der Migration innerhalb der EU auf die deutsche Wirtschaft' (2014) 49 Intereconomics 116.

[10] Jonne Lehtimäki and David Sondermann, 'Baldwin vs. Cecchini Revisited: The Growth Impact of the European Single Market' (2020) Working Paper Series No 2392.

[11] Paul de Grauwe, 'The European Central Bank as Lender of Last Resort in the Government Bond Markets' (2013) 59 CESifo Economic Studies 520.

[12] Helmut Siekmann, 'The Legality of Outright Monetary Transactions (OMT) of the European System of Central Banks' (2015) Working Paper Series No 90. See also the contributions by Thomas MJ Möllers, Christoph Degenhart, Helmut Siekmann, and Franz-Christoph Zeitler in Thomas MJ Möllers and Franz-Christoph Zeitler (eds), *Europa als Rechtsgemeinschaft—Währungsunion und Schuldenkrise* (Mohr Siebeck 2013).

governing the EMU can be made sense of from an economic perspective, how core principles of state organization—the distinction between federal and sub-federal competences—interact with the economic rationale for debt constraints, and how legal core provisions can reconcile legal interpretations respecting the telos of the norms, while at the same time not ignoring the macroeconomic contingencies in which these rules are embedded.

21
European Public Goods

There is no shortage of claims about what European public goods should be, how they should be delivered, or how they should be financed.[1] What remains lacking in the growing literature on European Public Goods is a clear definition and identification framework of these particular goods that is not circumstantial and that will stand the test of time, as well as a concept on how to govern the provision of these public goods in the EU. The underlying question is how much of public goods should be provided at the EU rather than at the Member State level. How should the EU decide when the benefits of EU-level provisions justify their potential costs in terms of reduced national sovereignty, differences in preferences regarding the nature and level of public goods, and the greater detachment of Brussels-based institutions from national and local concerns? To what extent could these costs be reduced through suitable institutional arrangements for governing the EU-level provision of public goods?

Often 'should public goods be provided at the national or European level?' may be the wrong question to ask. The right question is how to find institutional arrangements for public good provision that maximizes the benefits of public goods for EU members. In some cases, this will lead to EU decision-making and financing, in others to national decision-making and financing, with many possibilities in between. The chapter provides a framework, and a set of illustrations, that help identify the right arrangements.[2]

The first question is whether a particular good should be supplied by the private or by the public sector. The traditional definition of a public good considers non-rivalry (ie the consumption of the good by someone does not diminish the consumption of others), and non-excludability (ie the good can be consumed by anyone) to be essential features of public goods because they lead to free-riding and under-provision of the good, which justifies public intervention.[3] However, for the purpose of this analysis, the traditional definition of public goods is too restrictive,

[1] Thierry Breton, 'A Europe that protects its citizens, transforms its economy, and projects itself as a global power' (2024) Speech at the European Policy Centre, 10 January 2024; Mario Draghi, 'The Next Flight of the Bumblebee: The Path to Common Fiscal Policy in the Eurozone' (2023) 15th Annual Martin Feldstein Lecture, 11 July 2023; Marco Buti, 'When will the European Union finally get the budget it needs?' (2023) Analysis, 7 December 2023, Bruegel.

[2] This chapter draws from Gregory Claeys and Armin Steinbach, 'A conceptual framework for the identification and governance of European public goods' (2024) Working Paper 14/2024, Bruegel.

[3] Paul A Samuelson, 'The Pure Theory of Public Expenditure' (1954) 36 Review of Economics and Statistics 387.

EU Law and Economics. Armin Steinbach, Oxford University Press. © Oxford University Press 2025.
DOI: 10.1093/9780198920915.003.0021

as there are other coordination failures that can lead to the under-provision of a good compared to its optimal level, and that might require public intervention. A notable example is green transportation and in particular the transition towards electric vehicles (EVs). Consumers hesitate to purchase EVs due to the insufficient charging infrastructure, which restricts demand, while companies might be reluctant to develop a charging network without a sufficient number of EVs to justify their investment, thus leading to not enough supply. Contributing to the establishment of a dense network of EV charging points thus contributes to a public good, which is not related to the usual non-exclusion/non-rivalry market failure.

What is discussed in economics under the concept of public goods is reflected in legal debates about the concept of the common good or the public interest. Both terms have nothing to do with the traditional economic definition of public goods but are closely linked to theoretical debate about the legitimacy of state action. The concern for the common good, in the legal literature, has been likened with legitimizing statehood and the exercise of sovereign power.[4] The legal literature devoted to the common good has not produced a clear definition of what constitutes the common good, nor does a positive law definition exist.[5] For a start, it can be characterized as forming the basis of statehood, often likened to public interest. As an inherently open and indefinite concept, the common good creates a framework for justifying the legitimacy of state or sovereign action.

Given the discussion on the legitimacy of the European Union and the limitations of the economic definition of a pure public good, it seems reasonable to adopt a slightly broader definition: a public good will simply be defined as a good that is not supplied at an adequate level without public intervention (which could take various forms including direct provision/government expenditure, and regulation) because of coordination problems (not only non-exclusion/non-rivalry but also factors like network effects). This 'extended' notion of public goods is aligned with the general approach to public goods that is reflected both in the academic literature on fiscal federalism as well as in the policy discourse on European public goods.[6] A European Public Good can therefore be defined as a good not supplied at an adequate level without public intervention, and which should be provided at the EU level to internalize externalities, reap benefits of scale, while ensuring that local preferences are taken into account.

Both the legal quest for legitimacy as well as the economic concern for efficiency culminate in the question of whether a public good should be provided at the local, national, European, or global level. Early economic work has conceptualized the

[4] Christian Calliess, *Öffentliche Güter im Recht der Europäischen Union* (Bertelsmann Stiftung 2021) 7.

[5] J Öberg, 'Normative Justifications of EU Criminal Law: European Public Goods and Transnational Interests' (2021), 27 European Law Journal, 408; S Coutts, 'Supranational Public Wrongs: The Limitations and Possibilities of European Criminal Law and a European Community' (2017), 54 Common Market Law Review, 771, at 801 (equating European public interest with European public goods).

[6] Clemens Fuest and Jean Pisani-Ferry, 'A Primer on Developing European Public Goods' (2019) EconPol Policy Report, No 16.

answer to this question in the decentralization theorem, according to which '... in the absence of cost-savings from the centralized provision of a (local public) good and of inter-jurisdictional externalities, the level of welfare will always be at least as high (and typically higher) if Pareto-efficient levels of consumption are provided in each jurisdiction than if any single, uniform level of consumption is maintained across all jurisdictions'.[7] With more than one relevant factor, determining the appropriate governmental level for the organization and funding of public goods typically involves a trade-off.[8] On one hand, there is potential heterogeneity in preferences across geographical or political entities, which tends to favour the provision of goods at the local level (tailor-made in line with local preferences). On the other hand, there is the potential for improved efficiency through internalizing externalities and capitalizing on economies of scale, which pushes in the other direction. Decentralization is thus optimal when the costs of providing public goods at a lower level are lower than at a higher one either because there is no gain related to interjurisdictional spillovers or economies of scale or because these gains are lower than the costs associated with supplying uniform public goods rather than tailor-made public goods to take into account heterogenous preferences. Decentralized provision can also be beneficial due to better knowledge of preferences or higher democratic accountability. Put another way, the optimal level of provision of a public good is the one that reaps efficiency gains, while taking into account local preferences.

Where externalities are substantial and public goods and services are shared by large populations, their production and supply should be dealt with centrally.[9] For the EU, this can be framed in terms of intrajurisdictional efficiency. An optimal allocation is achieved when the bundle of collective goods supplied by Member States satisfy the collective demands of individuals at minimum cost, with costs comprising the costs of producing public services plus the transaction costs of the decision-making process, implementation costs, and agency-related control costs (see above Chapter 5).

a) Dealing with trade-offs

Determining the appropriate governmental level for the organization and funding of public goods typically involves a trade-off.[10] On one side, there are benefits from a larger size and internalization of spillover; on the other side, there are political costs associated with heterogeneous preferences of public goods and policies. Economies of scale intuitively occur in the provision of public goods, such as a common legal

[7] Wallace E Oates, *Fiscal Federalism* (Harcourt Brace Jovanovich 1972) 54.

[8] Alberto Alesina, Ignazio Angeloni and Ludger Schuknecht, 'What Does the European Union Do?' (2005) 123 Public Choice 275.

[9] Robert P Inman and Daniel L Rubinfeld, 'Economics of Federalism' in Francesco Parisi (ed), *Oxford Handbook of Law and Economics* (Oxford University Press 2017) 90.

[10] Oates (n 7); Alesina, Angeloni and Schuknecht (n 8).

and judicial system, foreign policy and defence, public health, transnational infrastructure, and a common monetary system. While the total costs of providing these goods EU-wide may be increasing, their average cost is decreasing in size because of shared fixed costs. In these cases, scale economies lead to lower prices per person.[11] Moreover, larger political unions can also internalize cross-regional externalities, as the literature on political integration and federalism has demonstrated[12]—in the EU, they can occur both by internalizing negative spillovers through reducing the level of Member States activities, or by reaping positive externalities by extending Member State activities or through Union activities. Yet, scale economies and internalization of externalities can be outweighed by costs associated with preferences and values along dimensions such as language, culture, religion, and ethnicity. Since many of these 'costs' are non-economic in nature, economic outcomes and political institutions can be fully understood only when social preferences and attitudes rooted in culture and history are taken into account[13]—an analytical angle which can be easily likened with the emphasis the German Constitutional Court has given to cultural divergences as factors that could bring the transfer of competences to an halt (see above Chapter 10 a)). Ultimately, the challenge is to account for the interplay between economic and non-economic factors, avoiding the over-emphasis of cultural and ethnic considerations at the expense of more material economic efficiency concerns (and vice versa).

However, the heterogeneity argument requires a closer look, specifically one should ask what the sources of heterogeneity are. The claim here is that cultural heterogeneity is not only associated with costs, but can also introduce significant benefits. Heterogeneity of traits and preferences can generate substantial benefits through innovation, specialization, and learning.[14] In particular, where production and exchange of *private* (ie rival) goods are concerned, heterogeneity may prove beneficial. A society composed of people with diverse tastes and preferences in private consumption is likely to function more efficiently and harmoniously than a society where everyone wants to consume the same identical goods and work at the same identical times. This is less obviously the case in relation to public goods, because they are supplied at a uniform level and a mismatch between policies and preferences create disagreements over public goods and policies, such as the design of social policies, family policies, or foreign and defence policies.[15]

[11] Alberto Alesina and Romain Wacziarg, 'Openness, Country Size and Government' (1998) 69 Journal of Public Economics 305.

[12] Wenche Hauge and Tanja Ellingsen, 'Beyond Environmental Scarcity: Causal Pathways to Conflict' (1998) 35 Journal of Peace Research 299; Wallace E Oates, 'An Essay on Fiscal Federalism' (1999) 37 Journal of Economic Literature 1120; Alberto Alesina, Ignazio Angeloni, and Federico Etro, 'International Unions' (2005) 95 American Economic Review 602.

[13] Alberto Alesina and Enrico Spolaore, *The Size of Nations* (The MIT Press 2005).

[14] Alberto Alesina and Eliana La Ferrara, 'Ethnic Diversity and Economic Performance' (2005) 43 Journal of Economic Literature 762.

[15] Enrico Spolaore, 'The Economic Approach to Political Borders' (2022) CESifo Working Paper No 10165.

Overall, on one side of the equation, there is the potential heterogeneity in preferences among different regions, which tends to favour the provision of goods at the local level. On the other hand, there is the potential for improved efficiency through internalizing externalities and capitalizing on economies of scale, which pushes in the other direction. Decentralization is thus optimal if heterogeneity of preferences and production costs are not larger at the local level than at a higher level (for costs this means there are no inter-jurisdictional spillovers or economies of scale), assuming that a lower level of government is better positioned to supply public goods (eg due to better knowledge of preferences or tailor-made supplies of public goods to locals) and/or that a higher level cannot provide a differentiated level of provision of the public good in different locations, either because of information asymmetries or for political/legal reasons. In other words, the optimal level of provision of a public good is the one that fully internalizes externalities and reaps benefits of scale, while taking into account local preferences.

One should emphasize that the trade-off equation may change over time. The elements of the trade-off may vary depending on the strength of the efficiency case (externalities, scale economies), the occurrence of external factors, the institutional framework, and the evolution of preferences in a society. Preferences in particular are the result of how they are accounted for in an institutional framework of governance which may, if well designed, lead to lower political costs from heterogeneity. Say that federal institutions are able to achieve democratic consensus more effectively than sub-federal institutions, this may have an impact on regional preferences. In other words, while the benefits of diversity can be maintained, the political costs associated with preference heterogeneity may be reduced by developing inclusive institutions that ensure the consideration of social, political, and economic preferences.[16]

Take the following two examples of how the trade-off does not remain constant over time. Brexit could be interpreted as a case in which the balance between efficiency and heterogenous preferences has evolved over time. While positive externalities and economies of scale were key motivations for the UK to be part of the EU for a long time, the global reduction in trade barriers made the efficiency of the EU less apparent for the UK. On the other hand, preference heterogeneity and dissatisfaction with the uniformity of EU rules finally outweighed the benefits of UK membership—at least for the citizens who voted 'leave' in the referendum. This is in line with the literature emphasizing that economic benefits from a larger domestic market shrink with lower barriers to international trade, which may lead to political disintegration.[17] The reverse may be true for EU border protection.

[16] ibid.

[17] Alberto Alesina, Enrico Spolaore, and Romain Wacziarg, 'Economic Integration and Political Disintegration' (2000) 90 American Economic Review 1276; Alberto Alesina, Enrico Spolaore, and Romain Wacziarg, 'Trade, Growth and the Size of Countries' (2005) 1 Handbook of Economic Growth 1499; Enrico Spolaore and Romain Wacziarg, 'Borders and Growth' (2005) 10 Journal of Economic Growth 331.

Border security has long been viewed as sensitive to national sovereignty concerns and thus remained under the control of Member States. However, new threats to security have strengthened the case for economies of scale and externality issues (with border security seen as a weakest-link public good (see above Chapter 6). Increasing external threats (eg military or geopolitical risks) may change attitudes towards joining forces in security and defence affairs, and ultimately make the efficiency gains of scale economies reverse the trade-offs equation.[18]

To make matters worse, in some cases, the decision on whether to centralize or decentralize may not always be obvious *ex ante*, which may lead to a suboptimal allocation of responsibilities. This may be the case when complementarities occur. Take financial regulation as an example: in some cases, centralized supervision and cross-border integration are complementary. Centralized supervision helps banks attract foreign funding, while conversely more reliance on foreign funding increases cross-border externalities (hence the need for centralized supervision).[19] The conditions which make centralization beneficial may not be satisfied *ex ante* but only *ex post*.

The adequacy of EU level governance could also lead to changes in preferences over time. Having institutions in place that account for minority positions (eg at the EU level through unanimity in the Council or through a greater role assigned to the European Committee of the Regions) may serve to overcome scepticism and resistance in Member States vis-à-vis centralized EU activity. Also, compensations to minorities who are 'farther' from European median preferences and policies may alter preferences, whether these compensations are institutionalized through specific rights (eg a stronger regional involvement in the subsidiarity test applied for EU law-making) or financial compensation (eg through regional and cohesion funds or individualized EU support schemes). In sum, the assessment of the trade-off should take account of the dynamic effects of external factors as well as internal institutional governance.

b) Identification of European public goods

In order for the theoretical approach to become meaningful in offering guidance on the identification of European public goods, different methods and economic tools must be implemented. Identifying them from an economic perspective should take the form of a four-step process.

First, externalities between national jurisdictions must be measured and assessed with the view to if and how these externalities can be internalized if the

[18] William H Riker, *Federalism: Origin, Operation, Significance* (Little, Brown and Company 1964); Enrico Spolaore, 'Adjustments in Different Government Systems' (2004) 16 Economics & Politics 117; Enrico Spolaore, 'The Economics of Political Borders' (2012) CESifo Working Paper No 3854.

[19] Jean-Edouard Colliard, 'Optimal Supervisory Architecture and Financial Integration in a Banking Union' (2019) Review of Finance 129.

public good is provided at the EU level. There are various methods to do that. For instance, looking at a shortlist of potential public goods, one can quantify the expected contributions and payoffs for each EU country in two scenarios (the status quo and a hypothetical provision at EU level, or vice versa), and argue that the level of provision (ie European or national) that leads to a higher correlation between countries' shares of benefits and costs of the policy is the level that best internalizes spillovers.[20]

Secondly, economies of scale and savings that could be reached by providing the good at the EU level must be measured. An indication for significant scale economies exists if fixed costs are too large for a given Member State. Again, there exist various methods to do that: Weiss and others, for instance, try to estimate (whenever possible) the slopes of cost or production functions of selected public goods to determine whether economies of scale exist.

Thirdly, one must measure heterogeneity of preferences among EU countries. It is necessary to consider two different forms of preference heterogeneity: the preferences on the level of provision of a specific public good (eg defence spending might be more important for Poland than for Ireland). Various instruments could be used to measure this: surveys or current expenditure levels (assuming that the national governance process that has led to these expenditures represent the preferences of citizens well). In light of the above discussion, it is likely that this element of preference is endogenous with respect to external events. Take the Russian assault on Ukraine—it is likely that such an event raises the preference for a higher level of provision of this public good overall, yet not at the same pace across all countries, as in some (neighbouring) countries the call for a higher level of defence may grow disproportionately (eg in countries neighbouring Russia). While this may increase the cross-border heterogeneity overall, there is a shared degree of preference for a certain minimum level of defence provision as a public good (eg small-scale joint defence activities). In addition to measuring the preference for the *level of public good provision*, it must also be measured on which *level of government* the good should be provided (eg two countries might have the same defence spending but prefer it to be provided only at the national level, considering it to be part of national sovereignty). Surveys should be the main tool for measuring this. This element of preference is likely to be endogenous to the institutional governance of regional preferences discussed above—the more that centralized government is able to account for minority rights and local preferences, the higher the likelihood that heterogeneity is reduced.

Finally, a more difficult task is to weigh up these three elements to decide if a public good should be provided at the EU level. Indeed, even though there are a few cases that are relatively clear (see Table 21.1: Goods A, C, and D for which

[20] Stefani Weiss and others, *How Europe Can Deliver: Optimising the Division of Competences among the EU and Its Member States* (Bertelsmann Stiftung 2017).

Table 21.1 What constitutes a European Public Good?

	Internalize externalities if provided at EU level	**Economies of scale if provided at EU level**	**Homogenous preferences across EU**	**European public good**	**Examples**	**Group**	**Currently provided at EU level**
Good A	Yes	Yes	Yes	Clear yes	Cross-border infrastructure; external border protection; pandemic prevention and health crisis-management; knowledge through research	1	Yes (eg COVID vaccine procurement: Schengen; Horizon Europe)
Good B	No	No	No	Clear no	Primary and secondary education; local cultural offers; local infrastructure	3	Primarily by Member States but also at EU level in some cases (eg local infrastructure through EU funds)
Good C	Yes	No	Yes	yes	Competitive markets; conservation of marine resources	1	Yes (eg competition policy)
Good D	No	Yes	Yes	yes	Administrative efficiency	1	Yes (eg customs)
Good E	No	Yes	No	Trade-off	Defence: procurement of military equipment	2	Primarily by Member States, for defence EU coordination and very limited EU budget support

Good F	Yes	No	No	Trade-off	Food security	2	Yes (elements of the CAP)
Good G	Yes	Yes	No	Trade-off	Climate protection; macroeconomic stability; economic resilience; defence: joint forces; external border protection, energy security; foreign security; economic security	2	Yes (eg EU Green Deal; ESM or banking supervision; investment screening)
Good H	No	No	Yes	Not needed	Local security (police, fire); local water supply	3	Primarily by Member States, but also at EU level (eg elements of the CAP: preservation of rural landscape)

Source: Gregory Claeys and Armin Steinbach, 'A conceptual framework for the identification and governance of European public goods' (2024) Working Paper 14/2024, Bruegel.

there are homogenous preferences and clear efficiency gains, or Good B which does not meet any of these conditions) in most cases, trade-offs arise. This is the case when efficiency gains could be made by providing a good at the EU level, but preferences clearly differ across countries (Goods E, F, and G in Table 21.1). This does not mean that these goods should be entirely excluded from the category of European Public Goods. Rather, it underscores the need for mechanisms to factor in varying preferences and address them. Dealing with these trade-offs should be done through the legal framework of European governance, one that is adapted to the variable trade-offs.

c) Legal options to deliver European public goods

European public goods vary in the degree to which they can be characterized as European or national goods. The consequence is that there is no 'one-size-fits-all' governance for all EU public goods. In other words, the governance of each public good should depend on the good's idiosyncrasies in terms of externalities, economies of scale, and preference heterogeneity. This calls upon the role of the law. While economics dominates the question of the identification of public goods, the law is vital to ensure that the public good is supplied in a fashion that corresponds to the good's economic rationale. Economic and legal analysis thus interact in optimizing an efficient outcome in delivering European public goods.

There is a large set of institutional and legal instruments, both within the EU treaties and outside, that can be used to manage this trade-off, in the sense of harnessing efficiency gains to the maximum extent while reflecting preference heterogeneity. These include: the allocation of competences within the margins of the Treaty; decision-making rules in the Council (unanimity versus qualified majority voting); provision of public goods at the level of clubs of Member States with similar preferences organized within or outside the Treaty; variable combination of centralization/decentralization of legislation, financing, and delivery of public goods; and compensation mechanisms to achieve greater alignment of preferences.

The EU's institutional and legal framework offers a diverse range of tools to bring the governance design of public goods in line with the economic rationale for public good provision at the EU level. Specifically, there are different governance design parameters that could be used to address trade-offs related to the provision of public goods in Europe.

Adjusting the scope of competence transfer from Member States to the EU

The most fundamental tool is to allocate the scope of competence between Member States and the EU. There is a spectrum of options for allocating the provision of a public good through the order of competences in the Treaties. On one side of the spectrum, competence for public good provision can reside at the country level without any involvement of the EU, no institutional or formalized coordination of Member States policies, and with financial resources entirely supplied at the country level. On the other side of the spectrum, the EU can have exclusive competence, legislating and enforcing centrally through EU institutions, and the public intervention can be financed through EU resources (eg monetary policy to deliver the public good of price stability).

Between these two extremes, the allocation of competences can vary. Legislation and enforcement can be centralized but give leeway for Member States authorities if their actions are not a risk for the provision of EU public goods (eg competition policy to deliver the public good of a competitive/undistorted market). Alternatively, a competence may remain with Member States, but the EU could oblige them to coordinate their domestic policies (eg the European Semester to deliver the public good of macroeconomic stability).

The power to legislate is the first level of competence allocation (before implementation or financing). The degree of competence transfer and the allocation of decision-making power should be adapted to the strength of the economic case for EU level provisions of public goods. Without Treaty change, the degree of competences can be shifted only for so-called 'shared competence'. In this area, if the policy actions pass the 'subsidiarity test' under Article 5(3) TEU, centralized action is possible.[21] The legal test requires that the policy objective cannot be sufficiently achieved at the Member State level, but be better achieved at the Union level. This would be the case when spillovers and scale economies suggest action at Union level.[22] For further competence transfers (eg from shared to exclusive EU competence), Treaty changes are necessary.

In many cases, however, there is no need to change the current rule-setting power by shifting competences, as group 1 public goods are often already governed by 'shared competence', where the subsidiarity principle does not create hurdles to Europeanization due to the strong efficiency case of these public goods (Table 21.1). In cases with a strong efficiency case for centralization (eg joint

[21] Christian Calliess (n 4) 22; Stephen Weatherill, 'Protecting the Internal Market from the Charter' in Sybe de Vries, Ulf Bernitz, and S Weatherill (eds), *The EU Charter of Fundamental Rights as a Binding Instrument: Five Years Old and Growing* (Hart Publishing 2016) 136.

[22] Fuest and Pisani-Ferry (n 6); Sigurd Naess-Schmidt and others, *Subsidiarity and Proportionality in the Single Market: An EU Fit for Inclusive Growth* (Bertelsmann Stiftung 2018).

procurement and interoperability in defence, good G), legislative power should be exercised at the EU level.

A shift to EU exclusive competence is desirable when externalities are significant, like in some Good A cases, such as pandemic prevention and crisis management. Indeed, there could be large spillovers because of the risk of contagion between countries if there is insufficient prevention and/or insufficient crisis action in one country against a pandemic. Health thus becomes a 'weakest-link' public good during pandemics. This contrasts with other elements of health policy, which is typically characterized by national idiosyncrasies and path-dependence (ie heterogenous preferences) and which should therefore remain in national hands. Accordingly, EU centralized power must be limited to preventing negative cross-border spillovers and untapping economies of scales. *Ex-ante* EU legislative power could oblige EU countries to acquire a necessary stock of medicine and vaccines, or harmonize vaccine requirements between countries, to ensure that there is no coordination failure or free-riding behaviour from a country. And during health crises the EU could also have a more important role to play in coordinating a response and acting swiftly (eg empowering the Commission to declare a state of emergency, rather than leaving this decision to the Council).

On the contrary, in other cases, such as Goods B and H, Member States' competences should be maintained (eg in cultural matters or primary education) or even re-established. For instance, one of the objectives of the Common Agricultural Policy (CAP) is to contribute to the 'preservation of rural areas'. However, there are no spillovers or economies of scale associated with a country having a 'vibrant rural life'. The same is true for local infrastructures, which are local public goods that are sometimes provided through the European Regional Development Fund, even in wealthy regions of the EU. For these goods, there is no real need for provision centralization. If anything, the EU could primarily function as a platform for sharing information, identifying best practices, and setting benchmarks.

Calibrating decision-making majority in the Council

With heterogeneity of preferences mainly determining the appropriate level of public good governance, account should be given to Member States' preferences to a variable degree through *design of decision-making* in the European Council between unanimity and qualified majority voting. The voting method should reflect the extent to which diverging preferences may block certain centralizing actions (which might be profitable for efficiency reasons). As a general rule, the more significant efficiency considerations there are—that is, the stronger spillovers and scale economies are—the more heterogeneity of preferences could be overruled (and vice-versa). While quality majority voting is the most widely used voting method in the Council today, with 80 per cent of legislation adopted through this method, for certain policy areas unanimity remains the default voting. Without Treaty changes, decision-making requirements can be adjusted using the 'passerelle clause', which gives some scope to move from unanimity to quality majority voting (Article 48(7) TEU). This move towards quality majority voting may, inter alia, extend in the existing Treaty framework to foreign and security policy (but not military and defence policies), taxation policy, environmental and energy policy, and social policy. However, passerelle clauses are ambivalent as they lead to a trade-off between democratic legitimacy and alignment with national preferences (through unanimity) on one hand, and necessary centralized action to mitigate efficiency concerns (spillovers and scale economies), on the other hand. That being said, passerelle clauses, when switching to quality majority voting, can claim to keep legitimacy and preference orientation at a high level because national parliaments are able to contradict and block moving to quality majority voting if necessary. Activating passerelle clauses should thus be the default option when efficiency considerations support it.

Preference heterogeneity is also taken into account through institutional safeguards to protect minority and regional rights. This could be done by strengthening national parliaments in the subsidiarity control mechanism which gives national parliaments the right to object to EU action when they see subsidiarity to be violated or by strengthening the Committee of the Regions in EU law-making.

Given that Group 1 public goods are characterized by relatively homogenous preferences, quality majority voting should be the rule to avoid strategic voting and inefficient bargaining between countries. With respect to the governance of Group 2 public goods, a unanimity requirement in the Council should be maintained if the heterogeneity of preferences weighs more heavily than the size of spillovers or scale economies. Conversely, if spillovers are considered more important than heterogenous preferences, quality majority voting should be sought after so that efficiency cases are not out-ruled by heterogenous preferences. Defence is a good example where there would be efficiency gains if it was centralized because of externalities and scale economies. It is also an example of a public good for which there is ground to distinguish voting requirements within the same public good. Common procurement of military equipment (with significant scale economies and limited preference heterogeneity) should be governed by quality majority voting, while a joint army should respect unanimity (due to strong preference heterogeneity on core sovereignty issues), at least if it involves the whole EU. Another approach to deal with this issue could be to pursue it only in countries with similar preferences, in which case quality majority voting could be used within this restricted group.

Variable participation in integration: 'club provision' of public goods

While modifications of the decision-making mode in the Council remains symmetrical in the sense that all Member States participate in the process, there may arise instances where efficiency and heterogeneity of preferences require an *asymmetrical process.* This could occur when the efficiency argument does not apply equally to all Member States or when certain countries have notably distinct preferences compared to others. This may lead to fragmentation in participation—moving from 'full participation' of all EU members to 'club cooperation'.

For some goods, club cooperation increases efficiency and reduces the under-provision of public goods. This would the case, for instance, if several EU countries decide to pool resources to coordinate their defence policies.[23] However, non-participating countries might free-ride on the efforts of the club members (eg a club's commitment to lower emissions by would be undermined if non-participating countries free-ride because they have no incentive to join the club). In such cases, club goods might not be feasible and other instruments—for example, compensation for potential losers from centralization, discussed below—may be necessary to incentivize participation and avoid free-riding behaviours.

From an institutional perspective, 'club cooperation' could take place within the EU institutional and legal framework or outside the framework. The choice between these options should depend on the economic case. While the passerelle clause (allowing to shift from unanimity to qualified majority voting) does not fragment the participation of Member States either geographically or temporally to achieve a more efficient result in which all Member States participate, 'variable participation' introduces some asymmetry.

This could be done in three ways. First, the least intrusive option, which is possible in the area of Common Foreign and Security Policy (CFSP), is through 'constructive abstention' under Article 31(1) TEU, which does not oblige a Member State to implement the decision but to accept that the decision commits the Union. Second, 'enhanced cooperation'—as one form of differentiating integration discussed above in Chapter 12 b)—can be established among a minimum of nine Member States to pursue action within a non-exclusive competence of the Union (Article 20 TEU). Although fragmented, 'enhanced cooperation' leaves the institutions of the EU intact, letting non-participating members easily join the club at a later stage. Third, in cases where 'club integration' is not politically feasible within the Treaty frame, willing states may pursue public good provision outside of the Treaty—like the Schengen Agreement, which was first pioneered by a few

[23] As discussed e.g. in Fuest and Pisani-Ferry (n 6).

countries, but later adopted by many and integrated as 'enhanced cooperation' into the EU Treaty. Deeper integration in defence policies (eg to build joint forces) may be implemented through intergovernmental cooperation.

Club provision may itself lead to an evolution of the trade-off between efficiency and preference heterogeneity, as preferences may gradually converge. While Schengen was initially inconceivable within the EU institutional and legal framework due to significant differences in preferences, the efficiency case of removing internal border controls (and the absence of significant negative experiences) changed preferences in such a way that Schengen was ultimately integrated into the EU legal framework. Similarly, some countries decided in 2012 to create the European Stability Mechanism (ESM) to solve the sovereign debt crisis, because the Treaty initially did not provide a legal basis for an institutionalized scheme for solvency-securing financial support. The ESM is not integrated into the EU institutional framework and is governed by its own international agreement, but it was made possible by the amendment of an article in the TFEU. This type of 'club integration' outside the main EU Treaties could also be pursued when the club has less than nine members, unlike 'enhanced cooperation' which requires a minimum of nine participants.

However, club integration is not suited to the provision of all public goods. This is the case when non-participating countries might free-ride on the efforts of club members. For instance, to achieve climate protection (an example of good G), the commitment to lower emissions by a club would be undermined if non-participating countries free-ride because they have no incentive to join the club. Similarly, to achieve economic security (another example of good G), all countries should participate in a minimal level of foreign direct investment screening to prevent some countries becoming a weakest link and undermining overall security standards in the EU.

Centralization versus decentralization of funding decisions and delivery of public goods

Besides the transfer of competence that shifts legislative power from Member States to the EU, there are two more levers through which the governance can be tailor-made to a specific European public good: its funding and its delivery. The extent to which all levers of governance should be centralized (legislation, funding, delivery) or whether elements of decentralization should be maintained depends on the specifics of each public good.

Combinations of legislation (discussed above), *funding*, and *delivery* of public goods can be achieved in several ways: in some cases, it may suffice to play by a uniform rulebook (eg to respect the single market) but leave funding and spending decisions at the national level to cater for national preferences (eg subsidies for cultural goods or industrial policy). A uniform rulebook may in some cases be sufficient to minimize potential externalities while respecting diverse preferences.

However, in other cases, the provision of a European public good may require both centralized regulation and centralized funding decisions and/or centralized delivery, as public funding and delivery at the national level may fail to account for the potential efficiency gains related to cross-border externalities or scale economies. NGEU is an example for a centralized funding tool (through the issuance of debt) and a uniform rulebook determining the spending priorities across the EU to deliver several European public goods (climate protection, macroeconomic stability, etc). At the same time, in that particular setup, delivery remained decentralized leaving the precise project selection to Member States.

When decentralized funding is inefficient, achieving efficiency may not necessarily require full funding at the EU level. Coordination of spending between countries or top-up funding from the EU may often be sufficient to achieve the right level of provision. This type of top-up funding would for instance be adequate to deliver the necessary green investments to achieve climate protection (good G) in the future. As discussed, this is what has been done, at least partly, with NGEU, but the programme will end in 2026, while efforts will have to continue until 2050. Another example of a public good that should be achieved at the EU level is economic resilience due to the increase in European countries' vulnerability to geopolitical shocks that has become apparent in recent years. A purely national 'de-risking' strategy would be inefficient as it would not internalize the spillovers from dependence on specific countries and would also forego scale economies. An answer to this lies in centralizing instruments to conclude EU trade agreements and unionizing inbound/outbound investment control and promotion of foreign trade and investment with the clear objective of increasing economic resilience for the EU as a whole. This should be complemented by top-up EU investments to reduce vulnerabilities related to dependence on specific countries, particularly by investing in relevant sectors, such as innovative technologies.[24]

In some cases, full budget centralization or centralized delivery might be necessary, in addition to a uniform legal rulebook. Centralization of funding is already the norm for subsidies provided to farmers to achieve food security (good F), which are provided centrally through the Common Agricultural Policy of the EU budget to avoid the negative externalities that could arise if subsidies were delivered at country level. Similarly, external border protection is an example of a 'weakest-link' public good creating externalities because insufficient border protection of only one EU member can reduce the security for all members. Impediments to effective border protection may be caused by financial unwillingness or political inability. Where border protection is not sufficient, the EU can exercise its existing

[24] Simone Tagliapietra, Reinhilde Veugelers, and Jeromin Zettelmeyer, 'Rebooting the European Union's Net Zero Industry Act' (2023) Policy Brief 15/2023, Bruegel.

legislative competence to border protection management and deliver it through Frontex in a centralized fashion. Centralization could be extended to other areas. Procurement concerning defence (eg joint large-scale military equipment) or health (eg preventing or combatting pandemic) should be delivered at the EU level. High-scale and risky research and development projects that would not be pursued at the country level because they are too expensive should also be funded and delivered at the EU level.

Finally, as discussed above, there are also public goods that are currently financed and/or delivered at the EU level that exhibit neither externalities nor economies of scale: local infrastructures with no cross-border spillovers or the preservation of rural areas. These should be financed and delivered at the national or regional levels.

Compensation to mitigate preference heterogeneity

When efficiency requires either full centralization or at least broad participation in the provision of public goods but some countries (or politically influential groups in the those countries) would be negatively affected, compensation schemes at the level of EU countries, regions, households, or companies may be a suitable tool to reap efficiency gains that would otherwise be blocked by the losing party, in particular in cases in which club good provision is not desirable (see above). Moreover, as discussed previously, financial compensation may also reshape preferences and make them more homogenous. To that end, the proceeds resulting from efficiency gains might have to be used (at least at the beginning) for distributional purposes.

This may be implemented through different channels: with the EU allocating budgets to individuals or companies administered by countries or regions in order to mitigate the impact of structural change on individuals (as it is already done through the European Globalisation Adjustment Fund,[25] or the recently agreed Social Climate Fund) or indirectly through compensation paid to EU countries (eg through the Just Transition Fund, or Structural and Cohesion Funds). These various funds and compensation schemes can be used to align local preferences with an efficiency-based need for centralization. For example, energy security is a public good of EU relevance because national decisions on power plants and renewable energies can impact other countries. There is certainly an efficiency case for allocating renewable energy where it can be produced most cost-efficiently. Centralized regulatory power should thus (at least partially) be allocated at the

[25] See, eg, Grégory Claeys and André Sapir, 'The European Globalisation Adjustment Fund: Easing the Pain from Trade?' in L Paganetto (ed), *Capitalism, Global Change and Sustainable Development* (Springer 2020) 97 (discussing how this fund can compensate potential losers from the EU's trade policies).

central level to untap efficiency gains that promote energy security (see above). This could however lead to high distributional effects between countries (as some countries may lack competitive advantages in solar or wind energy). To convince all EU countries to participate and influence their preferences, compensation schemes could be used to compensate potential losers and mitigate the distributional effects associated with the overall efficiency gains from centralization. Cohesion policies (eg through the Just Transition Fund) or policy-specific compensation programmes (eg through the Social Climate Fund) are instruments designed to mitigate these distributional effects.

d) Financing European public goods

The financing of European public goods should account for the particularities of the multilevel governance in the EU and the remaining preferences to supply public goods on the national level only. Without genuine taxing power at EU level, there is a challenge in bridging the limitations of national taxing power and European public goods delivery. Further challenging is the question of how European public goods should effectively be financed, taking into account that demand for public goods varies across countries displaying the heterogenous picture described above. In a system of multilevel governance with vertical differentiation between the EU and Member States as well as horizontal distinctions among Member States, the financing becomes increasingly complex if implicit fiscal transfers are to be avoided. At the same time, our analysis has shown that some European public goods exist and the question is how to finance them.

EU law is silent on offering guidance on how European public goods should be financed. What is certain is that Treaties do not support the provision of European public goods through EU revenues: apart from policy-specific rights to levy duties (eg in energy policy), the Treaties exclude the EU from generating revenue for public finance purposes. The EU's obligation to ensure balanced budgets (Article 310(4) TFEU) has largely precluded the EU from raising debt.[26] In terms of public finance, the EU is far behind the standing of a sovereign state. In that regard, the EU remains an international organization that is purely reliant on the sovereign borrowing power of its members. The EU's own resources are contributions made solely by Member States' will—not at the discretion or will of the Union institutions.

With EU law offering limited normative guidance, a conceptual approach can be offered by the theory of institutional and fiscal congruence as introduced by

[26] Sebastian Grund and Armin Steinbach, 'European Union Debt Financing: Leeway and Barriers from a Legal Perspective' (2023) Working Paper 15/2023, Bruegel.

Olson into public finance.[27] It departs from a political economy point of view by emphasizing that the incentive for government spending is stronger when it can externalize the costs for the public good while targeting the benefits at its electorate.[28] This is the traditional common pool problem,[29] and it is obviously one that plays out for the EU too—in the multilevel framework, each Member State seeks to secure the highest share of EU spending distributed among members for their respective constituencies at home. As a way out, Olson recommends institutional congruence, that is, 'that there can be a match between those who receive the benefits of a collective good and those who pay for it'.[30] By extension, fiscal congruence seeks to make those who demand a certain level of public goods provision pay. If this cannot be ensured, externalities occur by making citizens pay for public good services they dislike. If citizens were made to pay for public goods delivered to others (as is the political economy dynamic underpinning Olson's reasoning), this raises the overall demand for the public good to an inefficiently high level because those who demand the public good do not pay the full price for it (eg through taxes). To that end, institutional congruence requires three circles or groups to coincide—beneficiaries, decision-makers, and taxpayers—which brings into alignment risk, return, and control.[31]

We can thus draw a connection between fiscal equivalence and the fiscal federalism theory applied above. While fiscal federalism offers the criteria to determine *where* a public good should be delivered, that is at the European or at the Member State level, fiscal equivalence suggests *how* the financing of the public goods should be made. By tying the financing decision back to who the ultimate beneficiary is, fiscal equivalence relies on what we discussed above as preference heterogeneity. It is thus pivotal to take the citizens' willingness to pay for public goods as a benchmark for the adequate level of public good provision. Accordingly, the EU should not finance projects that supply local benefits only, especially when it is possible to impose a local tax. The construction of a new bridge in North Rhine-Westphalia provides benefits mainly to the local citizens. When the EU funds projects that are limited to producing local benefits, it implies an externalization of costs on outsiders. The rule here is capable of extension to other situations, whereby, for example, user fees can be imposed to maintain the costs of roads that might

[27] Mancur Olson, 'The Principle of "Fiscal Equivalence": The Division of Responsibilities among Different Levels of Government' (1969) 59 American Economic Review 479; David Christoph Ehmke, *Institutional Congruence the Riddle of Leviathan and Hydra* (Nomos Verlagsgesellschaft 2018) 38.

[28] Geert Jennes, 'Interregional Fiscal Transfers Resulting from Central Government Debt: New Insights and Consequences for Political Economy' (2021) 74 Kyklos 196, 198; PB Anand, 'Financing the Provision of Global Public Goods' (2004) 27 World Economy 215.

[29] Mancur Olson, *The Logic of Collective Action: Public Goods and the Theory of Groups* (Harvard University Press 1965)

[30] Mancur Olson, 'The Principle of Fiscal Equivalence: The Division of Responsibilities among Different Levels of Government' (1969) 59 American Economic Review 483.

[31] Charles B Blankart, Öffentliche Finanzen in der Demokratie: Eine Einführung in die Finanzwissenschaft (Vahlen 2011); Ehmke (n 27) 48.

otherwise come from other sources.[32] In that regard, there is plausibility to the EU unanimity requirement to raise taxes at the EU level. Unanimity raises direct costs (negotiation) but secures low external costs, as it avoids the externalization of public expenses to the detriment of local taxpayers.

Yet, divergent national preferences do not conceptually preclude the EU from public finance power. As discussed above, there is an efficiency case for certain goods to be supplied at EU level. This may be due to positive spillover or economies of scale generated by EU action (Good G in Table 21.1 above). By requiring equivalence between those paying and those consuming the goods, we can infer for the European case that what matters is the added value which member-only action would forego. The foregone efficiency gains represent an argument for taxing all EU citizens because this added value accrues in principle to all EU citizens. With the European case limited to financing the added value of EU supply of public goods, there will be a mixed financing structure shared between Member States and the EU, in particular for domains in which heterogenous preferences prevail. Hence, the rules should put both rule-making and financing in EU hand only in the limited cases where it is EU action alone that creates additional, not domestic-only, benefits. This means that excess demand in Member States to finance a higher level of public goods should be financed by individual Member States. For example, even if all Member States agree that having some sort of joint defence activity is beneficial, they may still diverge on the extent of security and defence strength. Economies of scale should be exploited by the EU leading to actions such as joint military forces, but members should retain control and responsibility over other elements of defence to account for their individual security preferences. Likewise, external border protection may be a sound example for a public good (see good A in Table 21.1), but members may wish for additional security which they can supply on their own. Top-up financing provided by the EU makes sense to reap benefits where members may otherwise provide a public good unsatisfactorily. For example, the EU should finance additional pandemic medicine that is not provided at sufficient levels in Member States. Fiscal equivalence also offers guidance for club public goods where cooperation fails because of insufficient preference alignment between all Members. Only Member States joining the provision of a public good should finance this endeavour, so others are not made to pay for it.

In terms of specific revenue creation, the question is whether the EU should be able to tax itself or to rely on Member States' contributions, the latter being the current rule. Again, fiscal congruence suggests that the circles of beneficiaries, decision-makers, and taxpayers should align—the decision-maker for EU public goods is at the EU level, and if benefits of EU law-making accrue to all citizens, a broad tax base should be put in place at the EU level (even if Member States

[32] Lee Epstein and Nicholas W Waterbury, 'Judicial Behavior' in William Thompson (ed), *Oxford Research Encyclopedia of Politics* (Oxford University Press 2020) 16.

participate through the Council). This is in line with the political economy motivation underpinning fiscal congruence which leads members to contribute as little as possible and benefit as much as possible from the funding.

Needless to say, the current EU Treaties are far from EU financing EU public goods.[33] However, some elements of the current member's contributions to the EU endorse the logic of weighted benefits. The residual and most important 'Own Resource' is the gross national income, which not only supplements other budget resources (eg custom duties, emission trading system revenues) but also constitutes the highest contribution to the budget. Gross national income represents a plausible proxy for benefits of EU public good provision at least to the extent that they are in line with burden-sharing based on economic strength. That this may produce net-payers and net-beneficiaries, this should be seen as inevitable in a multilevel union. Perfect institutional congruence would only be achievable (but unrealistic) if each resident is taxed individually based on each individual's consumption of public goods. In reality, some residents, regions, or even Member States may benefit disproportionally, depending on the public good in question.[34]

[33] Cristina Fasone, 'EU Budget and Spending Powers', in Alicia Hinarejos and Robert Schütze (eds), *EU Fiscal Federalism* (Oxford University Press 2023) 233, 237.

[34] Ehmke (n 27) 51.

22

Internal market: economic integration

The establishment of the European internal market is a central goal of the EU (Article 3(3), subpara 1, sentence 1 TEU) and was at the basis of the initial rationale of the European integration process. The idea of market unification or a 'common market' was the basis for various integration pushes brought about as part of Treaty changes. Since the Treaty of Lisbon, the concept of the internal market has dominated, which, according to Article 26(2) TFEU, is understood to mean an area without internal borders in which the free movement of goods, people, services, and capital is guaranteed.

From an economic perspective, ensuring market freedoms should ensure an optimal allocation of economic resources. An efficient market is fully integrated, that is, only direct production costs and preferences matter for individual companies and individuals making their decisions (absent of market failure and distortive public policies). The rationale of European integration then lies in efficient factor allocation and the existence of economies of scale. By reducing technical and economic boundaries, positive economies of scale can be created. Market integration is thus in principle concerned with the element of scale economies as discussed in Chapter 7 as one element of fiscal federalism theory. While it focuses on efficiency, it initially leaves aside considerations of externalities and preference heterogeneity. However, a heterogeneous order of preferences militates against a purely efficiency orientation and against the absolute eradication of market-hindering public policies. In fact, regions or Member States may diverge on the kind of collective goods that their citizens want their governments to supply, hence justifying different sets of public policies.

In the early stages of the European integration process, Member States believed they had ensured that EU law would align with national preferences by limiting the scope and competence of the EU institutions (in particular the European Commission, called the High Authority at that time) . Member States retained competences for those policy fields they considered necessary in order to align national preferences with domestic policies. National parliaments (as brokers of national preferences) could adopt national laws that would not be jeopardized by EU law. In this sense, preference diversity could continue to exist. This changed abruptly with the ECJ-driven doctrinal innovations of supremacy and direct effect, both of which were not explicitly anchored in the Treaties and both of which have harmonizing effects in practice, because they suppress legislative diverse choices at the domestic level. Supremacy leads uniform EU law to trump diverse Member

EU Law and Economics. Armin Steinbach, Oxford University Press. © Oxford University Press 2025.
DOI: 10.1093/9780198920915.003.0022

States' law—regional choices and diverse preferences enshrined in Member States' law no longer apply. Similarly, individuals invoking the direct effect of (economic) freedoms are in a position to seek harmonization towards eradicating Member States public policies. 'Negative integration' is the removal and absence of public policies that stand in the way of the individual right concerned. The result of both legal innovations was that Member States (and their legitimacy power) were no longer necessary to create a common market. With supremacy, economic integration was in the hands of the Commission and the ECJ. If they found that Member States' law was hindering the common market, they declared that Member States' law no longer applied. This led to a bias between EU competences and those of Member States—while the EU's predominantly economic competences were interpreted widely, leading to economic integration, the Member States' competences were interpreted more narrowly by the ECJ.[1]

A direct consequence of 'negative integration' was the removal of cross-border barriers. To achieve this goal, the EU Treaties stipulated explicitly only bans on discrimination across all freedoms. However, the ECJ declared not only discriminatory instruments to be trade-restrictive and thus forbidden, but even indiscriminate regimes applying to domestic and imported goods can be a barrier to free movement of goods. In principle, there are two ways to deal with this kind of barrier. First, it could be addressed through harmonization: this method safeguards members' preferences and ensures that harmonization occurs only if some minimum homogeneity exists to which Member States agree (though not as Pareto improvement because internal market harmonization may proceed with qualified majority voting). Yet it is a time-consuming and cost-intensive process that is susceptible to rent-seeking. Second and alternatively, the barrier could be tackled in a decentralized way by individuals invoking their individual rights, thus circumventing legislative action. In the former case, law-makers are central; in the latter they have no role and the individual trumps.

In fact, the principle of mutual recognition discussed above (see Chapter 13 b)), developed by the ECJ in *Dassonville*[2] and *Cassis de Dijon*,[3] led to the elimination of trade barriers without going through legislative harmonization. This judicial innovation introduced a market-opening mechanism by requiring Member States' recognition of foreign regulations. A Member State must allow a product lawfully produced and marketed in another Member State into its own market, unless a prohibition of this product is justified by mandatory requirements, such as health and safety protection. The advantage of mutual recognition over the harmonization approach is that trade restrictions are resolved decentrally at lower

[1] Dieter Grimm, *Europa ja—aber welches? Zur Verfassung der europäischen Demokratie* (CH Beck 2016) 109.

[2] Case C-8/74 *Dassonville* (1974) EU:C:1974:82 837.

[3] Case C-120/78 *Rewe-Zentral AG v Bundesmonopolverwaltung für Branntwein* (1979) EU:C:1979:42 0649.

transaction costs than through a harmonized standard. Mutual recognition works quasi-automatically; its implementation is not tied to political decisions, and thus it reduces political-economic distortions (eg through rent-seeking), and creates inter-jurisdictional competition between the Member States. 'Mutual recognition' thus became a lever for the effective enforcement of fundamental freedoms.

a) Free movement of goods

Since trade barriers create inefficiencies, Article 30 TFEU stipulates a general prohibition of tariffs, non-tariff measures, and any measures having equivalent effects. In line with economic free trade rationale, the ECJ has interpreted this prohibition extensively.[4] Yet, even if negative effects of tariffs are acknowledged,[5] there may be conflicts with national tax autonomy, which according to general insight of federalism theory should remain in Member States' autonomy or at least governed by unanimity (see above Chapter 21 c)).

Articles 34 and 35 TFEU prohibiting quantitative import and export restrictions and measures of equivalent effects follow standard insights of trade economics on adverse welfare effects of such measures. Article 36 TFEU offers the legal basis for exceptions to the general bans on trade restrictions, notably for grounds such as public morality, public policy, public security, and the protection of human health and life. The jurisprudence has given a narrow understanding to this rule, not allowing just any public policy concern and insisting that core state interests must be at stake.[6] This narrow reading is one that does not let any differences in preferences between Member States suffice to motivate trade barriers. One can interpret the Court's jurisdiction such that only core issues of sovereignty, that is, preferences regarding the supply of core public goods such as security and health, will be recognized as grounds justifying internal market barriers. There is thus a strong assumption built into the rule-exception relationship (which applies across the freedoms of goods, services, establishment, and capital) that the welfare-reducing effects of trade barriers outweigh gains be designing laws aligned with domestic preferences. The efficiency case clearly trumps the preference case here. As mentioned above, 'negative integration' by individual rights invalidating EU law-incompatible domestic measures shares with 'positive integration' by legislative harmonization at least some harmonizing effect, because national laws incompatible with EU freedoms cannot remain in effect. This extends even to non-discriminatory measures that are potentially trade hindering. Hence,

[4] Case 1/69 *Italy v Commission* (1969) EU:C:1969:34 193.

[5] Jacob Viner, *The Customs Union Issue* (Oxford University Press 1950).

[6] Marcus Klamert, Maria Moustakali, and Jonathan Tomkin, 'Article 36 TFEU' in Manuel Kellerbauer, Marcus Klamert, and Jonathan Tomkin (eds), *The EU Treaties and the Charter of Fundamental Rights* (Oxford University Press 2019).

even if the anti-competitive effect of discriminatory treatment is abolished, efficiency gains are presumed to be significant according to the *Dassonville* formula developed by the Court. The criticism against this judgment was that it meant that non-discriminating rules with little and uncertain potential effects on intra-Community trade could be tried before the ECJ.

With this extensive jurisprudence, which lets any potentially trade-hindering effect suffice to establish a violation of an economic freedom, the ECJ had arguably gone too far. From an economic perspective, this approach would preclude an extensive scope of public policy measures that would for example address market failures (eg environmental concerns or consumer protection) or reflect culturally persistent differences in preferences (eg in cultural or media policies). The ECJ's extensive jurisprudence was then modified and narrowed, for economically sound reasons. In *Cassis-de-Dijon*, the Court recognized that—only concerning non-discriminatory measures—certain 'mandatory requirements' could be acceptable grounds to justify trade-restrictive, non-discriminatory measures. 'Mandatory requirements' went beyond the interests listed in Article 36 TFEU and would allow Member States to take measures pursuing environmental protection, cultural aims, maintenance of press diversity, and the fight against crime. This relaxed legal standard offers more regulatory autonomy to Member States, in line with considerations of tackling market failures and accounting for heterogenous preferences in core areas.

In response to the criticism, in its *Keck* judgment, the Court drew a distinction between rules which relate to the product itself and those that relate to the method by which the product is being sold.[7] The notorious Sunday trading cases touched upon the question of whether mandatory closure of stores on Sunday would constitute a violation of economic freedoms.[8] In line with the modified definition which the Court developed in *Keck*, Sunday trading prohibitions would concern the general selling arrangements of a product, not the product as such. While this jurisprudence remained controversial and inconsistent,[9] the general economic logic behind this modification is one that accepts regulatory preferences concerning the general commercial environment of a good, thus measures that are characteristic of how certain goods should be marketed. Heterogenous policy preferences have more weight if they indeed concern *policy* issues rather than individual products. Consequentially, such non-discriminatory policy measures should remain in place.

Overall, the freedom to provide goods developed a differentiated regime that applies the strictest illegality regime for *de-jure* and *de-facto* discriminatory

[7] Joined cases C-267/91 and C-268/91 *Keck and Mithouard* EU:C:1993:905.

[8] Case C-145/88 *Torfaen Borough Council v B&Q plc* (1989) EU:C:1989:593 03851.

[9] Wolfgang Kerber and Roger van den Bergh, 'Unmasking Mutual Recognition: Current Inconsistencies and Future Chances' (2007) Marburger Volkswirtschaftliche Beiträge, No 2007,11.

treatment of imported goods. Illegality is justified by the obvious anti-competitive effect of discrimination, which favours few domestic suppliers of goods but creates harm for competitive pressure, consumers, and foreign suppliers. These kinds of restrictions are subject to the strictest regime of justification, and justification is only permitted when the external effects of the imported goods on the domestic economy or society are significant (eg by breaking laws, inflicting harm on health, or creating risks to life). Economic inefficiencies may result from non-discriminatory measures that potentially restrict trade, without however the additional anti-competitive effect of discriminations. The Court's wide interpretation of all potentially trade-restrictive measures to be in violation of the freedom was then narrowed by acknowledging leeway to account for heterogenous preferences on two different levels. First, it excluded selling arrangements that are disconnected to the product itself and are, as such, reflections of a more general collective policy choice. Second, it enlarged the scope of grounds to justify trade restrictions from the narrow externality-based regime of Article 36 TFEU (criminal laws, risks to health and life) to grounds reflecting heterogenous policy preferences more generally, albeit not unlimited. For historical, cultural, and political reasons, certain policy areas are characterized by persistent preference diversity. Among the areas recognized by the Court are cultural policy, maintenance of press diversity, the balance of the social security system, and the protection of fundamental rights. All of these exceptions developed in the jurisprudence point at policy areas which may claim particular connections to sovereignty concerns, as identified by the German Constitutional Court as areas which the German government could not transfer to the EU level (see above Chapter 10 a)). High sovereignty costs hinder a release of these policy areas from national prerogatives (see above Chapter 5).

b) Freedom to provide services

For the freedom of services, generally the same considerations apply as for the freedom to provide goods: from an economic perspective, discriminatory treatments of foreign services can only exceptionally be justified when strong negative externalities or market failures would occur of the kind referred to in Article 36 TFEU. Similar to the treatment of goods, EU primary law states in Article 56 TFEU a comprehensive prohibition of trade restrictions irrespective of their discriminatory or non-discriminatory nature. The ECJ has read this to encompass all measures 'which may prevent or otherwise obstruct the activities of the person providing the service'.[10]

[10] Case C-33/74 *Van Binsbergen v Bedrijfsvereniging voor de Metaalnijverheid* (1974) EU:C:1974:131 01299 [10], [12].

'Mutual recognition' plays an important role in the freedom of services. Numerous legislative initiatives have employed mutual recognition in areas where a balance between national regulatory autonomy and EU-wide harmonization must be found. Consider, for example, the mutual recognition of professional qualifications[11] or the posting of workers in the framework of the provision of services. Both are policy areas characterized by historical path-dependent idiosyncrasies reflecting national preferences. At the same time, labour migration and the effective use of freedom of workers heavily depends on how smoothly professional degrees are recognized in other jurisdictions. Likewise, the posting of workers is tightly connected to national social security and employment security issues (eg minimum wages, health and security standards at the work place, rest periods). With social policy as a genuinely 'harmonization-hostile' policy area (Article 153 TFEU), remaining under tight Member State control, account for heterogeneity across Member States is indispensable, which must be counterbalanced with the efficiency-enhancing effects of labour migration in the EU. Social policy concerns are in potential conflict with economic policy concerns. On one hand, concerns associated with 'social dumping' drive Member States to make sure that posted workers are not subject to working conditions abroad which undercut the domestic social standards. On the other hand, fixing minimum wages for services provided abroad and minimum working conditions would impair the comparative advantage of certain groups of labour supplier (eg of young and unqualified workers). Restrictions on the freedom to provide services could, from an economic standpoint, be justified if they tackle an information asymmetry, that is, if the lower minimum standards in the sending states are associated with a lower quality of the services delivered, which the buyers of the services cannot correctly assess.[12]

There remain multiple cross-border obstacles to the exercise of freedom to provide services in the EU.[13] In particular, traditional professional groups such as architects, lawyers, and doctors are subject to national admission requirements that are tied to proof of certain knowledge and skills. Such standards are economically justified if they are intended to compensate for information deficits on the side of the consumer. Information, disclosure, and qualification requirements then serve to create incentives to ensure the quality of services or to reduce information asymmetries.[14] However, reality often differs from this ideal of efficient regulation of services—in particular, the rent-seeking of affected interest groups can lead to protectionist effects in regulation. In an effort to break down the existing

[11] Directive 96/71/EC of the European Parliament and of the Council of 16 December 1996 concerning the posting of workers in the framework of the provision of services [1997] OJ L18/1.

[12] Hans-Jürgen Wagener and Thomas Eger, *Europäische Integration: Wirtschaft und Recht, Geschichte und Politik* (Vahlen 2014) 163.

[13] European Commission, 'Upgrading the Single Market: More Opportunities for People and Business' (2015) 8.

[14] Erik Canton, Daria Ciriaci, and Irune Solera, 'The Economic Impact of Professional Services Liberalisation' (2014) Economic Papers 533.

protectionist regulatory requirements, the EU Commission tabled in 2004 a Services Directive to, among other things, facilitate cross-border trade in services by generally applying the country of origin principle. Accordingly, the service provider would only be subject to the regulations in which they were established. The draft directive was met with massive resistance in various Member States and was adopted in a greatly modified form, according to which the country of origin principle had to be largely replaced by a country of destination principle.[15] This example illustrates how the market-opening effect has therefore receded in favour of the regulatory sovereignty of the destination countries in exercising their ability to protect domestic service providers against foreign competition.

Free movement of workers and freedom of establishment

From an economic perspective, reducing mobility restrictions for employees seeking to offer their work abroad has the function of putting workers to their most productive and therefore most efficient use. This has both allocative and distributional effects: in addition to increasing productivity through allocative efficiency, distributional effects ensue with wage levels and employment opportunities in immigration countries possibly changing significantly as a result of migration, which may consequently have political repercussions.

To date, labour mobility in the EU is comparatively low and is only around one fifth to one third of the level it is in the US, although regional income disparities are larger in Europe. In the US, shocks that lead to regional structural change and unemployment are at least partially absorbed by labour mobility, so that regional employment differences level out again within a decade.[16] The reasons for low mobility in the EU are diverse: monetary mobility incentives due to wage divergences between Member States are uncertain in view of the risk of unemployment, and non-economic aspects such as social and psychological factors influence decisions to migrate. In Europe, language diversity remains a significant barrier. However, the economic and financial crisis has shown how economic shocks may induce mobility. The crisis had worsened economic working conditions in many countries and increased the economic disparity within the Union. Migration movements from the crisis countries of Spain and Greece towards Germany were consequential. Empirical studies estimate that around 70 per cent of the increase

[15] Directive 2006/123/EC of the European Parliament and of the Council of 12 December 2006 on services in the internal market [2006] OJ L376/36.

[16] Wagener and Eger (n 12) 175; Zuzana Gáková and Lewis Dijkstra, 'Labour Mobility between the Regions of the EU-27 and a Comparison with the USA' (2008) European Union Regional Policy No 02/2008.

in immigration to Germany during the financial crisis can be attributed to the poor economic situation in other parts of Europe.[17]

Reducing mobility costs is particularly relevant for the euro zone, being a uniform currency area (see below Chapter 23). According to the theory of the optimal currency area, asymmetric shocks within a currency area can be balanced out if, among other things, an adjustment process occurs through the mobility of workers. Given the considerable degree of economic heterogeneity within the euro area, an adjustment channel is also required through labour mobility. With a view to smoothing the shocks in the euro area, labour mobility is one important channel, which is why reducing mobility costs in the EU is of primary concern. In fact, the mobility of workers was one of the initial projects of the European founding Treaties. The EEC Treaty of 1957 had already set itself the goal of a common market with free movement of people. This right has been continuously expanded through the adoption of secondary law and the case law of the ECJ: first by extending the initial limitation of the economically motivated exercise of freedom of movement to all persons seeking employment and engendering gradually to the freedom of movement of family members of job searchers who are not nationals of a Member State.[18] Today, the free movement of workers is provided in Articles 45 to 48 TFEU. These articles include a ban on discrimination and regulate the mobility aspects of freedom of movement in Article 45 para. 3 TFEU, which are subject to a public policy reservation that must be interpreted narrowly. The underlying economic rationale is consistent with the freedom to provide goods and services. Discriminatory treatments which overtly create inefficiencies by their anti-competitive and trade-reducing effects are subject to strict scrutiny, leaving leeway for restrictions only on the basis of severe negative externalities (eg health and crime). In turn, non-discriminatory restrictions on the freedom of workers can be justified on the basis of 'mandatory requirements' which give latitude to national public policies reflecting preference heterogeneity.

The freedom of establishment of natural persons and companies corresponds closely with the freedom of movement of workers. Both rights contribute to factor price flexibility and adjustment in the event of shocks and therefore act as adjusting mechanisms to align economic cycles within the EU. Article 49 TFEU promotes this by imposing a general prohibition of discrimination with regard to taking up and pursuing self-employment. According to Article 52 TFEU, restrictions are justified on grounds of public order, security, and health—they are narrowly interpreted as under other freedoms. For example, in the case of the freedom

[17] Simone Bertoli, Herbert Brücker, and Jesús Fernández-Huertas Moraga, 'The European Crisis and Migration to Germany: Expectations and the Diversion of Migration Flows' (2013) CERDI Working Papers No 7170.

[18] Herbert Brücker and Thomas Eger, 'The Law and Economics of the Free Movement of Persons in the European Union' in Thomas Eger and Hans-Bernd Schäfer (eds), *Research Handbook on the Economics of European Union Law* (Edward Elgar Publishing 2012) 146.

of workers, EU secondary law regulating harmonization and mutual recognition of national qualification requirements have been essential in practice, given that professional regulations can foreclose professional markets and imply significant migration restrictions. The EU has pursued different approaches towards the national policy space, ranging from the harmonization of minimum requirements for professional practice as well as the mutual recognition of national professional standards. In the area of freedom of establishment, too, the ECJ expanded the prohibition of discrimination enshrined in primary law into a general ban on restrictions, giving latitude for states to pursue 'mandatory requirements' provided that they are applied without discrimination.[19]

As a general trend, with a view to optimizing the mobility of persons and companies as a prerequisite for an optimal currency zone, the ECJ's efforts to reduce the restrictions that hinder access to employed and self-employed activities and facilitate bringing family members has an efficiency-enhancing effect. In addition, the Community legislature and the ECJ have eased the conditions under which intra-EU immigrants have access to social benefits from the host country. This includes improving the portability of pension insurance system benefits. What is problematic about this from an economic perspective is that it can lead to a situation in which employees are not guided by employment opportunities that help to bring the EU labour market closer to efficiency when making their decision to migrate, but are possibly guided by redistributional aspects such as by having access to more attractive social benefits. This can mean that workers migrate even though their marginal productivity in the host country is lower than in their country of origin. Low-productivity workers may be attracted to host countries with generous social security systems.[20] This phenomenon was feared when the EU expanded towards Eastern Europe. In fact, some increase in migration from the EU's eastern expansion countries has been empirically observed, but the feared drastic increase did not materialize.[21]

[19] Case C-55/94 *Reinhard Gebhard v Consiglio dell'Ordine degli Avvocati e Procuratori di Milano* (1995) EU:C:1995:411 [37].

[20] Wagener and Eger (n 12) 186.

[21] Statistik/Arbeitsmarktberichterstattung Bundesagentur für Arbeit, 'Auswirkungen der Migration auf den deutschen Arbeitsmarkt (Monatszahlen)' (2021).

23
Economic and monetary union

The European integration process has gone through various stages of economic integration. While the initial focus was on a customs union and free trade, the EU later developed into a common market and—within a limited circle of EU members—into the Economic and Monetary Union. The specific institutional design of the EMU, in particular its asymmetry between centralized monetary policy and decentralized fiscal policy, has been subject to economic controversy since the beginning of the monetary union. The problems arising out of the asymmetry have come to the fore in particular in times of crisis and have led to numerous policy innovations (eg in unconventional monetary policy) and reforms (eg of EU fiscal rules), in particular following the European solvency debt crisis.[1]

In principle, the creation of a monetary union implies a transfer of a Member State's 'property rights' over its national monetary policy to the supranational level (see above Chapter 2). Countries are the natural holder of this property right through their genuine exercise of public authority over national territory. The Westphalian order of international law assigns to the respective holder of public authority the property right of exercising authority over, inter alia, economic and monetary affairs on its territory. When states interact and trade authority with each other (through the conclusion of international treaties), in order to optimize their payoff function, states only agree to transferring their property rights (and accept the associated loss of sovereignty through the transfer of jurisdiction), if they can thereby achieve a gain.[2] Apart from the political added value of a monetary union as a precursor to a European political union, a common currency is a rationale for economies when transaction costs and exchange rate risks can be significantly reduced and macroeconomic shocks can be better cushioned through financial integration—and provided these advantages outweigh the loss of control over domestic currency. By subjecting Member States to a Treaty-based no-bailout clause and a set of fiscal rules, the prediction at the beginning of the monetary union was that a common currency in combination with a coordinated economic policy would not only, supported by an internal market, intensify trade within the Union, but also smooth business cycles across the euro area and thus make the currency

[1] André Sapir, 'Dealing with EMU Heterogeneity' in Francesco Caselli, Mário Centeno, and José Tavares (eds), *After the Crisis* (Oxford University Press 2016).

[2] Joel P Trachtman, *The Economic Structure of International Law* (Harvard University Press 2008) 10.

EU Law and Economics. Armin Steinbach, Oxford University Press. © Oxford University Press 2025.
DOI: 10.1093/9780198920915.003.0023

more resilient to shocks.[34] The conceptual basis for this prediction was the theory of Optimum Currency Area (OCA) which postulates that under certain conditions a geographical region maximizes economic efficiency with a shared currency. Efficiency gains are secured in an OCA only if labour and capital mobility exist. Regarding the EU, the Treaty-based economic freedoms discussed above are thus key for justifying a single currency under the OCA theory. Labour and capital mobility were restrained at the inception of the euro (and still are today), but the prevailing view was that despite remaining imperfections, the surrender of currency sovereignty would ultimately create welfare increases.[5] Member States of the EU joining the euro club considered these gains to be mutual and positive.

However, the transfer of property rights over the conduct of monetary policy means surrendering jurisdiction and authority of important economic adjustment tools to a central institution. As a consequence, while trade and commerce may flourish and unleash sizeable welfare effects, Member States' scope to adjust to economic shocks shrinks. As long as monetary policy is domestic, states can react to a shock with appreciation or devaluation of their currencies and thus influence their economy's competitiveness. Without monetary policy autonomy, the adjustment mechanisms shift to economic and fiscal policy, and price competitiveness adjustment runs through fiscal austerity and economic structural reforms, both of which can be politically costly. With fiscal policy being subject to legal constraints in the EU, adjustment processes in the event of shocks in the currency zone essentially take place via wages, product and capital market integration, and labour migration (in line with the OCA theory). Indeed, an increase in price and wage flexibility would lead to greater homogeneity in economic cycles and a decline in macroeconomic fluctuations. In practice, however, heterogeneity between European economies, illustrated by divergent business cycles, price levels, and current account imbalances, has increased rather than decreased.[6] In addition, heterogeneous economic structures within the eurozone (especially with divergent inflation levels) can be further reinforced by the effect of monetary policy transmission. If monetary policy impulses have different effects within the eurozone, there is a risk that monetary policy itself will generate asymmetric shocks.[7]

[3] Ansgar Belke and Frank Baumgärtner, 'Fiskalische Transfermechanismen und asymmetrische Schocks in Euroland' (2002) 71 Vierteljahrshefte zur Wirtschaftsforschung 384; Ansgar Belke and Jens Michael Heine, 'On the Endogeneity of an Exogenous OCA-Criterion: The Impact of Specialisation on the Synchronisation of Regional Business Cycles in Europe' (2001) HWWA Discussion Paper No 109.

[4] Claus Thustrup Kreiner, 'Do the New Keynesian Microfoundations Rationalise Stabilisation Policy?' (2002) 112 Economic Journal 384; Jochen Michaelis and Michael Pflüger, 'Euroland: Besser Als Befürchtet, Aber Schlechter Als Erhofft?' (2002) 71 Vierteljahrshefte zur Wirtschaftsforschung 296.

[5] Armin Steinbach, *Economic Policy Coordination in the Euro Area* (Taylor & Francis Ltd 2014), 21.

[6] Ibid 11.

[7] Junior Maih and others, 'Asymmetric Monetary Policy Rules for the Euro Area and the US' (2021) 70 Journal of Macroeconomics 103376; Guglielmo Maria Caporale and Alaa M Soliman, 'The Asymmetric Effects of a Common Monetary Policy in Europe' (2009) 24 Journal of Economic Integration 455.

At the same time, the monetary union created a 'club public good'. As with other public goods, the common currency created incentives for free-riding, inviting Member States to rely on the contributions of other Member States to maintain the stability of the currency. This also creates channels for spillovers—fiscal misconduct of an individual member becomes a threat to the common good. A country's fiscal behaviour affects the level of inflation, the stability of the currency, and through the refinancing conditions, the other members' economies. A country controlling its own currency can always service the debts incurred in this currency, if necessary through the central bank pursuing monetary financing. This means that the creditors of the individual country bear the inflation or exchange rate risk. In a monetary union, however, this risk is transferred to the eurozone as a whole, because it affects the common currency as a whole—the risk is mutualized, it is no longer differentiated as it was under individual currency regimes. In the wake of the sovereign debt crisis, the negative external effects of fiscal behaviour have come to the fore, with the lack of liquidity and the 'quasi-insolvency' of some countries jeopardizing the financial stability of the eurozone as a whole. Financial rescue programmes for distressed states were put together using bilateral loans conditioned on the implementation of reforms—an approach which was ultimately institutionalized as the European Stability Mechanism (ESM).

Typically, a macroeconomic perspective dominates the analysis of EMU. This perspective emphasizes factors influencing fiscal, financial, and monetary stability.[8] From a different angle, the institutional design and legal framework of EMU can be approached through federalism theory and institutional economics. They suggest inquiry of two issues: firstly, in a multilevel governance system such as the EU, the question is—descriptively—what incentives are associated with the current Treaty design in relation to fiscal policy decisions, and—normatively—how the liability framework enshrined in primary and secondary EU law should be designed such that negative external effects of Member States economic policy decision are internalized.

Unlike macroeconomic approaches to sovereign debt that seek to determine the sustainable level of debt for public finances purposes, the institutional economic perspective focuses on the legal institutions in which the state actors make their decisions. In the European multilevel context, the question is whether the decision-making process and the competence allocation between federal and subfederal levels are designed to serve the interests of citizens as ultimate principals. At the same time, constitutional economics seeks to offer insight about the expected consequences associated with the choice of alternative state liability regimes and decision-making procedures in the multilevel EU governance context.[9]

[8] See only Paul de Grauwe, *Economics of Monetary Union* (Oxford University Press 2022).

[9] Viktor Vanberg, 'Staatsverschuldung und konstitutionelle Ökonomik' in Christoph Engel and Martin Morlok (eds), *Öffentliches Recht als ein Gegenstand ökonomischer Forschung* (Mohr Siebeck 1998) 113.

In a monetary union characterized by central monetary policy but decentral fiscal policies, one core issue concerns how the design of fiscal policy coordination determines incentives to incur state debt. This question is led by the normative benchmark that sovereign debts should be maintained at a level that avoids negative external effects on other members of the euro area. Incentives for debt accumulation are critical in determining whether a specific form of fiscal policy coordination is appropriate. These incentives are in turn determined by the state organization principles that shape debt liability. From this perspective, we can distinguish two different ways of state organization that determine the incentives to incur debt both on the debtor and the creditor sides—*federal states* and *union states*.[10]

a) Fiscal policy coordination and state organization principles

For the purpose of highlighting the importance of state organization for the accumulation of state debt, we conceptualize that the primary difference between these two types of organization is the degree to which central government or sub-central governments incur liability for the debt of other state levels (federal versus sub-federal levels). In theory, in *federal states* there is no joint liability, meaning each individual member region is liable for its own debts—no other individual Member State assumes debt of another member, nor does the federal government level assume the debt of one of its sub-federal entities. We understand federal states as a self-organization of states that, albeit cooperation may have features of supranational character, maintains a logic of individual economic accountability which overrules a shifting of this accountability to other units. In a political dimension, this notion of federal states may be close to what the German Constitutional Court had characterized as a *Staatenverbund*, that is, an organization that goes beyond a mere confederation of states. In the EU, as *Staatenverbund*, there exists institutional supranational exercise of authority, while Member States retain sovereignty. By contrast, in *union states* the member regions or the central government can still take on their own debts individually, and those debts are first and foremost their own liability. But as a kind of guarantee, the other federal or sub-federal levels can ultimately be held liable for other members' debts. Hence, union states establish elements of mutualization.[11] Either sub-federal entities assume debt of the central level (or vice versa), or Member States offer guarantees for each other. In union state organization, whatever one level of state representation does, it can (to

[10] Charles B Blankart and Erik R Fasten, 'Wer soll für die Schulden im Bundesstaat Haften? Eine Vernachlässigte Frage der Föderalismusreform II' (2009) 10 Perspektiven der Wirtschaftspolitik 39, 40.
[11] David Christoph Ehmke, *Institutional Congruence the Riddle of Leviathan and Hydra* (Nomos Verlagsgesellschaft 2018) 202.

varying degrees) rely on the other members of the union to offer certain guarantees that the state's creditors are ultimately being served.[12] Clearly, this distinction between federal and union states is a theoretical one for the purpose of clarifying the associated incentive structure, with elements of both types of state organizations—the EU is illustrative for the combination of elements of both systems.

State debt in federal states

In federal states, no formal or factual liability links exist—federal and sub-federal governments are entirely liable for the debts they take on. A federal state, by the definition used in this analysis, is thus a state organization built on the autonomy of members within the federal union.[13] In contrast with union states, in federal states the central government is not liable to the regional governments' lenders, nor vice-versa; a 'no bailout' principle exists and is credibly applied. In federal states, lenders make their decisions by assessing only the credibility of the individual debtor country, because no other country guarantees repayment. Consequently, unlike in a union state, in theory there is a stronger correlation in a federal state between a government's financing costs and its debt level, which implies that higher debt translates directly into the country's disincentive to pile up debts, as governments are confronted with a rising interest rate curve, which in turn reduces the demand for debt. This correlation is presumably stronger because mutualization is not factored in.

This is the conceptual difference between a federal state and a union state: in a union state shared liability and risk taken on by the central government can lead to a higher level of total debt on sub-federal levels without significantly increasing the sub-federal governments' financing costs, because lenders offer interest rates that account for the higher solvency in a scenario of shared liability. This effect may also occur horizontally between sub-federal units if reciprocal liability exists. Since in a union state the regional governments share their risk, the total demand for debt is actually larger than the sum of the regional governments' demand for debt.

To take a historical example, the German Empire with its 26 sovereign states and around 40,000 municipalities was a federal state.[14] The states and municipalities had considerable spending and financial autonomy. There was no horizontal or vertical fiscal equalization, and, as a result, no shared liability among the regional states. The Empire was organized under the principle of fiscal equivalence (see above Chapter 21 d), meaning that the circle of beneficiaries, policy-makers,

[12] A third type of state is the unitary state. In unitary states the central government is liable for all debts throughout the state. As a result, only the central government can take on debt. The regional governments are just departments of the central government and cannot take on any debt.

[13] Ehmke (n 11) 58.

[14] Blankart and Fasten (n 10) 41.

and taxpayers in every sub-federal jurisdiction and on every level always perfectly overlapped. No one could live at the expense of their neighbours or could be forced to support their neighbours. Today, the US is an example where similar incentives are offered by a federal state. Instead of sharing liability as in a union state system, the central government offers no such safety net.[15] Instead, there is a great deal of uncertainty. For example, in 2010 California's request for a bailout from the United States government was rejected. This is still true even today despite the extensive debt taken over (in fact or implicitly) by the Federal Reserve and the US government in the course of various bailouts throughout the financial crisis. While liability for state debt thus remains individualized limiting shared liability, this does not mean that other fiscal policies are in place that implement inter-state solidarity with a strong economic equalization function. Interregional or vertical fiscal transfers designed to smooth macroeconomic shocks (in line with OCA theory) are to some extent a substitute for shared liability, though one that is more efficient because it engages in shock response without biasing incentives towards more debt inclination. For example, the United States has significant fiscal transfers in place to absorb asymmetrical regional shocks, with unemployment insurance as a channel for fiscal transfers. About 30 per cent of the states' expenditures (including Medicaid) consist of federal grants. 40 per cent of local government revenues come from the state governments (state grants). The risk of a bailout is thereby significantly mitigated by the existence of significant vertical financial assistance.

The eurozone has no automatic stabilizer in place that would be responsive to fluctuations in business cycles. The established EU transfer mechanisms seek to promote economic support of the economically weakest regions in Europe without however fulfilling an effective function regarding the business cycle (eg the Structural Fund and the Cohesion Fund).[16] Only more recently, transfer schemes such as SURE and NGEU have not only ensured a macroeconomic function of smoothing asymmetric shocks, specifically to counter the effects of the pandemic.[17] The transfer schemes have also introduced elements of union states by allowing the EU to take on debt that is ultimately secured by its Member States and which implied transfers between EU members.[18]

[15] The US experience of enforcing a no-bailout regime at the federal level vis-à-vis the US states has been controversially discussed, with more recent developments in US fiscal federalism being an indication of this provision being relaxed. See Peter Conti-Brown and David A Skeel, *When States Go Broke: The Origins, Context, and Solutions for the American States in Fiscal Crisis* (Cambridge University Press 2012); David Schleicher, *In a Bad State: Responding to State and Local Budget Crises* (Oxford University Press 2023).

[16] Berend Diekmann, Christoph Menzel, and Tobias Thomae, 'Konvergenzen und Divergenzen im "Währungsraum USA" im Vergleich zur Eurozone' (2012) 92 Wirtschaftsdienst 27; Cristina Fasone, 'EU Budget and Spending Powers' in Alicia Hinarejos and Robert Schütze (eds), *EU Fiscal Federalism* (Oxford University Press 2023) 256.

[17] Paul Dermine and Ana Bobic, 'Of Winners and Losers: A Commentary of the Bundesverfassungsgericht ORD Judgment of 6 December 2022' (2024) 20 European Constitutional Law Review 163, 175.

[18] Clemens Fuest, 'The NGEU Economic Recovery Fund' (2021) 22 CESifo Forum 3.

By contrast, in the US, a federal state, each state pays debt costs in line with its individual level of debt. To guard against debt costs rising too high, many states in the US have on their own initiative amended their constitutions to include debt limits of various kinds. The levels of government debt among the states in the US illustrate the results. While balanced budget rules have not prevented states running high deficits on a temporary basis, the overall debt of states has been contained. State debt in 2009 was as low as 7.3 per cent (California) and 4.9 per cent (Arizona).[19] That stands in stark contrast to Germany, a union state, where the level of debt ranged from about 7 per cent in Bavaria to almost 70 per cent of GDP in Berlin.[20]

State debt in union states

By contrast, the eurozone, while legally conceptualized as a federal entity, as *Staatenverbund*, which stipulates economic market accountability of each of its Member States, actually exhibits the features of a union state.[21] By definition, Member States of unions can take on their own debts, and those debts remain first and foremost their own liability. But as a guarantee, they can rely either on the centralized government or on other states in the union state that can be held liable for each other's debts. Whether this is channeled through formal joint and several liability or only by implicit liability of the state does not make a difference from an economic perspective (what matters are markets' beliefs). Whatever the governments do, there is some certainty that they can rely on other union members of a union state to step in and bail them out.

Contemporary Germany is an example of a union state. While formally no joint liability for debt means exists, in practice the *Bundesländer* can count on the federal government to step in if fiscal hardship occurs. While this bailout is subsidiary only and tied to strict conditions, the mutualizing effect is reflected in the debt costs paid by the *Bundesländer* in Germany's union system, as they remain largely independent of their individual debt levels. Their ratings ultimately depend on the rating of the federal Bund.

In a union state, the liability regime is protective of lenders. While shared liability in union states incentivizes debtors to take on excessive debt, the lender is well protected because their repayment claims can ultimately be satisfied

19 Randall Henning and Martin Kessler, *Fiscal Federalism: US History for Architects of Europe's Fiscal Union* (Bruegel 2012) 19.

20 Kai A Konrad and others, 'Wege aus der Europäischen Staatsschuldenkrise' (2010) 90 Wirtschaftsdienst 783, 802.

21 Armin Steinbach, 'Markets as an Accountability Mechanism in EU Economic Governance' in Mark Dawson (ed), *Substantive Accountability in Europe's New Economic Governance* (Cambridge University Press 2023).

by several (indirect and direct) debtors, not only the individual direct debtor. Through implicit joint liability the creditor's claims will be satisfied through a cascade of claims, starting with the primary debtor country but eventually extending to other members of the union or through institutionalized agencies channeling mutualization. The common debt assumed by the EU in the context of NGEU is illustrative: while the EU is the primary and direct debtor entering into contracts with creditors on capital markets, the repayment is backed by the EU budget (financed by Member States' contributions), and if one Member State fails to make its contribution, additional contributions can be drawn from other Member States (on a pro rata basis).[22]

This contrasts with a federal state where each sub-federal government takes on debts according to its individual debt demand curve, because lenders set their lending conditions based on each sub-federal government's likelihood to honour debts. In a union state, a pooling of the demand curves leads to a greater risk of default that may occur in sub-federal governments.[23] This is because in a union state the regional governments are expected to share their risk, making the total demand for debt actually larger than the sum of the sub-federal governments' demand for debt.[24] The incentive for debt accumulation is increased because the financing costs are lower, at least for many states within the union state. This is different for fiscally sound countries who face a deterioration of the financing conditions if markets perceive them as potentially bailing out other members of the union, because costs are determined by the solvency risks of all state entities who could possibly be held liable, not by the individual government debt level. This also makes fiscal consolidation efforts more unlikely, as due to the mutualization of solvency, each regional government's fiscal contribution to consolidation has only a limited effect on improving financing costs because the positive effects of consolidation are socialized across all states. Free-riding occurs—it may be rational from a member's perspective to wait for other countries to contribute to financial stability in the union, thus free-ride on their commitments by employing the additional debt space offered through other members' fiscal efforts. In sum, shared debt liability increases moral hazard.[25]

What has been described corresponds to the situation in Germany (particularly before it introduced sub-federal constitutional debt brakes aiming at preventing excess debt taking). Regional governments in Germany have no risk in the case of insolvency and can count on a bailout from the central government. In 1992, the German Federal Constitutional Court declared that the central government and

[22] Sebastian Grund and Armin Steinbach, 'European Union Debt Financing: Leeway and Barriers from a Legal Perspective' (2023) Working Paper 15/2023, Bruegel.

[23] William Oates, 'On the Evolution of Fiscal Federalism: Theory and Institutions' (2008) 62 National Tax Journal 313, 324.

[24] Blankart and Fasten (n 14) 45.

[25] ibid.

the regional governments in Germany are bound by a kind of community solidarity and are obligated to support one another.[26] As a result, the Court decided that the *Bund* and the *Bundesländer* must help and offer financial support when any member of the German state community was facing an extreme budget crisis. At that time, the judgment was criticized for incentivizing regional governments to deliberately precipitate a budget crisis in order to force other members to pay for their fiscal policy misconduct.[27] The Court's decision resulted in the regional state governments of the *Bundesländer* Bremen and Saarland receiving extensive aid from 1994 to 2004. In 2004, Bremen's debt level was still higher than that of any other regional state government. In Saarland as well, budget cuts did not have a long-lasting positive effect. But the Federal Court's decision of 1992 had clearly established that the central government and regional governments were jointly liable for each other's debts. The rating agencies' scoring of the local state governments shows that shared liability decisively influences the assessments of market participants. The Federal Constitutional Court confirmed the liability of the federal state as *ultima ratio* in its 'Berlin decision' in 2006. However, the Court sought to strengthen the regional state governments' responsibility by requiring a high level of budgetary emergency and imposing budgetary consolidation measures on the regional government as a precondition for budgetary aid. Notwithstanding the fiscal conditionality as a precondition for the solidarity principle to apply, the rating agencies maintained for both the central government and the regional state governments their highest rating indicating that *Bundesländer* ultimately enjoy a bailout-option. Since insolvency becomes less probable when bailouts are plausible options, even states with extremely high levels of debt (or non-sovereigns like the EU) can retain access to the credit market over an extended period. Under this condition, market-based refinancing interest rates do not accurately reflect a state's solvency, nor do markets function as a means of enforcing fiscal discipline.[28]

Incentives for debt consolidation in federal and union states

Organizing states as federal or as union states within the characteristics discussed above raises questions about the tools available for dealing with the public good dilemma that the EMU is facing—that is, to incentivize members of the common currency to engage in minimizing negative spillovers from fiscal conduct and to

[26] For the following, see Kai A Konrad and Holger Zschäpitz, *Schulden Ohne Sühne? Warum der Absturz der Staatsfinanzen uns alle Trifft* (CH Beck 2010) 186.

[27] Konrad and Zschäpitz (n 26) 187; Alexander Schulz and Guntram B Wolff, 'The German Sub-National Government Bond Market: Structure, Determinants of Yield Spreads and Berlin's Forgone Bail-Out' (2009) 229 Jahrbücher für Nationalökonomie und Statistik 61.

[28] Konrad and others (n 26) 802; For a different view see Blankart and Fasten (n 14) 51.

contribute to financial stability as a public good.[29] A core rationale for fiscal policy coordination is thus to mitigate externalities on public goods or 'club-goods' (like the stability of the euro currency). Since the 'pooling' of demand curves and default probabilities are a typical feature of federal states (where no credible no-bailout exist), all members of the currency area bear the costs of high state debt and raising interest rates—the effects of fiscal policy on the public good are socialized.

We focus on debt consolidation, as this has been in the past the major source of financial instability, while it is admitted that a sole focus on debt runs the risk of disregarding the necessary balancing with growth impulses and thus leeway for debt-based fiscal impulses. With this incentive-oriented focus on managing fiscal incentives, there are multiple ways of managing debt such as ceilings on deficit and debt, or methodologies computing debt sustainability—these instruments rely on a pre-defined set of thresholds or criteria, which are assessed and enforced by an (independent) agency. Rather than relying on the market's actual response to deficit and debt levels, this rules-based enforcement structure is implemented by a non-market-based enforcement of rule-makers' (discretionary) decisions. Statutory debt ceilings may try to reflect economically sustainable debt levels, but they are definitely different from relying on the market's verdict.[30]

A different approach is to either credibly exclude, by law, or at least create uncertainty that governments will be bailed out, with the aim of inducing markets to base their solvency judgements solely on an individual country's performance, hence using market-determined interest rates as disciplining tools.[31] Thus, the first approach is a discretion-based, non-market enforcement of fiscal policy and the latter relies on market-based enforcement, while both rely on the existence of a credible legal framework by determining the assessment and enforcement structure. In the EU, both approaches have been laid down in the EU Treaties: a deficit and debt ceiling approach with a rules-based mechanism of enforcement (Article 126 TFEU), more recently complemented by a regime determined by debt sustainability analysis, as well as a market-oriented no-bailout clause (Article 125 TFEU). The first approach limits regional governments' ability to take on debt put in place through statutory regulation and administrative enforcement (by the EU Commission). This approach does not necessarily alter the debtor's *preference* to take on debt (rather than increasing state revenue through taxation), but it limits the debt *space* through the decisions of an externally enforced limitation. In contrast, the second approach is aimed at reducing the debtor governments' preference

[29] Isabelle Joumard and Mathis Kongsrud, 'Fiscal Relations across Government Level' (2003) OECD Economics Department Working Papers No 375, 29.

[30] Daniel Kelemen and Terence Teo, 'Law, Focal Points, and Fiscal Discipline in the United States and the European Union' (2014) 108 American Political Science Review 355, 363; Geoffrey Woglom, 'Do Credit Markets Discipline Sovereign Borrowers? Evidence from US States' (1995) Journal of Money and Credit, and Banking 1046.

[31] Mark Hallerberg, 'Fiscal Federalism Reforms in the European Union and the Greek Crisis' (2010) 12 European Union Politics 127, 130.

for debt by leveraging market prices (interest rates) to influence the lender's willingness to loan.[32] The latter is a market-based strategy that uses the risk of insolvency to link the cost of credit as closely as possible to the risk of default.

Consequentially, the effectiveness of market-based no-bailout provisions critically depends on functionality of markets and the extent to which market-based interest rates are determined by fundamentals of the country concerned rather than being influenced by irrational market sentiments. The history of the EMU has shown that reliance on a statutory no-bailout clause in Article 125 TFEU is an insufficient tool to constrain debt incentives: over a decade since the beginning of the euro, markets did not view any divergence between Member States that was of relevance to members' solvency, as bond spreads were largely convergent. This market ignorance engendered underestimating different degrees of solvencies between EU members, and with the outbreak of the crisis, the bond spreads overreacted in a way that was not justified by the fundamental economic data (thus drastically overestimating divergences in solvency).[33] In turn, the effectiveness of enforcement-based approaches under Articles 121 and 126 TFEU depends on how existing rules deal with political economy and strategic behaviour, in particular how enforcement can be implemented effectively. Since its inception, the Treaty-based enforcement structure, implemented through the Stability and Growth Pact, has been subject to criticism due to its lack of effectiveness.

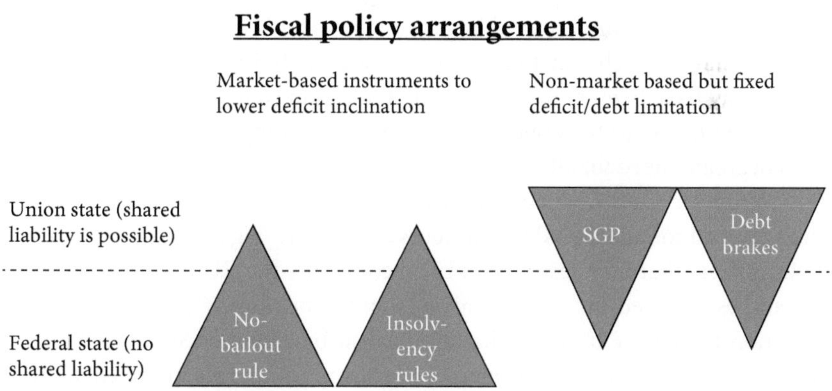

Fig 23.1 Fiscal policy arrangements
Source: Armin Steinbach, *Economic Policy Coordination in the Euro Area (Taylor & Francis Ltd 2014)* 83.

[32] Timothy D. Lane, 'Market Discipline' (1993) IMF Staff Papers No 53, 55; Fabrizio Balassone, Daniele Franco and Raffaela Giordano, 'Market-Induced Fiscal Discipline: Is there a Fall-Back Solution for Rule Failure?', Public Debt (Banca d'Italia 2004), 410.

[33] Paul de Grauwe, Yuemei Ji, and Armin Steinbach, 'The EU Debt Crisis: Testing and Revisiting Conventional Legal Doctrine' (2017) 51 International Review of Law and Economics 29.

Figure 23.1 shows how different state organization principles may have different methods of restricting sovereign debt accumulation. State organization principles can be distinguished by reference to shared liability as well as by reference to their market orientation. The suitability of each approach depends on the form of state organization that is legally implemented. A credible no-bailout provision and state insolvency procedure are better suited in a federal state setting building on a market-based system to contain debt.

In *federal unions*, debt is individualized and shared liability is precluded, and the markets assess only the solvency of an individual state—a logic that best suits a bailout-clause and state insolvency framework, that is, procedure to restructure debt.[34] The American experience with Chapter 9 of the American Bankruptcy Code shows that a formalized bankruptcy procedure can provide an incentive for fiscal consolidation. Certainly, market-based approaches could also be implemented in a union state, where shared liability determines the regional government's ability to take on debt, and one may argue that the EU is precisely such a case, as the Treaty-based bailout clause stands next to institutions such as the ESM, SURE, and NGEU, all of which have established some kind of shared liability. But market-based approaches are less effective in union states because shared liability undermines the market signal, not allowing market interest rates to be credible reflections of an individual state's solvency risk. Again, the EU is illustrative in this regard. During the first ten years of the eurozone, the strong convergence of sovereign bond interest rates suggested that markets assumed joint liability in the EU, as spreads were largely unconnected from underlying economic data. The market's belief in some kind of shared liability—despite the no-bailout clause—may have been at work. In turn, in a union state, in which market forces on an individual country's budgetary conduct are comparatively weak by design, there is a greater need for alternative debt containment in order to mitigate external effects. Without the disciplining force of markets that sanctions a state's solvency, there is a need for additional instruments containing negative external and destabilizing effects that may result from fiscal conduct—the EU has implemented the logic and established fiscal governance from the beginning of the euro. Revenue generation through EU bonds that are backed by Member States' contributions and ultimately secured by other members' solvency (as implemented in SURE and NGEU) is alien to the system in a pure federal organization due to the associated mutualization effects—while bonds allowing shared liability may be implemented for sound macroeconomic reasons to stabilize the currency area,[35] this instrument

[34] Jonathan P Thomas, 'Bankruptcy Proceedings for Sovereign State Insolvency and Their Effect on Capital Flows' (2004) 13 International Review of Economics & Finance 341.

[35] Gabriele Giudice and others, 'A European Safe Asset to Complement National Government Bonds' (2019) MPRA Paper No 95748.

weakens the market-based principle established through the no-bailout clause. Joint liability bonds engender a 'pooling' of demand curves.[36]

In turn, for a *union state*, shared liability bonds are the suitable tool to stabilize the character as a union state, because shared liability expenditure is an appropriate way of funding projects that address common concerns such as transnational public goods. The financing of transnational public goods (or European public goods, see above Chapter 21 d) is not obvious in a federal state with individual liability. Strictly speaking, members must contribute to European public goods according to the benefits they derive from them (fiscal equivalence). Common debt may facilitate financing public goods.

b) Debt limitation in the eurozone

The EU is not easily characterized as either a union or federal state. The EU is not a pure federal state, nor a union state. From a legal perspective, the EU has been characterized by the German Constitutional Court as an association of sovereign states (*Staatenverbund*), which highlights that the EU is more than just a loose group of states tied together through an international law Treaty, but is not a sovereign state in its own right. Formally, the EU has established a no-bailout principle (Article 125 TFEU) as well as a ban on monetary financing (Article 123 TFEU), both of which incorporate the idea of fiscal responsibility for each individual Member State of the EU—there is agreement in legal scholarship, both among scholars as well as in jurisprudence (of the ECJ and the German Constitutional Court), that the rationale of these core provisions of the EMU is to let market pressure be the disciplining force on Member States, thus emphasizing the EU's character as a federal state in which all union members remain responsible for their own fiscal fate.[37]

Experience has shown that the anti-crisis measures have put in question the binding force of these fiscal-monetary pillars of self-dependence. Financial turmoil threatening the financial stability of the eurozone has been seen to lead to detrimental effects (for all members of the eurozone) and injecting considerable flexibility to the rules as the only way to reconcile comprehensive financial assistance with statutory rules. Both a fiscal no-bailout provision as well as a monetary ban on state financing were turned away from a strict interpretation: a move that was motivated to divert negative effects that could result from state insolvency within the euro currency area. Hence, while a no-bailout clause builds the EU on the premise of a federal state, the statutory ban has incrementally softened towards a union state implementing elements of shared liability character. This leads

[36] Brady Gordon, *The Constitutional Boundaries of European Fiscal Federalism* (Cambridge University Press 2022) 350.

[37] ibid 122–130, 345.

markets to work only partially in constraining fiscal policy. The institutionalization of the crisis instruments in the EU Treaty, such as the legal basis for the ESM (Article 136 TFEU), have further established a permanent mechanism to provide financial aid when financial stability requires it.[38]

Despite weakening market pressure through these crisis instruments, the EU sought to offset the weakening of the bailout-clause by imposing fiscal conditionality as a *quid pro quo* for financial assistance. The consequence was a change from market accountability towards political accountability. As long as Article 125 TFEU was fully intact, Member States were held by markets accountable for their policies that affected their solvency, with markets sanctioning members for unsound fiscal policy.

The term 'economic accountability' captures the EU Treaties' choice of free market rules that subject the financing needs of private actors and states to the judgement of markets.[39] Economic accountability has been supplanted by subjecting receiving Member States to the judgement of other sovereigns' demands, with accountability to markets being incrementally replaced by accountability to other sovereigns or EU institutions. Creditor Member States, the EU Commission, and the European Central Bank act as providers of financial aid in return for conditional structural, economic, financial, and social reforms to be carried out by the debtor states. What has previously been pressured by markets is now (under the ESM) subject to political discretion of non-majoritarian institutions as well as from other sovereigns. It is against this background that a vast body of literature in political science emerged that focused on the problematic aspects of this shift from a legitimacy and acceptance perspective.[40] From an economic perspective, one can be neutral regarding who should be responsible for containing external effects—if the goal is to prevent Members to act in a fiscally imprudent fashion (Article 125 TFEU), a conditionality programme set up by non-majoritarian institutions is no worse than market pressure, provided that it is equally effective. A precondition for conditionality to be effective is that it is carefully calibrated so that it does not create bailout expectations.[41]

Taken together, there is no instrument in the EU that sufficiently minimizes the propensity to borrow. Since the eurozone was founded, sovereign bond interest rates have factored in the mutual commitment among eurozone countries, encouraging borrowing by offering relatively low rates. It was only during the sovereign debt crisis that rates reacted with hyper-sensitively, moving beyond the underlying

[38] Fabian Amtenbrink and Menelaos Markakis, 'Never Waste a Good Crisis on the Emergent EU Fiscal Capacity' in Alicia Hinarejos and Robert Schütze (eds), *EU Fiscal Federalism* (Oxford University Press 2023) 197.

[39] Steinbach (n 21).

[40] Ben Crum and Deirdre Curtin, 'The Challenge of Making European Union Executive Power Accountable' in Simona Piattoni (ed), *The European Union* (Oxford University Press 2015) 63; Deirdre Curtin, 'Challenging Executive Dominance in European Democracy' (2014) 77 Modern Law Review 1.

[41] Gordon (n 36) 354.

economic fundamentals.[42] In addition, there is also no insolvency regime that would restructure debt and require a plan for re-solvency.

If the EU wants to strengthen its federal element by reducing its Members' propensity to incur debt, a credible no-bailout and the possibility of insolvency for states would be suitable forms of coordination that aim at strengthening preventive market incentives. Insolvency proceedings create legal certainty for debtors and creditors. Having an insolvency procedure with restructuring requirements in place would further induce creditors to assess debtors' individual creditworthiness rather than counting on shared liability of union members. The introduction of collective action clauses (CAC) has been a major development in this regard. The main purpose of the euro area model CAC is to introduce a 'single-limb' voting mechanism. Restructuring decisions are thus binding on all holders of a series of debt securities aggregated in one voting group if the proposed modification is approved by holders of a majority of all securities aggregated in the voting group. Facilitating debt restructuring not only speeds up insolvency proceedings but also has a chilling effect on lending practices.

EU law has never relied exclusively on the bailout prohibition. In the absence of a credible ban, EU law sets out a comprehensive network of procedural and substantive fiscal obligations, led by the overarching goal to have 'sound public finances and monetary framework conditions' (Article 119 TFEU). This objective guides the fiscal policy regulations specified in Article 126 TFEU, the Stability and Growth Pact (SGP) specifying the implementation of numerical deficit and debt criteria, which was supplemented by the Fiscal Compact, an international Treaty requiring EU members to introduce national debt brakes.[43] National debt brakes fulfil a similar function to the SGP: they do not use market incentives for budget discipline, but rather impose (more or less) arbitrary debt and deficit limits set and administered by authorities. The SGP and the Member State debt brakes are therefore more suitable for a union state in which market forces are conceptually abandoned on strict terms. The same applies to shared liability bonds as implemented under the ESM, SURE, and NGEU. They amount, at least in part, to joint liability, even if—depending on their design—they mimic market pressure through conditionality.

On an economic account, it is questionable to what extent EU fiscal rules with their application of the rigid 'one-size-fits-all' approach using numerical benchmarks will promote the sustainability of its members' debt. Even if the distinction between 'good debt' and 'bad debt' is an unplausible market definition, there are instances when debt can be used for growth-enhancing purposes (thus stabilizing fiscal sustainability), and EU rules have shown certain flexibility for expenditures

[42] Paul de Grauwe and Yuemei Ji, 'Self-Fulfilling Crises in the Eurozone: An Empirical Test' (2012) 34 Journal of International Money and Finance 15.

[43] Steinbach (n 21) 84.

linked to structural reforms or for investments of transnational significance in the EU. The reform of the SGP moved in this direction,[44] notably shifting away from an isolated consideration of deficit and debt levels towards a more sophisticated debt sustainability analysis, which would build on established practices of the IMF and the Commission. The overall effect of a country-specific, non-numerical, and context-specific analysis would be to assess a country's ability to bear and reduce debt on a more diversified and robust basis.[45]

c) No bailout and monetary state financing

No-bailout clauses and the ban on monetary financing are core rules that aim mitigate negative external effects on club goods, such as currency stability, financial stability, price stability, and state refinancing conditions. EU jurisprudence developed in the *Pringle* judgment led to relaxations of the no-bailout clause, which prohibits states and Union institutions from assuming debt from other EU members. Accordingly, financial aid to crisis-struck EU Members under the ESM is permissible under certain conditions, provided that it is indispensable to secure the financial stability of the eurozone (Article 136 TFEU).[46]

The incentives associated with the interpretation of Article 125 TFEU matter. The Court emphasizes what economists have claimed to be the rationale of a no-bailout provision. States should remain under market pressure in order to create incentives for sound budgetary discipline.[47] This discipline ensures financial stability of the common currency and, consequently, any financial aid undermining this desirable effect should be prohibited under Article 125 TFEU.[48] The core of the Court's jurisprudence developed during the sovereign debt crisis in relation to inter-state financial aid (or transfers) is that conditionality attached to aid maintains the budgetary pressure on states.[49] This approach is plausible, as the empirical evidence suggests that market-determined interest rates are not solely determined by fundamental performance data of the states but to a large extent (at least during a crisis) are the result of market fears and risk aversion. In such situations, the logic of Article 125 TFEU does not apply, because there is no causal relationship between the fiscal conduct and the market-based bond spreads.

[44] The new fiscal framework builds on two regulations, Regulation (EU) 2024/1263) replacing the 'preventive arm' of the old system and Regulation 2024/1264 amending the excessive deficit procedure, and Directive 2024/1265, which sets out requirements Member States' budgets must comply with.

[45] Zsolt Darvas, Lennart Welslau, and Jeromin Zettelmeyer, 'The implications of the European Union's new fiscal rules' (2024) Policy Brief 10/2024, Bruegel.

[46] Case C-370/12 *Pringle* (2012) EU:C:2012:756.

[47] ibid [136]; Paul Craig, 'Pringle: Legal Reasoning, Text, Purpose and Teleology' (2013) 20 Maastricht Journal of European and Comparative Law 3.

[48] Case C-370/12 *Pringle* (2012) EU:C:2012:756, [136].

[49] ibid [137].

Decisively, the ECJ jurisprudence acknowledges politically determined conditionality as a substitute for market results. Political conditionality can have the same effect as market conditionality. As mentioned, one can interpret this jurisprudence as an interaction between two accountability regimes: between political accountability for supervising and legitimizing government action as a genuine core concept of accountability on the one hand, and the normative choice of the EU Treaties, which establish a regime of economic accountability under which states and private actors must subject their conduct to market mechanisms on the other hand. Throughout the financial crisis there has been a shift from economic to political accountability with an associated weakening of market mechanisms as a driving force in the formulation of national policy by public authorities. The political accountability that emerged from sovereign bailouts must mimic the logic of market pressure through discretional conditionality. Clearly, political economy considerations would put in doubt the equivalence of market pressure and political conditionality as tools to maintain the rationale of the no-bailout clause. Political discretion is loaded with considerations, assumptions, and preferences that are alien to markets, and with these political idiosyncrasies in mind, the conditionality of financial aid is likely to be guided by other parameters than solvency only.

Consider the macroeconomic harm of interpreting Article 125 TFEU too narrowly by not allowing any financial aid under any circumstances: the risk of contagion on inter-linked markets, the hyper-nervousness of market participants exacerbating the drift between bond spreads and fundamental data, suggest market failures that impose significant costs beyond the individual state concerned.[50] Yet, even if the short-term economically sound response may have been to allow a conditionality-based bailout, the long-term effect of this action must be effectively dealt with. Since the economic accountability regime required by EU Treaties has lost effect and was replaced by a political accountability regime of undemocratic design (as lawyers and political scientists have shown[51]), this shift should only be temporary in order to return to the desired state set forth by EU Treaties, which is the prevalence of market accountability.

A similar development can be observed in the interpretation of the ban on monetary state financing. The first relaxation of Article 123 TFEU was introduced by the Outright Monetary Transactions programme (OMT) in which the ECB committed to buy government bonds (if necessary for monetary policy reasons) provided that the countries concerned were subject to a conditionality programme under the ESM.[52] The ban on monetary financing follows a similar logic as the

[50] de Grauwe, Ji, and Steinbach (n 42).

[51] Mark Dawson, 'The Legal and Political Accountability Structure of 'Post-Crisis' EU Economic Governance' (2015) 53 Journal of Common Market Studies, 976, 989; Damian Chalmers, 'The European Redistributive State and a European Law of Struggle' (2012) 18 European Law Journal, 667, 692; Berthold Rittberger, 'Integration without Representation? The European Parliament and the Reform of Economic Governance in the EU' (2014) 52 Journal of Common Market Studies, 1174.

[52] ECB, 'ECB Monthly Bulletin September 2012' (2012) 8.

no bailout clause: it seeks to prevent Members from relying on monetary state financing and engaging in unsound budgetary policies. The provision seeks to ensure that what is necessary from a monetary policy perspective does not lift fiscal incentives to budgetary discipline, because legally the ECB must not engage in economic policy-making. What seems obvious from an economic perspective—the fact that there is an immediate effect from monetary policy decisions on economic policy parameters—is alien to a legal perspective that seeks to draw sharp lines between competences, that is, between EU exclusive competence on the one side (monetary policy) and Member States' policies on the other side (economic policies). Lawyers feel uncomfortable integrating spillovers between policy areas into their doctrine of competences.[53] In an attempt to reconcile the two perspectives, the Court acknowledged the occurrence of 'indirect effects' of monetary policy on economic policy, while at the same time requiring the ECB to implement 'safeguards' that would secure the market pressure on governments, which the ECB sought to secure by, inter alia, requiring that the country concerned must be subject to conditionality under the ESM.[54] Both conditionality (developed for financial aid in *Pringle*) as well as safeguards (attached to ECB's bond purchases in *Gauweiler* in relation to OMT) have market-substituting functions.[55]

While Articles 123 and 125 TFEU build on the premise of market accountability of states, an economic interpretation allows for temporary deviations of this premise by allowing political substitutes in order to mimic market pressure. More recently, the ECB introduced a so-called 'Transmission Protection Instrument' allowing it to engage exceptionally in government bond purchases when it considers irrational market behaviour to be a threat to the effectiveness of monetary policy. Again, the ECB must act in line with the ban on monetary financing and it thus considers eligible for bond purchases only states whose fiscal conduct is in line with EU fiscal rules. It remains a struggle to align effectiveness of monetary policy with legal norms that forbid monetary policy conduct to lift market pressure from states.

[53] Armin Steinbach, 'Effect-Based Analysis in the Court's Jurisprudence on the Euro Crisis' (2017) 42 European Law Review 255.

[54] Case C-62/14 *Gauweiler and others v Deutscher Bundestag* (2015) EU:C:2015:400 [46], [103].

[55] Steinbach (n 21) 1367.

Bibliography

Abbott KW, 'Modern International Relations Theory: A Prospectus for International Lawyers' (1989) 14 Yale Journal of International Law 335

——, 'Trust But Verify: The Production of Information in Arms Control Treaties and Other International Agreements' (1993) 26 Cornell International Law Journal 1

Abbott KW and Snidal D, 'Why States Act through Formal International Organizations' (1998) 42 Journal of Conflict Resolution 3

——, 'Hard and Soft Law in International Governance' (2000) 54 International Organization 421

Albi A and van Elsuwege P, 'EU Constitution, National Constitutions and Sovereignty: An Assessment of a "European Constitutional Order"' (2004) 29 European Law Review 741

Alesina A, Angeloni I, and Etro F, 'International Unions' (2005) 95 American Economic Review 602

Alesina A, Angeloni I, and Schuknecht L, 'What Does the European Union Do?' (2005) 123 Public Choice 275

Alesina A and La Ferrara E, 'Ethnic Diversity and Economic Performance' (2005) 43 Journal of Economic Literature 762

Alesina A and Spolaore E, *The Size of Nations* (The MIT Press 2005)

Alesina A, Spolaore E, and Wacziarg R, 'Economic Integration and Political Disintegration' (2000) 90 American Economic Review 1276

——, 'Trade, Growth and the Size of Countries' (2005) 1 Handbook of Economic Growth 1499

Alesina A and Wacziarg R, 'Openness, Country Size and Government' (1998) 69 Journal of Public Economics 305

Alford RP, 'The Self-Judging WTO Security Exception' (2011) 3 Utah Law Review 697

Allen L, Amacher RC, and Tollison RD, 'The Economic Theory of Clubs: A Geometric Exposition' (1974) 29 Public Finance = Finances publiques 386

Alonso-Sanz R, 'On a Three-Parameter Quantum Battle of the Sexes Cellular Automaton' (2013) 12 Quantum Information Processing 1835

Alter KJ, 'Who Are the "Masters of the Treaty"? European Governments and the European Court of Justice' (1998) 53 International Organization 121

——, 'The Multiple Roles of International Courts and Tribunals' in Jeffrey L Dunoff and Mark A Pollack (eds), *Interdisciplinary Perspectives on International Law and International Relations* (Cambridge University Press 2012)

Amtenbrink F and Lastra RM, 'Securing Democratic Accountability of Financial Regulatory Agencies—A Theoretical Framework' in Richard V de Mulder (ed) *Mitigating Risk in the Context of Safety and Security—How Relevant is a rational Approach?* (Erasmus School of Law 2009)

Anand PB, 'Financing the Provision of Global Public Goods' (2004) 27 World Economy 215

Andersen B, 'The crisis in Greece: missteps and miscalculations, European Stability Mechanism' (2020) Discussion Paper Series No 9

Armstrong KA, *Governing Social Inclusion* (Oxford University Press 2010)

Arnold NG and others, 'A Central Fiscal Stabilization Capacity for the Euro Area' (2018) Staff Discussion Notes No 2018/003

Arribas GV, 'Subsidiarity and EU Added Value: The Difficulty of Evaluating a Legal Principle in a Pragmatic Way' (2020) 3 European Court of Auditors Journal 30

Arrow KJ, *Kenneth Arrow, Social Choice and Individual Values, 1951* (Yale University Press 2012)

Atik J, 'From "No Bailout" to the European Stability Mechanism' (2016) 39 Fordham International Law Journal 1201

Avant DD, Finnemore M, and Sell SK, *Who Governs the Globe? (Cambridge Studies in International Relations, Series Number 114)* (Cambridge University Press 2010)
Baas T, 'The Macroeconomic Impact of Intra-EU Migration on the German Economy. Gefälligkeitsübersetzung: Der Makroökonomische Einfluss der Migration innerhalb der EU auf die deutsche Wirtschaft' (2014) 49 Intereconomics 116
Bagwell K and Staiger RW, *The Economics of the World Trading System* (The MIT Press 2004)
Balassone F, Franco D, and Giordano R, 'Market-Induced Fiscal Discipline: Is there a Fall-Back Solution for Rule Failure?', Public Debt (Banca d'Italia 2004) 410
Baraggia A and Bonelli M, 'Linking Money to Values: The New Rule of Law Conditionality Regulation and its Constitutional Challenges' (2022) 23 German Law Journal 131
Barber NW, 'Subsidiarity in the Draft Constitution' (2005) 11 European Public Law 197
Bar-Gill O and Fershtman C, 'Law and Preferences' (2004) 20 Journal of Law, Economics, & Organization 331
Barnard C, 'Social Dumping Revisited: Lessons from Delaware' (2000) 25 European Law Review 57
——, 'What the Keck? Balancing the Needs of the Single Market with State Regulatory Autonomy' (2012) 2 European Journal of Consumer Law 201
Barnett C, 'Culture, Policy, and Subsidiarity in the European Union: From Symbolic Identity to the Governmentalisation of Culture' (2001) 20 Political Geography 405
Bast J, 'On the Grammar of EU Law: Legal Instruments' (2003) Jean Monnet Working Paper 9/03
Beck G, *The Legal Reasoning of the Court of Justice of the EU* (Hart Publishing 2013)
Behrens P, 'The Ordoliberal Concept of "Abuse" of a Dominant Position and Its Impact on Article 102 TFEU' in Fabiana Di Porto and Rupprecht Podszun (eds), *Abusive Practices in Competition Law* (Edward Elgar Publishing 2018)
Belke A and Baumgärtner F, 'Fiskalische Transfermechanismen und asymmetrische Schocks in Euroland' (2002) 71 Vierteljahrshefte zur Wirtschaftsforschung 384
Belke A and Heine JM, 'On the Endogeneity of an Exogenous OCA-Criterion: The Impact of Specialisation on the Synchronisation of Regional Business Cycles in Europe' (2001) HWWA Discussion Paper No 109
Berlin I, *Four Essays on Liberty* (Oxford University Press 1969)
Berrisch GM, 'Zum "Bananen"-Urteil des EuGH Vom 5.10.1994' (1994) Europarecht 461
Bertoli S, Brücker H and Moraga JF-H, 'The European Crisis and Migration to Germany: Expectations and the Diversion of Migration Flows' (2013) CERDI Working Papers No 7170
Beukers T and van der Sluis M, 'Differentiated Integration from the Perspective of Non-Euro Area Member States' in Thomas Beukers, B De Witte, and C Kilpatrick (eds), *Constitutional Change through Euro-Crisis Law* (Cambridge University Press 2017)
Bhatia AV and others, 'A Capital Market Union for Europe' (2019) Staff Discussion Notes No 2019/007
Blankart CB, *Föderalismus in Deutschland und in Europa* (Nomos Verlagsgesellschaft 2007)
——, *Öffentliche Finanzen in der Demokratie: Eine Einführung in die Finanzwissenschaft* (Vahlen 2011)
Blankart CB and Fasten ER, 'Wer soll für die Schulden im Bundesstaat Haften? Eine Vernachlässigte Frage der Föderalismusreform II' (2009) 10 Perspektiven der Wirtschaftspolitik 39
Boadway R and Shah A, *Fiscal Federalism: Principles and Practice of Multiorder Governance* (Cambridge University Press 2009)
Boerger-De Smedt A, 'La Cour de Justice Dans Les Négociations Du Traité de Paris Instituant La CECA' (2008) 14 Journal of European Integration History 7
Börzel TA and Risse T, 'From Europeanisation to Diffusion: Introduction' (2012) 35 West European Politics 1
Bradford A, *The Brussels Effect: How the European Union Rules the World* (Oxford University Press 2019)
Bradford A, Chilton A, Linos K, and Weaver A, 'The Global Dominance of European Competition Law Over American Antitrust Law', (2019) 16 Journal of Empirical Legal Studies 731

Bradford A, Jackson Jr RJ, and Zytnick J, 'Is EU Merger Control Used for Protectionism? An Empirical Analysis' (2018) 15 Journal of Empirical Legal Studies 165

BrattonWWandMcCaheryJA,'TheNewEconomicsofJurisdictionalCompetition:Devolutionary the New Economics of Jurisdictional Competition: Devolutionary Federalism in a Second-Best World Federalism in a Second-Best World' (1997) 86 Georgetown Law Journal 201

Brennan G and Buchanan JM, *The Reason of Rules: Constitutional Political Economy* (Cambridge University Press 1985)

Breton A, 'The Existence and Stability of Interjurisdictional Competition' in Daphne A Kenyon and John Kincaid (eds), *Competition among States and Local Governments* (The Urban Institute Press 1991)

Breton T, 'Keynote Speech by Commissioner Breton—"A Europe That Protects Its Citizens, Transforms Its Economy, and Projects Itself as a Global Power"' (2024) European Commission, 10 January 2024

Brücker H and Eger T, 'The Law and Economics of the Free Movement of Persons in the European Union' in Thomas Eger and Hans-Bernd Schäfer (eds), *Research Handbook on the Economics of European Union Law* (Edward Elgar Publishing 2012)

Brummer C, 'Why Soft Law Dominates International Finance—and Not Trade' (2010) 13 Journal of International Economic Law 623

Brunnermeier MK, James H, and Landau J-P, *The Euro and the Battle of Ideas* (Princeton University Press 2017)

Buccirossi P and others, 'Deterrence in Competition Law' (2014) SFB/TR 15 Discussion Paper, No 285

Buchanan JM, 'An Economic Theory of Clubs' (1965) 32 Economica 1

——, *Fiscal Theory and Political Economy: Selected Essays* (The University of North Carolina Press 1954)

——, *Freedom in Constitutional Contract* (Texas A&M University Press 1977)

——, *The Limits of Liberty: Between Anarchy and Leviathan* (The University of Chicago Press 1977)

——, 'The Domain of Constitutional Economics' (1990) 1 Constitutional Political Economy 1

——, *The Economics and Ethics of Constitutional Order* (The University of Michigan Press 1991)

Buchanan JM and Brennan HG, *What Should Economists Do?* (Liberty Fund Inc 1979)

Buchanan JM and Tullock G, *The Calculus of Consent* (University of Michigan Press 1969)

Bucher A, 'Does Europe Need a Health Union?' (2022) Policy Contribution 02/2022, Bruegel

Budzinski O, 'Modern Industrial Economics and Competition Policy: Open Problems and Possible Limits' (2009) IME Working Paper, No 93

Bundesagentur für Arbeit S, 'Auswirkungen der Migration auf den deutschen Arbeitsmarkt (Monatszahlen)' (2021)

Buti M, 'When Will the European Union Finally Get the Budget it Needs?' (2023) Analysis, 7 December 2023, Bruegel

Calabresi G, *The Costs of Accidents: Legal and Economic Analysis* (Yale University Press 1970)

Calliess C, *Öffentliche Güter im Recht der Europäischen Union* (Bertelsmann Stiftung 2021)

Calvert RL, 'The Rational Choice Theory of Institutions: Implications for Design' in David L Weimer (ed), *Institutional Design* (Springer 1995)

Canton E, Ciriaci D, and Solera I, 'The Economic Impact of Professional Services Liberalisation' (2014) Economic Papers 533

Cao S, 'Quantifying Economic Reasoning in Court: Judge Economics Sophistication and Pro-Business Orientation' (2022) New Working Paper Series No 321

Caporale GM and Soliman AM, 'The Asymmetric Effects of a Common Monetary Policy in Europe' (2009) 24 Journal of Economic Integration 455

Caporaso JA, 'International Relations Theory and Multilateralism: The Search for Foundations' (1992) 46 International Organization 599

Carbonara E, Luppi B, and Parisi F, 'Self-Defeating Subsidiarity: An Economic Analysis' (2008) Minnesota Legal Studies Research Paper 1

Cason TN, Savikhin AC, and Sheremeta RM, 'Behavioral Spillovers in Coordination Games' (2012) 56 European Economic Review 233

Cecchini P, *The European Challenge 1992: The Benefits of a Single Market: European Challenge—Benefits of a Single Community* (Gower Publishing Ltd 1998)
Chalmers D, 'The European Redistributive State and a European Law of Struggle' (2012) 18 European Law Journal 667
Chayes A and Handler Chayes A, 'On Compliance' (1993) 47 International Organization 175
Checkel JT, 'Why Comply? Social Learning and European Identity Change' (2001) 55 International Organization 553
Chilton A and Linos K, 'Preferences and Compliance with International Law' (2021) 22 Theoretical Inquiries in Law 247
Chinkin CM, 'The Challenge of Soft Law: Development and Change in International Law' (1989) 38 International and Comparative Law Quarterly 850
Chiti E and Teixeira PG, 'The Constitutional Implications of the European Responses to the Financial and Public Debt Crisis' (2013) 50 Common Market Law Review 683
Claeys G and Sapir A, 'The European Globalisation Adjustment Fund: Easing the Pain from Trade?' in L Paganetto (ed), *Capitalism, Global Change and Sustainable Development* (Springer 2020) 97
Claeys G and Steinbach A, 'A Conceptual Framework for the Identification and Governance of European Public Goods' (2024) Working Paper 14/2024, Bruegel
Coase RH, 'The Problem of Social Cost' (1960) 3 The Journal of Law and Economics 1
——, 'The Institutional Structure of Production' (1992) University of Chicago Law Occasional Paper
Colliard J-E, 'Optimal Supervisory Architecture and Financial Integration in a Banking Union' (2019) 24 Review of Finance 129
Conti-Brown P and Skeel DA, *When States Go Broke: The Origins, Context, and Solutions for the American States in Fiscal Crisis* (Cambridge University Press 2012)
Conway G, 'Recovering a Separation of Powers in the European Union' (2011) 17 European Law Journal 304
Cooper I, 'National Parliaments in the Democratic Politics of the EU: The Subsidiarity Early Warning Mechanism, 2009–2017' (2019) 17 Comparative European Politics 919
Cooter R and Gilbert M, *Public Law and Economics* (Oxford University Press 2022)
Coutts S, 'Supranational public wrongs: The limitations and possibilities of European criminal law and a European community', 54 Common Market Law Review (2017), 771–800
Cox GW and McCubbins MD, 'The Institutional Determinants of Economic Policy Outcomes' in Stephan Haggard and Mathew D Mccubbins (eds), *Presidents, Parliaments, and Policy* (Cambridge University Press 2001)
Cozzi A-O, 'The Italian Constitutional Court, the Plurality of Legal Orders and Supranational Fundamental Rights: A Discussion in Terms of Interlegality' (2022) 1 European Law Open 606
Craig P, 'Pringle: Legal Reasoning, Text, Purpose and Teleology' (2013) 20 Maastricht Journal of European and Comparative Law 3
——, 'Institutions, Power, and Institutional Balance' in Paul Craig and Gráinne de Búrca (eds), *The Evolution of EU Law* (Oxford University Press 2021) 46
Craig PP and Markakis M, 'Gauweiler and the Legality of Outright Monetary Transactions' (2016) 41 European Law Review 4
Croley SP, 'Theories of Regulation: Incorporating the Administrative Process' (1998) 98 Columbia Law Review 1
Crum B and Curtin D, 'The Challenge of Making European Union Executive Power Accountable' in Simona Piattoni (ed), *The European Union* (Oxford University Press 2015) 63
——, 'The Challenge of Making European Union Executive Power Accountable' in Simona Piattoni (ed), *The European Union* (Oxford University Press 2015)
Crum B and Merlo S, 'Democratic Legitimacy in the Post-Crisis EMU' (2020) 42 Journal of European Integration 399
Curtin D, 'Challenging Executive Dominance in European Democracy' (2014) 77 The Modern Law Review 1
Cutler C, 'Critical Reflections on the Westphalian Assumptions of International Law and Organization: A Crisis of Legitimacy' (2001) 27 Review of International Studies 133

Dahl RA and Tufte ER, *Size and Democracy* (Stanford University Press 1973)
Dashwood A, 'The Relationship between the Member States and the European Union/European Community' (2004) 41 Common Market Law Review 355
Davies G, 'Subsidiarity: The Wrong Idea, in the Wrong Place, at the Wrong Time' (2006) 43 Common Market Law Review 63
Dawson M, 'The Legal and Political Accountability Structure of "Post-Crisis" EU Economic Governance' (2015) 53 Journal of Common Market Studies 976
de Búrca C, *EU Law: Text, Cases, and Materials* (Oxford University Press 2020)
de Grauwe P, 'The European Central Bank as Lender of Last Resort in the Government Bond Markets' (2013) 59 CESifo Economic Studies 520
de Grauwe P and Ji Y, 'Self-Fulfilling Crises in the Eurozone: An Empirical Test' (2012) 34 Journal of International Money and Finance 15
de Grauwe P, Ji Y, and Steinbach A, 'The EU Debt Crisis: Testing and Revisiting Conventional Legal Doctrine' (2017) 51 International Review of Law and Economics 29
de La Serre F and Wallace H, 'Flexibility and Enhanced Cooperation in the European Union: Placebo Rather than Panacea?' (1997) Research and Policy, Papers No 2
de Witte B, 'Using International Law in the Euro Crisis: Causes and Consequences' (2013) Arena Working Paper No 4
——, 'The Law as Tool and Constraint of Differentiated Integration' in Mark Dawson and Markus Jachtenfuchs (eds), *Autonomy without Collapse in a Better European Union* (Oxford University Press 2022) 63
Delaney E, 'Managing in a Federal System without an "Ultimate Arbiter": Kompetenz-Kompetenz in the EU and the Ante-Bellum United States' (2005) 15 Regional & Federal Studies 225
Delreux T and Adriaensen J, 'Principal–Agent Analysis and the European Union', *Oxford Research Encyclopedia of Politics* (Oxford University Press 2019)
Desomer M and Lenaerts K, 'New Models of Constitution-Making in Europe: The Quest for Legitimacy' (2002) 39 Common Market Law Review 1217
Diekmann B, Menzel C, and Thomae T, 'Konvergenzen und Divergenzen im' Währungsraum USA 'im Vergleich zur Eurozone' (2012) 92 Wirtschaftsdienst 27
Donnelly S, *Power Politics, Banking Union and EMU: Adjusting Europe to Germany* (Taylor & Francis Ltd 2018)
Dorf MC, 'Dynamic Incorporation of Foreign Law' (2008) 157 University of Pennsylvania Law Review 103
Douglas-Scott S, *Constitutional Law of the European Union* (Longman Pearson Publishers 2002)
Doukas D, 'The Frailty of the Stability and Growth Pact and the European Court of Justice: Much Ado about Nothing?' (2005) 32 Legal Issues of Economic Integration 293
Draghi M, '2023, 15th Annual Feldstein Lecture, Mario Draghi, "The Next Flight of the Bumblebee: The Path to Common Fiscal Policy in the Eurozone"' (2023) National Bureau of Economic Research, 11 July 2023
Droesse G, *Membership in International Organizations: Paradigms of Membership Structures, Legal Implications of Membership and the Concept of International Organization* (TMC Asser Press 2020)
Dupuch S, Jennequin H, and Mouhoub EM, 'EU Enlargement: What Does it Change for the European Economic Geography?' (2004) 91 Revue de l'OFCE, Presses de Sciences-Po 241
Easterbrook FH, 'Antitrust and the Economics of Federalism' (1983) 26 Journal of Law and Economics 23
——, 'Federalism and European Business Law' (1994) 14 International Review of Law and Economics 125
Eberlein B and Kerwer D, 'Theorising the New Modes of European Union Governance' (2002) 6 European Integration online papers
Eeckhout P, 'The Doctrine of Implied Powers', *EU External Relations Law* (Oxford University Press 2011)
Ehmke DC, *Institutional Congruence the Riddle of Leviathan and Hydra*, vol 16 (Nomos Verlagsgesellschaft 2018)

Ehrlich I and Posner RA, 'An Economic Analysis of Legal Rulemaking' (1974) 3 Journal of Legal Studies 257
Einav L and Yariv L, 'What's in a Surname? The Effects of Surname Initials on Academic Success' (2006) 20 Journal of Economic Perspectives 175
Eisenberg MA, *Foundational Principles of Contract Law* (Oxford University Press 2018)
——, *Foundational Principles of Contract Law* (Oxford University Press 2018)
Engel A, *The Choice of Legal Basis for Acts of the European Union: Competence Overlaps, Institutional Preferences, and Legal Basis Litigation* (Springer 2018)
Epstein D and O'Halloran S, 'Sovereignty and Delegation in International Organizations' (2008) 71 Law and Contemporary Problems 77
Epstein L and Waterbury NW, 'Judicial Behavior' in William Thompson (ed), *Oxford Research Encyclopedia of Politics* (Oxford University Press 2020)
European Central Bank, 'ECB Monthly Bulletin September 2012' (2012)
European Commission, 'A Blueprint for a Deep and Genuine Economic and Monetary Union: Launching a European Debate' (2012)
——, 'Upgrading the Single Market: More Opportunities for People and Business' (2015)
——, 'The Common Agricultural Policy at a Glance', 24 February 2022
——, 'EU Renewable Energy Financing Mechanism' (2023)
European Parliament and Council, 'Regulation (EU) 2016/679 of the European Parliament and of the Council of 27 April 2016 on the Protection of Natural Persons with Regard to the Processing of Personal Data and on the Free Movement of Such Data, and Repealing Directive 95/46/EC (General Data Protection Regulation)' (2016)
Esty DC and Damien G, *Regulatory Competition and Economic Integration. Comparative Perspectives* (Oxford University Press 2001)
Fabbrini F, *Economic Governance in Europe* (Oxford University Press 2016)
Fearon JD, 'Bargaining, Enforcement, and International Cooperation' (1998) 52 International Organization 269
——, 'Bargaining, Enforcement, and International Cooperation' (1998) 52 International Organization 269
Feldstein M, 'The Political Economy of the European Economic and Monetary Union: Political Sources of an Economic Liability' (1997) 11 Journal of Economic Perspectives 23
Ferguson J, *The Anti-Politics Machine: Development, Depoliticization, and Bureaucratic Power in Lesotho* (University of Minnesota Press 1994)
Ferry J-M, *La Question de l'État Européen* (Gallimard 2000)
Finnemore M, *National Interests in International Society* (Cornell University Press 1996)
Finnemore M and Sikkink K, 'International Norm Dynamics and Political Change' (1998) 52 International Organization 887
Forman S, 'Foreword' in David M Malone and Yuen Foong Khong (eds), *Unilateralism and U.S. Foreign Policy: International Perspectives* (Lynne Rienner 2003)
Franchino F, 'Efficiency or Credibility? Testing the Two Logics of Delegation to the European Commission' (2002) 9 Journal of European Public Policy 677
Franck TM, *The Power of Legitimacy among Nations* (Oxford University Press 1990)
Frankenreiter J, 'The Politics of Citations at the ECJ—Policy Preferences of E.U. Member State Governments and the Citation Behavior of Judges at the European Court of Justice' (2017) 14 Journal of Empirical Legal Studies 813
Frey BS and Stutzer A, 'The Role of Direct Democracy and Federalism in Local Power' (2004) Working Paper No 209
Friedman JW, 'A Non-Cooperative Equilibrium for Supergames' (1971) 38 Review of Economic Studies 1
Fudenberg D and Maskin E, 'The Folk Theorem in Repeated Games with Discounting or with Incomplete Information' (1986) 54 Econometrica 533
Fuest C, 'The NGEU Economic Recovery Fund' (2021) 22 CESifo Forum 3
Fuest C and Pisani-Ferry J, 'A Primer on Developing European Public Goods' (2019) EconPol Policy Report, No 16

Furby L and others, 'Public Perceptions of Electric Power Transmission Lines' (1988) 8 Journal of Environmental Psychology 19

Gáková Z and Dijkstra L, 'Labour Mobility between the Regions of the EU-27 and a Comparison with the USA' (2008) European Union Regional Policy No 02/2008

Gamble JK, 'Reservations to Multilateral Treaties: A Macroscopic View of State Practice' (1980) 74 American Journal of International Law 372

Garben S, 'Restating the Problem of Competence Creep, Tackling Harmonisation by Stealth and Reinstat-Ing the Legislator' in Sacha Garben and Inge Govaere (eds), *The Division of Competences between the EU and the Member States: Reflections on the Past, the Present and the Future* (Hart Publishing 2017)

Genschel P and Jachtenfuchs M, 'Introduction: Beyond Market Regulation. Analysing the European Integration of Core State Powers' in Philipp Genschel and Markus Jachtenfuchs (eds), *Beyond the Regulatory Polity?* (Oxford University Press 2013)

Genschel P, Jachtenfuchs M, and Migliorati M, 'Differentiated Integration as Symbolic Politics? Constitutional Differentiation and Policy Reintegration in Core State Powers' (2023) 24 European Union Politics 81

Genschel P and Tesche T, 'Supranational Agents as De-Commitment Devices: The ECB During the Eurozone Crisis' (2020) Amsterdam Center for European Studies Research Paper No 2020/02

Geradin D, Layne-Farrar A, and Petit N, *EU Competition Law and Economics* (Oxford University Press 2012)

Gersen J and Posner EA, 'Soft Law: Lessons from Congressional Practice Soft Law: Lessons from Congressional Practice' (2008) 61 Stanford Law Review 573

Gigerenzer G, *Bounded Rationality: The Adaptive Toolbox* (MIT Press 2002)

Gigerenzer G and Goldstein DG, 'Reasoning the Fast and Frugal Way: Models of Bounded Rationality.' (1996) 103 Psychological Review 650

Gilardi F, *Delegation in the Regulatory State* (Edward Elgar Publishing 2008)

Ginsburg T, 'Locking in Democracy: Constitutions, Commitment, and International Law' (2006) 38 New York University Journal of International Law and Politics 707

Ginsburg T and McAdams R, 'Adjudicating in Anarchy: An Expressive Theory of International Dispute Resolution' (2004) 45 William & Mary Law Review

Giudice G and others, 'A European Safe Asset to Complement National Government Bonds' (2019) MPRA Paper No 95748

Goldsmith JL and Posner EA, *The Limits of International Law* (Oxford University Press 2006)

Goldstein J and others, 'Introduction: Legalization and World Politics' (2000) 54 International Organization 385

Gordon B, *The Constitutional Boundaries of European Fiscal Federalism* (Cambridge University Press 2022)

Grimm D, 'Does Europe Need a Constitution?' (1995) 1 European Law Journal 282

——, *Constitutionalism: Past—Present—Future* (Oxford University Press 2006)

——, *Sovereignty: The Origin and Future of a Political and Legal Concept* (Columbia University Press 2015)

——, *Europa ja—aber welches? Zur Verfassung der europäischen Demokratie.* (CH Beck 2016)

Grimm D, Wendel M, and Reinbacher T, 'European Constitutionalism and the German Basic Law', in A Albi and S Bardutzky (eds), *National Constitutions in European and Global Governance: Democracy, Rights, the Rule of Law* (TMC Asser Press 2019) 407

Gruber L, *Ruling the World: Power Politics and the Rise of Supranational Institutions* (Princeton University Press 2000)

Grund S and Steinbach A, 'European Union Debt Financing: Leeway and Barriers from a Legal Perspective' (2023) Working Paper 15/2023, Bruegel

Guzman A, *How International Law Works* (Oxford University Press 2008)

——, 'The Consent Problem in International Law' (2012) 52 Virginia Journal of International Law 747

Guzman A and Simmons BA, 'To Settle or Empanel? An Empirical Analysis of Litigation and Settlement at the World Trade Organization' (2002) 31 Journal of Legal Studies 205

Hafner-Burton EM and Tsutsui K, 'Human Rights in a Globalizing World: The Paradox of Empty Promises' (2005) 110 American Journal of Sociology 1373

Hahn M, 'Interesting Times: Soft Law in International Economic Governance' in Manjiao Chi, Marc Bungenberg, and Andrea K Bjorklund (eds), *Asian Yearbook of International Economic Law 2022*, vol 2022 (Springer 2022)

Hakimi M, 'Unfriendly Unilateralism' (2014) 55 Harvard International Law Journal 105

Hanf D, 'Flexibility Clauses in the Founding Treaties, from Rome to Nice' in Bruno de Witte, Dominik Hanf, and Ellen Vos (eds), *The Many Faces of Differentiation in EU Law* (Intersentia 2001)

Hallerberg M, 'Fiscal Federalism Reforms in the European Union and the Greek Crisis' (2010) 12 European Union Politics 127

Hartley TC, *The Foundations of European Community Law: An Introduction to the Constitutional and Administrative Law of the European Community* (3rd edn, Clarendon Press 1994)

Hathaway JC, 'America, Defender of Democratic Legitimacy?' (2000) 11 European Journal of International Law 121

Hauge W and Ellingsen T, 'Beyond Environmental Scarcity: Causal Pathways to Conflict' (1998) 35 Journal of Peace Research 299

Heckathorn DD, 'Collective Action and the Second-Order Free-Rider Problem' (1989) 1 Rationality and Society 78

Heinkelmann-Wild T, Zangl B, Rittberger B, and Kriegmair L, 'Blame Shifting and Blame Obfuscation: The Blame Avoidance Effects of Delegation in the European Union' (2023) 62 European Journal of Political Research 221

Helfer LR, 'Exiting Treaties' (2005) 91 Virginia Law Review 1579

Hemrajani R and Hobert T, 'The Effects of Decision Fatigue on Judicial Behavior: A Study of Arkansas Traffic Court Outcomes' (2024) 2024 Journal of Law and Courts 1

Henkin L, *International Law: Politics and Values*, vol 18 (Brill 1995)

Henning R and Kessler M, *Fiscal Federalism: US History for Architects of Europe's Fiscal Union* (Bruegel 2012)

Hilpold P, 'So Long Solange? The PSPP Judgment of the German Constitutional Court and the Conflict between the German and the European "Popular Spirit"' (2021) 23 Cambridge Yearbook of European Legal Studies 159

Hinarejos A, *The Euro Area Crisis in Constitutional Perspective* (Oxford University Press 2015)

Hix S, 'Parties at the European Level', in Paul Webb, David Farrell, and Ian Holliday (eds), *Political Parties in Advanced Industrial Democracies.* Comparative Politics. (Oxford University Press 2002) 280–309

Hix S and Follesdal A, 'Why is There a Democratic Deficit in the EU? A Response to Majone and Moravcsik' (2006) 44 Journal of Common Market Studies 533

Hodson D, 'Reforming EU Economic Governance: A View from (and on) the Principal-Agent Approach' (2009) 7 Comparative European Politics 455

——, 'The EMU Paradox: Centralization and Decentralization in EU Macroeconomic Policy' in Jeremy Richardson (ed), *Constructing a Policy-Making State?* (Oxford University Press 2012)

Holcombe RG, 'Make Economics Policy Relevant Depose the Omniscient Benevolent Dictator' (2012) 17 The Independent Review 165

Hollis DB, 'Why State Consent Still Matters—Non-State Actors, Treaties, and the Changing Sources of International Law' (2005) 23 Berkeley Journal of International Law 137

Holzinger K, Knill C, and Schäfer A, 'Rhetoric and Reality? "New Governance" in EU Environmental Policy' (2006) 12 European Law Journal 403

Hooghe L, 'Supranational Activists or Intergovernmental Agents? Explaining the Orientations of Senior Commission Officials Toward European Integration' (1999) 32 Comparative Political Studies 435

——, 'Images of Europe: Orientations to European Integration among Senior Officials of the Commission' (1999) 29 British Journal of Political Science 345

Howarth D and Quaglia L, *The Political Economy of European Banking Union* (Oxford University Press 2016)
Huber PM, 'Das Kooperationsverhältnis zwischen BVerfG und EuGH in Grundrechtsfragen' (1997) Europäische Zeitschrift für Wirtschaftsrecht 517
Hurka S and Steinebach Y, 'Legal Instrument Choice in the European Union' (2021) 59 Journal of Common Market Studies 278
Hutt WH, *Plan for Reconstruction: A Project for Victory in War and Peace* (Kegan Paul 1943)
Inman RP and Rubinfeld DL, 'Rethinking Federalism' (1997) 11 Journal of Economic Perspectives 43
——, 'Economics of Federalism' in Francesco Parisi (ed), *Oxford Handbook of Law and Economics* (Oxford University Press 2017)
Ipsen HP, 'Der deutsche Jurist und das Europäische Gemeinschaftsrecht', *Verhandlungen des 43. Deutschen Juristentages* (1994)
Ipsen HP and Nicolaysen G, 'Haager Kongreß für Europarecht und Bericht über die aktuelle Entwicklung des Gemeinschaftsrechts' (1964) Neue Juristische Wochenschrift 339
Jacob MA, *Precedents and Case-Based Reasoning in the European Court of Justice: Unfinished Business* (Cambridge University Press 2014)
Jennes G, 'Interregional Fiscal Transfers Resulting from Central Government Debt: New Insights and Consequences for Political Economy' (2021) 74 Kyklos 196
Johns L, 'The Design of Enforcement: Collective Action and the Enforcement of International Law' (2019) 31 Journal of Theoretical Politics 543
Joumard I and Kongsrud M, 'Fiscal Relations across Government Level' (2003) OECD Economics Department Working Papers No 375
Juncker J-C, 'The Five Presidents' Report: Completing Europe's Economic and Monetary Union' (2012)
Kahneman D and Tversky A, 'Prospect Theory: An Analysis of Decision under Risk' (1979) 47 Econometrica 263
Kaplow L, 'Rules Versus Standards: An Economic Analysis' (1992) 42 Duke Law Journal 557
——, 'General Characteristics of Rules', *Encyclopedia of Law and Economics* (National Bureau of Economic Research 1997)
Kassim H and Menon A, 'The Principal-Agent Approach and the Study of the European Union: Promise Unfulfilled?' (2003) 10 Journal of European Public Policy 121
Kelemen D and Teo T, 'Law, Focal Points, and Fiscal Discipline in the United States and the European Union' (2014) 108 American Political Science Review 355
Kelley J, 'International Actors on the Domestic Scene: Membership Conditionality and Socialization by International Institutions' (2004) 58 International Organization 425
Keohane RO, *After Hegemony: Cooperation and Discord in the World Political Economy* (Princeton University Press 2005)
Kerber W and Bergh R van den, 'Unmasking Mutual Recognition: Current Inconsistencies and Future Chances' (2007) Marburger Volkswirtschaftliche Beiträge, No 2007, 11
Kindleberger CP, 'Dominance and Leadership in the International Economy: Exploitation, Public Goods, and Free Rides' (1981) 25 International Studies Quarterly 242
Kiššová S, 'Overview of the Doctrine of Ultra Vires from the Perspective of the German Federal Constitutional Court and the Polish Constitutional Court' (2022) 2 Slovak Yearbook of European Union Law 33
Klamert M, Moustakali M, and Tomkin J, 'Article 36 TFEU' in Manuel Kellerbauer, Marcus Klamert, and Jonathan Tomkin (eds), *The EU Treaties and the Charter of Fundamental Rights* (Oxford University Press 2019)
Kleine M, *Informal Governance in the European Union: How Governments Make International Organizations Work* (Cornell University Press 2013)
Kleine M, Arregui J, and Thomson R, 'The Impact of National Democratic Representation on Decision-Making in the European Union' (2022) 29 Journal of European Public Policy 1

Kochenov DV and Lavranos N, 'Achmea versus the Rule of Law: CJEU's Dogmatic Dismissal of Investors' Rights in Backsliding Member States of the European Union' (2022) 14 Hague Journal on the Rule of Law 195

Konrad KA and others, 'Wege aus der Europäischen Staatsschuldenkrise' (2010) 90 Wirtschaftsdienst 783

Konrad KA and Zschäpitz H, *Schulden ohne Sühne? Warum der Absturz der Staatsfinanzen uns alle Trifft* (CH Beck 2010)

Koremenos B, *The Continent of International Law: Explaining Agreement Design* (Cambridge University Press 2016)

Koremenos B, Lipson C, and Snidal D, 'The Rational Design of International Institutions' (2001) 55 International Organization 761

Korobkin RB and Guthrie CP, 'Heuristics and Biases at the Bargaining Table' (2004) 87 Marquette Law Review 795

Koutsoukis N-S and Roukanas SA, 'The GrExit Paradox' (2014) 9 Procedia Economics and Finance 24

Krasner SD, *International Regimes* (Cornell University Press 1983)

Kreiner CT, 'Do the New Keynesian Microfoundations Rationalise Stabilisation Policy?' (2002) 112 Economic Journal 384

Kreps D, *A Course in Microeconomic Theory* (Princeton University Press 1990)

Kroll DA and Leuffen D, 'Enhanced Cooperation in Practice. An Analysis of Differentiated Integration in EU Secondary Law' (2015) 22 Journal of European Public Policy 353

Lane TD, 'Market Discipline' (1993) IMF Staff Papers No 53

Larch M, Malzubris J, and Santacroce S, 'Numerical Compliance with EU Fiscal Rules: Facts and Figures from a New Database' (2023) 58 Intereconomics 32

Lasek-Markey M, 'Poland's Constitutional Tribunal on the Status of EU Law: The Polish Government Got All the Answers It Needed from a Court It Controls' (*European Law Blog*, 21 October 2021)

Lastra RM, *International Financial and Monetary Law* (Oxford University Press 2015)

Lastra RM and Skinner CP, 'Sustainable Central Banking' (2023) 63 Virginia Journal of International Law 397

Lebeck C, 'Implied Powers beyond Functional Integration—the Flexibility Clause in the Revised EU Treaties' (2007) 17 Journal of Transnational Law & Policy 303

LeBoeuf J, 'The Economics of Federalism and the Proper Scope of the Federal Commerce Power' (1994) 31 San Diego Law Review 555

——, 'Unilateralism in International Law: A United States-European Symposium' (2000) 11 European Journal of International Law 1

Lehne S, *Is There Hope for EU Foreign Policy?* (Carnegie Endowment for International Peace 2017)

——, 'Making EU Foreign Policy Fit for a Geopolitical World' *Carnegie Europe* (14 April 2022)

Lehtimäki J and Sondermann D, 'Baldwin vs. Cecchini Revisited: The Growth Impact of the European Single Market' (2020) Working Paper Series No 2392

Lejour AM, Solanic V, and Tang PJG, 'EU Accession and Income Growth: An Empirical Approach' (2009) 16 Transition Studies Review 127

Levit JK, 'A Bottom-Up Approach to International Lawmaking: The Tale of Three Trade Finance Instruments' (2005) 30 Yale Journal of International Law 125

Levy JS, 'Prospect Theory and International Relations: Theoretical Applications and Analytical Problems' (1992) 13 Political Psychology 283

Liao W, *The Application of the Theory of Efficient Breach in Contract Law: A Comparative Law and Economics Perspective* (Intersentia Ltd 2015)

——, *The Application of the Theory of Efficient Breach in Contract Law: A Comparative Law and Economics Perspective* (Intersentia 2015)

Lipscy PY, 'Explaining Institutional Change: Policy Areas, Outside Options, and the Bretton Woods Institutions' (2015) 59 American Journal of Political Science 341

Lipson C, 'Why are Some International Agreements Informal?' (1991) 45 International Organization 495

Linos K, 'A Theory of Diffusion Through Democratic Mechanisms' in Katerina Linos (ed), *The Democratic Foundations of Policy Diffusion: How Health, Family, and Employment Laws Spread Across Countries* (Oxford University Press 2013)

——, 'How can international organizations shape national welfare states? Evidence from compliance with European Union directives' (2007) 40 Comparative Political Studies 547

Loeper A, 'Cross-Border Externalities and Cooperation among Representative Democracies' (2017) 91 European Economic Review 180

Loughlin M, 'The Silences of Constitutions' (2018) 16 International Journal of Constitutional Law 922

Lundmark T, MacCormick DN, and Summers RS, 'Interpreting Precedents: A Comparative Study' (1997) 46 The American Journal of Comparative Law 211

Macey JR, 'Corporate Social Responsibility: A Law & Economics Perspective' (2014) 17 Chapman Law Review 331

Maciariello E, 'EU Agencies and the Issue of Delegation: Conferral, Implied Powers and the State of Exception' (2019) 4 European Papers 723

Mader O, 'Enforcement of EU Values as a Political Endeavour: Constitutional Pluralism and Value Homogeneity in Times of Persistent Challenges to the Rule of Law' (2019) 11 Hague Journal on the Rule of Law 133

Mahlmann M, 'Constitutional Identity and the Politics of Homogeneity' (2005) 6 German Law Journal 307

Maih J and others, 'Asymmetric Monetary Policy Rules for the Euro Area and the US' (2021) 70 Journal of Macroeconomics 103376

Mair P, *Ruling the Void: The Hollowing of Western Democracy* (Verso 2013)

Majone G, 'Nonmajoritarian Institutions and the Limits of Democratic Governance: A Political Transaction-Cost Approach' (2001) 157 Journal of Institutional and Theoretical Economics 57

——, 'Two Logics of Delegation' (2001) 2 European Union Politics 103

——, *Dilemmas of European Integration: The Ambiguities and Pitfalls of Integration by Stealth* (Oxford University Press 2005)

——, *Europe as the Would-Be World Power: The EU at Fifty* (Cambridge University Press 2009)

Malferrari L, 'The Functional Representation of the Individual's Interests Before the EC Courts: The Evolution of the Remedies System and the Pluralistic Deficit in the EC' (2005) 12 Indiana Journal of Global Legal Studies 667

Malone DM and Khong YF, 'Unilateralism and U.S. Foreign Policy: International Perspectives' in David M Malone and Yuen Foong Khong (eds), *Unilateralism and U.S. Foreign Policy: International Perspectives* (Lynne Rienner 2003)

Mangiameli S, 'The European Union and the Identity of Member States' (2013) 369 L'Europe en Formation 151

Martinico G and Repetto G, 'Fundamental Rights and Constitutional Duels in Europe: An Italian Perspective on Case 269/2017 of the Italian Constitutional Court and Its Aftermath' (2019) 15 European Constitutional Law Review 731

Mathis K, *Law and Economics in Europe: Foundations and Applications* (Springer 2014)

Mayhew D, *Congress: The Electoral Connection* (Yale University Press 2004)

McLaughlin Mitchell S and Hensel PR, 'International Institutions and Compliance with Agreements' (2007) 51 American Journal of Political Science 721

Mearsheimer JJ, *The Tragedy of Great Power Politics* (Updated Edition, Norton & Company 2014)

Mengus E, 'Asset Purchase Bailouts and Endogenous Implicit Guarantees' (2023) 142 Journal of International Economics 103737

Menon A and Weatherill S, 'Transnational Legitimacy in a Globalising World: How the European Union Rescues its States' (2008) 31 West European Politics 397

Messina M, 'Strengthening Economic Governance of the European Union through Enhanced Cooperation: A Still Possible, but Already Missed, Opportunity' (2014) 39 European Law Review 404

Michaelis J and Pflüger M, 'Euroland: Besser als befürchtet, aber schlechter als erhofft?' (2002) 71 Vierteljahrshefte zur Wirtschaftsforschung 296
Milgrom PR, North DC, and Weingast BR, 'The Role of Institutions in the Revival of Trade: The Law Merchant, Private Judges, and the Champagne Fairs' (1990) 2 Economics & Politics 1
Moe TM, 'Political Institutions: The Neglected Side of the Story' (1990) 6 Journal of Law, Economics, and Organization 213
Möllers TMJ and Zeitler F-C, *Europa als Rechtsgemeinschaft – Währungsunion und Schuldenkrise* (Mohr Siebeck 2013)
Moon BE, *Dilemmas of International Trade* (Routledge 2018)
Moravcsik A, 'Taking Preferences Seriously: A Liberal Theory of International Politics' (1997) 51 International Organization 513
——, 'The Origins of Human Rights Regimes: Democratic Delegation in Postwar Europe' (2000) 54 International Organization 217
——, 'In Defence of the Democratic Deficit: Reassessing Legitimacy in the EU' (2002) 40 Journal of Common Market Studies 603
Morgenthau HJ, 'Positivism, Functionalism, and International Law' (1940) 34 American Journal of International Law 260
——, *Politics Among Nations: The Struggle for Power and Peace* (5th edn, Alfred A Knopf 1978)
Moser C and Rittberger B, 'The CJEU and EU (de-)Constitutionalization: Unpacking Jurisprudential Responses' (2022) 20 International Journal of Constitutional Law 1038
Mueller DC, *Public Choice II* (Cambridge University Press 1989)
Naess-Schmidt S and others, *Subsidiarity and Proportionality in the Single Market: An EU Fit for Inclusive Growth* (Bertelsmann Stiftung 2018)
Nettesheim M, 'Grundrechtliche Prüfungsdichte Durch Den EuGH' (1995) Europäische Zeitschrift für Wirtschaftsrecht 106
Neumayer E, 'Qualified Ratification: Explaining Reservations to International Human Rights Treaties' (2007) 36 Journal of Legal Studies 397
Newman AL and Posner E, *Voluntary Disruptions: International Soft Law, Finance, and Power* (Oxford University Press 2018)
Nicolaïdis K, 'The New Constitution as European "Democracy"?' (2004) 7 Critical Review of International Social and Political Philosophy 76
Niskanen WA, *Bureaucracy and Representative Government* (Routledge 2017)
Oates WE, *Fiscal Federalism* (Harcourt Brace Jovanovich 1972)
——, 'An Essay on Fiscal Federalism' (1999) 37 Journal of Economic Literature 1120
——, 'On The Evolution of Fiscal Federalism: Theory and Institutions' (2008) 61 National Tax Journal 313
Öberg J, 'Subsidiarity as a Limit to the Exercise of EU Competences' (2017) 36 Yearbook of European Law 391
Öberg J, 'Normative Justifications of EU Criminal Law: European Public Goods and Transnational Interests', 27 European Law Journal (2021), 408–425
Oliver-Lalana AD, 'Legitimacy through Rationality: Parliamentary Argumentation as Rational Justification of Laws' in Luc J Wintgens (ed), *The Theory and Practice of Legislation* (Routledge 2005) 239
Olson M, 'The Principle of "Fiscal Equivalence": The Division of Responsibilities among Different Levels of Government' (1969) 59 The American Economic Review 479
Orts EW, 'Shirking and Sharking: A Legal Theory of the Firm' (1998) 16 Yale Law & Policy Review 265
Paasch J, 'Revisiting Policy Preferences and Capacities in the EU: Multi-level Policy Implementation in the Subnational Authorities' (2022) 60 Journal of Common Market Studies 783
Paetz C and Watzka S, 'The Macroeconomic Effects of Re-Applying the EU Fiscal Rules: Returning to the Status Quo Ante or Moving to Expenditure Rules?' (2023) 264 National Institute Economic Review 59

Pär Hallström, 'The European Union—From Reciprocity to Loyalty' (1999) 39 Scandinavian Studies in Law 79

Parisi F and Fon V, *The Economics of Lawmaking* (Oxford University Press 2008)

Peers S, 'Towards a New Form of EU Law? The Use of EU Institutions Outside the EU Legal Framework' (2013) 9 European Constitutional Law Review 37

Pelc KJ, 'Seeking Escape: The Use of Escape Clauses in International Trade Agreements' (2009) 53 International Studies Quarterly 349

Pelkmans J, 'Mutual Recognition in Goods and Services: An Economic Perspective' in Fiorella Kostoris Padoa Schioppa (ed), *The Principles of Mutual Recognition in the European Integration Process* (Palgrave Macmillan 2005)

——, 'Testing for Subsidiarity. Bruges European Economic Policy (BEEP) Briefing 13/2006' (2006)

Peters A, 'International Organizations and International Law', *The Oxford Handbook of International Organizations* (Oxford University Press 2017)

——, 'The Constitutionalisation of the European Union—Without the Constitutional Treaty' in Sonja Puntscher Riekmann and Wolfgang Wessels (eds), *The Making of a European Constitution* (VS Verlag für Sozialwissenschaften 2006)

Petersmann E-U, *Multilevel Constitutionalism for Multilevel Governance of Public Goods: Methodology Problems in International Law* (Hart Publishing 2019)

——, 'Constitutional Pluralism, Regulatory Competition and Transnational Governance Failures', *Constitutionalism and Transnational Governance Failures* (Brill/Nijhoff 2024)

Petersmann E-U and Steinbach A, 'Neo-Liberalism, State-Capitalism and Ordo-Liberalism: "Institutional Economics" and "Constitutional Choices" in Multilevel Trade Regulation' (2021) 22 Journal of World Investment & Trade 1

Petrocik JR, *Party Coalitions: Realignment and the Decline of the New Deal Party System* (Chicago University Press 1981)

Phelan W, 'What is Sui Generis about the European Union? Costly International Cooperation in a Self-Contained Regime' (2012) 14 International Studies Review 367

Pierson P, 'Increasing Returns, Path Dependence, and the Study of Politics' (2000) 94 American Political Science Review 251

Pisani-Ferry J, Tagliapietra S, and Zachmann G, 'A New Governance Framework to Safeguard the European Green Deal' (2023)

Pollack MA, 'Delegation, Agency, and Agenda Setting in the European Community' (1997) 51 International Organization 99

——, *The Engines of European Integration* (Oxford University Press 2003)

Polyak P, 'The Silent Losers of Germany's Export Surpluses. How Current Account Imbalances Are Exacerbated by the Misrepresentation of Their Domestic Costs' (2024) 22 Comparative European Politics 31

Portuese A, 'Principle of Proportionality as Principle of Economic Efficiency' (2013) 19 European Law Journal 612

Posner E and Sykes AO, *Economic Foundations of International Law* (Harvard University Press 2013)

Posner EA, 'Human Rights, the Laws of War, and Reciprocity' (2010) John M Olin Program in Law and Economics Working Paper No 537

Posner RA, 'The Chicago School of Antitrust Analysis' (1979) 127 University of Pennsylvania Law Review 925

——, *The Economics of Justice* (Harvard University Press 1983)

——, 'Judicial Behavior and Performance: An Economic Approach Judicial Behavior and Performance: An Economic Approach' (2005) 32 Florida State University Law Review 1259

——, 'The Role of the Judge in the Twenty-First Century' (2006) 86 Boston University Law Review 1049

Potacs M, 'Effet Utile als Auslegungsgrundsatz' (2009) 44 Europarecht 465

Priestley T and Evans GW, 'Resident Perceptions of a Nearby Electric Transmission-Line' (1996) 16 Journal of Environmental Psychology 65

Program on International Policy Attitudes, *Americans on Globalization: A Study of US Public Attitudes* (PIPA 2000)
Psaroudakis G, 'The Scope for Financial Stability Considerations in the Fulfilment of the Mandate of the ECB/Eurosystem' (2018) 4 Journal of Financial Regulation 119
Putnam RD, 'Diplomacy and Domestic Politics: The Logic of Two-Level Games' (1988) 42 International Organization 427
Rachlinski JJ and Wistrich AJ, 'Judging the Judiciary by the Numbers: Empirical Research on Judges' (2017) 13 Annual Review of Law and Social Science 203
Rawls J, *A Theory of Justice* (Harvard University Press 1971)
Reisman M, 'The Concept and Functions of Soft Law in International Politics' in Emmanuel G Bello and Prince Bola A Ajibola (eds), *Essays in Honour of Judge Taslim Olawale Elias* (Brill 1992)
Rhinard M, 'The Crisisification of Policy-making in the European Union' (2019) 57 Journal of Common Market Studies 616
Richmond C, 'Preserving the Identity Crisis: Autonomy, System and Sovereignty in European Law' (1997) 16 Law and Philosophy 377
Riker WH, *Federalism: Origin, Operation, Significance* (Little, Brown and Company 1964)
Risse T, 'Neofunctionalism, European Identity, and the Puzzles of European Integration' (2005) 12 Journal of European Public Policy 291
Rittberger B, 'Integration without Representation? The European Parliament and the Reform of Economic Governance in the EU' (2014) 52 Journal of Common Market Studies, 1174
Rodden J, 'Strength in Numbers?' (2002) 3 European Union Politics 151
Roeben V, 'A Concept of Shared Principles and the Constitutional Homogeneity in Europe: The Case of Subsidiarity' (2021) 4 Cardozo International & Comparative Law Review 903
Rogoff K, 'The Optimal Degree of Commitment to an Intermediate Monetary Target' (1985) 100 Quarterly Journal of Economics 1169
Romeo G, 'What's Wrong with Depoliticization?' (2022) 1 European Law Open 168
Rosas A, 'Separation of Powers in the European Union' (2007) 41 The International Lawyer 1033
Rose-Ackerman S, Egidy S, and Fowkes J, *Due Process of Lawmaking: The United States, South Africa, Germany, and the European Union* (Cambridge University Press 2015)
Rosendorff BP and Milner HV, 'The Optimal Design of International Trade Institutions: Uncertainty and Escape' (2001) 55 International Organization 829
Ross G, *Jacques Delors and European Integration* (Oxford University Press 1995)
Šadl U, 'The Role of Effet Utile in Preserving the Continuity and Authority of European Union Law: Evidence from the Citation Web of the Pre-Accession Case Law of the Court of Justice of the EU' (2015) 8 European Journal of Legal Studies 18
Samuelson PA, 'The Pure Theory of Public Expenditure' (1954) 36 Review of Economics and Statistics 387
Sandler T and Tschirhart J, 'The Economic Theory of Clubs: An Evaluative Survey' (1980) 18 Journal of Economic Literature 1481
Sapir A, 'Dealing with EMU Heterogeneity' in Francesco Caselli, Mário Centeno, and José Tavares (eds), *After the Crisis* (Oxford University Press 2016)
Sauter W, 'Proportionality in EU Law: A Balancing Act?' (2013) 15 Cambridge Yearbook of European Legal Studies 439
Schaefer H-B, 'Legal Rules and Standards' in Charles K Rowley and Friedrich Schneider (eds), *The Encyclopedia of Public Choice* (Springer 2004) 671
Schafer A, 'Resolving Deadlock: Why International Organisations Introduce Soft Law' (2006) 12 European Law Journal 194
Scharpf FW, 'Economic Integration, Democracy and the Welfare State' (1997) 4 Journal of European Public Policy 18
Schimmelfennig F and Winzen T, *Ever Looser Union?* (Oxford University Press 2020)
Schleicher D, *In a Bad State: Responding to State and Local Budget Crises* (Oxford University Press 2023)

Schmidt VA, *Europe's Crisis of Legitimacy: Governing by Rules and Ruling by Numbers in the Eurozone* (Oxford University Press 2020)
Schmidtchen D, Neunzig AR, and Schmidt-Trenz H-J, 'One Market, One Law: EU Enlargement in Light of the Economic Theory of Optimal Legal Areas' (2001) CSLE Discussion Paper, No 2001-03
Schulz A and Wolff GB, 'The German Sub-National Government Bond Market: Structure, Determinants of Yield Spreads and Berlin's Forgone Bail-Out' (2009) 229 Jahrbücher für Nationalökonomie und Statistik 61
Scopelliti A, 'The Political Decision-Making Process in the Council of the European Union Under the New Definition of a Qualified Majority' (2008) 73 Il Politico 180
Scott RE and Stephan PB, 'Self-Enforcing International Agreements and the Limits of Coercion' (2004) 2004 Wisconsin Law Review 551
Scott RE and Stephan PB, *The Limits of Leviathan* (Cambridge University Press 2006)
Shaffer G and Ginsburg T, 'The Empirical Turn in International Legal Scholarship' (2012) 106 American Journal of International Law 1
Shapiro SP, 'Agency Theory' (2005) 31 Annual Review of Sociology 263
Shavell S, 'Damage Measures for Breach of Contract' (1980) 11 Bell Journal of Economics 466
Shelton DL, 'Introduction' in Dinah L Shelton (ed), *Commitment and Compliance: The Role of Non-Binding Norms in Commitment and Compliance: The Role of Non-Binding Norms in the International Legal System* (Oxford University Press 2000)
Shepsle KA and Weingast BR, 'The Institutional Foundations of Committee Power' (1987) 81 American Political Science Review 85
Siekmann H, 'The Legality of Outright Monetary Transactions (OMT) of the European System of Central Banks' (2015) Working Paper Series No 90
Simmons B, 'Treaty Compliance and Violation' (2010) 13 Annual Review of Political Science 273
Simon HA, *Reason in Human Affairs* (Stanford University Press 1983)
Sitkoff RH, 'An Economic Theory of Fiduciary Law' in Andrew S Gold, and Paul B Miller (eds), *Philosophical Foundations of Fiduciary Law* (Oxford University Press 2014)
Slaughter A-M, 'Remarks, The Big Picture: Beyond Hot Spots & Crises in Our Interconnected World' (2012) 1 Penn State Journal of Law & International Affairs 286
Slaughter A-M, Tulumello AS, and Wood S, 'International Law and International Relations Theory: A New Generation of Interdisciplinary Scholarship' (1998) 92 American Journal of International Law 367
Smeets S and Beach D, '"It Takes Three to Tango": New Inter-Institutional Dynamics in Managing Major Crisis Reform' (2022) 29 Journal of European Public Policy 1414
Smeets S, Jaschke A, and Beach D, 'The Role of the EU Institutions in Establishing the European Stability Mechanism: Institutional Leadership under a Veil of Intergovernmentalism' (2019) 57 Journal of Common Market Studies 675
Snidal D, 'The Limits of Hegemonic Stability Theory' (1985) 39 International Organization 579
——, 'Coordination versus Prisoners' Dilemma: Implications for International Cooperation and Regimes' (1985) 79 American Political Science Review 923
Snyder F, 'The Effectiveness of European Community Law: Institutions, Processes, Tools and Techniques' (1993) 56 Modern Law Review 19
Spolaore E, 'Adjustments in Different Government Systems' (2004) 16 Economics & Politics 117
——, 'The Economics of Political Borders' (2012) CESifo Working Paper No 3854
——, 'The Economic Approach to Political Borders' (2022) CESifo Working Paper No 10165.
Spolaore E and Wacziarg R, 'Borders and Growth' (2005) 10 Journal of Economic Growth 331
Spruyt H, 'Institutional Selection in International Relations: State Anarchy as Order' (1994) 48 International Organization 527
Starke JG, *Introduction to International Law* (Butterworths 1989)
Starr-Deelen D and Deelen B, 'The European Court of Justice as a Federator' (1996) 26 Publius: The Journal of Federalism 81

Staudt NC, Friedman B, and Epstein L, 'On the Role of Ideological Homogeneity in Generating Consequential Constitutional Decisions' (2008) 10 University of Pennsylvania Journal of Constitutional Law 361

Stein E, 'Lawyers, Judges, and the Making of a Transnational Constitution' (1981) 75 American Journal of International Law 1

Steinbach A, *Economic Policy Coordination in the Euro Area* (Taylor & Francis Ltd 2014)

——, 'The Trend towards Non-Consensualism in Public International Law: A (Behavioural) Law and Economics Perspective' (2016) 27 European Journal of International Law 643

——, 'Effect-Based Analysis in the Court's Jurisprudence on the Euro Crisis' (2017) 42 European Law Review 255

——, 'EU Economic Governance after the Crisis: Revisiting the Accountability Shift in EU Economic Governance' (2019) 26 Journal of European Public Policy 1354

——, 'Markets as an Accountability Mechanism in EU Economic Governance' in Mark Dawson (ed), *Substantive Accountability in Europe's New Economic Governance* (Cambridge University Press 2023)

——, 'Constitutional Economics and Transnational Governance Failures', *Constitutionalism and Transnational Governance Failures* (Brill/Nijhoff 2024)

Steinbach A and Grund S, 'Next Generation EU – Auf dem Weg in die Fiskal- und Transferunion?' (2023) Neue Juristische Wochenschrift 425

Steinberg RH, 'Wanted—Dead or Alive', *Interdisciplinary Perspectives on International Law and International Relations* (Cambridge University Press 2012)

Stephan PB, *Economics of European Union Law* (Edward Elgar 2007)

Stone RW, *Controlling Institutions: International Organizations and the Global Economy* (Cambridge University Press 2011)

Sullivan K, 'The Justices of Rules and Standards' (1992) 106 Harvard Law Review 22

Sunstein CR, 'Problems with Rules' (1995) 83 California Law Review 953

——, 'Problems with Rules' (1995) 83 California Law Review 953

——, *Are Judges Political? An Empirical Analysis of the Federal Judiciary* (Brookings Institution Press 2006)

Svetiev Y, 'The Limits of Informal International Law: Enforcement, Norm-Generation and Learning in the International Competition Network' in Joost Pauwelyn, Ramses Wessel, and Jan Wouters (eds), *Informal International Lawmaking* (Oxford University Press 2012)

Sweet AS and Sandholtz W, 'European integration and Supranational Governance' (1997) 4 Journal of European Public Policy 297

Swenson DL, 'Why Do Developing Countries Sign BITs?' in Karl P Sauvant and Lisa E Sachs (eds), *The Effect of Treaties on Foreign Direct Investment* (Oxford University Press 2009)

Sykes AO, 'Protectionism as a Safeguard: A Positive Analysis of the GATT Protectionism as a Safeguard: A Positive Analysis of the GATT Escape Clause with Normative Speculations' (1991) 58 University of Chicago Law School 255

——, 'Externalities in Open Economy Antitrust and Their Implications for International Competition Policy Competition, Free Markets, and the Law-Symposium on Law and Public Policy-1999' (1999) 23 Harvard Journal of Law and Public Policy 89

——, 'The Economics of Public International Law' (2004) John M Olin Program in Law and Economics Working Paper No 216

Tagliapietra S, Veugelers R, and Zettelmeyer J, 'Rebooting the European Union's Net Zero Industry Act' (2023) Policy Brief 15/2023, Bruegel

Tallberg J, 'Delegation to Supranational Institutions: Why, How, and with What Consequences?' (2002) 25 West European Politics 23

Tams CJ, 'Erga Omnes Enforcement Rights and Competing Enforcement Mechanisms' in Christian J Tams (ed), *Enforcing Obligations Erga Omnes in International Law* (Cambridge University Press 2005)

Taylor C, *Wieviel Gemeinschaft braucht die Demokratie? Aufsätze zur Praktischen Philosophie* (Suhrkamp Verlag 2019)

Terpan F, 'Soft Law in the European Union - The Changing Nature of EU Law' (2015) 21 European Law Journal 68

Thatcher M and Sweet AS, 'Theory and Practice of Delegation to Non-Majoritarian Institutions' (2002) 25 West European Politics 1

Thatcher M, Sweet AS, and Rangoni B, 'Reversing Delegation? Politicization, De-delegation, and Non-majoritarian Institutions' (2023) 36 Governance 5

——, 'Reversing Delegation? Politicization, De-delegation, and Non-majoritarian Institutions' (2023) 36 Governance 5

Thomas JP, 'Bankruptcy Proceedings for Sovereign State Insolvency and Their Effect on Capital Flows' (2004) 13 International Review of Economics & Finance 341

Thompson A, 'Coercive Enforcement of International Law' in Jeffrey L Dunoff and Mark A Pollack (eds), *Interdisciplinary Perspectives on International Law and International Relations* (Cambridge University Press 2012) 502

Thomson R, 'National Actors in International Organizations' (2008) 41 Comparative Political Studies 169

Tiebout CM, 'A Pure Theory of Local Expenditures' (1956) 64 Journal of Political Economy 416

Tierney MJ and others, *Delegation and Agency in International Organizations* (Cambridge University Press 2006)

Toope SJ and Brunnée J, *Legitimacy and Legality in International Law: An Interactional Account* (Cambridge University Press 2010)

Trachtman J, 'Regulatory Competition and Regulatory Jurisdiction' (2000) 3 Journal of International Economic Law 331

——, *The Economic Structure of International Law* (Harvard University Press 2008)

——, *The Future of International Law: Global Government* (Cambridge University Press 2013)

——, 'Economics of International Organizations' in Francesco Parisi (ed), *The Oxford Handbook of Law and Economics: Volume 3: Public Law and Legal Institutions the Oxford Handbook of Law and Economics: Volume 3: Public Law and Legal Institutions*, vol 1 (Oxford University Press 2017)

Tucker P, *Unelected Power: The Quest for Legitimacy in Central Banking* (Princeton University Press 2020)

Tullock G, 'Federalism: Problems of Scale' (1969) 6 Public Choice 19

Tuori K, 'Legislation Between Politics and Law' in Luc J Wintgens (ed), *Legisprudence: A New Theoretical Approach to Legislation* (Hart Publishing 2002) 99

van Aaken A, 'Behavioral Aspects of the International Law of Global Public Goods and Common Pool Resources' (2018) 112 American Journal of International Law 67

——, 'Behavioral International Law and Economics' (2014) 55 Harvard International Law 421

——, 'Effectuating Public International Law through Market Mechanisms?' (2009) 165 Journal of Institutional and Theoretical Economics 33

van Aaken A and Broude T, 'The Psychology of International Law: An Introduction' (2019) 30 European Journal of International Law 1225

van Aaken A and Trachtman JP, 'Political Economy of International Law: Towards a Holistic Model of State Behavior' in Alberta Fabricotti (ed), *Political Economy of International Law: A European Perspective* (Edward Elgar 2016)

van den Bergh R, 'The Subsidiarity Principle in European Community Law: Some Insights from Law and Economics' (1994) 1 Maastricht Journal of European and Comparative Law 337

van Elsuwege P, 'The EU Constitution, National Constitutions and Sovereignty: An Assessment of a "European Constitutional Order"' (2004) 29 European Law Review 741

Vanberg VJ, 'Staatsverschuldung Und Konstitutionelle Ökonomik' in Christoph Engel and Martin Morlok (eds), *Öffentliches Recht als ein Gegenstand ökonomischer Forschung* (Mohr Siebeck 1998)

——, 'Market and State: The Perspective of Constitutional Political Economy' (2005) 1 Journal of Institutional Economics 23

Vaubel R, 'The Public Choice Analysis of European Integration: A Survey' (1994) 10 European Journal of Political Economy 227

Vermeule A, *Common Good Constitutionalism: Recovering the Classical Legal Tradition* (Polity 2022)

Viner J, *The Customs Union Issue* (Oxford University Press 1950)

Violante T, 'Bring Back the Politics: The PSPP Ruling in Its Institutional Context' (2020) 21 German Law Journal 1045

Virzo R and Ingravallo I, *Evolutions in the Law of International Organizations* (Brill/Nijhoff 2015)

Voeten E, 'Making Sense of the Design of International Institutions' (2019) 22 Annual Review of Political Science 147

Voigt S, 'Iudex Calculat: The ECJ's Quest for Power' (2003) 22 *Jahrbuch für Neue Politische Ökonomie* 77

——, 'The Economics of Informal International Law - An Empirical Assessment' in Thomas Eger, Stefan Oeter, and Stefan Voigt (eds), *The Economics of Informal International Law* (Mohr Siebeck 2011) 81

——, 'Spielräume Des EuGH—Eine Ökonomische Analyse' in Peter Behrens, Thomas Eger, and Hans-Bernd Schäfer (eds), *Ökonomische Analyse des Europarechts* (Mohr Siebeck 2012) 37

von Bogdandy A, 'The Prospect of a European Republic: What European Citizens Are Voting On' (2005) 42 Common Market Law Review 913

——, *Strukturwandel des öffentlichen Rechts: Entstehung und Demokratisierung der europäischen Gesellschaft* (Suhrkamp Verlag 2022)

Voßkuhle A, *Europa, Demokratie, Verfassungsgerichte* (Suhrkamp 2021)

Wagner G, 'The Economics of Harmonisation: The Case of Contract Law' (2002) 3 ERA Forum 77

Wagener H-J and Eger T, *Europäische Integration: Wirtschaft Und Recht, Geschichte Und Politik* (Vahlen 2014)

Walker N, 'The Idea of Constitutional Pluralism' (2002) 65Modern Law Review 317

Weale Albert and Nentwich M, *Political Theory and the European Union: Legitimacy, Constitutional Choice and Citizenship* (Routledge 1998)

Weatherill S, 'Protecting the Internal Market from the Charter' in Sybe de Vries, Ulf Bernitz, and Stephen Weatherill (eds), *The EU Charter of Fundamental Rights as a Binding Instrument: Five Years Old and Growing* (Hart Publishing 2016)

——, 'The Limits of Legislative Harmonization Ten Years after Tobacco Advertising: How the Court's Case Law has become a "Drafting Guide"' (2011) 12 German Law Journal 827

——, 'Why Harmonise?' in Takis Tridimas and Paolo Nebbia (eds), *European Union Law for the Twenty-First Century: Rethinking the New Legal Order* (Hart Publishing 2003) 11

Weiler JHH, 'The Transformation of Europe' (1991) 100 Yale Law Journal 2403

——, 'The State "über alles" Demos, Telos and the German Maastricht Decision' (1995) Jean Monnet Working Papers 1995/19

——, 'Does Europe Need a Constitution? Demos, Telos and the German Maastricht Decision' (1995) 1 European Law Journal 219

——, *The Constitution of Europe: 'Do the New Clothes Have an Emperor?' And Other Essays on European Integration* (Cambridge University Press 1999)

Weiss S and others, *How Europe Can Deliver: Optimising the Division of Competences among the EU and Its Member States* (Bertelsmann Stiftung 2017).

Wendt A, 'Constructing International Politics' (1995) 20 International Security 71

Williamson OE, 'The Economics of Organization: The Transaction Cost Approach' (1981) 87 American Journal of Sociology 548

——, *The Economic Institutions of Capitalism: Firms, Markets, Relational Contracting* (The Free Press 1985)

Wintgens LJ, 'Rationality in Legislation—Legal Theory as Legisprudence: An Introduction' in Luc J Wintgens (ed), *Legisprudence: A New Theoretical Approach to Legislation* (Hart Publishing 2002) 1

——, 'The Rational Legislator Revisited. Bounded Rationality and Legisprudence' in Luc J Wintgens and A Daniel Oliver-Lalana (eds), *The Rationality and Justification of Legislation: Essays in Legisprudence* (Springer 2013) 1

Woglom G, 'Do Credit Markets Discipline Sovereign Borrowers? Evidence from US States' (1995) 27 Journal of Money and Credit, and Banking 1046

Wonka A, 'Technocratic and Independent? The Appointment of European Commissioners and Its Policy Implications' (2007) 14 Journal of European Public Policy 169

——, 'Die Europäische Kommission in EU-Entscheidungsprozessen, in: Die Politische Ökonomie Des EU-Entscheidungsprozesses' in Torsten Selck and Tim Veen (eds), *Die politische Ökonomie des EU-Entscheidungsprozesses* (VS Verlag 2008)

Wörsdörfer M, 'Louis D. Brandeis and the New Brandeis Movement: Parallels and Differences' (2023) 68 The Antitrust Bulletin 440

Wright DS, 'Fiscal Federalism' (1974) 68 American Political Science Review 1777

Wyplosz C, 'Europe's Quest for Fiscal Discipline' (2013) European Economy—Economic Papers 2008—2015 No 498

Zglinski J, 'The End of Negative Market Integration: 60 Years of Free Movement of Goods Litigation in the EU (1961–2020)' (2024) 31 Journal of European Public Policy 633

Zilioli C and Ioannidis M, 'Climate Change and the Mandate of the ECB: Potential and Limits of Monetary Contribution to European Green Policies' (2022) 59 Common Market Law Review 363

Ziller J, 'European Union Law in the Jurisprudence of French Supreme Courts: Europe-Friendliness with a French Touch' (2015) 21 European Public Law

Zsolt D, Welslau L, and Zettelmeyer J, 'The Implications of the European Union's New Fiscal Rules' (2024) Policy Brief 10/2024, Bruegel

Zürn M, 'Democratic Governance Beyond the Nation-State' (2000) 6 European Journal of International Relations 183

Index

For the benefit of digital users, indexed terms that span two pages (e.g., 52–53) may, on occasion, appear on only one of those pages.